W9-AGV-092

Quantitative Analysis of Movement

DISCARDED
JENKS LRC
GORDON COLLEGE

Quantitative Analysis of Movement

MEASURING AND MODELING POPULATION REDISTRIBUTION IN ANIMALS AND PLANTS

Peter Turchin

University of Connecticut

JENKS L.R.C.
GORDON COLLEGE
255 GRAPEVINE RD.
WENHAM, MA 01984-1895

Sinauer Associates, Inc. Publishers
Sunderland, Massachusetts

QH
541.15
.S62
T87
1998

The Cover

The flight trajectories of nine individual male fireflies of the genus *Photinus* are tracked by the species-specific patterns of their light flashes. Drawing by D. Otte, from J. E. Lloyd, 1966, "Studies on the flash communication system in *Photinus* fireflies." *Miscellaneous Publications of the Museum of Zoology, University of Michigan* 130: 1–95. Courtesy of James E. Lloyd.

QUANTITATIVE ANALYSIS OF MOVEMENT:
MEASURING AND MODELING POPULATION REDISTRIBUTION
IN ANIMALS AND PLANTS

Copyright © 1998 by Sinauer Associates, Inc.

All rights reserved. This book may not be reproduced in whole or in part without permission from the publisher. For information address Sinauer Associates, 23 Plumtree Road, Sunderland, MA 01375 U.S.A.

Fax: 413-549-1118
E-mail: publish@sinauer.com
World Wide Web: www.sinauer.com

Library of Congress Cataloging-in-Publication Data

Turchin, Peter, 1957–
   Quantitative analysis of movement : measuring and modeling population redistribution in animals and plants / Peter Turchin
     p.   cm.
   Includes bibliographical references and index.
   1. Spatial ecology--Mathematical models. 2. Population biology--Mathematical models.   I. Title.
QH541.15.S62T87   1998
577.8'8'0151--dc21   98-4838
                                              CIP

Printed in U.S.A.   5   4   3   2

To my teachers

Contents

Preface

In the last two decades it has become increasingly clear that the spatial dimension, and, in particular, the interplay between environmental heterogeneity and individual movement, is an extremely important aspect of ecological dynamics. Ecologists are currently investing an enormous amount of effort in quantifying movement patterns of organisms. Connecting these data to general issues in metapopulation biology and landscape ecology, as well as to applied questions in conservation and natural resource management is, however, not a trivial task. One of the main impediments to a theoretical/empirical synthesis in the field of spatial ecology appears to be a lack of a single source describing and systematizing quantitative methods for analyzing and modeling movement of organisms in the field.

The most important goal of this book is to provide such a source for empirical ecologists interested in quantifying movement in an ecological context. In fact, I attempted to go beyond a simple compendium of existing approaches, by presenting a general and (hopefully) coherent framework for studying and modeling movement that melds together individual-based simulations, reaction-diffusion models, and empirical curve-fitting approaches.

I also have two secondary goals. First, I wanted to provide a popular account of the mathematical aspects of movement models that are relevant to ecologists. There is much mystique surrounding diffusion equations, but the underlying logic, I think, can be understood without first taking a course in partial differential equations (although such a course would not hurt). My second, more general goal is to forge better links between theory and empiricism in spatial ecology. I have tried to clearly identify areas that need more theoretical development. On the other hand, there is much theory that has never been rigorously tested in the field, and my hope is that this book will stimulate empirical ecologists to do so.

This book was written primarily for active researchers and graduate students interested in spatial ecology, including applications in conservation biology, pest control, and fisheries. Generally, I assume that readers are familiar with college calculus and elementary differential equations. I have tried to make this book not too intimidating to an empirical ecologist. Nevertheless, population ecology, and its spatial aspects in particular, remain a heavily mathematical subject, and nonmathematical readers (the majority, I would hope) should expect a steep learning curve when trying to understand and use the quantitative tools described here. Developing quantitative skills requires time and effort, but this investment will pay for itself with dividend. Note also that different kinds of analytical approaches may vary greatly in their mathematical difficulty. In fact, there are many problems in spatial ecology, for which no cut and dried answers exist, and I may be able to suggest no more than an idea for a potential approach. When tackling such difficult problems, the only recourse is to colaborate with a mathematician, in which case I hope that this book will help you formulate your problem in a language familiar to your mathematical counterpart. Some of the finest examples used in this book were a result of such a collaboration between a mathematician and a mathematically literate ("numerate") ecologist.

The methodological approaches discussed in the book will be useful to ecologists working with all taxonomic groups. Case studies have been selected from a wide variety of organisms, including plants (seed dispersal, spatial spread of clonal plants), many kinds of insects, and vertebrates (fish, birds, and mammals). Unicellular organisms, however, are outside the scope of this book, although we will find useful some of the mathematical approaches to modeling movements of these entities.

Acknowledgments

Many people read single chapters or large portions of this book and made very useful comments: Andrea Belgrano, Michael Cain, Jerome Casas, Dan Doak, Barbara Ekbom, Steve Ellner, Jim Gilliam, Nick Haddad, Jane Hayes, Peter Kareiva, Mark Lewis, Kristian Omland, Steve Pousty, John Reeve, Tomas Roslin, and Rich Wilkens. To all of you, many thanks. Mary Jane Spring provided invaluable help with illustrations.

I thank all the people with whom I collaborated on studying movements and dispersal of particular organisms, and who continuously challenged me to come up with new approaches to the analysis and modeling of movement. Here is a partial list of them: Ron Stinner, Greg Simmons, Frank Stermitz, Tim Schowalter, Julia Parrish, Jim Cronin, and Zvi Mendel. I am particularly indebted to François Odendaal, with whom I spent many enjoyable hours chasing diverse organisms in diverse environments, from butterflies in Colorado mountains to marine snails on a Cape Town beach.

To a very large degree this book is a culmination of a research program on which I embarked when I was a graduate student at Duke University, and then a postdoctoral scientist at University of Washington. I owe a huge debt of gratitude to Mark Rausher, who was probably the ideal Ph.D. adviser for me—letting me go in any direction that I would choose, but providing a lot of guidance and feedback on how to get there. The importance of doing postdoctoral research with Peter Kareiva hardly requires a comment (just check the bibliography). This whole book would certainly not happen if I never met him.

Finally, if not for my wife Olga, who kept my sights clear on the ultimate goal, this book would probably not see the light until the next millenium.

Storrs, Connecticut
1997

Chapter 1

Why Study Movement?

1.1 Population Dynamics in Space and Time

Population ecology is the study of the distribution and abundance of organisms (Elton 1927, Andrewartha and Birch 1954). The primary variable of interest for a population ecologist is the spatio-temporal density of organisms, that is, the number (or biomass) of organisms located within a unit of area or volume at certain spatial coordinates at a certain point in time. Traditionally, distribution and abundance have been studied separately, although as Andrewartha and Birch (1954) point out, they are two different aspects of the same problem. Studies focusing on distribution ignore the temporal aspect of population dynamics by taking a "snapshot" of the spatial density of a population at a particular point in time, or by averaging the population density over time. Similarly, studies of abundance ignore the spatial component and focus on temporal fluctuations in the number of organisms at a particular spatial point, or averaged over a large area. Developments in mathematical ecology followed a similar division between the spatial and temporal approaches. The situation was further confounded by separate traditions in animal and plant ecology (see, e.g., Pielou 1977). Thus, models of animal population dynamics traditionally focused on temporal fluctuations in abundance (reviewed in Pielou 1977: Part I). On the other hand, statistical methods for the study of plant populations have traditionally focused on the distribution in space (reviewed in Pielou 1977: Parts II and III). Such a separation should not be surprising because studying multidimensional problems that involve both temporal and (possibly more than one) spatial coordinates is much more difficult than an approach focusing on either time or space. As necessary as this abstraction can be for methodological reasons, however, "the separation should never be allowed to persist in the final synthesis" (Andrewartha and

Birch 1954).

Developments in ecological theory over the last two decades make it increasingly clear that the interplay between environmental heterogeneity and individual movements can have far-reaching consequences for the ecology of organisms. As a result, there has been a paradigmatic shift in the view of nature held by the majority of ecologists, from the aspatial equilibrium view of the "balance of nature" to a spatially explicit view—thus the popularity of such fields as metapopulation biology and landscape ecology. This shift in the way ecologists view nature is also percolating through conservation biology and natural resources management.

1.2   Movement and Spatial Dynamics

The temporal change in the population density of organisms at certain spatio-temporal coordinates can occur as a result of births, deaths, and movement (immigration and emigration). Methodologically it is easier to study birth and death processes because they are essentially a one-dimensional problem. Movement, however, involves at least two scales—temporal and spatial—which makes its study intrinsically more difficult (Schneider 1989). Conceptual and practical difficulties in studying movement resulted in an "avoidance behavior" by ecologists (Southwood 1972, Hughes 1979, Kennedy and Way 1979, Rabb 1979, Dye 1983).

Unlike the well-developed and codified methodologies for measuring population density, survival, and mortality, we have no comparable compendia for population movement. For example, consider various treatises on insect ecology (keeping in mind that insects are the taxon for which movement is perhaps best understood). In his *Ecological Methods*, Southwood (1978) devotes only 15 pages (out of more than 500) to dispersal. Probably the best general source on insect ecology (Price 1984) devotes only 5 pages out of 600 to dispersal. Neglect of movement also extends to modeling. For example, a recent primer on modeling insect population dynamics (Goodenough and McKinion 1992) devotes specific chapters to modeling insect development, mortality, and recruitment. There is, however, no corresponding chapter on insect movement. Only 1 out of 13 chapters explicitly addresses movement, and it is not a general treatment of how to model insect movement, but instead deals with a narrow subtopic—long-distance dispersal of moths in relation to weather patterns.

Ecologists working on a wide variety of organisms have realized that movement is a critical but little understood process affecting population numbers. Movement subtracts or adds individuals to a population, can alter (or even reverse) the outcome of species interactions, provides crucial genetic variability, and can rescue populations from extinction. However, to know whether any of these postulated effects are of practical importance, we need to be able to quantify dispersal, and to understand how spatial heterogeneity, distributions of other species, and conservation plans will enhance or reduce movement. In short, we need to find solutions to the conceptual and methodological problems associated with studying movement. I hope that by collecting various approaches to studying movement in one place, this book will help to identify gaps in our knowledge and stimulate research to fill these gaps.

A NOTE ON TERMINOLOGY   Many of the terms that I use in this book have a very specific meaning that does not necessarily conform to the widespread usage; all such special terms are defined in the Glossary. In particular, I use the term *movement* in its most general sense: the process by which individual organisms are displaced in space over time. *Population redistribution* in space is the population-level consequence of movement by individual organisms. I should note that the majority of ecologists use the term *dispersal* when talking about movement and population redistribution. I prefer to reserve *dispersal* for one kind of population redistribution, the one that leads to spatial spread. Movement can also result in *aggregation*, or population concentration: when organisms gather together in a certain location. Aggregation, as well as one particular mechanism leading to it, *congregation* (see Section 4.5), are relatively neglected topics in population ecology, and I will have a lot more to say about them later. *Dispersion*, often used as a synonym for dispersal, should be reserved for describing static spatial patterns. Finally, I will use *diffusion* to denote a specific kind of mathematical models useful in representing spatial redistribution of organisms, rather than equating it to "random movement."

1.3   Models, Data, Theory

Population ecology is essentially a mathematical subject (Pielou 1977). This is because population ecologists deal with numbers, rates of change, and fluxes. Rather than saying that "there are deer in the forest," we usually need to know how *many* deer are in that forest. Thus, it is much more useful to state that there are, for example, 1.8 ± 0.5 deer km^{-2}. That ecology is, and should be, a quantitative science becomes especially clear when we begin considering issues that are relevant to the society within which we live—the same society that provides funds for our research. For example, it is not enough to know the general principle that habitat fragmentation promotes extinction. We are often required by society (or rather its instruments—legislative bodies, government agencies, and the courts) to make quantitative predictions, e.g., how high is the extinction probability of a population of spotted owls given a certain level of habitat destruction and fragmentation. Today one challenge for the science of ecology is to be more quantitative and predictive.

Population ecology studies very complex systems. A population may be affected by physical factors, by its age or stage structure, by population density feedbacks, and by biotic interactions with other populations. These factors do not act additively, but interact with each other in complex, nonlinear ways. The human brain cannot deal with such complexities unaided. We need help from mathematical formalism and computers.

These considerations about population ecology in general apply doubly to spatial population dynamics and movement, because we now have additional spatial dimensions to consider. Quantitative understanding of the consequences of movement for population dynamics is practically impossible without constructing and testing mathematical models. For this reason, models of movement and population redistribution occupy a large portion of this book, in both theoretical and empirical chapters.

Of course, without an empirical link, the utility of models is severely restricted. Empirical information is necessary to parameterize models, and to enable us to choose between alternative models by testing their predictions against data. The connection between models and data works in the other direction as well. Complex data can often be interpreted only by making assumptions and constructing models (even if they are statistical models, such as regression, or the lowly *t*-test). In fact, the interplay between models and data is the key process for developing theory. *Theory*, in my opinion, is not just a collection of models, but a quantitative understanding brought about by both data and models.

Another point to keep in mind is that any particular model's conclusion can be affected not only by biological assumptions, but by its mathematical form. For example, sometimes results from discrete versus continuous models may be at variance with each other (see Section A.4 in the Appendix). The aim of the theory, as opposed to a specific model, is to gain a general insight into the problem at hand.

To illustrate this idea, let us consider the theory of predator-prey interactions. This is an example of a relatively mature theory: predator-prey interactions have been modeled as continuous differential equations (Lotka 1925, Volterra 1926), as discrete difference equations (Nicholson and Bailey 1935), as individual-based simulations (Stone 1990), and as cellular automata (Hassell et al. 1991), to name just a few mathematical approaches. One insight remains robust: predator-prey systems have an inherent tendency to undergo oscillations. The details vary—it could be a neutrally stable cycle in the Lotka-

Volterra model, or diverging oscillations in the Nicholson-Bailey model, or an oscillatory approach to a stable equilibrium in some more realistic modifications of the Nicholson-Bailey model (Hassell 1978)—but the general message remains the same.

Another hallmark of the mature theory is an understanding of why different mathematical formulations may lead to somewhat differing conclusions. After all, different mathematical frameworks may reflect different assumptions about biological properties of population systems. For example, difference equation models are most appropriate for annual species that reproduce once a year, while continuous differential models are most appropriate to continuously reproducing populations with overlapping generations. Thus, the different kinds of dynamic behavior exhibited by the two kinds of models may well be represented in the two kinds of biological systems.

1.4 Empirically Based Models

My philosophy of science dictates that after the preliminary stage, when we learn the basic natural history of the studied organism and begin to formulate initial hypotheses, we approach any serious data gathering with a more or less specific model in mind. The idealized approach runs something like this. First, we should have a specific and as simple as possible model in mind. This model will almost certainly be wrong, unless we are inordinately lucky, but as Francis Bacon said (quoted in Hull 1988), in science it is better to be wrong than confused. The model is designed to predict one set of phenomena (e.g., the spatio-temporal distribution of organisms) based on quantitative knowledge of some other phenomena (e.g., organism movement patterns). Often the explanatory variables will relate to a lower level of organization than the variables to be explained; when dealing with movement, therefore, we use mechanisms based on individual behaviors to explain and predict patterns at the population level.

The first empirical stage is geared to estimating model parameters. When studying movement, this stage will typically focus on short-term behavioral responses. As we collect data, we may quickly see ways in which the model fails. We then modify the model, redesign the fieldwork, and use the data to estimate the parameters of the revised model. This is a circular approach that does not constitute a test of the model. We are not yet ready to test the model; we are still at the development stage.

The purpose of the second empirical stage is to test the model more rigorously. Here we use the model to predict something novel, something that we would not be able to do without it. The more striking and detailed the predictions, the better. We then design a field experiment to collect data that will be compared with the model's predictions. At the analysis stage, one thing we do *not* do is a goodness-of-fit test designed to "reject" or "accept" a model. We do not need a test to know that our model is wrong—it is (all models, by definition, are wrong). What we need to know is how wrong our model is, and whether we can find or design a better alternative. I say *an* alternative because we are not testing one model in this program, but a whole series of them. By the time we get to the point of testing we have probably already rejected some alternatives in favor of the current version of the model. In some situations, we will be testing explicit alternatives that *a priori* will appear equally likely, and thus we need an experiment to decide which one is better. For example, if we are interested in understanding why diverse plant communities suffer less herbivore damage than monocultures (Root 1973), we might advance two very different models, one based on movement patterns of herbivores, and the other on differential patterns of mortality due to natural enemies. This is a good situation to be in, because instead of a subjective decision to test "novel" or "striking" predictions, we can now choose variables to be predicted by the alternative models objectively—those where their predictions disagree the most.

Returning to the data for model testing, we now calculate a measure of the deviations between the data patterns and the patterns predicted by the model (or by each alternative model). We can calculate a single measure of fit (e.g., the sum of squares of deviations, or the average absolute value of deviations), but it is better to plot the data and model predictions against each other. For example, if the model predicted the spatial distribution of organisms, we want to see where predictions are accurate and where they are wrong because this may suggest an alternative model to try. The end result of the test is one model that is best supported by data (actually, the one that is least wrong), and a measure of how well the model predicts the data. If this best model was one suggested by patterns in the data, we will need to do at least one more round of model testing, ideally collecting different kinds of data, to further challenge the model.

When do we stop this cycling between model development and empirical testing? One way is to set an arbitrary cut-off point for the accuracy of model predictions. In ecology, getting within 10% of data is considered the equivalent of hitting the bull's eye. For those who want to squeeze out the last drops of understanding, another approach is to determine whether there are still some systematic deviations between model predictions and data patterns. In other words, are deviations simply a result of inherent randomness present in any data set, or is there a signal in them?

This is the idealized program that I advocate, consisting of building empirically based models and, on a parallel track, collecting model-motivated data. It is certainly achievable in practice (for a fascinating account of one such long-term program, see Murdoch 1994). My advice to graduate students is: at the very least, construct a model before you start collecting the data for your thesis. Once you have a model, you may find that in your empirical plan you have left our measurement of some key variable!

Clearly, not all ecologists support the program I have outlined here. In fact, ecologists who attempt to combine models with data are still a distinct (although rapidly growing) minority. Also, we do not always have the time or the funds necessary for completing the full sequence from generating initial ideas to successfully testing a model that explains how our system works. Often we have some data, limited in one way or another, and we need answers now. Nevertheless, my contention is that we should approach the analysis with a spectrum of explicit models in mind. Put a different way, I advocate that we build empirically based models instead of traditional analysis relying on hypothesis testing. You will see this philosophy (or bias, if you will) throughout this book, especially in Chapters 5–7. To a very great extent, this book is about building empirically based models of movement and population redistribution among animals and plants.

Chapter 2

Data for Measuring Movement

2.1 Introduction

Data on the movement and spatial redistribution of organisms comes in a variety of shapes and forms. The most basic distinction is whether our focus is on the movements of an individual organism, or whether we are quantifying spatial redistribution of a population. This basic dichotomy reflects the two conceptual approaches to modeling movement, Lagrangian and Eulerian (see Section 3.1.2).

In many ways, direct observation of movement behavior is the most powerful approach for quantifying movement. It has several advantages over the other frequently used methodology, mark-recapture. At worst, mark-recapture studies just tell us the rate at which organisms are disappearing, without allowing us to separate death from emigration rate. At best, they provide information on the overall displacement of an organism between the points of release and recapture. The actual movement track of a recaptured individual between these two points, as well as environmental factors that affect the track, remain unknown. A mark-recapture study, therefore, cannot reveal the identity of proximal cues used by organisms in guiding their movements. Another serious problem is with recapture rates. We shall see in Section 2.3.5 that maximization of the recapture rate is often self-defeating. Low recapture rates, however, may raise doubts about the validity of results based on a small subsample of the marked population (this point will be more fully discussed in Chapter 6).

Unfortunately, recording movement behaviors and paths of individual organisms is very labor-intensive, and there are many organisms (probably the majority) to which this method cannot be applied. The method can be unsuccessful for a variety of reasons. Following moving organisms may be impossible if they are too small to be easily seen. Organisms may also move too fast, or enter regions inaccessible to humans (for example, when they fly to a high altitude, or when they burrow into the ground). Modern technology can extend our ability to follow moving organisms, but in many cases we have no recourse but a mark-recapture study.

Another consideration is that we often do not require the very detailed information that can be collected by following individuals, but, instead, wish to quantify population-level redistribution processes. In such cases, an Eulerian approach is indicated, *mass mark-recapture* (MMR). I distinguish the *mass-marking* component of this general approach from *individual mark-recapture* (IMR) because, as we shall presently see, the approaches to analyzing MMR and IMR data can be quite different (e.g., diffusion models for MMR, but uncorrelated random-walk models for IMR). As the name suggests, the IMR approach is intermediate between following individuals and mass-marking and recapturing them (see Chapter 7).

In this chapter I discuss methods of collecting movement data in the field, starting with individual-based methods and then moving on to mark-recapture. I advise the reader, however, to read the chapters following this one before jumping into data collection. Analysis of movement data is inextricably intertwined with modeling movement, and collecting data without a clear idea of how it will be analyzed will almost certainly be a waste of time (see Provine 1986:358).

2.2   Methods for Recording Paths

Recording movement activity of organisms in the lab is much easier than in the field. Simple methods include tracing an animal's image on a digitizing tablet (Bond 1980, Bell et al. 1985), or actually tracking an animal's movements on a transparent substrate with felt-tipped pen (Dethier 1989). More sophisticated methods use videotaping and locomotion compensators (for a review see Bell 1991). However, because laboratory data are collected under artificial conditions, they are more difficult to interpret (and generalize from) than field data. Of all ecological processes, movement is probably the least amenable to laboratory experimentation, because laboratory conditions (unless we are dealing with very minute and sessile organisms) will always impose limits on the range of an animal's normal movements. In the following sections, I will concentrate on methods for tracking organisms under natural or seminatural conditions. Other methodology reviews (which should be consulted because their biases differ from mine) are Schaefer and Bent (1984), Aluja et al. (1989), Bell (1991), and Kearns and Inouye (1993).

2.2.1 Following individuals

The simplest method for obtaining paths is to follow an individual organism as it swims, walks, hops, or flies around. Observers are required to (1) track the organism without losing it, (2) keep up with it as it moves, (3) record its behaviors, and (4) obtain a spatio-temporal representation of its track. Practically all studies use some kind of technological apparatus to aid in one or more of these tasks.

There are a number of methods that enhance the ability of observers to keep track of moving organisms visually. For example, marking an organism can make it more visible to the human eye. In situations where there are a number of conspecifics in the area, marking the tracked organism will help to distinguish it from conspecifics (Odendaal et al. 1988). However, care should be taken that the marking method does not affect the behavior of the tracked organism.

An opto-electronic device is necessary to be able to track nocturnal or crepuscular organisms that move under poor light conditions (Drake 1991). Moths flying at dusk or after dark have been traced using night-vision goggles, which can be used in combination with infrared lights (Lingren et al. 1978, Fitt and Boyan 1991).

Other devices have been developed to permit tracking organisms even when they cannot be followed by eye. For example, Mascanzoni and Wallin (1986) tagged ground beetles with tiny electronic diodes that reflect microwave beams, and then traced them with a portable harmonic radar system. They were able to follow a number of beetles at night simultaneously by recording the position of each beetle at 15-minute intervals. Various radiotelemetry methods have been developed over the past several decades (White and Garrot 1990). Although typically used to locate an animal at infrequent time intervals (see Section 2.3.2), these techniques can also be used for continuous tracking.

Keeping up with moving organisms may also present a difficulty. Chasing butterflies in a mountainous terrain requires excellent physical shape! In other cases, following has to be done from a car or an airplane. For example, Griffin and Hock (1949) used an airplane to follow movements of homing gannets.

The simplest method for recording behaviors of followed organisms is dictating to a portable cassette recorder (e.g., Stanton 1982b). Although a recorder leaves the hands free, the disadvantage of using it is that the data has to be manually transcribed later. A hand-held computer is more convenient because it stores the data in a digitized, computer-readable form. For example, we (Turchin et al. 1991) recorded behaviors of butterflies on a hand-held TRS-80 computer. The current trend to ever smaller and more powerful hand-held computers bodes well for future data collection. As voice recognition software improves, I expect that eventually one will not even need to spare a hand to operate these devices.

CAVEATS   The uncertainty principle, first propounded by the physicist Werner Heisenberg, states that just the act of observing an event will change it. In behavioral studies the presence and actions of the observer can modify the behavior of the observed. More specifically, following directly behind the organism may lead to it being "herded" in a direction it would not otherwise move. Alternatively, certain herbivorous insects searching for food plants may be attracted to any upright object, including a standing human being. When standing in the middle of a southern pine beetle infestation, I have been bitten on numerous occasions by beetles fooled into accepting me as a host tree by thick concentrations of congregation pheromones and my vertical shape. Herding, attracting, or disturbing organisms in other ways should be minimized by staying as far away from them as practical. You should also vary your position in relation to the organism (for example, do not always stand behind the subject). When flags are used to mark stopping points, they should be placed after the organism has moved on, usually after a delay of one or two moves. Finally, the effect of an observer's presence should be tested wherever possible. For example, Root and Kareiva (1984) compared certain characteristics of butterfly movement when followed by an observer, and when flying alone while being observed with binoculars from a tower.

2.2.2   Mapping paths

Two commonly used methods that do not require expensive or complex apparatus are sequentially numbered flags to mark stopping points, and prearranged grids. More technologically sophisticated methods include tracking organisms with theodolites, surveying with electronic distance-measuring equipment, and using video equipment.

NUMBERED FLAGS   In the field, a path can be demarcated by placing numbered flagged clothespins (Root and Kareiva 1984), small brightly colored disks (Cain et al. 1985), surveyor's flags (Turchin et al. 1991), or flagged toothpicks (Wiens et al. 1993a). The path can subsequently be recorded by either measuring the spatial coordinates of each flag, or by measuring the spatial attributes (e.g., distance and direction) of each move (a *move* is a segment of the path between two consecutive stopping points). If measurement were error-free, these

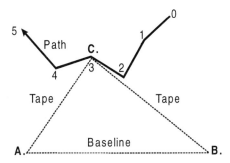

Figure 2.1: Triangulation with measuring tape. The baseline AB should be approximately as long as the linear dimensions of the area that includes all flags, and it should lie completely outside of that area. The zero-end of the measuring tape is attached at point A. One investigator stretches the tape from A to C, the n-th landing point, and the other stretches the tape from C to B. Both read and record the numbers off the tape (which give the distances AC and ACB, respectively). The procedure is repeated for all landing points, always using A and B as fixed points.

two methods would be equivalent because move distances and directions are readily calculated from the spatial coordinates, and vice versa. However, since there is an error associated with any measurement, translating move distances and directions into spatial coordinates leads to decreased accuracy for landing points near the end of the path (Turchin et al. 1991). This happens because the spatial coordinates after n moves are calculated from the coordinates after $(n-1)$ moves, and so on. As a result, the errors accumulate as more moves intervene between the starting point and the point under consideration.

There are various methods for measuring the coordinates of stopping points. The simplest is triangulation with measuring tape (Figure 2.1). The data (consisting of two measurements, AC and ACB) are translated into the spatial coordinates specifying landing points, using the trigonometric relationships. First, calculate distance CB = ACB−AC. Then, supposing that A is the origin of the coordinate system and the x-axis stretches from A in the direction of B, $x = (\mathrm{AC}^2 + \mathrm{AB}^2 - \mathrm{BC}^2)/2\mathrm{AB}$ and $y = \sqrt{\mathrm{AC}^2 - x^2}$.

The same task can be accomplished by triangulation with a compass, by stationing the investigator at point C and taking compass sightings to A and B. This procedure can be utilized when the dimensions of the area containing the path are too large for tape triangulation. Its additional advantage is that it requires only one person, but this advantage can be defeated by heavy underbrush or complex topography. A disadvantage of triangulation by compass is that it is less accurate than triangulation with tape.

Another simple procedure for mapping spatial points using measuring tapes and double right-angle prisms was described by Reed et al. (1989).

A more efficient and accurate, albeit expensive, methodology for mapping flag positions is to survey flag locations using an electronic distance-measuring instrument (Wiens et al. 1993a). The measurement error of this device is about ±5 mm, which is negligible compared to the accuracy of observers in placing flags at an insect's stops. The instrument can be connected to a data logger, and the data can be ported to a computer. See Wiens et al. (1993a) for more details.

PREARRANGED GRIDS   An alternative methodology used to record successive positions of an organism is to observe its movement within a prearranged grid. The position of the animal at any given time is approximated by recording the nearest grid node. The advantage of this technique is that it does not require mapping paths. However, its resolution is limited by the distance between the neighboring grid nodes. Very fine grids increase the probability of misreading the coordinates and are laborious to construct. In addition, the grid can only enclose a finite area (or volume) of space, and thus observations must stop when an animal leaves its confines.

A one-dimensional (1D), regularly spaced grid was used by Kaiser (1976), who observed dragonfly movement along pond shorelines. Kaiser (1976) divided pond shorelines into 1-m segments and recorded dragonfly positions within this grid at 1.5-s intervals. Smith (1974) used a 2D grid of marker pegs laid out on the meadow to study foraging movements of thrushes. A regular twine grid with lines 15 cm apart was employed by Heinrich (1979) in a study of pollinator foraging.

Grids can also exploit features of the environment. For example, coordinates of landing points made by insect herbivores within regular arrays of host plants can be approximated by the coordinates of the nearest plant (Turchin 1986). The procedure for constructing a 3D grid for tracing foraging movements of apple maggot flies within fruit trees was proposed by Aluja et al. (1989), who divided a tree into imaginary cubes of space (dimensions: 20 cm). Each cube was scanned and all plant parts within it were marked with masking tape strips, on which Aluja et al. recorded the 3D coordinates of the cube. Fly movement was recorded by noting which cubes the fly visited during a foraging bout.

THREE-DIMENSIONAL TRACKING WITH THEODOLITES   A very accurate, but technologically more demanding, method of measuring paths was described by Zalucki et al. (1980). They employed a pair of fixed theodolites that were focused on a moving butterfly and measured changes in the butterfly angular displacement relative to the theodolites. The angular readings were translated by a computer program into a set of 3D spatial coordinates of the butterfly position. Readings were taken at 0.75 s intervals. Like grid-based techniques, this approach is limited to a specific area covered by the theodolites.

2.2.3   Using video equipment

Although video equipment has been primarily used under laboratory conditions, it is starting to find application in the field. One of the pioneering studies was performed by Okubo and coworkers (Okubo and Chiang 1974, Okubo et al. 1977, 1981) who studied midge swarming. The midge *Anarete pritchardii* swarms in the daytime, and can be induced to swarm above a white marker. Chiang employed a 16 mm movie camera to record midges swarming under field conditions, and Okubo analyzed the data. These investigators found that by using high speed film they could keep track of individual midges. Originally, they did not intend to use the movies to calculate 3D tracks of midges, but during the analysis they noticed that each midge was throwing a shadow on the white marker. They realized they could use the positions of both the midge and the shadow to calculate the midge's 3D coordinates (the method is described in Okubo et al. 1981).

Some of the best analyses of flight behavior have been applied to male moths who use sex pheromones when searching for females. For example, Murlis et al. (1982) used a cine camera and an image intensifier (a night-vision device) to record paths of male *Spodoptera littoralis* under field conditions, and at night. They found that it was necessary to illuminate their observation area with infra-red light in order to increase the contrast of moth images against the background. It is believed that infra-red is invisible to moths, and should therefore have no effect on their flight behavior (Murlis et al. 1982).

Due to limitations of technology, the researchers cited above were restricted to a manual analysis of the film frame by frame. In recent years, developments in computer image analysis have greatly streamlined data collection, although often at the expense of giving up realistic, field conditions. For example, Gibson (1985), asking questions similar to Okubo and Chiang's, used a video camera and a digitizing board to record trajectories of mosquitos swarming in a 1.2 m cage. Hoy et al. (1983) developed a system that was capable of tracking movements of minute arthropods (such as mites, less than 1 mm long) traveling at speeds up to three body lengths per second, in an arena approximately 50 body lengths across. The system consisted of a video camera, a digitizer, and a microcomputer, and its output was a sequence of 2D coordinates of the moving animal taken 6 times per second.

A powerful system for automatic remote sensing of insects under natural conditions was developed by Schaefer and Bent (1984). In this system, IRADIT, flying insects are irradiated by an intense beam of near-infra-red radiation and detected using an image intensifier linked with a video camera. The video signals are then processed by a computer. In field tests, IRADIT was capable of tracking insects with only 1.5 mm^2 wing area flying against the noon sky, with a maximal range of up to 15 m. For larger insects, and without interference from the daylight, Schaefer and Bent (1984) expect a range of up to 100 m.

2.2.4   Some practical recommendations

If movement data are collected with the goal of quantitative analysis or modeling, then it is essential to unambiguously define the spatio-temporal sequence of the followed organism's positions. This means that each point should be characterized by three numbers if the organism moves on a surface, or four numbers if it moves within a volume. For an organism moving on a plane (2D space), each path point will need one temporal coordinate, such as the time from the beginning of observations, and two spatial coordinates. Given a sequence of these three numbers, we can reconstruct the path, and calculate other secondary quantities, such as displacement, speed, and the turning angle of each move.

This recommendation may sound obvious, but too many studies in the past did not collect a complete set of coordinates, making a quantitative reanalysis of the data difficult, if not impossible. It is unfortunate that the popular random walk formula of Kareiva and Shigesada (1983), by not including the time component explicitly, has encouraged the tendency to ignore the temporal dimension (Turchin 1991). The problems associated with omitting the temporal dimension are also discussed by Bell (1991:292).

An important question is at what resolution to collect data, for example, how often should fixes of an organism's location be taken? The answer to this question will be postponed until Section 5.2.

There is also a question of the resolution at which to measure the environment through which the organism has moved. In one extreme example, the investigator may want to record all host and non-host plants over which an insect herbivore flew, as well as all plants on which it has landed. Such a *micro-cue* based approach is appropriate in behavioral studies in which the investigator wishes to understand in detail the mechanisms governing the herbivore's searching behavior. When movement data is collected for the purpose of understanding spatio-temporal population dynamics (the main focus in this book) a more coarse approach will usually suffice. When addressing spatial population dynamics issues, we only need to measure average conditions characterizing a certain portion of the organism's path comprising several moves. For example, the environment can be divided into a host patch, and an area with low or no host presence (e.g., the *Euphydryas anicia* case study in Section 5.4.3). In fact, when estimating diffusion model parameters from path data, we explicitly make an assumption that we are concerned with an average effect of space and gradients that are somewhat larger than the length of an individual move.

How long organisms should be followed, or the rule for terminating observations, will depend on the details of the system. However, it is not very efficient to attempt to obtain very long paths (i.e., paths consisting of many moves). First, there seems to be a consensus that the basic unit of analysis should be not a single move but a complete path, because there could be statistical interdependences between consecutive moves within the same path (Turchin et al. 1991, Wiens et al. 1993a). The degrees of freedom, therefore, will be determined by the number of paths, rather than the total number of moves. Too much of an emphasis on long paths will be detrimental to obtaining an adequate statistical sample. Second, it is inevitable that some organisms will be lost while being followed. If the number of moves at which observations are stopped is set unrealistically high, then there is a danger that the data set will contain several long paths from easy-to-follow individuals, and many short paths from difficult-to-follow individuals. In this case, the data on easy-to-follow individuals will dominate the results, since they will contribute more moves to the dataset. This is another reason for using each path as a statistical unit rather than each move, whenever possible.

Wiens et al. (1993a) also suggest that the minimum number of observed moves should set the number of useful moves from which statistics are gathered from any of the paths. In other words, if the shortest path happens to have only three moves, then only the first three moves in all other paths can be used. Their reason is that longer paths will bias measures of net displacement both in duration and in length (net displacement is the distance from the beginning to the end point of a path). I would argue that net displacement is a poor statistic with which to compare different paths, precisely because it is so sensitive to path duration. A better and theoretically more sound statistic is the rate of increase in net squared displacement per unit of time. Because the net squared displacement is expected to increase linearly with time for a variety of random walk formulations (Chapter 4), the rate of its increase should be approximately independent of total path duration. Using statistics whose expected value varies little or not at all with path duration will allow the investigator to avoid discarding data. Finally, displacement is not the only path-level descriptor. Other path statistics, such as average speed and directional persistence, will be discussed in Chapters 4 and 5.

2.2.5   Synthesis

Designing an optimal program for measuring individual movements of organisms is an exercise in balancing trade-offs. It should only be tackled after thinking through the steps of how the collected data will be analyzed. In other words, read Chapter 5 before going in the field. One of the most important decisions that needs to be made is to determine at what resolution to measure the spatio-temporal paths of organisms. The choice of temporal resolution should avoid both undersampling and oversampling (see Section 5.2.1). The choice of spatial resolution depends on the questions motivating the study, and particularly, on how movement will be modeled. Flagging and measuring actual stopping points will obviously provide more detailed data. However, if movement will be modeled as random walk within a discrete 2D or 3D grid, then it should also be quantified in the same fashion using prearranged grids (e.g., see Aluja et al. 1991 for data collection, and Casas and Aluja 1997 for modeling). Similarly, the resolution with which environmental heterogeneity is to be measured depends on how data will be analyzed and modeled. In most population-level analyses of movement, we will not need fine-scale measures of spatial variation in environmental variables. Care should be taken that a representative sample of individuals is followed, and that no single subgroup (such as one age or size class) dominates the data set. Finally, some technological solutions may be worse than the problem they are supposed to solve if time invested in getting them to work is greater than collecting data manually.

2.3   Mark-Recapture Methods

2.3.1   Mass-marking organisms

Methods for mass-marking organism have been extensively described by Southwood (1978), and more recently reviewed by Akey (1991), Kearns and Inouye (1993), and Dingle (1996: Chapter 4). Below I will briefly review some of the common marking methods. Traditionally, mass-marking techniques have been primarily used on arthropods, and particularly insects; but seed dispersal can be, and often is, studied using this approach. Vertebrate movement, by contrast, is usually studied using individually marked organisms. Of course, one can employ techniques used for marking individual organisms (see Section 2.3.2) and then treat the data as though it came from mass-mark recapture, although individual marking is typically more labor-intensive than mass marking.

COLOR MARKING   Coloring organisms, or some part of them, has been the most widely used method for mass-marking. Various liquid paints have been used in marking: artist's oil paint, model airplane paint, fluorescent lacquer enamels, nail polish, and reflecting paints. See Southwood (1978: Section 3.1) for an extensive discussion with bibliography. Liquid paints can be applied to each individual insect with an entomological pin, a sharpened match stick, or a single bristle (Southwood 1978). However, this is a laborious process, especially when large numbers of marked insects are required. An alternative method for mass-marking is spraying, e.g., with a hand atomizer (Southwood 1978). Mortality as a result of spraying may be reduced by quickly drying insects with an electric fan immediately after spraying (Southwood 1978). By using a spray gun, this technique can be used under field conditions (Davey 1956).

Marking with micronized fluorescent dusts is almost as venerable in studying insect movement as the use of liquid paints. Although originally it was thought that fluorescent dusts were primarily useful for hairy insects (Southwood 1978), it is now apparent that even insects with few hairs usually retain enough particles for identification (Kearns and Inouye 1993, and my own personal experience). Fluorescent dusts have several advantages over liquid paints, and they are becoming the preferred technique for color-marking insects. This technique allows for rapid and inexpensive marking of large numbers of insects. Insects on flowers can be marked by applying fluorescent dust directly to their bodies, without causing them to leave flowers (Kearns and Inouye 1993). An alternative technique is to gently puff insects with dust by using a hand atomizer (Heinrich 1981, Turchin and Kareiva 1989). Larger numbers of insects can be sprayed with fluorescent dusts using pesticide applicators. It is also possible to capture insects and shake them in a container with powder (Crumpacker 1974). Flies subjected to such treatment are heavily marked with dust. They will usually spend some time grooming after they are released (which still leaves plenty of dust to identify them as marked), and then appear to behave normally. I have observed the same behavioral pattern with southern pine beetles. Because fluorescent dusts absorb radiant energy from ultraviolet light and convert it into a longer wave lengths that we can see (Kearns and Inouye 1993), they are easily detectable under a black light lamp (at night or in the laboratory), even if dust particles are present only in minute quantities. Insects are affected little or not at all by dusting (e.g., Crumpacker 1974, McMullen et al. 1988, Cook and Hain 1992). An additional advantage of fluorescent dusts is that this technique can be modified to allow insects to self-mark. Norris (1957) covered the soil containing fly puparia with a mixture of fine sand and fluorescent powder. As the flies emerged, a small quantity of dust adhered to the ptilinum. Self-marking with fluorescent dust works very well with bark beetles (e.g., McMullen et al. 1988, Turchin and Thoeny 1993). Further references to mass-marking with fluorescent dust can be found in Southwood (1978) and Kearns and Inouye (1993).

Another mass-marking technique is to use dye as part of larval diet. Many dyes have been tried, but most of them are either rapidly excreted or prove toxic (Southwood 1978). One dye that appears to be useful is Calco oil red N-1700 (Southwood 1978, Kearns and Inouye 1993).

RADIOACTIVE ISOTOPES   Although external dying or dusting has several advantages (primarily, ease of application and low cost), it often requires extensive handling of organisms, and can potentially disrupt locomotion activity. Thus, beginning in the 1940s, ecologists started looking for other, less invasive techniques. Radioactive isotopes proved to be useful, and their use exploded in 1950s (Akey 1991). Southwood (1978) provides a number of references for this extensively used method. One drawback of this mass-marking technique is the considerable expense in obtaining radioisotopes and detecting equipment. Even more importantly, radioactive labels can cause radiation injuries to experimental animals (e.g., Baars 1979). Finally, elaborate precautions must be taken to ensure the safety of personnel and to avoid contamination of the environment. Because of safety concerns many investigators switched to using elemental markers (e.g., Stimmann 1991). Currently, the use of radioisotopes as markers appears on the decline, and they are not even mentioned in the most recent review of Kearns and Inouye (1993) (but see the review of the use of radioisotopes in the study of small mammal dispersal, Stenseth and Lidicker 1992: Appendix 3).

ELEMENTAL MARKERS   Use of elemental markers has been rapidly increasing over the recent years (Akey 1991). Rare elements, such as cesium, strontium, and, most frequently, rubidium, are introduced into a larval diet, and are subsequently taken up into the organism's tissues. Additionally, adults can be marked by feeding them treated food, for example, nectar. The advantages of this technique include the ability to mass-mark large numbers of organisms nondisruptively. Rubidium (Rb), for example, acts as a surrogate of potassium. It can be simply sprayed on crops (Hayes 1991), or injected into host trees (Fleischer et al. 1991). Larvae feeding on Rb-enhanced foods subsequently incorporate the elemental marker in their tissues. The primary disadvantage of this technique is the cost—both the rare elements and the equipment used to detect it (atomic absorption spectrophotometer) are expensive. A very useful collection of articles on the use of elemental markers in the study of arthropod movement has been published in *the Southwestern Entomologist*, Supplement No. 14 (Akey et al. 1991).

A related technique to elemental enrichment is *chemoprinting*. This approach relies on natural variation in elemental composition of insects originating from different areas. So far this techniques has proved to be of limited value in measuring dispersal (Akey 1991, Kearns and Inouye 1993).

Finally an *elemental marker* such as a small piece of metal can be physically inserted into an organism or propagule, and later detected with a metal detector. For example, Sork (1984) inserted a small nail into acorns in such a way that no part of the nail was exposed above the surface. Metal-tagged acorns placed at release sites in October were removed by rodents over winter. Next summer, investigators searched the area around the release points with a Fischer metal detector, and locations of both metal-inserted acorns and isolated metal pieces were recorded.

GENETIC MARKERS Genetic markers have been used since the very beginning of quantitative study of insect dispersal. In their classic study on the dispersal of *Drosophila*, Dobzhansky and Wright (1943) used a recessive genetic marker "orange," which produces a brilliant red eye color. Care should be taken that the genetic marker does not affect the vigor and behavior of the marked organisms. Unfortunately, organisms with genetic markers often have to be reared in the laboratory, which may have deleterious side effects on their ability to disperse (Dobzhansky and Wright 1943). Another potential disadvantage of genetic markers is that they require careful preparatory investigative work (Akey 1991). Despite these disadvantages, however, genetic markers are sometimes the best overall method for quantifying dispersal as, for example, in studies of pollen dispersal (Manasse 1992). In general, this approach has a great potential in the near future, as technical advances now make it possible to survey genetic variation rapidly and inexpensively in large numbers of individuals by the RAPD method of the polymerase chain reaction (PCR), by DNA fingerprinting of minisatellite or microsatellite DNA, or by restriction enzyme digests of DNA amplified by PCR (Hoy 1994; for the review of the methods, see Chapter 14 of her book).

USING UNMARKED ORGANISMS   Under certain circumstances, marking study organisms may not be necessary. For example, when a point release is performed in an area completely devoid of conspecifics, clearly we do not need to mark organisms. An inferior variation of this technique is to mass-release organisms in an area with a sparse resident population. The density of the resident population becomes a key parameter in analyzing and interpreting such data. Basically, we will not be able to detect the shape of the tail of dispersal curve once the density of dispersers falls below the average density of the resident population. In addition, we have to be careful in attributing all population density gradients to the released organisms, since the resident population is unlikely to be distributed evenly, but will usually be aggregated in response to various features of heterogeneous environment. Due to difficulties associated with marking seeds, studies of plant dispersal often rely on this technique by looking at spatial gradients in seed deposition or seedling density around isolated standing trees (e.g., Guevara and Laborde 1993).

Another variation of this technique is to identify a natural population source near an area that is devoid of organisms, because (1) it is hostile habitat, so that there is no reproduction, (2) the organisms went extinct naturally, or (3) organisms were removed by the investigator. For example, Antolin and Strong (1987) inferred long distance dispersal of a parasitoid *Anagrus delicatus* from their appearance on offshore islands, where the parasitoid was previously extinct. Another example is the study of Thomas et al. (1990) who sprayed a field with pesticide, and then studied the diffusion of linyphiid spiders into it. Studies of plant dispersal often take advantage of land use changes, for example, pine invasion of moorlands or heathlands (Welch et al. 1990).

Finally, population redistribution models can be fitted to a temporal sequence of spatial distributions (see Section 6.4) that have been completely unmanipulated by the investigator. For example, Ribbens et al. (1994) calibrated tree seedling recruitment functions by comparing seedling distributions with adult distributions. In general, studies involving unmarked organisms are characterized by lesser degrees of experimental control, and thus are more difficult to analyze than studies employing marked organisms. An exception is provided by the data on the spread of invading organisms, where we are certain that the only source of organisms is behind the advancing front.

2.3.2   Marking organisms individually

Ecologists, especially those working with arthropods or plant seeds, have historically paid more attention to methods for mass-marking organisms (e.g., see Southwood 1978: Chapter 3). Currently, however, methods for marking individuals are becoming increasingly more common. A recent handbook on ecological census techniques (Sutherland 1996a) provides a good source for various marking techniques.

PAINTS AND LABELS Many organisms can be easily marked with various kinds of paints or labels. When working with the Mexican bean beetle (a phytophagous coccinellid), I have obtained good results with Testors brand enamel paint (Turchin 1986, 1987). Other possibilities include colored "Liquid Paper" typewriter correction fluid and Floquil hobby paints. [See Kearns and Inouye (1993) for a discussion of various methods for applying paints to insects.] Insects are marked individually by applying small dots of different colors to different parts of their bodies; typically, elytra or pronotum for beetles, and wings for butterflies. Brussard (1971) is a good reference to check for suggestions about individually marking butterflies with "Sharpie" pens. Using a combination of different-colored spots in different positions, literally thousands of insects can be marked individually (see Southwood 1978 and Kearns and Inouye 1993 for various numbering methods).

Many investigators have successfully employed numbered labels or tags. A simple method that will work with larger hard-bodied insects is to paint a label with white typewriter-correction fluid, and then to write a number on it with a fine pen. There are also commercially-available tags. For example, Kearns and Inouye (1993) describe small plastic tags that can be used for marking bumblebees. Other investigators have used tags made by photo-reducing a computer-generated spreadsheet filled with numbers, metal tags that could be automatically collected in magnetic traps, and electronic tags (for references to these methods, see Kearns and Inouye 1993). A very useful method for larger insects was developed by Mascanzoni and Wallin (1986) (see also Wallin and Ekbom 1988 and Wallin 1991). They glued a tiny diode to the thorax of carabid beetles, and employed a portable harmonic radar to locate each marked beetle at regular time intervals (15 min). One advantage of this technique is that it allowed them to follow beetle movements at night when they are most active. Harmonic radar can also locate individuals that have burrowed into the soil, or under detritus, and thus would be invisible to an unequipped observer.

Marking vertebrates usually presents fewer problems, simply because of their larger size. Any of the above methods, such as panting and tagging can be adapted to marking vertebrates (see Kearns and Inouye 1993 for suggestions on marking hummingbirds and bats). Vertebrate groups have been marked with an array of different approaches. For example, amphibians have been marked with elastic waistbands, knee tags, skin transplants or staining, tatooing, and branding (see Table 1 in Halliday 1996). Birds can be marked with color-coded leg bands, neck collars, and wing tags (Bibby et al. 1992).

MUTILATION   Another possible method is mutilation, or removing parts of an organism in a certain pattern. Hard-bodied insects can be marked by either scraping patches (Murdoch 1963) or cutting notches in their elytra. A technique useful for burrowing arthropods, for whom any type of external painting rapidly wears off, is minute perforations of the elytra made with the tip of an insect needle (Unruh and Chauvin 1993). Taking advantage of the "map" created by grooves and ridges on the elytron, one can achieve several hundreds of combinations even on quite small beetles.

A mutilation technique, toe-clipping, is often used in dispersal studies of salamanders, frogs, lizards, and small mammals (e.g., Wells and Wells 1976). The basic techniques are described in Halliday (1996).

INDIVIDUAL RECOGNITION   This approach works only with few species, typically vertebrates. For example, female crested newts have highly individual color patterns on their bellies (Halliday 1996). The method is particularly useful when studying mammal carnivores—wild dogs, lions—or whales (Sutherland 1996b).

TELEMETRY   Collars equipped with radiotransmitters are often the only way to track shy, difficult to find mammals (Cochran et al. 1965). Disadvantages of radiotelemetry include expense, substantial upfront investment of time to learn the techniques, limitations on the accuracy of measuring an animal position (Lee et al. 1985), and limitations on the numbers of animals that can be equipped with radiotransmitters. These are all outweighed by the advantage of knowing the ultimate fate of the radio-collared individual (assuming that the transmitter does not fail). Thus, long-distance dispersal events can be distinguished from death by predation. As a result, telemetry provides a much better data base for studying dispersal than data obtained by trapping (Jones 1987). Radio-tracking is a widely used method in mammal and bird population research, and handbooks are available (e.g., Mech 1983). A particularly useful book is White and Garrott (1990), who cover all stages of a radio-tracking study, from design to data analysis.

As technology improves, telemetry becomes feasible for ever smaller animals, for example, passerine birds (Naefdaenzer 1994) and insects (Roland et al. 1996). Recent developments in GPS technology hold even greater promise for detecting long-distance movements than could be obtained using traditional radio-collars (e.g., Morreale et al. 1997; Koenig et al. 1996 provide some additional references). However, the potential of radiotracking data for a quantitative measurement of dispersive movements of vertebrates has hardly been tapped. Thus, in an otherwise excellent book, the best White and Garrott (1990) can do when discussing analysis of movement is to cite the formula of Kareiva and Shigesada (1983). Approaches to quantitative analysis of radio-tracking data will be discussed in Chapter 7.

2.3.3 Handling and releasing marked organisms

One of the greatest worries in marking and releasing organisms is that the technique will affect (typically negatively) the survival, dispersal ability, and other aspects of their biology. An attempt should always be made to measure any negative impact of marking and handling on the study organisms. This may be checked in the laboratory or in field cages by comparing survival of marked and unmarked organisms (Southwood 1978). This approach, however, will not detect any difference in dispersal ability between marked and unmarked individuals. An alternative is to use two (or more) very different methods of marking, release both groups of organisms together, and determine whether their dispersal patterns (as measured by how many and where they are recaptured) are different. The logic of this *double-marking* approach is that the two marking methods are very different and are expected to affect different aspects of the biology of the study organisms. If there are no differences between the dispersal of the two groups, then we can assume that the influences of marking are minor. This approach was used by Dobzhansky and Wright (1943), whose primary marking technique relied on a genetic marker and laboratory-bred flies; the secondary or test technique was to mark wild-caught flies with a spot of nail polish. Dobzhansky and Wright (1943) found that marked wild flies displayed the same behavior as the flies with "orange" eyes.

In our work on dispersal of southern pine beetles, we followed a similar approach to test for potential side effects of our primary marking technique, fluorescent dust (Turchin and Thoeny 1993). We released insects that were marked with fluorescent dust only, with the elemental marker rubidium, and with both markers (Thoeny et al. 1992), and found that all groups behaved essentially identically. Yet another method to test the effects of marking on dispersal is to contrive a release of both marked and unmarked insects during a period when no wild insects are flying. For example, Elkinton and Cardé (1980) released equal numbers of laboratory-reared marked and unmarked male gypsy moths in September, after the flight of wild males had ended. They also found no effect of marking on recapture probability.

Handling insects during marking can cause a substantial degree of mortality. The best methods for marking and releasing insects allows them to mark themselves and initiate flight in a natural way (*self-marking*). This is where techniques such as elemental marking are especially advantageous, since they often allow self-marking of organisms during, for example, larval feeding. However, external marking techniques can also be adapted for self-marking. For example, in our work with the southern pine beetle (Turchin and Thoeny 1993) we located beetle-infested pine trees, cut them into bolts, carried the bolts to the release point in the center of a study area, and dusted the outside of the bolts with fluorescent dust. Beetles completed their development within the bolts, and as they emerged, they picked up fluorescent dust marker. There was no handling of individual beetles, and thus their flight initiation differed from natural take-off only in that they were taking off from bolts, rather than from dead trees. When self-marking is not possible, one of the techniques reviewed by Southwood (1978) should be employed to minimize the effects of handling.

The release of marked organisms should not be casually undertaken (Southwood 1978). After being held in containers, handled, marked, and finally dumped onto the release point, most insects will exhibit enhanced levels of movement activity, known as the *agitation dispersal*. Several approaches can be used to minimize agitation dispersal. Organisms should be released during their inactive period (if such exists). Night releases are best for organisms active during daylight hours. Insects may be restrained from flying immediately after release by covering them with small cages that are gently removed after some time has passed, and the released insects have quieted down. Another technique for avoiding agitation dispersal is chilling insects before releasing them. Thus, cool temperatures at night may be an additional reason to prefer night releases.

One factor that is often ignored in dispersal studies is the effect of population density at the release point. All too often, especially in point-release studies, insects are released at extremely high local densities, possibly causing enhanced density-dependent dispersal. For example, I found that Mexican bean beetles had a much higher probability of initiating movement when large numbers were released on the same host plant (Turchin 1987). Many insects are characterized by initially high diffusion rates that decline as time after release increases. Such a pattern can be a result of many factors: agitation dispersal, density-dependent dispersal, or gradual "leaching" of active individuals from the population. It is possible to test for density-dependent dispersal by releasing insects at various initial densities. If density-dependent dispersal is indicated (or suspected) it is worthwhile to consider alternatives to point-releasing organisms. For example, releasing animals in a circular area at constant density can still be handled by statistical analysis (see Section 6.2.2).

2.3.4 Recapturing organisms

In contrast to IMR methods, where we are interested in obtaining a time sequence of spatial positions of an individual, the basic purpose of recapturing in MMR is to obtain an estimate of spatial density of marked organisms. We may attempt to estimate the absolute density of marked animals (e.g., numbers per unit of area), or be content with a relative density estimate (e.g., density-distance curves). In either case, these density estimates will serve as basic data for fitting various spatial models.

Southwood (1978) provides an exhaustive review of various methods for obtaining absolute and relative estimates of population density. Another, more recent source is the handbook on ecological census techniques edited by Sutherland (1996a), which includes chapters on plants and invertebrates, as well as all the major classes of vertebrates. Any of these techniques can be used in MMR; we simply focus on marked organisms (although there is value in recording the densities of unmarked organisms, too; see below). With one exception, I will not attempt to review these methods, and instead refer the reader directly to Southwood (1978) and Sutherland (1996a). The exception is the use of attractive (baited) traps.

Baits (food, potential mates, attractive pheromones) may affect movements of organisms in a variety of ways, such as directed attraction and flight arrestment. The important point for MMR studies is that baits can increase by orders of magnitude the number of marked animals captured in a trap, thus allowing sampling of very sparse population densities. For example, "active" (pheromone baited) traps typically capture up to 100 times as many bark beetles as passive traps (Schlyter 1992: Table 3). Such amplification of recapture rates is an absolute necessity for studying movement of organisms characterized by moderate to long average dispersal distances (on the order of 100 m and more). Unless the movement of organisms is restricted to one-dimensional space, their density will be subject to the *area dilution effect*: as distance from the release point increases, the number of insects that reach that distance will be spread over a progressively greater area. To give a numerical example, suppose we release 100,000 marked beetles that will spread out according to the diffusion-death model (Equation A.55) with diffusion rate $D = 1 \text{ km}^2/\text{day}$ and death rate $\delta = 1.38/\text{day}$ (these values were chosen to give median dispersal distance of 1 km). If we then recapture marked beetles with passive traps that sample 1 m^2 of area, then the expected cumulative catch of a trap (see Equation A.56) at 1 km from the release point (that is, at the median dispersal distance) is less than 0.01 insects! Increasing the number of released individuals ten-fold, will bring the expected number of recaptures to less than 0.1 insects. Clearly, attempting to quantify the dispersal of such insects with passive traps would be hopeless.

Some caveats about pheromone-baited traps used in recapturing insect populations are in order, however. The lures used in traps can be broadly classified into kairomones that most often are chemicals associated with food, and pheromones (Southwood 1978). Attractant pheromones can be further subdivided into sex and congregation pheromones, with sex pheromones attracting only one sex, usually males. As males typically are the wider ranging sex in insects, the pattern of male recaptures may not provide a good picture of the spatial distribution of females, of eggs that females lay, and, consequently, of the damage to host plants. Thus, traps baited with sex pheromones may not be an optimal recapture method in a movement study. By contrast, congregation pheromones attract both sexes (although not necessarily equally), and thus provide much better data on population density of marked organisms in the vicinity of a trap. Various aspects of field trapping with pheromone-baited traps have been reviewed by Cardé and Elkinton (1984). The most common types use a sticky surface to capture an attracted insect. Sticky traps are often sufficient for monitoring, when we simply need to detect presence or absence of pests in an area. They are less suitable for dispersal studies, especially if insects are locally abundant. As the sticky surface becomes covered with captured insects, its ability to retain new arrivals becomes limited (Cardé and Elkinton 1984). Thus, another caveat is that sticky traps provide biased estimates of population density, and the bias gets worse as local density increases. A better alternative for dispersal studies is some variation of a no-exit trap, typically supplemented by a vaporous insecticide. Other concerns in pheromone trapping such as trap placement, rate of pheromone release, and avoiding pheromone contamination are reviewed in Cardé and Elkinton (1984). A useful overview of insect pheromones and their practical applications is found in Klassen et al. (1982).

RESIGHTING ORGANISMS   Resighting means that the spatio-temporal coordinates of the marked organism can be determined without recapturing it. This is desirable for two reasons. First, many methods of recapture result in the organism's death. Thus, we cannot obtain information of what its subsequent movement would be like. Second, even if we can recapture an organism without killing it, we cannot avoid disrupting its normal pattern of dispersal.

2.3.5 Designing spatial trapping grids

Spatial arrangement of traps is one of the most critical aspects in a MMR study. The following points are worth keeping in mind when designing trapping grids.

1. The trapping grid should extend far enough to sample a substantial proportion of disperser end points. Ideally, the farthest traps should enclose an area encompassing 90–95% of dispersers (this information, of course, will not be available at the very beginning of the study, but can be obtained only as a result of preliminary experiments). However, there is no point in putting traps so far from a release point that they will not capture any marked animals. Usually, it will not be possible to enclose *all* potential dispersers (there is always a very small but non-zero chance that one marked organism will end up in Antarctica). Thus, some extrapolation beyond the recapture grid will be necessary. Hopefully, however, only a small proportion of the population will be affected by extrapolation errors.

2. There is some disagreement as to whether rectangular or concentric (radiating trap lines) grids are best. In my opinion, neither basic design is superior in all possible situations. Data from either type of grid can be analyzed with any model discussed in this chapter. However, if the investigator is interested in analyzing the effects of dispersal distance separately from dispersal direction, then the analysis will be simpler and more intuitive if the data are collected on a concentric grid. By contrast, if one wants to fit a diffusion equation to spatio-temporal density of marked organisms, then it is better to sample the density on a rectangular, evenly spaced grid (and also use regular temporal intervals).

3. Traps are usually in limited supply (or we could be limited by the number of traps that we can "service"). Thus, it is important to arrange traps in a way that will maximize the chance of distinguishing between rival hypotheses, or that will allow the most accurate estimate of model parameters. One common mistake is to have too few distance treatments. For example, suppose we have 24 traps for recapturing marked insects released from a central point. If we arrange traps in eight cardinal directions, then for each direction we will have only three different distances. Suppose, further, that we detect no effect of direction on the numbers of recaptured insects. If we decide to fit one of the theoretical functions to our density-distance data, we will have only three distance levels. Thus, any three-parameter curve will fit the means for each distance exactly, and we will not be able to determine which relationship best fits the data, since they will all provide equal fits. We would do much better if we used four directions and six different distances. This would still allow us to test for directionality, but we would have a much better idea of the shape of the density-distance curve.

4. Ecologists often worry about low recapture rates in MMR studies. However, it is a mistake to attempt to maximize the proportion of released organisms that are recaptured. The primary goal of recapturing marked animals in

MMR is to obtain a good estimate of their spatial density. However, by trapping marked individuals, we remove them from the population and thus affect their density. This is another manifestation of the Heisenberg effect. Consider what would happen if we used very powerful traps. Traps in the vicinity of the release point would then capture a high proportion of marked organisms, depleting the numbers that would otherwise reach more distant traps. The end result is that the density-distance curve obtained from such a study would be deformed from its true shape.

These considerations suggest that, especially at locations near the release point, our traps should capture no more than a few percent of the marked population. This is especially true if we use pheromone traps to study dispersal. By placing pheromone traps too close to the release point we will simply ensure that all (or most) insects that are primed to respond to the pheromone will end up in these traps—we will certainly not be able to conclude anything about dispersal. However, using weaker traps, we run into the opposite problem of too few insects captured at distant traps, which results in difficulties for the statistical analysis of data. There are several possible ways of dealing with this dilemma. One is to use weak traps near the release point, and more powerful traps far away from it. One should be careful when using pheromone traps, however, because the relationship between the rate of pheromone release and the increase in trap catch is often nonlinear, and can be quite complex (Cardé and Elkinton 1984). By overlapping weak and strong traps at some intermediate density, it is possible to quantify their relative drawing powers. Another approach is to use more traps at greater distances from the release point. For example, in a mark-recapture study of the southern pine beetle dispersal, we used only 2 pheromone traps nearest the release point, and 8 traps at farthest distances (Figure 2.2). Finally, it is also possible to explicitly model the effects of trapping on the spatial population density of marked organisms. This approach, however, results in a more complex analysis of data.

The basic assumption that we make in a MMR analysis is that the recaptured animals are a representative sample of the marked and released population. As in any other study that relies on random sampling, we should test this assumption if possible. In particular, we need to worry about whether we disproportionately recapture many slow-moving individuals as opposed to widely-ranging ones. If we use pheromone traps, then we should be concerned with population variability in response to the pheromone. In many bark beetle species, some proportion of individuals at emergence are not responsive to the congregation pheromone, but become more responsive after dispersal (Mason 1969, Bennet and Borden 1971, Hagen and Atkins 1975, Hain and Anderson 1976, Andryszak et al. 1982, Forsee and Solbreck 1985). When such

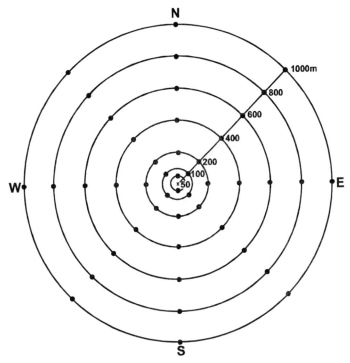

Figure 2.2: A spatial arrangement of traps for recapturing marked insects. (After Turchin and Thoeny 1993.)

complications arise, they may have to be treated explicitly in the analysis. For example, if insects are shown to require a certain period of dispersal before becoming receptive to pheromone bait, then this behavioral pattern can be included in a random-walk or a diffusion model, and its effects on the spatial distribution of recaptures quantified. What one should not do, is to attempt to recapture all released organisms. We may feel good about recapturing 30% as opposed to 2% of marked animals, but we will still miss the individuals that are not responding to the pheromone, and obtain an incorrect measure of the dispersal rate. The recapture efficiency should be not maximized, but optimized: we need to recapture enough marked animals to be able to statistically analyze the data, but not so many that we would significantly distort their spatial distribution.

2.3.6   Synthesis

Designs of individual versus mass mark-recapture studies are governed by very different considerations. Read Chapter 7 before collecting any IMR data. Otherwise, most considerations in Section 2.2 apply to an IMR study because the analysis will often follow a similar route. Thus, recording several consecutive moves is better than simply recapturing each organism once after release. We want to mark a representative sample of organisms, and avoid any biases associated with some kinds of organisms being easier to recapture than others. One basic difference, however, is that in an IMR study we do not know the actual track of an organism between the release and the recapture points (or two consecutive resighting positions). Thus, an investigation of effects of spatial heterogeneity on movement is severely limited in the resolution with which we can measure spatial heterogeneity. Essentially, the smallest scale at which we can quantify environmental gradients is the one that encloses both the starting and the ending point of a move.

Before designing a mass mark-recapture program, study Chapter 6. The key point to keep in mind is that we are measuring population density at various distances, directions, and times from the release point. Do not worry about recapturing a small proportion of marked organisms. Instead work to ensure that you recapture a representative sample (check this by comparing sex, age, and size structure of the released to the recaptured populations). If you plan to fit instantaneous density data (Section 6.2.2), you will need to simultaneously maximize the number of different distances, directions, and times at which you will measure the density of marked organisms. If you use time-averaged methods (Section 6.2.5), then only the number of distances and directions need to be maximized. In most applications, increasing the number of distance treatments yields a greater amount of information then doing the same for directions or times, but this is not a hard rule. The greatest challenge is usually in quantifying the tail of the density-distance curve. Increased recaptures at distances far from the release point may be achieved by releasing greater numbers of marked organisms, and by increasing the trapping power of recapture devices, although both approaches may have hidden problems.

Chapter 3

Modeling Movement

3.1 Introduction

Models of movement and spatial population dynamics range from very simple to extremely detailed and complex. They may employ different kinds of mathematical formalism and be applicable at different levels of biological organization. In order to judge the usefulness of a model, however, the very first thing we need to know is its purpose. Thus, I begin this chapter by reviewing some of the common objectives of mathematical models in ecology.

3.1.1 Modeling objectives

FORMAL STATEMENT OF THE PROBLEM Formulating a model is always useful for clarifying one's ideas. This descriptive exercise forces one to think about which aspects of the problem are important, and thus must be included in the model, and which aspects may be unimportant, and can be left out (at least initially). This is one benefit of formulating a model, even when there is no intent to confront it with the data or to use it in advancing theory. The necessity of stating the assumptions of the model is another benefit. A mathematical description of a problem forces one to be very clear about what the different variables and parameters in the model are, and how they are interrelated.

IDENTIFYING KNOWLEDGE GAPS The act of writing down the model forces one to think about what the functional forms and numerical values of the model's parameters may be. It may turn out that good quantitative data are available to estimate some functions and parameters but not others, immediately suggesting a focus for the empirical program. When there are many gaps, one has to decide which parameters need to be estimated precisely, and for which parameters "guesstimates" will do. This can be done by means of a sensitivity analysis. Such an analysis would typically indicate that variation in some parameters may have only a slight effect on the model's output, while other key parameters will have a disproportionate effect. Clearly, it would be advisable to concentrate on such key quantities.

GAINING THEORETICAL INSIGHTS   There is a large class of models that are never intended to be directly confronted with data. These models are sometimes called "strategic" or "explanatory," and they typically ask: If certain assumptions were true, how would the system behave? The purpose of such models is to gain insights into possible causal interconnections between various factors and, in general, extend our intuition. Strategic theoretical models attempt to be general—that is, applicable to a wide variety of situations. Their predictions tend to be qualitative. For this reason, they are not very useful for formulating specific hypotheses for particular systems.

QUANTITATIVE TESTS OF THEORY   A qualitative prediction may be "the factor X will increase as a result of an increase in the factor Y." A qualitative prediction allows one to test the theory that generated it, but it does not provide a very strong test. Because there are only a few possible outcomes in a qualitative situation (e.g., factor X will either increase, stay the same, or decrease), the probability that the "correct" outcome will happen by chance is correspondingly high. A quantitative prediction, on the other hand, can be a much stronger test of the theory, because it will not only say that X will increase, but by how much. Furthermore, it may specify the shape of the functional relationship between X and Y, and even how factor Z would affect this shape. Quantitative predictions, however, are sometimes difficult to obtain from general strategic models that lack biological detail. This observation suggests a role for more detailed models as system-specific links to data. Such realistic (but complex) models can be derived from strategic models by adding biological detail specific to the system.

INTERPRETING THE DATA   Sometimes an investigator is motivated not by a desire to test general theory, but by the necessity of measuring some specific quantity. This is a situation often encountered in applied ecology. For example, suppose that we need to estimate mortality in a population in which we cannot follow individuals, so that we have to resort to mark-recapture methods. The problem is to distinguish between the organisms that die and those that move away. Caging animals is out of question, since restricting emigration would completely change the natural behavior of individuals. In such (quite typical) situations, our only recourse may be to explicitly model the processes of mortality and movement, and to estimate the parameters that quantify these two rates by fitting the model to mark-recapture data (see Chapter 6). The answer will be model-dependent, and may be influenced by the model choice. This is not an insurmountable problem, however, since there are objective, data-based methods for selecting among several candidate models.

FORECASTING AND PREDICTION   Finally, the most powerful, but also the most elusive goal of modeling is forecasting and prediction. *Forecasting* is weaker then prediction, and uses the knowledge of the past behavior of the system to forecast its future state. Forecasting does not necessarily require an in-depth understanding of the system's dynamics, and can be done at the phenomenological level. However, forecasting will most likely fail if the system's dynamics change. I use *prediction* in its strongest sense: that is, to predict a situation that was not encountered in the past. For example, it may be necessary to generate predictions about how a system's behavior will change as a result of a certain human intervention. Prediction, in general, requires a mechanistic understanding of the system. The ability to predict should be the ultimate goal and the most powerful test to which a model could be subjected. This does not mean, however, that non-predictive models or science are worthless—prediction is, after all, only one of the modeling goals listed above.

This classification of modeling purposes roughly follows the classical spectrum of description–explanation–prediction. Thus, *formal statement of the problem* and *identifying knowledge gaps* are descriptive goals; *gaining theoretical insights* and *interpreting the data* are explanatory; while *forecasting and prediction* and *quantitative test of theory* address predictive aspects of modeling.

Finally, a comment is due on one nonbiological motivation of modeling. As Pielou (1977) remarked, it is now an established tradition in applied mathematics to "raid" the subject matter of ecology for illustrative material. Although many articles begin by paying lip service to one or another ecological problem, their purpose is to examine the properties of abstract mathematical objects, or "prove theorems." This is essentially a mathematical activity, and often has no immediate relevance for ecology. Nevertheless, we are fortunate that ecology has been such a fertile ground for mathematicians, because many of the models formulated and solved by mathematicians for the mathematical audience have turned out to be very useful for ecologists, although not necessarily in the context within which they were formulated. Thus, many formulas used in this book were developed without ecological motivation, but proved invaluable in investigations of ecological movement (see also a commentary by Levin [1980] on the relationship between mathematicians and biologists).

3.1.2   Lagrangian and Eulerian approaches

In addition to differing in their goals, movement models can be classified in many other ways: analytical versus simulation; simple versus detailed; stochastic versus deterministic; and by their mathematical structure (whether key variables such as the population density, space, and time are discrete or continuous, see Section 3.7). However, one basic distinction I want to stress here is that between Lagrangian and Eulerian models.

The *Lagrangian* point of view is centered on the moving individual. For example, an individual's movement could be characterized by velocity and acceleration. Acceleration (which includes turning) may be influenced by the spatial coordinates of the organism (via environmental influences such as the distribution of resources, and presence of natural enemies). A typical example of a Lagrangian model is a computer simulation of individuals moving through heterogeneous environments. Being individual-based, all Lagrangian models represent population numbers as a discrete variable.

The *Eulerian* point of view, by contrast, is centered on a point in space. The spatial point is characterized by densities (or numbers) and fluxes of moving organisms. A typical example of the Eulerian approach is a diffusion model. Thus, Lagrangian and Eulerian points of view roughly correspond to the individual and population level of organization. Because they are two sides of the same coin, these two approaches to modeling movement are not isolated, but are related to each other. Thus, to a certain degree, a model formulated within one approach can be translated into a corresponding model within the other. These links will be discussed in greater detail in Chapter 4.

3.2   Linear Dispersal

At large spatial scales, movement paths of real organisms rarely resemble straight lines. Nevertheless, an assumption of linear movement greatly simplifies the model mechanics, and such models have been used to gain theoretical insights. I will review two of these models later in this section.

At small spatial scales, however, paths of real organisms can be approximately represented by straight lines without a great loss of biological realism. Linear representation can be thought of as one extreme case of path idealization, with an infinitely wriggly trajectory assumed by diffusion as the opposite extreme. Moreover, many organisms tend to move relatively straight for a

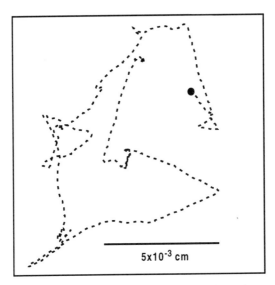

Figure 3.1: A digitized path of a bacterium *Escherichia coli* ranging in a homogeneous isotropic medium. (After Berg 1983.)

period of time, and then make a turn and move in another direction. The bacterium *Escherichia coli* is one of the best examples of this type of movement (Figure 3.1). These bacteria make "runs" that have an average duration of 1 s, periodically interrupted by short periods (about 0.1 s) of "tumbling" (Berg 1983). During tumbling, motion is very erratic, and the direction of the next run is largely independent of the previous one.

Movement of other organisms can also be approximately represented by a sequence of straight runs. Examples include the blowfly *Phormia regina* (Dethier 1989), thrushes (Smith 1974), and checkerspot butterflies (Turchin et al. 1991). Another example is passive dispersal of wind-borne organisms such as aphids—as long as the wind direction stays constant. It is important to keep in mind, however, that a straight-line representation is still an approximation, even in a very simple organism such as bacteria. Thus, runs of *E. coli* are not completely straight, and the movement direction of bacteria during a run tends to drift, with an average change of 27° (Berg 1983). In general, studies of ranging animals suggest that most species are incapable of moving very far in a straight line without the assistance of some external cue (Bell 1991).

Models of linear movement can be useful for gaining insights into the interaction between small-scale (that is, smaller than the average length of a straight-line move) environmental heterogeneity and organism movement. For

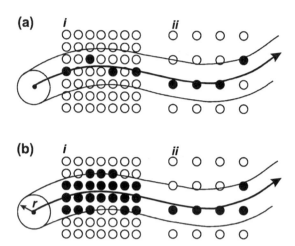

Figure 3.2: Herbivore search for patchily distributed host plants. A herbivorous insect flies from left to right, and perceives all plants within a distance r from its track. In case (a), the herbivore flies a constant distance after visiting one host plant before it lands on another. (Black circles indicate plants on which the herbivore landed.) In case (b), the herbivore lands on all plants that it perceives. Thus, in case (a) the herbivore lands on the same number of plants in both the dense patch i and in the sparse patch ii, but an individual plant in the dense patch has a lower probability of being landed on. In case (b), more plants are landed on in patch i, and the probability of being attacked is the same in both patches. (After Stanton 1982a.)

example, is there an optimal search direction for an animal flying or swimming in a wind or current? Using a simple model of linear movement, Dusenberry (1989) found that the optimal direction of search is influenced by the shape of the *active space* around a resource item (such as the shape of a chemical plume). While the optimal search direction for a spherical active space was downwind, the optimal heading while searching for highly elongated active spaces was nearly cross-flow. Another example is the conceptual model used by Stanton (1982a) to gain insights into effects of spatial distribution of host plants on the probability that individual plants will be found and attacked by herbivores. In particular, she considered the effect of host density in a patch on herbivore attack rate. These ideas are illustrated in Figure 3.2.

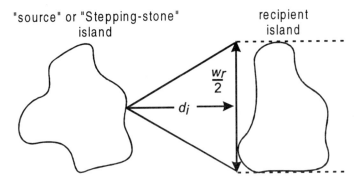

Figure 3.3: The stepping-stone model. (After MacArthur and Wilson 1967.)

STEPPING-STONE DISPERSAL   One of the best known and most influential examples utilizing the assumption of linear dispersal is the stepping-stone model of MacArthur and Wilson (1967: Chapter 6). MacArthur and Wilson were interested in understanding how the rate of species exchange between two islands was affected by the distance separating them. They approached this problem by constructing a simple dispersal model, described below.

MacArthur and Wilson's model assumes that a propagule moves in a constant direction—for example, an insect carried by wind over sea (Figure 3.3). If there is a constant probability per unit of time that the propagule will stop movement (e.g., fall from the air to the ground or sea), then the dispersal distance r follows the exponential distribution with the probability density function proportional to $\exp[-br]$ (where b is a constant). With the purpose of exploring how various assumptions on the mode of movement affect model predictions, MacArthur and Wilson also examined the consequences of normal distribution of dispersal distances. However, they incorrectly state that this distribution is expected when propagules fly through the air on a randomly changing course like diffusing particles. Under the assumption of random walk, the redistribution of particles will be approximately described by a diffusion equation. Thus, a Gaussian surface would describe the *instantaneous* spatial distribution of propagules undergoing random walk. In the Appendix (Section A.3.5) I discuss a model describing the settling of helminth larvae that undergo random walk. Using a very similar model for a particles moving according to random walk having a constant probability of falling out of air, we can calculate that the number of propagules will be proportional to

$$\exp[-\sqrt{\delta/D}\, r]/\sqrt{r}$$

where D is the diffusion rate, and δ is the probability of falling to the ground (or in the sea) per unit of time. Interestingly, the frequency distribution of dispersal distances implied by this relationship is almost identical in mathematical form to the exponential distribution implied by the model with linear dispersal, differing only by a factor of $r^{-1/2}$.

THE Δ MODEL   Another simple model of movement was advanced by L. R. Taylor and R. A. J. Taylor, who wanted to draw the attention of ecologists to the importance of the spatial component of population dynamics, and in particular, to the role of density-dependent movement in population regulation (Taylor and Taylor 1977, R. A. J. Taylor 1981a,b). Taylor (1981a) assumed that displacement of an individual is governed by two opposite forces, or "behavioral pressures": repulsion and attraction between conspecifics. He further assumed that these two forces are related to the distance separating individuals by an inverse power law. Translating (in a rather *ad hoc* fashion) interindividual distances into population density, and equating the net force Δ to the distance moved by an organism, Taylor (1981a) arrived at the following equation relating the distance moved to population density:

$$\Delta = \epsilon[(\rho/\rho_0)^p - (\rho/\rho_0)^q] \qquad (3.1)$$

Here ϵ and exponents p and q are constants; ρ_0 is the population density below which movement is dominated by congregation, while above it movement is dispersive.

Despite an interesting initial concept of including influence of population density on movement, the consequent development of the Δ model suffers from a number of inconsistencies and errors, as detailed in the review of Thorarinsson (1986). Although this model continues to be cited in ecological literature, as far as I know, it has not stimulated further theoretical or empirical work.

Synthesis

Simple models of linear movement, such as that of MacArthur and Wilson (1967), are typically not meant as realistic descriptions of movement of any particular organism (although the distribution of dispersal distances is often well fitted with the negative exponential function; see Section 3.3). Their primary value is in stimulating ecologists to think more explicitly about the interplay between movement and spatial population dynamics, e.g., the effect of spatial relations between source and target islands, or other habitat patches (MacArthur and Wilson 1967), or the effects of population density on dispersal (Taylor and Taylor 1977).

3.3 Empirical Models

Phenomenological models describing relationship between the organism density and distance from the point of release, or from the population source, were among the first quantitative tools employed by ecologists to study dispersal, beginning in the 1940s (see below). The basic premise of this approach is that as the distance from the source of the dispersers increases, disperser density will decline. This density decline is a result of two factors: (1) because few organisms will travel very far, as a result of tendency to settle, or because of limited life span; and (2) dilution of organism numbers by greater area at increased distances from the center. Intuitively it is clear that by measuring density versus distance curves we can learn something, and maybe a lot, about the extent of dispersal. (There are some pitfalls and caveats, however, that will be addressed in Chapter 6.)

An important advantage of empirical models over earlier approaches is that they are *quantitative*, and can be used to quantify movement of organisms under natural conditions. Their primary role, however, is descriptive. The empirical relationships are used to summarize data trends, and to extract certain useful statistics. For example, making certain additional assumptions, a fitted density-distance curve can be used to calculate the median dispersal distance, that is, the radius of a circle enclosing 50% of dispersal distances (Freeman 1977; more on this in Section 6.2.5). Density-distance curves abstract from the detail of individual movement, and thus can be used as an elemental building block (the redistribution module) in a model of spatial population dynamics. They are particularly suitable for spatial models discrete in time, but continuous in space (e.g., Pacala and Silander 1985).

A bewildering variety of *ad hoc* functional relationships has been used by investigators. A little order can be created out of the confusion by considering these relationships to be particular cases of the response surface methodology (RSM) of Box and Draper (1987). RSM is a general and very powerful approach to fitting phenomenological models (that is, when the functional form is unknown). RSM is basically a polynomial approximation of the functional relationship between the response variable u and the predictor variable r, but both u and r are transformed using the Box-Cox transformation (Box and Cox 1964). For example, using the first-degree (linear) polynomial and only one predictor variable, the RSM model is:

$$u^{(\phi)} = \alpha + \beta r^{(\theta)} \tag{3.2}$$

The Box-Cox transformation is the same as the power-transformation, but supplemented by the log-transformation when the exponent (θ or ϕ) is equal to zero. It includes as special cases most common statistical transformations,

Table 3.1: Correspondence between functional forms used in empirical models and RSM transformation parameters ϕ and θ.

	Function	ϕ	θ	References
I	$u = a\exp[-br]$	0	1	Frampton et al. 1942
II	$u = a - b\log r$	1	0	Wadley and Wolfenbarger 1944
III	$u = ar^b$	1	b	Wilson and Baker 1946
IV	$u = a - b/r$	1	-1	Paris 1965
V	$u = \exp[a - br^2]$	0	2	Ito and Myashita 1965
VI	$u = \exp[a - br^{\frac{1}{2}}]$	0	$\frac{1}{2}$	Wallace 1966
VII	$u = \exp[a + br^c]$	0	c	Taylor 1978
VIII	$u = a + b\log r + c/r$	–	–	Wadley and Wolfenbarger 1944
IX	$u = \exp[a - b\sqrt{r}] - ct + dr\log t]$	–	–	Freeman 1977
X	$u = \exp[a - br^c - d\log r]$	–	–	Taylor 1980, Portnoy and Wilson 1993

e.g., square-root ($\theta = 1/2$), logarithmic ($\theta = 0$), inverse ($\theta = -1$), and no transformation ($\theta = 1$).

It turns out that most of the functional forms proposed for describing the relationship between the density of dispersers (or numbers recaptured in a trap) u and the distance from the release center r are special cases of the RSM model (Equation 3.2). For example, the negative exponential function $u = a\exp[-br]$ (Frampton et al. 1942, Kettle 1951), that, when log-transformed, is $\log u = \log a - br$, corresponds to the response surface model with $\phi = 0$ and $\theta = 1$. Other models are summarized in Table 3.1. The last three models go beyond the general functional form of RSM—model VIII combines log-transformed with inverse-transformed r, model X adds together a power and log-transformed r-terms, while model IX mixes the spatial with temporal coordinates. Note that model X is an attempt at a general form, like RSM (it also has the same number of parameters). Interestingly, model X has some mechanistic justification, being the model that Portnoy and Wilson (1993) derived as an approximate description of the tail of the distribution of dispersal distances (see Section 6.3.4).

There has been a number of empirical analyses using the models in Table 3.1 (Wolfenbarger 1946, Gregory and Read 1949, Kettle 1951, Ito and

Miyashita 1965, Paris 1965, Wallace 1966, Freeman 1977, Taylor 1978, 1980). No consensus has emerged as to which model should be preferred, or under what conditions we should prefer one model over another. The general problem is that empirical curve fitting lacks a mechanistic basis. More specifically:

1. Most previous analyses of density-distance curves suffer from a number of statistical problems. Little attention has been devoted to error structure in the data. Yet inappropriate assumptions about the distribution of residuals may lead to a serious bias in the fitted relationship (Turchin and Thoeny 1993). Another statistical problem is that different models have different numbers of parameters. Thus, it is not surprising that the three-parameter model VII outperformed the two parameter models I, V, and VI, that are special cases of VII in the analyses of Taylor (1978). A related problem is that published comparisons often do not report at how many distances the density of dispersers was measured. This is critical information, because if there are, for example, only three distances, then any model with three or more parameters will fit the mean density at each of three distances perfectly.

2. More importantly, comparisons between various phenomenological models, such as the ones listed in Table 3.1, cannot result in any progress towards understanding movement processes. It is always difficult to make inferences about underlying mechanisms from observing patterns. If we construct two or more *mechanistic* models, then we can confront them with patterns observed in the data, and possibly reject one model in favor of another. (We can never prove that our best model is true, because there always are an infinite number of other models that could produce exactly the same pattern in the data.) Rejecting one phenomenological model in favor of another does not result in a similar advance.

3. This weakness of empirical models—their phenomenological rather than mechanistic basis—did not go unnoticed by the investigators that used them. In fact, there were several attempts to interpret various functional components in terms of possible mechanisms. For example, Wadley (1957) suggested that the term $b \log r$ in models II and VIII accounted for disappearance of organisms. The term b/r in Model IV was interpreted by Paris (1965) as dilution of density due to increased area at greater r. Model V is typically interpreted as the expected form when movement is "random," because it is basically the same as the Gaussian distribution that describes a population diffusing from a single point. Unfortunately, such *ad hoc* interpretations are always vague, and sometimes wrong.

As an example, Taylor (1978) made an observation that model V is a special case of his general function (model VII) with the exponent $c = 2$. He argued that model V is a parametric form of the Gaussian distribution, and thus corresponds to the case of "random motion." He then fitted model V to the density of *Drosophila* flies averaged over a 10 day period, and found that the model fitted very badly, concluding that fly movement was non-random. However, the Gaussian curve describes the spatial distribution of diffusing particles *at any given point in time*. *Time-averaged* spatial distribution of diffusing particles has a completely different functional form, more similar to model I than V (see Box 6.2 and Section A.3.5). Thus, Taylor's result had no bearing on whether or not fly movement is nonrandom.

Taylor (1978) furthermore postulated that a deviation in the fitted parameter c from 2 is a measure of nonrandomness in movement. He suggested that $c > 2$ (flattened curves, or platykurtosis) is an indication of attraction between individuals, while $c < 2$ (leptokurtosis, characterized by a narrow peak with fat tails) should be an indication of repulsion among individuals. This interpretation is incorrect because, first, when data are time-averaged (all Taylor's data were average numbers at a distance, see caption of Table 1 in Taylor 1980), we expect to see leptokurtic distributions without respect to behavioral interactions. Second, it is not true that repulsion should result in leptokurtosis. On the contrary, repulsion among individuals should quickly level off a sharp peak observed in leptokurtic distributions, rather than create one. The point is that attempts to assign meaning to various empirical models that argue by analogy can be highly misleading.

4. Because of their lack of a firm mechanistic basis, many empirical relationships have mathematical flaws. It has been pointed out, for example, that functions involving $\log r$ and $1/r$ terms become infinite as $r \to 0$. This is not such a serious problem, as long as the integral of the density u over the whole space is finite. Existence of the integral is important if we want to go beyond curve fitting and interpret the fitted function as a frequency distribution of dispersal distances (probabilities of all possible events must sum to one). Recasting the fitted function as a probability distribution allows us to infer the mean or median dispersal distance, and the distribution can be directly employed in modeling individual movements. Thus, it is much more important that the empirical function be well-behaved out at the tails, rather then in the center, because the area affected by tails is infinitely large. For this reason, the real problem lies with models whose tails do not go to zero, either becoming negative (e.g., model II and VIII), or tending to a positive asymptote (e.g., model IV).

Synthesis

Empirical models constitute an important stage in the historical development of quantitative methods for analysis of movement. They lack, however, a firm mechanistic basis, and attempts to assign meaning to various functions *post hoc* have not enjoyed much success. It is much more profitable to build mechanistic models from the ground up (see Chapter 4), and to use them to infer the expected functional forms for data analysis. We now have a suite of such mechanistically-grounded models, and thus there is no further need to employ phenomenological models.

3.4 Diffusion

Diffusion models and random walks are closely connected, although distinct mathematical topics. In particular, diffusion models are often derived as continuum approximations of discrete random walk processes (see Section 4.2). Diffusion models have been of enormous value in both theoretical and empirical investigations of spatial aspects of population ecology. Their value for ecological theory is that they provide a natural spatial extension of Lotka-Volterra models. Traditionally, ecological models for population growth and interactions have been formulated as ordinary differential equations. To add a spatial dimension, one needs to take only two logical steps: (1) redefine population density as a function of both time and space, and (2) replace the system of ordinary differential equations with a partial differential equation system. The spatial model has all the same growth, death, and interaction terms, but in addition there are diffusion terms that redistribute the population in space without changing total population numbers.

From the empirical point of view, diffusion models have been especially useful in situations where we cannot follow individuals and observe their movement behaviors. When we attempt to quantify movement by measuring how population numbers vary in space and time (e.g., by recapturing marked individuals with traps) we essentially adopt an Eulerian point of view, and thus we need Eulerian models to analyze the data. In such investigations, however, it is important not to forget that the diffusion approach is much more general and flexible than the simple diffusion equation.

3.4.1 A brief history

Application of random walks and diffusion models to ecological problems has a long history. Much of the mathematical framework for treating dispersal was available by the end of last century, and in fact was utilized by Maxwell in developing a kinetic theory of gases based on the behavior of an infinity of perfectly elastic spheres moving at random (Skellam 1951). In 1905, Albert Einstein developed the mathematical theory of Brownian motion. The first explicit description of a random walk was given by Karl Pearson in the same year (Weiss 1983). Early applications of the random-walk framework in biology were made by Pearson and Blakeman (1906) to the problem of random migration of species, and by Brownlee (1911) to the spread of an epidemic. Random walks often serve as the microscopic model for the phenomenon of diffusion, and there are very close links between these two classes of mathematical models (Weiss 1983). Mathematical methods for random walk and diffusion were steadily improved during the first half of this century, in part stimulated by developments in spatially structured evolutionary theory (Fisher 1937, Kolmogorov et al. 1937), but it was not until the early fifties that these tools were used in mathematical population ecology.

In 1951 Skellam published his seminal paper on random dispersal in theoretical populations. Skellam's paper made a number of contributions. It provided a heuristic derivation of the diffusion equation as an approximation of a simple random walk. Skellam included diffusion in models of population growth and competition between two species in heterogeneous habitats. Finally, Skellam applied the diffusion framework to the problem of the spread of an invading species and critical patch size. Skellam's paper is the single most important influence on the theory of spatially structured populations. Many of his ideas introduced in the 1951 paper are still being actively developed by theoretical ecologists.

Another pioneering paper was published two years later by Patlak (1953a). Patlak approached ecological diffusion from a different viewpoint than Skellam (1951). Instead of investigating the consequences of random dispersal to spatial population dynamics, Patlak was interested in developing a more realistic model of movement behavior that mixed stochastic and deterministic elements. Thus, Patlak's approach includes the ability to model realistic features of movement behavior, such as area-restricted search and long-distance attraction to resource patches. Unlike Skellam's paper, Patlak's contributions were virtually ignored by theoretical ecologists until the 1980s (Okubo 1980, Doucet and Wilschut 1987, Turchin 1989b), and his approach was not tested with field data until recently (Turchin 1991). Nevertheless, Patlak's approach has much to offer to both theoretical and field ecologists who are interested in movement models more realistic than simple diffusion. I will return to this paper in Chapters 4 and 5.

Empirical application of diffusion to ecological movement began in the 1940s, primarily focusing on insects. Curiously, early studies were motivated not by issues in insect population ecology, but instead were prompted by evolutionary concerns—measuring the effective population size (Timofeef-Ressovsky and Timofeef-Ressovsky 1940, Dobzhansky and Wright 1943, 1947); or by applied problems—the spread of insect-transmitted diseases in crops

(Frampton et al. 1942) and contamination of seed crops by alien pollen borne by insect pollinators (Bateman 1947a,c). The classic work of Dobzhansky and Wright (1943) had as much influence on the empirical aspect as Skellam's had on the theoretical aspect of ecological diffusion. Despite being more than 50 years old, the Dobzhansky and Wright (1943) paper is still one of the best introductions to the technique, potential problems, and statistical analysis of mark-recapture experiments.

3.4.2   The bugbear of "randomness"

Because diffusion models are closely connected with random walks, ecologists often identify diffusion with random movement. It is worthwhile, however, to discuss what "random" actually means. Anybody who has observed animals searching for a patchily distributed resource (food, mates, or oviposition sites) notices that there almost always is an irregular, apparently unpredictable, element in their movements. In animals with poorly developed sensory systems, like many insect herbivores, the impression of randomness is overwhelming. "Although their survival depends on finding a suitable host, many herbivores bumblingly search in a haphazard fashion and must literally bump into a host plant before they recognize it as food" (Kareiva 1985b). However, animals with highly developed sensory systems also search in an apparently random manner when there are no directional cues available to them because the target is too distant (e.g., trajectories of homing birds, Griffin and Hock 1949).

Of course, we do not know that animals truly move at random, like flipping coins to decide whether to turn right or left. Each individual could be a perfect automaton, rigidly reacting to environmental cues and its internal states in accordance with some set of behavioral rules. However, even if this were true, we might still choose to model behavior of such animals stochastically, because we would not have the perfect knowledge of all the deterministic rules driving these animals. Even if we did, we might not want to include them all in our dispersal model, since such a model would have an enormous number of parameters and would require a very accurate representation of all environmental "micro-cues." The point is that randomness is a modeling convention. Because it is impractical, and not even helpful, to attempt to model individual movement deterministically, we use a more parsimonious probabilistic model. This approach is aptly termed *behavioral minimalism* (Lima and Zollner 1996). In essence, we adopt a thermodynamic approach: the behavior of individuals is erratic, or irregular, but the redistribution process at the population level has many regular features. There is a direct analogy with thermodynamic theory. The motion of each gas molecule is chaotic and essentially unpredictable, and can only be described probabilistically. When dealing with large numbers of molecules, however, the laws at the aggregate level are for all intents and purposes deterministic. Similarly, the problem of biological dispersal can be treated by starting with a probabilistic description of individual movements (in other words, formulating the problem as a random walk), and then approximating the redistribution process of the ensemble of individuals with a deterministic equation, diffusion.

The thermodynamic approach to dispersal does not have to assume that the movement of each "particle" is completely random. The important feature of this approach is that we can control the degree of realism in the model. Environmental factors that have strong effects on movement can be included explicitly in the model, while other factors that have weak effects (or about which we have no information) are included in the stochastic component. An example of representing the movement of individuals as a sum of deterministic and random elements was discussed by Okubo (1986) in the context of dynamical models of grouping. A systematic application of this approach to constructing more behaviorally sophisticated models (as called for by Lima and Zollner 1996) will be found in Chapter 4.

The term *random* has been used in so many different contexts, and has acquired so many different meanings, that I prefer to avoid it wherever possible (unless it is part of a mathematical designation such as *random walk*). Instead, I will use *stochastic* to describe the random element or component of movement, and *simple random walk* for a model of completely random movement. When "random" is used in the sense "random with respect to direction," I will use *undirected*.

3.4.3   The uses of diffusion

Diffusion models provide continuum approximations of discrete random walks (see Section A.1.1 in the Appendix, and more generally Chapter 4). Why should we bother with an approximation instead of simply simulating movement of organisms using the computer? This issue will be taken up again in Section 4.1. Here it suffices to say that the diffusion equations are more amenable to analytical solutions (Goel and Rychter-Dyn 1974). Partial differential equations arise in many physical applications, and thus there is a wealth of analytical results available for them that can be mined for ecological applications (see Section A.2). Solutions of these diffusion models for various boundary and initial conditions provide ready-made formulas for analyzing mass mark-recapture data (Chapter 6).

Full spatio-temporal solutions may not be available for more realistic, and thus more complex diffusion models. However, even when dealing with such complex models we often can obtain *equilibrium solutions* that describe the spatial distribution of organisms as time approaches infinity. Equilibrium solutions are particularly useful in situations where we can neglect birth and death terms (because they occur on a slower time scale than movement) and are interested in understanding the interplay between spatial heterogeneity and movement. The spatial distribution of organisms resulting from their movements can then be characterized using the concept of the *residence index* (see Section 4.2.5). The residence index provides a connection between (1) the individual movement patterns and (2) population-level redistribution. First, it is expressed in terms of individual movement parameters. As an example, it is the inverse of *motility* in the Fokker-Planck equation (see Section 4.2.5)—the faster organisms move through some portion of habitat, the lower is their expected density there. In other models the residence index has a more complex form (see Section 4.4.3). Second, it directly specifies the spatial distribution to which the population density will tend with time because equilibrium population density at any given point in space is proportional to the residence index.

3.4.4 Synthesis

Diffusion is often equated with "random" movement. However, it is possible for movement to be highly nonrandom, and still to be well approximated by a simple diffusion model at some spatial scale. Moreover, simple diffusion, which corresponds to a completely random walk, is only one kind of a diffusion model. Including various realistic features of individual movement leads to more complex diffusion models (reviewed in Chapter 4). Generalized diffusion models are among the most powerful tools for analyzing and modeling movement in population ecology. They are particularly useful in the analysis of mass mark-recapture experiments, and in providing a connection between the behavioral responses to spatial heterogeneity at the individual level, and the spatial distribution of organisms at the population level.

Diffusion models play an important role in the general framework for quantitative analysis of movement that I advocate in this book. They provide the "glue" between detailed descriptions of movement provided by individual-based models (see Section 3.5) and overall descriptions of population spread, such as density-distance curves (see Section 3.3). The diffusion connection is not infallible—we will not be able to approximate a random walk of arbitrary complexity with a diffusion equation, nor is it possible to obtain analytical solutions for all generalized diffusion models. In such cases, we have to resort to simulation and numerical solutions. Nevertheless, analytical solutions exist for a surprising variety of diffusion models, and many quite complex random walks can be approximated with a diffusion equation. Finally, even where diffusion cannot handle the complexity of the world it still provides a common language for building general theory.

3.5   Individual-Based Movement Models

Ecologists interested in movement were among the pioneers in developing individual-based models (e.g., Siniff and Jessen 1969, Jones 1977) although, at the time, their models were referred to as "computer simulations" rather than individual-based models. Historically, computer simulations of individual-based movement models (IBMMs) and random walk models have been treated as distinct fields (the first primarily biological, the second primarily mathematical). However, both of these approaches to modeling movement rely on the same basic conceptual framework (see Chapter 4).

IBMMs, by definition, adopt the Lagrangian point of view, since the focus is always on the individual, its actions, and its trajectory through space. The basic assumption in IBMMs is that each action during the movement process (e.g., whether to stop or to continue movement, or what direction to take) is a mixture of stochastic and deterministic elements (see Section 3.4.2). For example, whether or not an organism will stop in a certain locality could be a probabilistic process. But in some localities (for example, with abundant food) the probability of stopping might be much higher than in localities where food is absent. In some places the probability of stopping may even be one, in which case the action becomes deterministic. (Note that in biological literature such distinctions are sometimes not made, so that "random walk" often means "completely random walk," see Section 3.4.2.)

IBMMs provide a very "feature-rich" framework for modeling individual movement. Death and birth events are easily incorporated within the framework. In a way, however, this richness is both a strength of IBMMs and a limitation. Attempting to model too many behaviors and too many individuals can strain both the capacity of the computer to simulate the model, and the capacity of the human brain to interpret the results.

Construction and simulation of IBMMs is a very individualistic activity. The strength of IBMMs is in their close connection to specific empirical systems that allows an investigator to build a data-based model and to test it with some independent data set from the same system. The obverse side of the coin is that as a result of individualistic approaches chosen by investigators, it is usually difficult to compare different models for different systems in terms of their structure or results. Thus, little if any general theoretical progress has resulted from IBMMs. However, these models can be very useful when combined with other, less detail-specific approaches, such as the diffusion-approximation models I discuss in Chapter 4. For example, it is not always clear how to translate individual behaviors into population models. IBMMs can be used to generate specific predictions on how spatio-temporal density of, for example, predator and prey will change on a short time scale, depending on various assumptions about individual behavior (e.g., predator foraging tactics, and prey avoidance or defense behaviors). These predictions are then compared to the population rates of change assumed by various population-level models, and a match between behavioral assumptions and population-level assumptions is sought. This is an example of a hierarchical modeling approach. Detailed IBMMs are employed at the smaller spatio-temporal scale with limited numbers of interacting individuals. Population-level models that distill behavioral assumptions with a few key parameters are used to model the spatio-temporal dynamics of the system at a larger spatial scale and for longer periods of time (e.g., generations or years).

Because IBMMs are such individualistic approaches to modeling movement, few other general points can be made about them. Instead of attempting a general overview, in the rest of this section I describe several specific IBMM examples from different ecological and taxonomic perspectives.

3.5.1 A simulation of butterfly search

The work of R. E. Jones on movement patterns and egg distribution in cabbage butterflies (Jones 1977, Jones et al. 1980) provided one of the first demonstrations of how a model based on individual movement behaviors could be used to explain and predict large-scale spatial distribution patterns. Jones began with detailed behavioral observations of female butterflies searching for oviposition sites within spatial arrays of host plants (kale, cauliflowers, and radish). These data served as a basis for a simulation model of butterflies flying, landing, and ovipositing on their host plants.

The space was represented in the model as a discrete rectangular grid of points with the distance of 1 m between points. Each position could be occupied by a host plant, a nectar source, or be left unoccupied ("grass"). The model simulated movement of females as a series of unitary steps between two adjacent grid points (a butterfly could move to one of eight possible neighbors). The direction of each step was determined by an interplay between three factors (Figure 3.4). If one or more of the eight adjacent positions had a host plant, then the butterfly was more likely to move there. In the absence of hosts, the direction of successive moves were autocorrelated. Finally, each butterfly had a preferred direction, randomly chosen from an empirically measured distribution at the beginning of each simulation run (Figure 3.4). The probability that any encountered host would be oviposited on was governed

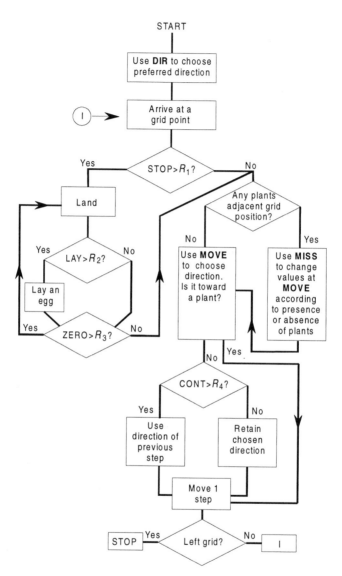

Figure 3.4: Flow chart of the individual-based movement model for cabbage butterflies. R_i are random uniformly distributed variables between 0 and 1. (After Jones 1977.)

by, first, the probability of landing on it, and, second, the probability of laying an egg given that landing occurred. All the model parameters were estimated from the field observation data, and several parameters were allowed to vary with the host species, plant size and age, and the number of eggs that the female carried.

An especially interesting aspect of this research was that Jones used the model to predict the spatial distribution of eggs resulting from individual behaviors of females searching within spatially heterogeneous environments. In one experiment, she manipulated host plant species, age, and density (spacing between plants) and measured the average number of eggs laid per plant in each of these treatments. In the second experiment, Jones et al. (1980) tested the model predictions at a large spatial scale. Females were fed on an artifical diet containing a dye, and upon reaching maturity, they were released within a large (1 km^2) array of cabbage plants. The distribution of colored eggs laid by experimental females was compared with the distribution predicted by the model. Although no statistical tests were performed, a visual comparison between model predictions and data suggested that the model accurately mimicked the observed egg distribution.

This study by Jones and colleagues was a truly pioneering work and exerted an important influence on the developing field of insect movement. Their model was closely tailored to the characteristics of the studied species, the cabbage butterfly. The model parameters were estimated directly using the behavioral data. Finally, and most importantly, the model was constructed using observations of individual movements at a small spatial scale (20 × 40 m and 20 × 90 m patches of host plants), but was tested by predicting spatial distribution of eggs at a large spatial scale (1 km × 1 km).

3.5.2 Clonal growth in the white clover

Many clonal plants move as they grow: although ramets within a clone are sedentary, the clone itself (the genet) often is mobile. The situation may be further complicated because in many species the connections between ramets can be lost over time. The end result is a complex spatial mosaic of clonal fragments (sets of interconnected ramets) of varying sizes (Cain et al. 1995). Cain et al. developed a stochastic simulation of how clones of the white clover, *Trifolium repens*, spread through space. Their basic conceptual framework for representing growth and movement in clover stolons is very similar to a correlated random walk (Figure 3.5).

The stochastic simulation model of Cain et al. (1995) assumed that each stolon grew independently of other stolons in its clonal fragment. The growth of an apical meristem was density-dependent (Figure 3.6) and, therefore, the

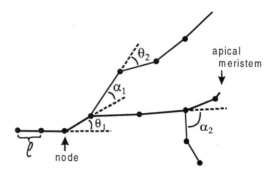

Figure 3.5: An approximate representation of growth and movement in white clover. Black circles represent nodes, thick lines the primary stolon, and thinner lines are secondary stolons. (After Cain et al. 1995.)

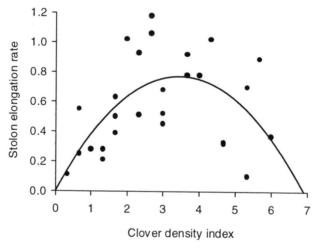

Figure 3.6: Stolon elongation rate observed in the field as a function of local clover density. The curve is a second order polynomial fitted to the data. (After Cain et al. 1995.)

simulation first determined the local density of nodes with leaves. It then calculated the stolon elongation rate based on the quadratic relationship between the elongation rate and density observed in the field. The stolon length at time $t + \Delta t$, $S(t + \Delta t)$, was calculated from the exponential relation (because the magnitude of stolon elongation increased with initial stolon length):

$$S(t + \Delta t) = S(t) \exp[b\Delta t] \tag{3.3}$$

where $S(t)$ is the stolon length at the previous time step, b is the stolon elongation rate, and Δt is the time step in the simulation (set to 2 weeks). A node was added when the cumulative stolon growth since the previous node exceeded the internode distance (determined at the time when the previous node was created). When a new node was added, a new internode length (until the next node) and an angle of growth (θ_i, see Figure 3.5) were chosen randomly from empirically derived distributions. In addition, there was a certain probability that a branch stolon would be initiated from a node.

Stolon dieback rates were independent of local clover density. The dieback rate was assumed to be a uniformly distributed random variable on the interval $(0, 0.0112)$. For each time step, the model used a randomly selected dieback rate to calculate the length of stolon (including nodes) to remove, using an equation analogous to Equation 3.3. When a node with a branch point died, the simulation treated the resulting two colonial fragments as separate entities.

In summary, the model of Cain et al. (1995) illustrates how the random walk framework, originally applied to animal movements, can be adapted to modeling clonal plant growth. The major features of the framework are retained: the assumption of discrete "moves" (from node to node) characterized by length, turning angle, and temporal duration (how many time steps were needed). The clover simulation model then extends the random walk framework in two ways: (1) by allowing branches, and (2) by keeping track not only of the stolon elongation at the front end, but also of stolon contraction at the rear end *via* the process of dieback. Despite these extensions, the philosophy underlying the application of this model to data is very similar to that in the cabbage butterfly example. An individual movement model is formulated and its parameters are estimated in the field using short-term experiments. The functional dependence of move attributes on spatial heterogeneity is quantified (in this case, the relationship between the stolon elongation rate and local clover density; Figure 3.6). Finally, spatial patterns in clover distribution predicted by the model are compared to an independent long-term data set. Once again, this example illustrates the strength of the IBMM approach in providing a direct approach to data—both for fitting parameters and for testing model predictions.

3.5.3 Ungulate winter foraging

The last example, from Turner et al. (1993, 1994), is conceptually similar to the model of Jones (1977), although it is more complex, and has a somewhat different focus, emphasizing energetics of individual foragers rather than their movements. Turner et al. (1993, 1994) simulated movements and grazing of large ungulates (elk and bison) within large-scale random and actual landscapes. The space was represented in the model as a discrete rectangular 100×100 grid, with each 1 ha cell classified as one of four grassland or two forest types, each characterized by a different initial value of forage quantity. In addition to the influence of habitat type, the amount of forage was affected by whether and when the area was burned in the 1988 Yellowstone fires. The distribution of landscape types and states (burned or unburned) was taken from the Yellowstone Park geographic information system database. Initial amount of forage in each cell can be depleted through winter by ungulate consumption. Each cell is also affected by snow conditions (depth and density).

Ungulates were assumed to always forage in groups; thus, the quantity moved around in the simulation is not an individual animal, but a whole group. Turner et al. (1993) examined three different algorithms for group movement, but in their 1994 paper, they focused on one. The algorithm assumes that animals possess knowledge of the state of each cell within the landscape. The group examines the landscape within the radius of a maximum distance that it can move, identifies the nearest resource site with at least some forage available, and moves there. If there are several cells with forage at the same distance, then the group moves to the one with the highest quantity of food. The movement submodel, thus, is rather simplistic, but more complex alternatives would be difficult to justify until more data are available on what these animals actually do under various conditions.

The submodel dealing with ungulate energetics is more sophisticated (probably because better data are available). Maximum forage intake, achieved in cells with abundant forage and no snow, is a function of the body weight of the animal. This maximum is reduced by two factors: decreased forage biomass and increased thickness of snow cover. Daily energetic balances are computed as a difference between the energy gain due to food intake, and the energy loss due to maintenance and travel.

Turner et al. (1994) tested their model by comparing simulated and observed elk and bison mortalities in three winters. The simulations were in agreement with the data, although this comparison was not completely rigorous since substantial mortality was observed only in one winter (1988–1989), and that winter's data were used to calibrate values of two model parameters.

A factorial simulation experiment suggested that the dominant factor in ungulate survival is winter severity. Under mild winter conditions even very large fires had no effect on survival. However, when winter conditions were average to severe, fire size and pattern became important. Interestingly, ungulate survival was higher with a clumped, rather than with a fragmented fire pattern (Turner et al. 1994). This result suggests that fire-fighting efforts, if they result in a pattern of many small fires instead of one large one, may be counterproductive from the point of view of ungulate populations (although this may not be an important management goal at the Yellowstone Park).

In summary, Turner et al. (1993, 1994) developed a detailed individual-based simulation of movement and foraging of ungulate herds in heterogeneous landscapes. Their model can be useful in informing ungulate management decisions. The model also points out two areas where further empirical work is critical: better understanding of movement rules used by ungulate groups, and the need for a rigorous field test of the model using independent data.

3.5.4   Synthesis

Individual-based simulations have many attractive features that made them the modeling tool of choice for empirical ecologists. They do not require much mathematical background and can be made as detailed and complex as their creator desires. They are unparalleled in the ease with which they can be connected to an empirical investigation, as the three examples in this section show. Of the three general approaches to quantifying movement (the other two being diffusion and empirical curve-fitting), individual-based simulation is the most versatile one—it is possible to imagine a book like this one in which most, if not all, analyses would employ simulation models.

If we only use simulation models, however, then we would have no general theory in spatial ecology, because simulation models are a terrible medium for communicating ideas and for obtaining general insights. The simulation approach is also a miserable way to begin analyzing data. What we need in the early stages of analysis is a set of tools that can quickly give us general ideas about how the empirical system may work. The answers may be based on approximations, but that is not a problem because they can always be sharpened later. Attempting to construct a simulation model before some general intuition about the system is developed runs the danger of getting lost among the trees, and never seeing the forest. In the later stages of analysis, by contrast, we are likely to employ specific simulation models, because at that point we need their precision to discriminate between increasingly more complex and detailed hypotheses about movement mechanisms (assuming our data are good enough to get us that far).

These are the reasons, therefore, for *not* basing this book on simulation models. In fact, in the pages to follow I devote relatively little space to simulation models and their mechanics. I do that not because I find little worth in them, but because (1) this is not a programming textbook, and (2) constructing a simulation model is conceptually a simple task—all you need is a fast computer and a stout heart. Constructing a *useful* simulation model, a model that would increase your understanding of the empirical system, is much harder, and that is where this book should help.

3.6   Passive Dispersal

Passive dispersal is distinguished from active movement by the source of energy used in accomplishing spatial displacement: in the first case the energy comes from the environment, while in the second case it comes from within the organism itself (Wolfenbarger 1975). Thus, passive dispersal is largely determined by movements of the medium—typically, air, water, or another organism (in the case of phoresy). Okubo (1980) similarly distinguishes between passive and active diffusion. Passive *dispersal* is somewhat of a misnomer, however, since it does not necessarily lead to population spread in space. For example, convergent wind patterns may concentrate, rather than disperse certain insect populations, like migratory locusts (Rainey 1979, Pedgley 1982).

Terrestrial organisms usually have some degree of control over their displacement during passive dispersal, because they can control when to initiate movement and, to a certain extent, when to terminate it. Additionally, organisms may take advantage of certain properties of the fluid or gaseous medium that carries them. For instance, organisms can use vertical wind (or water current) shear to control the speed of displacement. In fact, there is no sharp boundary between passive dispersal and active locomotion, since actively moving organisms frequently take advantage of media motion, for example, soaring birds riding on updrafts.

3.6.1   Wind-mediated dispersal of seeds

Seed dispersal is one of the three fundamental processes (in addition to fecundity and survivorship) that determine spatio-temporal dynamics of plant populations (e.g., Pacala and Silander 1985). Many plants disperse seeds, pollen, or spores by wind. Thus, models of wind-mediated dispersal have been primarily formulated in the context of plant ecology, although they can be equally well applied to passive dispersal of other small airborne organisms, including minute insects and mites.

Until fairly recently, most widely used models of seed or spore dispersal have been phenomenological in nature (Okubo and Levin 1989). For example, Pacala and Silander (1985) suggested that a dispersal module of a plant population dynamics model may be obtained by empirically fitting a dispersal function relating the number of seeds to the distance from the source (see Section 6.5.2 for an example). As Okubo and Levin (1989) point out, however, "such models provide no way to extrapolate from one situation to another based on independently measured physical parameters, and no understanding of the underlying mechanisms." Recently, several authors have developed mechanistic models of plant dispersal by wind (e.g., Okubo and Levin 1989 and Greene and Johnson 1989, who apparently were unaware of each others work, but ended up publishing their articles cheek-to-jowl in the same journal issue; see also Portnoy and Wilson 1993). Here we will look in detail at one of these papers, Okubo and Levin (1989).

Okubo and Levin (1989) discuss several mechanistic approaches to modeling wind-mediated dispersal, borrowed from literature on atmospheric diffusion of pollutants. The first one, the *Gaussian plume model* (Figure 3.7a), assumes that particles move under the influences of two forces: advection due to wind, and diffusion due to turbulent movement of air. This model, however, makes no allowance for gravitational settling of seeds. The *tilted plume model* corrects that omission (Figure 3.7b), by assuming that seeds settle towards the ground with a constant velocity. Okubo and Levin (1989) calculate the number of seeds that will settle at distance x from the seed source in the downwind direction, $Q(x)$ (this quantity is also known as the *crosswind-integrated deposition*):

$$Q(x) = \frac{N_0 W_s}{\sqrt{2\pi}\bar{u}\sigma_z} \exp\left[-\frac{(H - W_s x/\bar{u})^2}{2\sigma_z^2}\right] \tag{3.4}$$

Here N_0 is the rate of seed release at the source, H is height above ground of the seed source, $\bar{u}$ is the mean wind speed, W_s is the settling velocity of seed, and σ_z is the vertical component of variance in seed random motion, or equivalently, the variance in wind speed in the vertical direction.

Interestingly, Greene and Johnson (1989) arrive at a somewhat similar expression:

$$Q(x) = \frac{N_0}{\sqrt{2\pi}x\sigma_x} \exp\left[-\frac{(\ln[W_s x/H\bar{u}_g])^2}{2\sigma_x^2}\right] \tag{3.5}$$

Here $\bar{u}_g$ is the geometric mean wind speed and σ_x^2 is the variance of wind speed in the *downwind* direction (not in the vertical direction, as assumed by Okubo and Levin 1989). The difference between Equations 3.4 and 3.5 apparently results from the different assumptions they make about how turbulence affects the trajectory of falling seed.

The final *advection-diffusion-deposition* model that Okubo and Levin discusses is the most realistic. It allows the wind speed and vertical eddy diffu-

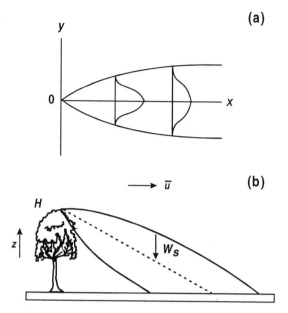

Figure 3.7: (a) Distribution of wind-deposited seeds according to the Gaussian plume model (viewed from above). (b) The tilted plume model. Symbols explained in the text. (After Okubo and Levin 1989.)

sivity to depend on height above ground, and has more realistic boundary conditions representing deposition of seeds at the earth's surface. Okubo and Levin (1989) were unable to obtain an exact general solution of this model, but instead derived a formula for the mode (maximum) of the distribution of seeds, r_m:

$$\lambda \frac{r_m}{H} = \frac{\bar{u}}{W_s} \tag{3.6}$$

This result basically says that the mode r_m scaled by the height H at which seeds are released is directly proportional to the wind speed $\bar{u}$ scaled by the settling speed W_s. The constant of proportionality is the dimensionless quantity λ that measures the relative importance of gravitational settling and vertical diffusion. For heavy seeds, deposition will be primarily affected by their settling velocity, and $\lambda \to 1$. Deposition of light seeds will be dominated by the vertical diffusivity, and $\lambda \gg 1$. Interestingly, both of these limiting cases result in the same relationships that were derived from the tilted plume model, but the models differ slightly for the intermediate values of λ (Okubo and

Levin 1989). This suggests that the simpler tilted plume model succeeded in capturing the key features of wind-mediated seed dispersal.

3.6.2 Atmospheric circulation models for insect dispersal

Models of wind-mediated dispersal primarily focus on the intricacies of turbulent motion of particles as well as their settlement and deposition rates, while the influence of air motions is modeled simply by a constant advection term (the *mean field approximation*). By contrast, atmospheric circulation models focus on complex air movements, in effect assuming that the trajectories of air parcels will largely determine the trajectories of organisms. While wind-mediated dispersal models are primarily meant for local seed or spore movements, atmospheric circulation models attempt to understand and predict long-distance dispersal of organisms on the geographic scale of hundreds and thousands of kilometers.

Entomologists in particular have long realized that weather systems can be extremely important in long-distance migrations of insects. By the time C. G. Johnson wrote his monumental treatise on insect migration, he could review a number of case studies that had established the importance of large-scale weather motions in migration of such insects as leaf-hoppers, aphids, noctuid moths, and locusts (Johnson 1969: Chapters 20-22). The important features of atmospheric movements relevant to insect migration were described by Wellington (1945), Johnson (1969: Chapter 19), Pedgley (1982), and most recently in a thorough review by Drake and Farrow (1988). Drake and Farrow review such important meteorological concepts as the planetary boundary layer and the motions of air within it, and the synoptic-scale weather patterns. One of the most interesting synoptic features (from the point of view of insect ecology) is the area of convergence formed by trade winds arising in the low latitudes of each hemisphere called the intertropical convergence zone. The presence of this weather system provides the basis for the theory of Rainey (1951) that explains the adaptive significance of downwind displacement of locusts. By letting themselves be carried by winds into the intertropical convergence zone, locusts ensure that they will end up in areas receiving plenty of rain that are suitable for the production of offspring. Dingle (1996), however, points out that the situation may be more complex than is suggested by Rainey's model. For a recent review of long-range insect migration in relation to weather systems, see also Pedgley et al. (1995).

By connecting the atmospheric circulation (in other words, population redistribution) module to the appropriate modules of local reproduction and mortality, it is possible to construct models of spatial population dynamics. Furthermore, when supplemented by a wide-area network of sampling units,

these models can be used for forecasting outbreaks and incursions of insects
utilizing atmospheric motions for long-distance movement (Pedgley 1982). For
example, forecasting schemes have been employed for the desert locust, the
African armyworm, and the black bean aphid (Pedgley 1981, Odiyo 1979, Way
et al. 1981; see also Part III of Drake and Gatehouse 1995).

3.6.3 Oceanic transport models

Models of passive transport in oceans are similar in spirit to atmospheric circulation models, but are more sophisticated mathematically and better tested
empirically. Biological questions addressed by these models include spatial
redistribution of planktonic organisms, such as algae and larvae of benthic
invertebrates and fish (Wroblewski et al. 1989, Gregg and Walsh 1992, Koehl
et al. 1993, Schultz and Cowen 1994).

Mathematically, these models are usually framed as advection-diffusion
equations, but with several interesting twists. First, motion components along
the vertical and the horizontal directions are very different. For example, horizontal turbulence is of considerably greater scale than that along the vertical
direction, and therefore horizontal diffusion is much more important (Okubo
1980). The vertical component is, thus, dominated by the advection (sinking
or upwelling) term. Second, the Fickian diffusion model is a poor descriptor
of turbulent diffusion. Okubo (1978, 1980:22-23) gives three representative
solutions for turbulent diffusion, depending on the form of horizontal diffusivity, K_h. Horizontal variances in the particle distribution, corresponding to
these three solutions, increase as the first, second, or third power of time, respectively. Data for limnological and oceanic diffusion tend to support either
the second or third power, but not the first (which corresponds to the Fickian
diffusion). Third, the horizontal diffusion is not necessarily isotropic (*isotropic
diffusion* means that the diffusion coefficient is the same in both the x and
the y direction). Typically, the extent of diffusion is greater in the direction
of flow (advection) as a result of *shear diffusion* (Okubo 1980). Koehl et al.
(1993) empirically confirmed this result by observing behavior of dye "blobs"
in a wave-swept surge channel.

An attempt to include all of these features of water motion would lead to
a very complex model for passive transport of biological entities in the ocean.
Some authors, therefore, choose to focus on the most important components of
transport, and make simplifying assumptions about the rest. For example, the
model of larval dispersal of marine organisms of Possingham and Roughgarden (1990) ignored the vertical dimension of motion, assumed that horizontal
diffusion was isotropic, and represented the coast with a straight line. This
is, of course, an appropriate modeling strategy for the general, qualitative

questions that these authors were interested in addressing (what are the effects of habitat size and the pattern of current flow on population increase or decrease?).

When quantitative and specific predictions are desired, then a more complex and detailed model is needed. An example is the simulation by Gregg and Walsh (1992) of the 1979 spring phytoplankton bloom in the Mid-Atlantic Bight (the US coastal region between Cape Hatteras and Cape Cod). This simulation employed a very sophisticated redistribution model, incorporating both horizontal and vertical terms for advection and diffusion of the medium, plus another vertical term accounting for sinking phytoplankton cells. The boundary conditions were imposed by the actual geography of the coastline and the topography of the sea bottom. These redistribution terms were coupled to the biological process terms: growth and death of the phytoplankton and uptake and excretion of nutrients. This model is an impressive effort which puts together much of what is known about the physical and biological processes in the ocean, and it was gratifying that its predictions were generally in line with the data (chlorophyll observations from Coastal Zone Color Scanner imagery).

Finally, some approaches follow a more empirical track, taking patterns in the ocean circulation as a given (instead of modeling it explicitly), and then attempting to infer their effect on larval dispersal. One example is the calculation by Schultz and Cowen (1994) of the time required for the transport of coral-reef fish larvae to Bermuda from the nearest possible source population (Cape Hatteras). Assuming that transport occurs first via Gulf Stream, and then by cold-core rings thrown off by the Stream, Schultz and Cowen (1994) showed that transport times are much longer than the duration of the pelagic larval stage, suggesting that such transport events would be an infrequent occurrence. In another application of the same idea, Hare and Cowen (1996) developed a scenario for how bluefish larvae and pelagic juveniles could be transported from the South Atlantic Bight, where the adults spawn from March to May, to estuaries in the Middle Atlantic Bight, where juveniles recruit in late May–early June.

3.6.4 Synthesis

Most movement models focus on terrestrial animals who are characterized by active locomotion, and thus they share a certain mechanistic unity. By comparison, dispersal of plants and aquatic organisms has been relatively neglected. This section collects together several modeling approaches that attempt to plug this gap. The approaches are a rather heterogeneous set, both biologically (since we are addressing such different kinds of organisms) and mathematically (because different kinds of media behave in different ways, and have to be modeled using different approaches). There appears to be little opportunity for any meaningful synthesis yet since the field is so young. We will, however, review the progress in the empirical investigation of plant dispersal (Section 6.5).

3.7 Models of Spatial Population Dynamics

In the last section of this chapter we shift our focus from movement models to models of spatial population dynamics that incorporate both movement (population redistribution) terms and birth/death terms. There are three kinds of variables in a spatially explicit population model: population density (possibly of more than one interacting species), space (from one to three dimensions), and time. Each variable can be continuous or discrete, giving a total of eight possible combinations. Curiously, different approaches to modeling spatial dynamics have utilized all of the possible combinations ranging from continuum models (in which all variables are continuous) to cellular automata (in which all variables are discrete).

Choosing to model any variable as either discrete or continuous often has a profound influence on the results. In general, models with continuous variables are easier to solve analytically. On the other hand, in order to be solved numerically on the computer, the model has to be discrete, so any continuous variables must be "discretized." Sometimes, apparently the same model gives different answers depending on whether a particular variable is discrete or continuous. In such cases, it is important to relate the two alternative mathematical formulations to corresponding biological assumptions. For example, suppose that we obtain different results depending on whether time is represented as continuous or discrete. Discrete-time models are appropriate for annual species that breed once per year (semelparity), while continuous-time models may be more appropriate to continuously breeding species with overlapping generations (iteroparity). Thus, it is possible that different mathematical formulations reflect a real difference in life-history characteristics, which would explain why we obtain different results. (For specific examples in the context of spatial dynamics models see Section A.4.)

Continuum models often serve as approximations of discrete models. Continuous population density, for example, is an idealization, since most organisms come in discrete packages—individuals. For the purposes of modeling, it may be convenient to "smear" discrete individuals and deal with their (idealized) spatio-temporal density. This approach often works if we desire to model some average dynamical behavior of the system. If we are interested in stochastic effects, however, it is necessary to employ models that are discrete in population density. Thus, discrete density is a hallmark of stochastic population models.

What follows is a review of various mathematical approaches to modeling spatio-temporal population dynamics, with examples. The classification scheme is based on whether each variable is discrete or continuous, and is an expansion of that in Caswell and Etter (1993). To impose a little structure on this overview, I begin with continuum models in which all variables—density, space, and time—are continuous, and proceed to the next class by making discrete one variable at a time. This sequence will focus on deterministic models. When I come to cellular automata, I will review a sequence of stochastic models in the reverse order (from discrete to continuous in space and time).

3.7.1 Continuum reaction-diffusion models

Continuum models are usually formulated as partial differential equations (PDE), and less frequently as integro-differential models. Chapter 4 and Appendix A discuss in detail the PDE framework and, in particular, generalized diffusion as models of ecological movement. Birth/death terms are incorporated in a straightforward manner by adding them to the right side of a diffusion model (however, sometimes this simple procedure fails, see Durrett and Levin 1994a). For example, the simplest continuum reaction-diffusion model is the Skellam model of simple diffusion with exponential growth (Section A.2.5):

$$\frac{\partial u}{\partial t} = D\frac{\partial^2 u}{\partial x^2} + \alpha u \tag{3.7}$$

where D is the diffusion constant, and α is the intrinsic rate of population increase. Equation 3.7 says that population density in any particular locality, $u(x,t)$, can change as a result of both population redistribution and local population increase.

In non-diffusion continuum models, such as the telegraph equation (Section 4.3.1) adding birth/death terms is less straightforward. For example, suppose that local population dynamics are characterized by population growth rate $f(u)$. Then, the one-dimensional *reaction-telegraph model* will be (Holmes 1993):

$$\frac{\partial^2 u}{\partial t^2} + 2\lambda\frac{\partial u}{\partial t} = \gamma^2\frac{\partial^2 u}{\partial x^2} + \frac{\partial f(u)}{\partial t} + 2\lambda f(u) \tag{3.8}$$

The extra term involving a time derivative of $f(u)$ arises because the telegraph equation includes a $\partial^2 u/\partial t^2$ term (Holmes 1993).

Continuum models have proved to be a very fruitful approach for investigations of spatially-structured population dynamics, and a variety of analytical results are available. The study of reaction-diffusion models originated in theoretical chemistry (where this category of models acquired its name). The first systematic application of reaction-diffusion models to ecological problems was in the classical work of Skellam (1951). An excellent overview of reaction-diffusion results relevant to ecological applications can be found in Okubo (1980: Chapter 10). Many potentially useful results for general reaction-diffusion models are presented in books by Glansdorff and Prigogine (1971), Aris (1975), and Denn (1975), and in more recent volumes edited by Brown and Lacey (1990) and Lam and Naroditsky (1991). However, these sources are tough going even for a mathematically literate biologist. I found the book by Grindrod (1991) a very helpful exposition of the underlying mathematical techniques that does not demand a high degree of mathematical sophistication from the reader.

Because Equation 3.7 is linear in both the diffusion and population growth terms, it can be solved analytically. However, this simple model can exhibit only two kinds of dynamics: either exponential decline leading to eventual population extinction, or exponential growth with the population spreading out from the center. Nonlinear diffusion-reaction models, by contrast, are capable of an astonishing variety of spatio-temporal dynamics: stable spatial patterns, antiphasic spatio-temporal oscillations (standing waves), spatio-temporal chaos, and various kinds of traveling waves, including frontal waves and more complex spiral waves. However, analysis of nonlinear reaction-diffusion models is much more challenging, and is usually limited to a qualitative characterization of long-term solutions. There are two basic ways in which nonlinearity can enter Equation 3.7. Most attention so far has been focused on nonlinearities in reaction terms. More recently, mathematicians have begun paying attention to the role of nonlinear diffusion (congregation) in spatial pattern formation (e.g., Grindrod 1988).

3.7.2   Reaction-diffusion networks

Reaction-diffusion networks result from a modification of continuum models in which space is represented as a discrete variable. Mathematically, reaction-diffusion networks are systems of ordinary differential equations, with one continuum (continuous time and density) equation for each patch. To reduce the dimensionality of the problem, so that it can be studied analytically, these models often consider a limited number of patches (the absolute minimum being two). Reaction-diffusion networks were used by Turing (1952) in his famous study of pattern formation during morphogenesis. In ecological applications, this class of models has been used to study conditions under which dispersal in patchy environments can maintain coexistence of competing species (Caswell and Etter 1993). One of the first applications of reaction-diffusion networks in ecology was Levin's (1974) model of two competing species inhabiting two patches. The within-patch dynamics of each population is modeled by the Lotka-Volterra competition model. In addition, the patches exchange emigrants, with organisms leaving their home patch at a constant dispersal rate.

Levin's model employed the simplest possible spatial configuration—two patches connected by dispersal. By adding more equations and appropriate dispersal terms, it is possible to model a variety of more complex patch networks. Thus, patches may be arranged linearly, or on a two-dimensional grid, with only neighboring patches exchanging migrants. Kareiva (1990) refers to such formulations as *stepping-stone models* (not to be confused with the MacArthur and Wilson model). Alternatively, dispersal may be non-local, allowing migrants to move beyond neighbor patches. In the extreme, all patches may be equally accessible to migrants originating from any patch (*island models* of Kareiva 1990). Such *mean-field* models are easier to analyze, but they lack an explicit spatial component.

3.7.3 Coupled map lattices

Making yet another variable discrete, time, we obtain coupled map lattices. Mathematically, these models are systems of difference equations (hence *maps*, since difference equations are often called maps in the mathematical literature). Dynamics of coupled map lattices are easily studied numerically by solving them on the computer. Recently there has been a lot of interest in extending the study of nonlinear oscillations and chaos to spatio-temporal dynamical systems. Coupled map lattices offer a natural medium for explorations of this kind (see Hassell et al. 1991). An example of an ecological coupled map lattice is the model of Hassell et al. (1991). The space in their model is represented by a two-dimensional rectangular lattice of patches. Each patch is inhabited by hosts and parasitoids. The dynamics of the model occur in two steps. In the first step, populations of host and parasitoids interact in each patch according to the Nicholson-Bailey model. In the second step, a fixed proportion of the hosts and the parasitoids in each patch is distributed to the eight neighboring patches (with each neighboring patch receiving the same number of migrants). Hassell et al. (1991) explored the behavior of this model numerically, and showed that it is capable of exhibiting a variety of dynamics: extinction of both species, fixed spatial patterns ("crystal lattices"), spatio-temporal chaos, and spiral waves.

3.7.4   Cellular automata

Reducing population density in a coupled map lattice to a discrete variable we end up with a cellular automata (CA) model, in which all variables are discrete. A cellular automaton is a collection of interconnected cells, usually arranged as a regular spatial grid. At any given time, each cell is characterized by one of a number of states. Often there are just two states (interpreted in ecological terms they correspond to either presence or absence of population at the spatial location). However, other representations are also possible (e.g., absence, low density, high density; or species 1, species 2, both species, no species present). Mathematically, CA models are formulated by specifying rules for how the state of a cell is changed at each time step, depending on its own previous state, and states of its neighbors. Rules can be purely deterministic (this is most common in applications), or stochastic.

An example of a CA model is John Conway's game of "life." Each cell can be in one of two states (*off* or *on*). The transition rules are very simple. A cell that is *on* will stay in this state if two or three of its neighbors are also *on*; otherwise, it is turned *off*. An *off* cell is turned *on* only if three of its neighbors are *on*.

Simple CA models, such as the game of life can exhibit four types of long-term dynamics: (1) homogeneity, with the initial pattern dying out; (2) a fixed periodic pattern; (3) a chaotic pattern; (4) complex patterns consisting of homogeneous regions and regions containing complex localized structures, that could travel across the CA domain (Wolfram 1983).

It is very difficult to obtain analytical solutions for interesting CA models, and thus most results are generated by computer simulation. Because the population state is a discrete variable, it is easy to include stochasticity into a CA model. However, many CA models employ purely deterministic transition rules, probably because their authors wish to study the simplest possible formulations. It is commonly found that CA models with very simple deterministic rules, such as the game of life, can generate very complex, almost random-looking spatio-temporal patterns. Because even simplest CA are capable of extremely rich and complex behaviors, they have been used to study complexity (Caswell and Ritter 1993). Because of the simplicity of their transition rules (and thus, lack of realism), however, CA models are more useful in generating broad theoretical insights rather than in making specific predictions (Phipps 1989, Molofsky 1994).

3.7.5 Interacting particle systems

Interacting particle systems are stochastic equivalents of deterministic CA models. Population density and space are modeled as discrete variables, while time can be either discrete (in which case these models are equivalent to cellular automata), or continuous. The latter formulation makes obtaining analytical results easier (Durrett and Levin 1994a). The motivation for developing the mathematical theory of interacting particle systems came from dissatisfaction with two aspects of continuum models: their determinism and the assumption of local mixing. Discrete representation of population numbers is necessary for modeling stochastic effects, while dividing space into a discrete grid of cells allows us to separate local from long-distance interaction effects (Durrett and Levin 1994b). I will discuss the issue of local versus long-distance dispersal in reaction-diffusion models in Section 3.7.6, which deals with spatial contact processes.

Durrett and Levin (1994a) explain why the mathematical theory of interacting particle systems becomes simpler if time is continuous rather than discrete:

> Suppose first that we are simulating a system on $\{0, 1, \ldots, L-1\}^d$ with some boundary conditions. In discrete time we go from time t to time $t+1$ by setting $\xi_{t+1}(x) = i$ with probability $p_i(x, \xi_t)$[1], with the choices being made independently for each x. In continuous time, we change one site at a time: if the current state is ξ, we pick a site x at random, and change its state to i with probability $p_i(x, \xi_t)$, and repeat the process, with cL^d changes corresponding to one unit of time, where c is a constant that describes the overall rate at which transitions are occurring. The main difference then is that we update one site at a time rather than all sites at once. In the terminology of the theory of cellular automata we use *asynchronous* rather than *synchronous* updating. Asynchronous updating makes it easier to prove theorems since the state of the system changes gradually rather than abruptly. From a modeling point of view asynchronous updating is simpler since we do not need "collision rules" to decide what should happen when several events try to influence a site at once.

An example of a simple interacting particle system in continuous time is the following model in Durrett and Levin (1994a):

1. The space is a linear array of cells, indexed by x. Each cell can contain at most one particle.

---

[1] $\xi_t(x)$ is the state of the system at t, for example, the values *on* or *off* for all cells

2. Particles die at rate δ.

3. Particles give birth to another particle at rate α.

4. The daughter particle born at x is sent to y chosen at random from the 2 or 4 nearest neighbors (depending on whether the space is one- or two-dimensional).

5. If y is already occupied, the newly born particle is killed.

In addition to illustrating the general theory with a number of examples, Durrett and Levin (1994a) discuss how three previously advanced ecological models fit within the framework of interacting particle systems: the spread of wild daffodils (Barkham and Hance 1982), competition between annuals and perennials (Crawley and May 1987), and the competition of different genets of a perennial (Inghe 1989).

A closely related approach is percolation. One example of an ecological application is Gardner et al. (1989), who used a simple percolation model to generate two-dimensional random maps in their investigation of the influence of habitat heterogeneity on movement of organisms.

3.7.6   Spatial contact processes

Spatial contact processes is a general class of models that is related, on one hand, to interacting particle systems and percolation models, and, on the other hand, to continuum reaction-diffusion models. The key component of a spatial contact process is the contact distribution that describes the spatial relation between the positions of a parent and its offspring. The term *contact distribution* comes from epidemiology where it refers to the frequency distribution of distances between the donor and the recipient of a disease. Much of the mathematical development of contact models occurred in the context of epidemics. However, this mathematical framework proved to be quite general and useful in modeling such disparate phenomena as fungal disease spread (van den Bosch et al. 1988a,b,c), geographic spread of invading species (Hengeveld 1989), forest fires (Green 1989), tumor growth (Williams and Bjerkness 1972), and the spread of farming in Neolithic Europe (Ammerman and Cavalli-Sforza 1973).

Mollison (1986) distinguishes four classes of spatial contact models, depending on whether they are stochastic or deterministic, and linear or nonlinear. An example of a **linear stochastic contact model** is the *contact birth process* (Mollison 1977). Each individual i is located at a fixed spatial location $x(i)$ (for simplicity, I will use one-dimensional space in this example). As in an interacting particle model, individuals give birth with probability α, and the offspring is placed at a distance s, chosen from a particular probability distribution $V(s)$ (here, however, space is continuous). The probability of a new individual appearing at location x, then, is proportional to a weighted average over all possible parents, with a parent at y having a weight $dV(x-y)$ (Mollison 1977). Thus, the probability of a new individual arriving at location x during $(t, t+dt)$ is

$$\Pr(N \to N+1) = \alpha \bar{N}(x,t)dt \tag{3.9}$$

where $N(x,t)$ is the number of individuals at location x at time t, and $\bar{N}(x,t)$ is the convolution $\int N(x-s,t)dV(s)$ (the integration is carried over the whole spatial domain of the process). This equation basically says that in order to arrive at x, an organism had to be born at some location s [with probability $\alpha N(s,t)dt$] and then travel the distance $x-s$ [with the probability specified by the contact distribution $V(s)$]. In discrete space, in place of the convolution integral there would be a sum over all possible localities.

A **linear deterministic contact model** can be viewed as an approximation of the underlying linear stochastic contact model (Mollison 1977). This deterministic connection is most easily traced in a simple model such as the contact birth process. We simply replace the stochastic model (Equation 3.9) by an integro-differential model

$$\frac{du}{dt} = \alpha \bar{u} \tag{3.10}$$

The bar over u again indicates a convolution integral. Note that in this equation, $u(x,t)$ is a continuous variable, rather than the number of discrete individuals $N(x,t)$ (in other words, we have made a transition from an individual based—Lagrangian—model, to a population-based—Eulerian—one). In the case of the contact birth process, u has a clear interpretation as the expected number of individuals at x, $E(N)$, since Equation 3.10 is exactly the same as the equation governing the expected numbers of the stochastic process (Mollison 1977). In general, there is a direct connection between a linear stochastic process and a linear (or sometimes nonlinear) deterministic model (Mollison 1977, 1986). The deterministic model can usually be viewed as an approximation of the stochastic process.

We can further approximate the weighted average $\bar{u}$ by expanding the convolution integral into a Taylor series. If V is symmetric, then the first-order term vanishes. Discarding terms of third and higher order, we obtain $\bar{u} \approx u + 1/2\sigma^2 \partial^2 u/\partial x^2$. Here σ^2 is the variance of V. Thus, the diffusion approximation of the stochastic model (Equation 3.9) resulted in the following equation:

$$\frac{\partial u}{\partial t} = \frac{\alpha \sigma^2}{2} \frac{\partial^2 u}{\partial x^2} + \alpha u \tag{3.11}$$

We see that Equation 3.11 is the model of simple diffusion with exponential growth. Equation 3.11 would exactly describe the evolution of the expected population density in the stochastic birth process (Equation 3.9), if the contact distribution V had all its moments but the second equal to zero.

Returning for a moment to Equation 3.10, note that it has a rather sophisticated spatial component, since the contact distribution $V(s)$ can represent a wide variety of dispersal processes. However, its temporal component is very simple—in particular, this model does not incorporate any effects of age structure. In Section A.4.4 I will discuss a more general mathematical approach based on the reproduction and dispersal kernel model, which allows one to model both the spatial and age structure of the population.

A simple example of a **nonlinear stochastic contact model** is a modification of the contact birth process in which we introduce a probability of failure of a newborn individual proportional to the number already occupying its chosen location, $N(x, t)/K$ (assuming discrete space—in continuous space we would need to sum individuals within some spatial neighborhood). Here K is analogous to the local carrying capacity. This model is known as the *simple epidemic* (Mollison 1977):

$$\Pr(N \rightarrow N + 1) = \alpha \bar{N}(1 - N/K)dt \tag{3.12}$$

In the context of epidemiology, the density dependent failure rate arises because each new infection at x reduces the number of susceptible individuals. The contact distribution V specifies how the probability that an infected individual will pass the disease to a susceptible one will depend on the spatial separation between the two.

The connection between the expected numbers in a stochastic process and density in a deterministic model does not carry in the nonlinear case (Mollison 1991), because expectation of the product of two random variables is not, in general, equal to the product of expectations. This is a pity, because the **nonlinear stochastic** class is the most realistic approach to modeling the spread of invading species or epidemics. Yet, obtaining analytical results beyond a few simple cases is very difficult, and the only remaining recourse is simulation.

3.7.7   Synthesis

Although the primary focus of the book is on movement, the ultimate purpose of collecting movement data and of building empirically based movement models, at least in an ecological setting, is to understand and predict dynamics of populations in space. Assuming that we succeed in building and testing movement modules, how difficult is the next step going to be? This section reviews mathematical approaches that combine movement with birth, death, and population interaction processes. The prognosis is good: the theory is well developed, and appears to be ready to incorporate whatever quantitative information about movement we can provide. In fact, it is amazing how many different kinds of models for spatial population dynamics have been proposed and analyzed. We are certainly not limited to traditional reaction-diffusion models, nor to individual-based simulations, although both approaches continue to be very productive. Particularly interesting are recent developments in stochastic models, such as interacting particle systems and spatial contact processes. Some of the recent results from these approaches are of particular importance to empirical investigations of spatial spread (see Section 6.3; some theoretical results are also reviewed in the Appendix, Section A.4).

Chapter 4

Building Behaviorally Based Models

4.1 The Problem

Investigations into the consequences of movement for population dynamics have traditionally been conducted within one of the three general frameworks: (1) empirical studies that have described dispersal data with various (typically phenomenological) models; (2) theoretical analyses usually based on diffusion models; and (3) mechanistic (individual-based) approaches tailored to specific organisms, and usually employing computer simulations. Each approach has its strengths and limitations. Empirical approaches are very useful in quantifying dispersal in the field, but cannot provide us with sharp answers about mechanisms of population redistribution. Reaction-diffusion models yielded many general insights into spatial population dynamics, but usually make oversimplifying assumptions about movement of real organisms. Individual-based movement models are mechanistic and can be tightly linked to careful field observations of organism movements, but generalizations from these situation-specific studies have been slow to emerge.

At first glance, mechanistic simulation studies have the best claim as the most powerful approach to studying movements of organisms, and thus it is worth discussing why they have not displaced other approaches. One problem is a lack of a commonly accepted framework for simulating movement. Paucity of general insights, thus, is partly due to an incompatibility between the various schemes of quantifying individual movement patterns employed by different investigators. As a result, comparisons between different simulation studies, even of the same species, are often impossible. For example, the studies of both Jones (1977) and Root and Kareiva (1984) recognized that movements of cabbage white butterflies have a directional component. Jones (1977), however, represented the movement of cabbage whites as a biased random walk with no correlations among moves, while Root and Kareiva (1984) modeled movement as an unbiased correlated random walk. Each set of assumptions leads to quite different consequences for population redistribution. The problem with simulation models as the general framework is further compounded by the tendency of their creators to err on the side of complexity and to not report full details of computer implementation. Thus, it is usually impossible to determine just what the model does. Finally, simulations provide predictions limited to a particular combination of parameters, and exploration of the parameter space may be impractical due to a large number of parameters.

The limitations of the simulation approach have long been recognized (Kareiva and Shigesada 1983, Marsh and Jones 1988, Gross et al. 1992). Marsh and Jones (1988) proposed two possible solutions. One is for workers interested in building movement simulations to agree on a set of standard structures for coding movement models. As Marsh and Jones (1988) noted, this approach may be premature as these standard structures would need to be flexible enough and elaborate enough to accommodate a variety of organisms. Another solution (first proposed by Kareiva and Shigesada 1983) is to develop formulas that fall between general diffusion models and detailed behavioral simulations tailored to specific systems. The advantage of these formulas over simulation models is their greater degree of generality. This was the approach that Marsh and Jones (1988) followed in their paper.

The problem with this approach, however, is that at the end of the process we are left with one (or several) descriptive statistics, such as the expected net squared displacement after n moves (Kareiva and Shigesada 1983), or a test statistic that distinguishes between various random walk assumptions, such as the one proposed by Marsh and Jones (1988). These statistics are useful in summarizing patterns of animal movements and for interspecific comparisons. However, they cannot be used to explicitly describe and predict the redistribution and spatial dynamics of organisms. Neither can they be of help in analyzing density-distance curves resulting from a mark-recapture experiment.

My conclusion is that it is neither possible nor desirable to exclusively focus on any single approach to the study of movement. The need for a unifying framework is nevertheless genuine. I argue that such a framework can be constructed by establishing explicit connections between the various approaches. In particular, we need to establish two kinds of connections: (1) diffusion to empirical curve-fitting, and (2) individual movement behaviors to diffusion. The first connection was already discussed in Section 3.3, where I pointed out that instead of using phenomenological models lacking a mechanistic basis, we should fit curves that are solutions of specific diffusion models tailored to the particular experimental conditions. Many such solutions are listed in Appendix A, and we will be applying this approach in Chapter 6. The second connection, between mechanistic individual-based models and diffusion, is provided by the *diffusion-approximation* approach—the subject of this chapter.

My goal in this chapter is to systematically use the method of diffusion approximation on a series of random-walk models representing different ways in which moving individuals may interact with various features of spatially-variable landscapes, as well as each other. I will start with fairly simple formulations, and then move to more realistic and complex ones. In each case the end result is a *generalized diffusion model*, the coefficients of which are expressed in terms of random-walk parameters. These parameters can be measured by direct observation of individual movement behaviors, and therefore provide direct links to the data. The coefficients of the model, and how they depend on the environment, provide a concise summary of the movement pattern of the organisms that can be used in interspecific comparisons of movement patterns. Finally, the diffusion model itself can be used to predict the spatial redistribution of organisms resulting from their movements (with the movement pattern described by the original random-walk formulation). In some cases, analytical time-dependent solutions will be available. When no time-dependent solutions are available, it may be possible to solve the equations for equilibrium (this is useful in situations where population redistribution occurs on a faster time scale than birth, death, and population-interaction processes).

Even when no analytical solutions are known, there is an advantage in numerically solving the diffusion model compared to simulating the random-walk process from which it was derived. This is because a diffusion-approximation model will typically have fewer parameters than the random-walk process, making exploration of the parameter space much more feasible. In addition, stochastic simulations need to be repeated hundreds of times before their average behavior can be characterized, while a deterministic diffusion model needs to be solved only once for each combination of parameters and the initial and boundary conditions. Of course, the opposite side of the coin is that the diffusion model cannot predict the variance associated with predictions. Moreover, in cases where stochasticity enters in a nonlinear manner, the deterministic approximation may give biased results. Thus, diffusion approximation is not the "silver bullet." It should always be checked by judiciously chosen simulations, especially when predictions are needed for a specific set of parameters and conditions, which is often the case in studies tailored to specific systems.

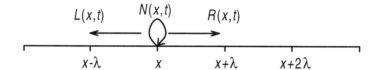

Figure 4.1: Random walk in one-dimensional space.

Finally, there are situations in which diffusion-based models are known to fail (e.g., population spread, see Section 6.3.1). What I wish to establish in this chapter is that diffusion approximation is an extremely useful tool, but only one of many in the toolkit of the sophisticated movement analyst.

4.2   Movement without Directional Persistence

4.2.1   Fixed move length, heterogeneous space

We start by considering a fairly simple case of movement in heterogeneous environments in which there is no directional persistence, that is, the direction of the current move does not affect the direction of the next move. For many organisms this assumption will not hold. However, not having to deal with directional persistence greatly simplifies the math, and, as we shall see in Chapter 7, the resulting diffusion-approximation model turns out to be very useful in analyzing data from individual mark-recapture studies. Because I assume no directional persistence, I will call this model *uncorrelated random walk.*

Although the general approach in this book is to avoid derivations, in this section I plan to present the intermediate steps of the algebraic manipulations connecting initial assumptions of the model to the final equation. The reason for breaking the rule is that I am interested not in the specific result, but rather in the process that will get us to it. The same general procedure can be used in obtaining a diffusion approximation of many other kinds of random walk formulations. For example, I will use this approach to derive a diffusion model for congregating individuals (Section 4.5.1). To follow the algebra is not very difficult, although it will require some work on your part. For a gentler introduction to deriving a diffusion equation, read Section A.1.1 in the Appendix. You might also read about the Taylor expansion (any good textbook on calculus covers it).

Our first goal is to formulate the laws of movement using the random-walk framework. Let us assume that our organism is moving on a lattice of spatial positions (Figure 4.1). We can imagine, for example, a phytophagous beetle moving within a row of crop plants such as cabbages. Cabbages are planted in a regular array, and the distance between the neighboring plants is λ. Let us further assume that during the time interval τ the beetle can move at most to the next plant. Thus, it can make a step of length λ right with probability $R(x,t)$, left with probability $L(x,t)$, or make no move with probability $N(x,t)$.

Several realistic features distinguish this formulation from that in Section A.1.1: (1) the organism is allowed to rest at a spatial point [with probability $N(x,t)$]; (2) probabilities of moving right and left are not the same, allowing for directional bias; and (3) most importantly, all parameters can vary with space and time. For example, cabbages may vary in their quality and beetles may respond to this variation by leaving poor-quality plants at a faster rate than high-quality plants. The simplifying assumptions of this formulation, on the other hand are (1) one-dimensional space, (2) organisms move in steps of fixed length, (3) there are no correlations between subsequent moves, and (4) organisms move independently of each other.

The second step is to write a recurrence equation for the probability of finding the beetle at any spatial location x at any time t, $p(x,t)$. The reason we want to do this is that the probability distribution of finding any individual at (x,t) translates directly into the spatial population density of an ensemble of individuals, if all individuals start in the same locality at $t = 0$, employ identical movement rules, and do not affect the movement of each other. Thus, if we can derive a formula governing the time evolution of $p(x,t)$, then we will also have the formula for the spatio-temporal population density, $u(x,t)$.

A beetle found at any particular location x, could come from one of only three possible locations in one time step: $x - \lambda$, x, or $x + \lambda$ (because the maximum move length is λ). Thus,

$$p(x,t) = N(x,t-\tau)p(x,t-\tau) \quad + \quad R(x-\lambda,t-\tau)p(x-\lambda,t-\tau)$$
$$+ \quad L(x+\lambda,t-\tau)p(x+\lambda,t-\tau) \quad (4.1)$$

This equation simply states that the probability of finding the organism at the specific location x at time t is the probability that before the last move it was at either x, $x - \lambda$, or $x + \lambda$, multiplied by the probabilities of not moving, moving right, or moving left, respectively.

The third step is to translate this recurrence equation into a differential model. Our goal is an equation expressed in term of derivatives of $p(x,t)$.

Instead, we have terms depending on $x \pm \lambda$ and $t - \tau$. To get rid of these terms, we expand them in a Taylor series:

$$p(x, t - \tau) \quad = \quad p - \tau\frac{\partial p}{\partial t} + O(\tau^2)$$

$$p(x - \lambda, t - \tau) \quad = \quad p - \tau\frac{\partial p}{\partial t} + O(\tau^2) - \lambda\frac{\partial p}{\partial x} + \frac{\lambda^2}{2}\frac{\partial^2 p}{\partial x^2} + O(\lambda^3)$$

$$p(x + \lambda, t - \tau) \quad = \quad p - \tau\frac{\partial p}{\partial t} + O(\tau^2) + \lambda\frac{\partial p}{\partial x} + \frac{\lambda^2}{2}\frac{\partial^2 p}{\partial x^2} + O(\lambda^3)$$

where p is a short-hand notation for $p(x, t)$, and $O(\cdot)$ denotes higher order terms, that is, terms multiplied by τ^2, τ^3, λ^3, λ^4, etc. Terms involving N, R, and L are expanded in the same manner. Substituting Taylor expansions of p, N, R, and L into Equation 4.1, and gathering together similar terms, we obtain

$$
\begin{aligned}
p \quad = \quad & p(N + R + L) - \tau\frac{\partial p}{\partial t}(N + R + L) - \tau p\frac{\partial}{\partial t}(N + R + L) \\
& -\lambda\frac{\partial p}{\partial x}(R - L) - \lambda p\frac{\partial}{\partial x}(R - L) \\
& +\frac{\lambda^2}{2}\frac{\partial^2 p}{\partial x^2}(L + R) + \lambda^2\frac{\partial p}{\partial x}\frac{\partial}{\partial x}(L + R) + \frac{\lambda^2}{2}p\frac{\partial^2}{\partial x^2}(L + R) \\
& +O(\tau^2 \text{ and } \lambda^3)
\end{aligned}
$$

We notice that in the first line, $N + R + L = 1$. The second line is the first spatial derivative of the product of p and $R - L$ (times the constant λ), while the third line is the second spatial derivative of $p(R + L)$ (times $\lambda^2/2$). Thus, if we neglect the terms involving λ^3, τ^2, and their products, we can write

$$\tau\frac{\partial p}{\partial t} \approx -\frac{\partial}{\partial x}(\lambda(R - L)p) + \frac{\partial^2}{\partial x^2}\left[\frac{\lambda^2(R + L)p}{2}\right] \tag{4.2}$$

Now define *bias* $\beta = \lambda(R - L)/\tau$ and *motility* $\mu = \lambda^2(R + L)/2\tau$. Note that bias is proportional to the difference between the probabilities of moving right versus left, while motility is proportional to the probability of *moving*, since $R + L = 1 - N$. Bias and motility can vary with spatial position and with time. Substituting these definitions into Equation 4.2, leads to

$$\frac{\partial p}{\partial t} = -\frac{\partial}{\partial x}(\beta p) + \frac{\partial^2}{\partial x^2}(\mu p) \tag{4.3}$$

Both β and μ appear inside the partial derivatives because, in general, they are functions of space and time. Finally, multiplying the probability of finding an individual at location x at time t, $p(x,t)$, by the total number of moving organisms, N, we rewrite the above equation in terms of spatio-temporal population density, $u(x,t) \equiv Np(x,t)$. We now arrive at our goal, a diffusion-approximation model for a population of organisms moving according to an uncorrelated random walk in a heterogeneous environment

$$\frac{\partial u}{\partial t} = -\frac{\partial}{\partial x}(\beta u) + \frac{\partial^2}{\partial x^2}(\mu u) \qquad (4.4)$$

This equation is known as Fokker-Planck, or forward Kolmogorov equation.

4.2.2 Variable move lengths

Although the random walk formulation developed above can be applied to some experimental systems (see Section 4.2.6), in most field situations the assumptions of fixed move length would not hold. Thus, we need to generalize the model to accommodate variable step length. The final product will be flexible enough to be useful in the analysis of movement data from a variety of realistic field situations, provided that there is no autocorrelation in the move direction, and no behavioral interactions among insects.

Let us again consider movements of cabbage beetles, but this time we will not assume that beetles move at discrete time intervals and use discrete spatial steps. Instead, a beetle can make a move at any point in time, and its movement rate $\pi = \pi(x,t)$ depends on its spatial position and on time. The movement rate is defined indirectly by setting the probability of moving in a short period of time τ equal to $\pi\tau$. By selecting a very small τ we can minimize the probability that multiple moves will occur during the same interval.

When movement occurs, the beetle can move in either a positive or negative direction, with the probability of a particular step length λ described by the frequency distribution $M(\lambda, x, t)$ (Figure 4.2). In general, the distribution of move lengths $M(\lambda, x, t)$ will vary with space and time. If M is symmetric, than the random walk is unbiased (i.e., there is no drift). Since M is a probability distribution, $\int_{-\infty}^{\infty} M(\lambda, x, t)\, d\lambda = 1$. This distribution can be characterized by its moments, e.g., the n-th moment: $m_n = \int_{-\infty}^{\infty} \lambda^n M(\lambda, x, t)\, d\lambda$. Note that instead of discrete-time, discrete space random walk process of the previous section, we have formulated the problem as a continuous-time, continuous-space random walk (known as a *Brownian motion* stochastic process, Karlin and Taylor 1975).

Using the same logic as in the previous section, we write the recurrence relationship for $p(x,t)$, the probability of finding the beetle at location x at time t

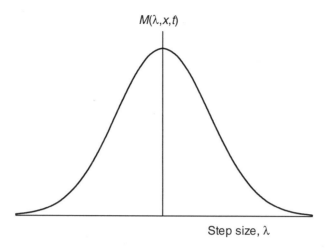

Figure 4.2: An example of frequency distribution of move length.

$$
\begin{aligned}
p(x,t) \;=\;& p(x,t-\tau)[1-\pi(x,t-\tau)\tau] \qquad\qquad\qquad (4.5)\\
+\;& \int_{-\infty}^{\infty} p(x-\lambda,t-\tau)\pi(x-\lambda,t-\tau)\tau M(\lambda,x-\lambda,t-\tau)\,d\lambda
\end{aligned}
$$

The first term on the right side is simply the probability of the beetle being at position x at time $t-\tau$, multiplied by the probability of *not* moving during τ. The second term, the integral, is a continuous analog of the last two terms in Equation 4.1. Again we consider all the possible positions from where the beetle could move to x (see Figure 4.2). For example, if the beetle was at the position $x-\lambda$, then by moving λ spatial units (to the right if λ is positive, or to the left if it is negative) the beetle will arrive at the position x. Thus, the probability that the beetle will move to x is the product of the probability of being found at $x-\lambda$, the probability of moving from that position, and the probability of moving λ units. The integral in Equation 4.5 sums this product over all possible positions from where the beetle could reach x.

There are several ways to proceed with Equation 4.5. One way to derive the diffusion-approximation model is to use the mathematical approach of the previous sections. The intermediate steps are detailed in Section A.1.2. A more rigorous mathematical approach for achieving the same result is the method of generating functions used in the derivation of the Fokker-Planck equation for the analysis of the Brownian motion (e.g., Skellam 1973). Interested readers should also consult Okubo (1980:75-78), and Goel and Richter-Dyn (1974:33-36). Whatever approach we use, we eventually arrive at the following partial-differential equation for the evolution of p:

$$\frac{\partial p}{\partial t} = -\frac{\partial}{\partial x}(\pi m_1 p) + \frac{1}{2}\frac{\partial^2}{\partial x^2}(\pi m_2 p) + \cdots \qquad (4.6)$$

4.2.3 How many terms to retain in the approximation?

Let us rewrite Equation 4.6 in its exact form using an infinite sum of spatial derivatives (Goel and Richter-Dyn 1974:36)

$$\frac{\partial u}{\partial t} = \sum_{k=1}^{\infty} \frac{(-1)^k}{k!}\frac{\partial^k}{\partial x^k}(\pi m_k u) \qquad (4.7)$$

In real-life applications, we can (and need) only use a finite number of terms. The question is, how many? There is no general answer to this question that would fit all possible applications. Sometimes the bias (as measured by m_1) may be so strong that it would dominate the population redistribution. In that case, one may want to entirely ignore diffusive movements around the advection term and just use the equation

$$\frac{\partial u}{\partial t} = -\frac{\partial}{\partial x}(\pi m_1 u)$$

As Skellam (1951) noted, "a slight systematic drift, no matter how small, is *ultimately* the most important cause of displacement," that is, when t is sufficiently large.

If we keep the first two terms we obtain the Fokker-Planck, but *not* Fickian, diffusion equation

$$\frac{\partial u}{\partial t} = -\frac{\partial}{\partial x}(\pi m_1 u) + \frac{1}{2}\frac{\partial^2}{\partial x^2}(\pi m_2 u) \qquad (4.8)$$

We see that $\pi m_1 = \beta$ is the bias, and $\pi m_2 = \mu$ is the motility (analogous to the diffusion rate in the Fickian formulation). Goel and Richter-Dyn (1974:36-38) describe a wide class of dynamical stochastic processes for which $m_k = 0$ for all $k > 2$. In most real-life applications, however, the Fokker-Planck equation will be an approximate rather than the exact model governing population redistribution. The success of diffusion equations in many field studies argues that in most cases the second-order approximation (the Fokker-Planck equation) is adequate.

Nevertheless, in some applications we might need higher order terms. For example, Skellam (1973) thought that the role of higher order terms in accelerating invasions may not be negligible. Higher-order terms may also be helpful in preventing ill-posedness in congregation-diffusion models (Section 4.5). A generalized diffusion model involving fourth-order terms has been proposed and analyzed by Cohen and Murray (1981). Finally, some random walk formulations lead to extra terms involving higher-order *temporal* derivatives (see Section 4.3.1).

4.2.4   The form of the diffusion-approximation model

The Fokker-Planck equation for ecological diffusion that we have derived in this chapter is of the following form (assuming no bias):

$$\frac{\partial u}{\partial t} = \frac{\partial^2}{\partial x^2}\left(\mu(x)u\right) \tag{4.9}$$

The Fickian diffusion equation that appears in many physical and chemical applications, has a different form:

$$\frac{\partial u}{\partial t} = \frac{\partial}{\partial x}\left(D(x)\frac{\partial u}{\partial x}\right) \tag{4.10}$$

(for a derivation of this model using flux consideration, see Appendix Section A.1.3). Motility, μ, and diffusivity, D, are parameters that determine the rate of population spread. However, the Fokker-Planck μ appears inside both partial x derivatives on the right side of Equation 4.9, while the Fickian D is outside one of the derivatives. The two diffusion equations are identical if the diffusivity, or motility does not vary in space. In heterogeneous environments, however, the two models predict very different distributions of organisms. Fickian diffusion leads to spatially uniform distribution at the equilibrium, even if D varies in space. By contrast, the Fokker-Planck model predicts spatially non-uniform distribution, with $\tilde{u} = \text{const}/\mu(x)$ (Section A.3.2).

Some confusion arose in the past because the Fickian equation was indiscriminantly applied to movements of both physical (molecules) and biological entities (cells and organisms) (see Lapidus and Levandowsky 1981). Currently, it has become widely accepted (Okubo 1980, Kareiva and Odell 1987) that while the Fickian equation is appropriate for modeling molecule diffusion, movements of cells and organisms should usually be represented with the Fokker-Planck equation. The reason for this choice is that a variety of random walk formulations (such as the ones already considered in this chapter) lead to the Fokker-Planck rather than the Fickian model. Why Fokker-Planck is the form that usually arises in ecological applications is explained by Okubo

(1980:83-86), who also develops a general diffusion model that includes both Fickian and Fokker-Planck forms as special cases.

The general lesson, however, is that no particular diffusion model should be used thoughtlessly, including the Fokker-Planck form. The form, as well as content, of a diffusion-approximation model is determined by the assumptions about the mode of movement built into the random walk formulation, which in turn reflects properties of biological organisms.

4.2.5 Residence index

As was noted in the previous section, the equilibrium solution of Equation 4.9) is

$$\tilde{u}(x) = \frac{\text{const}}{\mu(x)} \tag{4.11}$$

Here tilde (the squiggle above u) indicates the equilibrium density distribution of organisms (as $t \to \infty$). The Fokker-Planck model, therefore, predicts that organisms will eventually accumulate in localities where their rate of movement (motility) is low, while in localities where motility is high population density will decline. If we define the *residence index* $\rho(x) = 1/\mu(x)$, then we can rewrite Equation 4.11 as follows:

$$\tilde{u}(x) \sim \rho(x) \tag{4.12}$$

This equation says that the equilibrium population density at any given point in space is proportional to the residence index.

Because the residence index is used for comparative purposes ("the density of organisms in patch i is three times that in patch j"), there is an undefined constant multiplier associated with it. To obtain an absolute estimate of equilibrium population density, we will need to divide the relative distribution, given by the residence index, by the total number of organisms within the modeled spatial domain.

The residence index provides a connection between the individual movement patterns (because it is expressed in terms of random walk parameters) and population-level redistribution (because it predicts how population density will vary in space). For the random walk with fixed move length (Section 4.2.1) residence index is

$$\rho(x) = \frac{2\tau}{\lambda^2[R(x) + L(x)]}$$

Since the residence index is a relative quantity, we can drop the part that does not vary in space, and write:

$$\rho(x) = [R(x) + L(x)]^{-1}$$

Using this formula, we can test whether the model predicts the distribution of organisms as follows. First measure how random walk parameters $R(x)$ and $L(x)$ vary in space, then calculate the residence index for different spatial localities, and finally compare the spatial distribution of organisms predicted by the model to the observed distribution (see next section for an example).

For simple random walk models, such as the one with fixed move length, calculation of the residence index is a rather trivial step (in fact, we could simply use the inverse of motility to achieve the same result). My purpose in introducing ρ at this stage is to provide an illustration of this concept in a simple setting, unencumbered by the complexities with which we will have to deal later (e.g., Section 4.4). Some technical matters associated with the residence index are discussed in the Appendix (Section A.3.3).

4.2.6   Example: flea beetles in collard patches

The random walk and the diffusion approximation developed in this section, although fairly simple, has enough realism to serve as a reasonable model for quantifying movements of some organisms. For example, it fits well the experimental system of Kareiva (1982), who studied the flea beetle (*Phyllotreta* spp.) movements within one-dimensional arrays of collard patches. I will use some of Kareiva's data to illustrate how the diffusion-approximation framework developed in this section can be applied in a realistic field setting.

Kareiva (1982) performed two sets of experiments. In the first (1977), he released marked beetles in centers of homogeneous one-dimensional arrays of collard patches. Beetles were recaptured 24 h after release. In the second set of experiments (1978), Kareiva studied flea beetle movement in heterogeneous arrays of alternating "lush" and "stunted" patches. Marked beetles were released in different kinds of patches, and movement of beetles was recorded 1 h later. Although Kareiva varied the distance between patches and studied two different *Phyllotreta* species, for the purpose of illustration I will focus here only on experiments in which the distance between patches was 2 m, and on only one species (*P. cruciferae*).

I will first use the 1978 short-term experiments to estimate the parameters of the random walk model. Because movement from the release patch was scored 1 h after release, practically no beetles moved farther than a neighboring patch. Thus, the conditions of this experiment fit the assumption of the random walk model developed in this section. Kareiva (1982: Table 3) lists the proportion of beetles that stayed in the patch of release, F_{sd}, and the proportion that moved to one of the neighboring patches, F_{mv}. The proportions do not add up to one, because Kareiva was unable to recapture all beetles within the patches. Thus, in order to estimate the probability of moving, $(R + L)$, we need to adjust F_{mv} by the proportion of beetles recaptured:

$$(R+L) = \frac{F_{mv}}{F_{mv} + F_{sd}} \qquad (4.13)$$

In other words, I am assuming that movement probabilities for recaptured beetles did not differ from those of not recaptured ones. For beetles that were released in lush patches, $(R+L) = 0.181/(0.181+0.417)$ (Kareiva 1982: Table 3; using July data). The bias β is zero, since there was no preferred direction in flea beetle movement. The motility is $\lambda^2(R+L)/2\tau$, with $\lambda = 2$ m, and $\tau = 1$ h (see Equation 4.2). Putting these numbers together, we find that the motility in lush patches was $\mu_l = 0.61$ m^2/h in July. In August it was almost the same, $\mu_l = 0.63$ m^2/h. Calculating the motility in stunted patches we find $\mu_s = 1.63$ and 1.60 m^2/h in July and August respectively.

Second, we can compare the motilities calculated using the short-term 1978 experiments with the motility estimated by fitting simple diffusion equation to the data from 1977 experiments. Taking the diffusion coefficient for 2 m-arrays of patches from Kareiva (1982: Table 2), and equating it to μ, we obtain an estimate of $\mu = 1.88$ m^2/h. This coefficient should be intermediate in value between μ_l and μ_s, because the quality of collard patches used in 1977 was intermediate between lush and stunted. However, the estimates of μ based on 1978 data substantially underestimate the diffusion coefficient observed in 1977. This may be due to differences in experimental conditions (different numbers of collards per patch, different years and beetle populations). Alternatively, the rate of population spread may be affected by the heterogeneous versus homogeneous composition of patch arrays.

Finally, we can use the estimated values of μ_l and μ_s to calculate the expected residence index in lush versus stunted patches, and therefore the expected equilibrium distribution of beetles among lush and stunted patches. The predicted ratio of residence indices is

$$\frac{\rho_l}{\rho_s} = \frac{\mu_s}{\mu_l} = 2.67 \qquad (4.14)$$

in July and 2.54 in August. The observed ratios were $2.75/0.88 = 3.13$, and $5.25/2.13 = 2.46$ in July and August, respectively (Kareiva 1982: Table 5). Correspondence between the predicted and observed values is excellent, especially considering that the observed values came from an independent experiment, in which initially empty arrays were allowed to accumulate flea beetles by immigration and population redistribution.

4.2.7   Synthesis

This section showed how random walk models can be approximated with diffusion equations. Deriving a diffusion-approximation model for an uncorrelated random walk is not very difficult (although it may involve a lot of algebra), and yields at least two insights. First, population redistribution should be modeled differently from molecular diffusion (Fokker-Planck versus Fickian diffusion equations). Second, we can express the parameters of the diffusion model in quantities that can be estimated by observing individuals. This section also introduces the concept of residence index that translates quantitative measures of individual movement into the patterns of population redistribution.

4.3   Movement with Persistence: 1D Space

The random walk models considered so far in this chapter have assumed that the direction of each move performed by an organism is statistically independent of the direction of the previous move. Under some circumstances this may not be a bad assumption. For example, a beetle landing on a host plant may spend quite some time on it, feeding or looking for mates, so that by the time it is ready to fly again all memory of direction where it came from is lost. On the other hand, consider a butterfly flying through an array of plants. Such an organism is almost certain to have some degree of directional persistence, so that each successive move will take the butterfly in generally the same direction as the previous one.

The degree of correlation between subsequent steps is a property of the organism, the environment it moves through, but also the scale at which we observe its movements. If we record the organism position at very frequent time intervals, there is going to be a high correlation between the directions of subsequent moves. Alternatively, by recording organism position infrequently we allow the autocorrelations to die out, and thus the directions of subsequent displacements may be uncorrelated with each other. This suggests that one way to deal with direction autocorrelation is to view organism movements at a larger spatio-temporal scale. This may be a reasonable approach for some kinds of questions.

In other situations, however, we do not want to take this route, because autocorrelation in direction may convey much biologically relevant information. For example, one kind of area-restricted search is a result of an organism increasing its turning magnitude and frequency in response to resource presence or other cues. Thus, we would like to know how changes in consumer turning behavior would affect their aggregation within a landscape of heterogeneously distributed resources. This provides a motivation for formulating random walk models that explicitly take into account correlations between moves, and deducing population-level consequences from such *correlated random walk* (CRW) models.

CRW models are much easier to formulate and analyze in one-dimensional space because we deal only with two possible directions (e.g., positive and negative), while in two or more dimensions we have an infinity of possible directions to consider. To understand the effect of correlated moves, we begin with simpler one-dimensional CRW models in this section. The more powerful but also more complex models of two-dimensional CRW will be considered later.

4.3.1 The telegraph equation

We begin by considering the simplest CRW model, using the random walk of Section 4.2.1 as a starting point (this CRW model was analyzed by Taylor 1921, and then further elaborated by Goldstein 1951; see also Okubo 1980 and Holmes 1993). For simplicity, I will assume that space is homogeneous and that the organism (beetle) moves within a one-dimensional spatial array of, for example, host plants.

During a time interval τ the beetle moves one step of length λ. Thus, the speed of the beetle, $v = \lambda/\tau$, is a constant. Unlike the previous formulation, however, we also allow the current move direction to be affected by the previous direction. In particular, let Q be the probability that the beetle will continue moving in the same direction as before, and R be the probability of reversing direction ($Q + R = 1$). We assume that the partial autocorrelations between move directions separated by more than one time interval are all zero, so that the autocorrelation function of directionality will decay exponentially. In other words, only the direction of the previous move matters.

Consider now N beetles that start at the origin at $t = 0$, one half of them initially moving left, and the other half right. The insects will spread out symmetrically from the origin. Initially there may be two heaps of beetles at $x = \pm vt$, but unless the directionality is very strong (Q very near 1), each beetle will "forget" its initial direction of movement after a few steps, and the distribution of beetles will begin to resemble a bell-shaped clump centered at the origin. This clump will then spread out in a fashion that very much resembles the spread of organisms undergoing a simple (uncorrelated) random walk.

To put these observations on a more quantitative basis we need to approximate the random walk with a continuum differential equation. This was done by Goldstein (1951). To follow his approach, we begin shrinking τ, the time

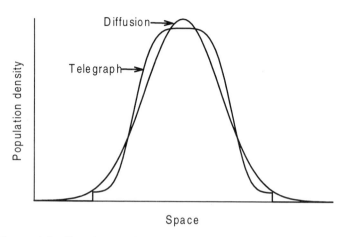

Figure 4.3: Population distribution resulting from spread from a central release point predicted by diffusion and telegraph equations. (After Holmes 1993.)

interval at which we record the beetle's positions. However, the smaller the time interval the less likely it is that the beetle will reverse its direction during it. Thus, the probability of direction reversal R should also be shrinking as τ decreases. We assume that in the limit,

$$\lim_{\tau \to 0} \frac{\tau}{R} = T \tag{4.15}$$

where T is the characteristic time of directional persitence (Okubo 1980: 69). Small T implies frequent direction reversals and wiggly paths. In contrast, large T implies straightened-out, smooth paths. Given these assumptions, the continuum approximation for the CRW model is (Goldstein 1951):

$$\frac{\partial^2 u}{\partial t^2} + \frac{2}{T}\frac{\partial u}{\partial t} = v^2\frac{\partial^2 u}{\partial x^2} \tag{4.16}$$

known in the applied mathematics literature as the *telegraph equation*. The telegraph equation is a curious mixture of diffusion (the first time derivative of u) and wave equation (the second time derivative). The dynamics of telegraph spread have both elements of wave-like and diffusion motion (Figure 4.3). Note that, unlike the diffusion model, the telegraph equation does not predict infinitely long tails. In the diffusion model, infinitely long tails arise because the diffusion limit implies infinite velocity, while the telegraph equation assumes finite velocity.

The relative importance of the wave versus diffusion terms is measured by T. When reversal frequency is high (low correlation between moves), $1/T$ will be large, and the diffusion term ($\partial u/\partial t$) will dominate. This makes sense since the diffusion equation is the continuum counterpart of the uncorrelated random walk. For low frequency of direction reversals, $1/T$ will be small, and the wave-equation term involving the second time derivative will dominate. Nevertheless, as time $t >> T$, eventually the diffusion term will become important (Okubo 1980). This echoes the point I made above, that when organism movement is viewed at a spatio-temporal scale much larger than the characteristic time of correlation, redistribution is approximately diffusion.

To see the connection between telegraph and diffusion approximations more clearly, let us rewrite Equation 4.16 as follows:

$$\frac{T}{2}\frac{\partial^2 u}{\partial t^2} + \frac{\partial u}{\partial t} = \frac{v^2 T}{2}\frac{\partial^2 u}{\partial x^2} \tag{4.17}$$

If we now take a limit with $T \to 0$, the first term will vanish, and Equation 4.17 will become the diffusion equation. However, notice that in order to keep the right-hand side from going to zero, we need to assume that the speed becomes infinite. This somewhat pathological consequence of the diffusion limit is discussed in the Appendix (Section A.1.1). We see that the correlated random walk makes a more intuitively appealing starting point for deriving diffusion approximations, at least if we insist on taking limits with τ and λ going to zero. With CRW, we *do not* have to assume an infinite speed of movement, and infinitely wriggly paths (Section A.1.1). Instead, we make an intuitively pleasing assumption that as we shrink the spatio-temporal scale, the path becomes increasingly smoother (the probability of direction reversal goes to zero). These observations apply equally strongly to two- and higher-dimensional space.

The price we pay for greater realism, however, is an extra term involving the second temporal derivative of population density. Such a development should be expected. In Section 4.2.2 we relaxed the assumption of a fixed step length, and, as a result, ended up with more terms involving spatial derivatives. Thus, the more realistic features we include in the random walk formulation, the more terms we will have in the resulting continuum approximation, akin to retaining more terms in the Taylor expansion.

Clearly, we can go on adding more and more terms, but this would be self defeating. I advocate truncating the Taylor expansion after the first temporal and the second spatial derivatives, unless we have a very compelling reason to retain higher order terms (for a possible example, see Section 4.5). On one hand, this approach gives us enough flexibility in accommodating various random walk formulations, both in form (e.g., Fickian versus Fokker-Planck) and in content (the way diffusion model parameters are expressed in terms of random walk quantities). On the other hand, by keeping the mathematical structure of the model reasonably simple we retain some hope of obtaining analytical solutions. Accordingly, in the following sections we will concentrate on diffusion approximations of CRW that neglect higher-order temporal derivatives.

4.3.2 Models for chemotaxis and "preytaxis"

Section A.1.3 in the Appendix explains how the simple diffusion equation can be derived by using an empirical relationship (Fick's Law) that relates the flux to the gradient in particle concentration. An alternative is to use a combination of methods in Sections A.1.3 and 4.2.1 to derive an expression for flux from considerations of microscale behavior (in other words, from a random walk formulation). This approach was developed by Segel (1977) in his study of chemotactic aggregation in *Escherichia coli* bacteria.

Again, consider a population of animals continuously moving in a one-dimensional space. The animals move with a constant speed v. Let $r^+(x, t)$ be the probability of direction reversal per unit time for animals moving in the positive direction (to the right) at (x, t), and $r^-(x, t)$ the direction reversal probability for animals moving to the left at (x, t). Note that the probability of direction reversal can now vary in space and time. It can be shown that regardless of the mechanism by which r^+ and r^- are determined, the flux density of animals is approximated by the following expression (Segel 1978):

$$J = -\left(\frac{v^2}{r^- + r^+}\right)\frac{\partial u}{\partial x} + \left(v\frac{r^- - r^+}{r^- + r^+}\right)u \tag{4.18}$$

Substitution of this expression for flux into

$$\frac{\partial u}{\partial t} = -\frac{\partial}{\partial x}J \tag{4.19}$$

leads to a diffusion equation.

The basic result of Segel (1978), Equation 4.18, was further developed and elaborated by Kareiva and Odell (1987). Kareiva and Odell were interested in population-level consequences of area-restricted search by predatory beetles (ladybugs). They assumed that the natural state of each predator is persistent motion, occasionally punctuated by direction reversals (that is, there is a non-zero correlation between the direction of subsequent moves). The frequency of changes in the direction increases each time a predator consumes a prey. Kareiva and Odell proposed that the turning rate depends on gut fullness: starving predators move long distances in the same direction, while satiated predators make frequent turns. Intuitively, we may guess that this simple mechanism should lead to the aggregation of predators in localities where prey are abundant. To put this intuitive conclusion on a more rigorous basis Kareiva and Odell developed the following model.

Let S be a measure of gut-fullness: 0 indicates empty, while 1 corresponds to full digestive tract. According to the assumption above, the probability of changing direction r is a function of gut fullness, $r = R(S)$. S changes as a result of prey consumption and excretion, thus the rate of change in gut fullness is a function of both S and the victim density V, so that

$$\frac{\partial S}{\partial t} = f(S, V) \tag{4.20}$$

Kareiva and Odell were primarily interested in how prey density affects predator behavior, not in the dynamics of gut fullness *per se*. Thus, they assumed that gut fullness S quickly equilibrates in the presence of constant prey density

$$S = S_0(V) \tag{4.21}$$

In other words, gut fullness is primarily a function of prey density V. The probability of direction reversal is a function of gut fullness, and thus indirectly of prey density: $R = R[S_0(V)]$. Using these assumptions, Kareiva and Odell calculated how the quantities $r^- + r^+$ and $r^- - r^+$ (see above) can be expressed in terms of predator speed v, the reversal frequency R, and the rate of change in gut fullness, f. Substituting these expressions into Equation 4.18, they obtained

$$J = -\frac{v^2}{2R}\frac{\partial u}{\partial x} + u\left[\frac{v^2}{R(2R - \partial f/\partial S)}\right]\frac{\partial R}{\partial S}\frac{\partial S_0}{\partial V}\frac{\partial V}{\partial x} \tag{4.22}$$

Here J and u are the flux and the density of predators, respectively. Functional dependencies of various parameters ($R = R(S_0)$, $S_0 = S_0(V)$, $f = f(S_0, V)$, and $V = V(x, t)$) have been suppressed for better "visibility." Speed v is a constant.

Expression 4.22 looks somewhat complicated, but in reality it is closely related to other diffusion models. To see this, we first rewrite it as a diffusion model:

$$\frac{\partial u}{\partial t} = \frac{\partial}{\partial x}\left(D\frac{\partial u}{\partial x}\right) - \frac{\partial}{\partial x}\left(\chi\frac{\partial V}{\partial x}u\right) \tag{4.23}$$

where

$$D = \frac{v^2}{2R}$$

$$\chi \; = \; \frac{v^2}{R(2R - \partial f/\partial S)} \frac{\partial R}{\partial V}$$

We see that this equation belongs to the class of diffusion-advection models. The first term on the right hand side is diffusion (in the Fickian form, since D is outside one of the spatial derivative). The second term is advection, with the bias parameter $\chi \partial V/\partial x$. Essentially the same model was proposed by Keller and Segel (1970, 1971) to represent redistribution of *Escherichia coli* bacteria moving up a chemical gradient. The concentration of the chemical to which the bacteria respond is V, which is analogous to the prey density. Keller and Segel postulated that the advection term is proportional to the *gradient* of V, $\partial V/\partial x$, rather than the concentration itself. The derivation by Kareiva and Odell put this proposition on a firm mechanistic basis. Note that Kareiva and Odell did not assume that predators can sense gradients in prey population density. The flux of predators up the prey gradient, instead, is a consequence of predators modifying turning rate as a function of their gut fullness. The parameter χ is the coefficient of chemotactic sensitivity. Predators characterized by high values of χ are more efficient at traveling up gradients of prey density.

The expression for diffusivity in terms of random walk parameters makes intuitive sense (Kareiva and Odell 1987)—faster travel (greater v) means more rapid dispersal. On the other hand, more frequent direction reversal should slow down the population spread. We also recognize that R is the inverse of the average run time (time between direction changes), $R = \tau^{-1}$. In homogeneous space $\partial V/\partial x = 0$, so that Equation 4.23 reduces to

$$\frac{\partial u}{\partial t} = \frac{v^2 \tau}{2} \frac{\partial^2 u}{\partial x^2} \tag{4.24}$$

This equation is identical to the diffusion model that we obtained from the telegraph equation when we neglected the second time derivative (Section 4.3.1). This suggests that Kareiva and Odell dropped the second temporal derivative term as part of their derivation.

The expression for chemotactic (or *preytactic*) sensitivity is less transparent. The preytactic sensitivity increases with speed, suggesting that faster moving predators will be more successful at moving up prey density gradients. The other term in the numerator is $\partial R/\partial V$. This also makes intuitive sense: the faster direction-reversal frequency changes with prey density, the more sensitive the predator aggregative behavior should be. The denominator, however, does not appear to have an obvious intuitive interpretation.

If the partial derivative of f with respect to S were zero, that would greatly simplify the model. Using the chain rule, we could rewrite the flux as:

$$J = -\frac{v^2}{2R}\frac{\partial u}{\partial x} + \frac{v^2}{2R^2}\frac{\partial R}{\partial x}u \qquad (4.25)$$

Note that we now have only one variable coefficient, R, which is expressed directly as a function of space. Furthermore, combining both terms within the spatial derivative, we have

$$J = -\frac{v^2}{2}\frac{\partial}{\partial x}\left(\frac{u}{R}\right) \qquad (4.26)$$

which, in turn implies that at equilibrium ($J = 0$) the population density of consumers is directly proportional to R (that is, the residence index ρ is simply equal to R). Unfortunately, this simplification cannot be justified on either theoretical or empirical grounds. On theoretical grounds, Kareiva and Odell argue that $\partial f/\partial S$ should not be set to zero because it would imply that the a predator's satiation level has no effect on its feeding rate—an assumption that is certainly incorrect when applied to their experimental system, and possibly to many other predators. Empirically, the model yielding $\rho = R$ would substantially underestimate the degree of ladybug aggregation, as we shall see later.

EMPIRICAL TEST OF THE PREYTAXIS MODEL   Kareiva and Odell (1987) applied their model to a system consisting of the ladybug, *Coccinella septempunctata*, and its prey, the goldenrod aphid, *Uroleucon nigrotuberculatum*. They performed two short-term foraging experiments to estimate the parameters of the diffusion equation for predator redistribution. In one experiment, marked adults were starved for measured time intervals, and then released into rows of goldenrod plants with spatially uniform aphid densities. Observations on how many aphids these ladybugs killed were used to estimate the model parameters that characterize ladybug ingestion and digestion of aphids, and thus, the rate of change in the variable S. The second experiment focused on quantifying trajectories of ladybugs. Marked ladybugs were released into goldenrod rows containing uniform aphid densities, allowed to "equilibrate" for half a day, and then their movement behavior was observed. The data from this experiment allowed Kareiva and Odell to estimate the ladybug speed v, and the functional dependence of reversal frequency R on prey density V.

The complete model of the spatio-temporal dynamics of the ladybug-aphid interaction also needs an equation for the prey density. Kareiva and Odell assumed that (1) prey redistribute themselves according to simple diffusion, (2) the prey death term is due to predation involving type II functional response, and (3) the prey population growth is logistic. The prey diffusion rate was estimated by point releases of aphids into empty goldenrod arrays, and the parameters of logistic growth were estimated by transplanting groups of aphids onto single isolated goldenrod stems, and censusing them over time. Finally, the killing rate of predators was estimated using the data from the short-term predator foraging experiments. The fully parameterized model was solved numerically to obtain predictions.

The predictions of the model were tested by experimentally setting up uneven spatial profiles of aphid density within 10 m strips of goldenrod plants, and releasing ladybugs at an initially uniform density (Figure 4.4). The spatio-temporal dynamics in each experiment were followed by censusing aphids and ladybugs in each meter of the goldenrod array 1 and 2 days after the release. The qualitative predictions of the model that ladybugs would aggregate within aphid clumps were borne out by the data, although the quantitative predictions tended to underestimate somewhat the strength of ladybug aggregative response (Figure 4.4).

4.3.3   Synthesis

This section is an introduction to correlated random walks and the associated diffusion-approximation models. The approach here focuses on 1D spatial domains, in which the tasks of both formulating random walks and deriving diffusion models is greatly simplified compared to 2D or 3D situations. An approximation of the correlated random walk with a partial differential equation leads, strictly speaking, not to a diffusion model but to a model that has features of both diffusion and wave equations. A further approximation is required to obtain a diffusion model. A somewhat different approach is taken by Kareiva and Odell (1987), who derive their diffusion model for ladybug movement in one step.

4.4   Persistence and Directional Bias: 2D Space

We now move on to more complex and flexible models of random walk. The major innovation in this section is that we will consider movement with persistence and directional (external) bias in a two-dimensional space. As was already stated in Section 4.3, restricting a CRW process to one-dimensional (1D) space greatly simplifies the task of diffusion approximation. In 1D space we simply need to track two subpopulations of individuals: those moving to the right, and those moving to the left. Directional persistence is automatically built in, since each organism continues to move in the same direction until it makes a turn. Imposing an external directional bias (long-distance

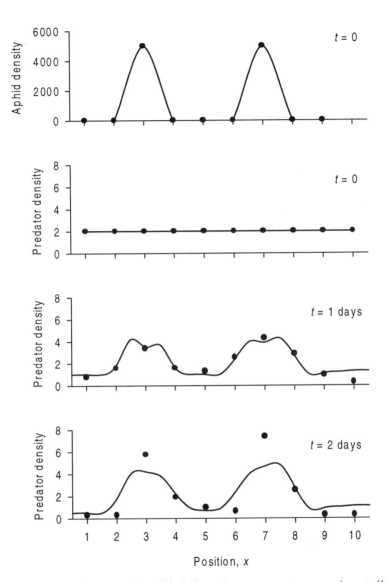

Figure 4.4: Aggregation of ladybugs in response to experimentally created aphid clumps (the July 1985 experiment). The average of three experimental goldenrod arrays is shown. Solid lines: predictions; dots: observations. (After Kareiva and Odell 1987.)

attraction) is also simple. For example, right-moving organisms are less likely to reverse their direction than left-moving organisms.

In 2D space, construction of a random walk model is conceptually more difficult. We have not just two, but an infinite number of directions to keep track of, and, therefore, cannot divide organisms into a finite number of "direction-groups." An additional conceptual difficulty is modeling the combined effect of directional persistence and directional bias. To illustrate this, consider a butterfly in 2D space that moves with persistence in a direction (that is, according to CRW) when it does not perceive a resource patch. After perceiving a patch, it also biases its movements towards it. Now suppose that the previous move of the butterfly happened to be in the general direction toward the patch. If the next move is also toward the patch, did it happen because of directional persistence? Or because the butterfly perceived the patch and biased its movement toward it?

Due to this conceptual difficulty, I will first consider a CRW model without directional bias. Approaches to combining directional persistence and external bias will be discussed later.

My focus in this section will be on two-dimensional models. In fact, models for 3D space are not much more complex, since the major increase in complexity occurs when we pass from one- to two-dimensional correlated random walks. I will not discuss the three-dimensional case, however, because in most terrestrial habitats we are concerned with only two spatial dimensions, and because the formulas for the three-dimensional space are only minor variations of two-dimensional formulas.

4.4.1   The Patlak model

Consider a butterfly flying through a landscape containing patches of resources such as host plants. At irregular intervals of time the butterfly lands (for example, to explore a plant for oviposition). Let us assume that by connecting landing points with straight lines we can obtain a reasonably accurate discrete representation of the butterfly's continuous and curvilinear path. (Section 5.2 will deal with various methods for discrete representation of continuous paths.) Thus, we represent each *path* traced by the butterfly as a series of *moves*, with each move characterized by three numbers: one temporal and two spatial coordinates; for example, move duration, length, and direction (Figure 4.5). We need two spatial coordinates because we have assumed that the butterfly is moving within a two-dimensional space, or a plane. Let us also define two other useful quantities, the speed of straight-line displacement, which is the ratio of move length to its duration, and the turning angle, which is the direction of the move measured relative to the direction of the previous

(a)

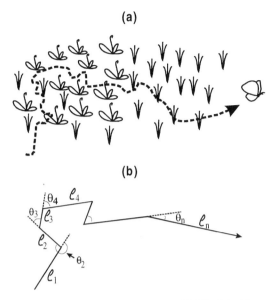

(b)

Figure 4.5: Movement represented as a CRW. (a) The actual path traced by the butterfly. (b) The discrete representation of the path.

move (Figure 4.5). Since the movement process is probabilistic, the values of move components (length, speed, duration, etc.) are not fixed. Instead, each move component has an associated probability density function that specifies how likely any given value be realized.

The five move components defined above are interrelated. For example, we would expect that move length and duration are correlated: longer moves generally require more time. Since derivation of the diffusion approximation is much easier if one deals with uncorrelated quantities, we need to select a subset of the movement components that are statistically independent of each other. Let us assume that an organism chooses move speed and duration independently of each other (this, in turn, determines the move distance). This takes care of the temporal and one of the spatial components. Since we wish to take into account the correlation in the direction of subsequent moves, we do not want to use move directions but, instead, the turning angle as the second spatial component. Let us further assume that turning angles are distributed symmetrically about $0°$ (for example, the probability of a $10°$ turn to the left equals the probability of a $10°$ turn to the right).

We now have the following conceptual scheme for the movement process of the butterfly. At the beginning of each move, the butterfly randomly "chooses" its speed, the duration of its move, and its turning angle (in relation to the direction of the previous move). After a move defined by these three components is completed, the process is repeated again. In sum, each path is characterized by three frequency distributions: move speeds, move durations, and turning angles. Each path "realization" is a result of repeated random and independent sampling from these three distributions. The frequency distributions of the three move components are allowed to vary in space. For example, in areas where resources are plentiful, the butterfly will make shorter and slower moves, and it may also make sharper turns between moves.

Given the initial position of an organism and its initial movement direction, and given the frequency distributions of move speed, duration, and turning angle, it is possible to specify the probabilities of finding the organism at any point in space at any time. If there is a large number of organisms moving around in identical fashion without influencing the movement of one another, then the probability of finding an individual at the position x, y at time t translates directly into the population density of organisms, $u(x, y, t)$. The following diffusion equation for the population redistribution of organisms moving according to this CRW process was derived by Patlak (1953a):

$$\frac{\partial u}{\partial t} = \frac{1}{n} \nabla \cdot \left[\frac{1 + \psi(2\frac{m_1^2}{m_2} - 1)}{1 - \psi} \nabla \left(\frac{m_2}{2\tau} u \right) - \frac{\psi m_1^3}{\tau m_2 (1 - \psi)} \nabla \left(\frac{m_2}{m_1} \right) u \right] \quad (4.27)$$

Here ∇ is the gradient operator, $\nabla = (\partial/\partial x, \partial/\partial y)$, n is the dimension of the space ($n = 2$ for two-dimensional space), and m_1, m_2, τ, and ψ are CRW parameters. The parameters m_1 and m_2 are the first and the second moments of the frequency distribution of the move length: m_1 is the average move length, while m_2 is the average *squared* move length. Parameter τ is the average move duration. The directional persistence is quantified by the mean cosine of the turning angle, ψ. Cosines of turning angles near zero (small changes in direction) are close to 1, while cosines of angles near π (direction reversals) are close to -1. Thus, if there is persistence in movement direction between consecutive moves, small turning angles will predominate and ψ will be greater than zero. By contrast, if the organism tends to reverse its direction very frequently, then ψ will be negative. No persistence implies $\psi = 0$.

4.4.2   Relationship to other diffusion approximations

At first glance, Equation (4.27) may look intimidating. However, we immediately observe two facts. First, there are only four random walk parameters (or functions, since these parameters can vary in space). It turns out that we do not need to know the shapes of the frequency distributions of move components exactly. It is sufficient to know the average move length m_1, the average squared move length m_2, the mean move duration τ, and the mean cosine of the turning angle ψ. Second, Equation 4.27 has strong links to the framework of diffusion-approximation models developed earlier in this chapter.

UNCORRELATED RANDOM WALK   No directional persistence implies $\psi = 0$. Assuming for simplicity 1D space ($n = 1$), Equation 4.27 simplifies to

$$\frac{\partial u}{\partial t} = \frac{\partial^2}{\partial x^2}\left(\frac{m_2}{2\tau}u\right) \tag{4.28}$$

This is the Fokker-Planck diffusion equation with motility $\mu = m_2/2\tau$. Simplifying even further, let us assume that the organism makes moves of fixed length, λ. Then $m_2 = \lambda^2$, which implies that $\mu = \lambda^2/2\tau$. This is the same as the formula for μ derived in Section 4.2.1, $\mu = \lambda^2(R + L)/2\tau$ (because $R + L = 1$ in the CRW formulation since movement is continuous).

TELEGRAPH EQUATION   If the random walk is confined to 1D space, then every change in direction is a direction reversal, with the turning angle $\theta = \pi$. This implies that the persistence $\psi = -1$. Furthermore, the CRW formulation leading to the telegraph equation (see Section 4.3.1) assumed that the probability of reversing direction was independent of the length of movement since the last reversal. This implies that the distribution of move durations is exponential. Finally, the velocity of movement was assumed to be constant. Therefore, move length distribution is also exponential. The ratio of the second moment to the squared first moment in the exponential distribution is $\gamma = m_2/m_1^2 = 2$. Using these relationships, Equation 4.27 simplifies to

$$\frac{\partial u}{\partial t} = \frac{\partial}{\partial x}\left[\frac{\partial}{\partial x}\left(\frac{m_1^2}{2\tau}u\right) + \frac{m_1}{2\tau}\frac{\partial m_1}{\partial x}u\right] \tag{4.29}$$

Substituting the velocity $v = m_1/\tau$ yields

$$\frac{\partial u}{\partial t} = \frac{v^2}{2}\frac{\partial}{\partial x}\left[\frac{\partial}{\partial x}(\tau u) + \frac{\partial \tau}{\partial x}u\right] \tag{4.30}$$

Finally, in homogeneous space, the second term vanishes, and we obtain the diffusion approximation of the telegraph equation (compare with Equation 4.17):

$$\frac{\partial u}{\partial t} = \frac{v^2\tau}{2}\frac{\partial^2 u}{\partial x^2} \tag{4.31}$$

SQUARED DISPLACEMENT IN CRW   Squared net displacement after n moves, R_n^2, is the most convenient and theoretically sound parameter with which to quantify dispersal (Skellam 1973, Okubo 1980, Kareiva and Shigesada 1983). If a population of organisms moves according to CRW in two-dimensional space, then their average, or expected squared displacement, $E(R_n^2)$, for large n is approximately (Kareiva and Shigesada 1983):

$$E(R_n^2) \approx nm_2 + 2n\frac{\psi}{1-\psi}m_1^2 \qquad (4.32)$$

We can check this formula using the Patlak model. Rewriting the Patlak equation for homogeneous two-dimensional space, we obtain:

$$\frac{\partial u}{\partial t} = \frac{m_2 - \psi m_2 + 2\psi m_1^2}{4\tau(1-\psi)}\nabla^2 u \qquad (4.33)$$

We see that in homogeneous space, the Patlak model is equivalent to a simple diffusion equation, with the diffusion coefficient

$$D = \frac{m_2 - \psi m_2 + 2\psi m_1^2}{4\tau(1-\psi)}$$

The expected squared displacement for diffusion is

$$E(R_n^2) = 4Dt = 4Dn\tau \qquad (4.34)$$

where n is the number of moves, as above. Substituting the formula for D we obtain a result identical to Kareiva and Shigesada.

Note that persistence enters this formula in a nonlinear way as $\psi/(1-\psi)$. When ψ is close to zero, $\psi/(1-\psi) \sim \psi$, and squared net displacement will be dominated by the second moment of the move length distribution. As $\psi \to 1$, $\psi/(1-\psi) \to \infty$, and displacement will be dominated by the first moment m_1. Thus, the closer ψ is to 1, the more variation in ψ will affect net displacement.

PREYTAXIS MODEL OF KAREIVA AND ODELL (1987)   When we assumed that the $\partial f/\partial S$ is set to zero (see Section 4.3.2), the expression for the flux in the Kareiva-Odell preytaxis model simplified to

$$J = -\frac{v^2}{2R}\frac{\partial u}{\partial x} + \frac{v^2}{2R^2}\frac{\partial R}{\partial x}u \qquad (4.35)$$

To compare this equation to the Patlak model, we substitute $R = \tau^{-1}$, obtaining

$$J = -\frac{v^2}{2}\left(\tau\frac{\partial u}{\partial x} + \frac{\partial\tau}{\partial x}u\right) \qquad (4.36)$$

The Patlak expression for the flux, extracted from Equation 4.30 is:

$$J = -\frac{v^2}{2}\left(\frac{\partial}{\partial x}(\tau u) + \frac{\partial \tau}{\partial x}u\right) \tag{4.37}$$

The advection terms in these two expressions are the same, but the diffusion terms differ: Fickian in the simplified Kareiva-Odell model, while Fokker-Planck in the Patlak model. Thus, these two models are not equivalent. They make different assumptions about how individual movements are translated into a diffusion model. As a consequence, the two models make different predictions about the equilibrium distribution of organisms.

RELATIONSHIP TO CHEMOTAXIS MODELS   The above comparisons suggest some reparameterizations of Equation 4.27. First, we have identified $m_2/2\tau$ as the motility μ. Second, we can use the quantity $\gamma = m_2/m_1^2$ to simplify the expression. This parameter reflects the shape of the frequency distribution of move lengths. If the probability of terminating a move is independent of how long an organism has been moving since its last stop, then the distribution of move lengths will be exponential, and $\gamma = 2$. If the organism makes steps of fixed move length, then $\gamma = 1$. Alternatively, if the move-length distribution is characterized by a long tail, then $\gamma > 2$. Finally, we have already encountered the parameter $v = m_1/\tau$, the average speed. Using these parameters, we can rewrite Equation 4.27 as follows (assuming 2D space):

$$\frac{\partial u}{\partial t} = \frac{1}{2}\nabla \cdot \{\delta[\nabla(\mu u) - \chi\nabla(\gamma m_1)u]\} \tag{4.38}$$

where

$$\delta = 1 + \frac{2}{\gamma}\frac{\psi}{1-\psi}$$

$$\chi = \frac{v}{2 + \gamma(1-\psi)/\psi}$$

Apart from the factor δ, this form is identical to the diffusion-advection equation that we have already encountered on numerous occasions, with motility μ and bias $\chi\nabla(\gamma m_1)$. Note that δ does not affect the population redistribution at equilibrium, but only the speed with which equilibrium distribution is approached. The shape of the bias term in Equation 4.38 resembles the shape of the bias in chemotactic and preytactic models (see Section 4.3). It also consists of two parts, one involving a gradient of some environmentally varying quantity, $\nabla(\gamma m_1)$, and the other the coefficient χ that determines how sensitively organisms react to the gradient. The sensitivity χ is proportional to the speed v with which organisms move (cf. Section 4.3.2). Note that both δ and χ involve ψ in the form $\psi/(1-\psi)$.

4.4.3 Equilibrium distribution and the residence index

The Patlak model (Equation 4.38) is too complex to solve analytically, and thus time-dependent solutions have to be obtained numerically. In many cases, however, all we need is an equilibrium distribution of organisms in space resulting from their movements. For example, our butterflies searching for patchily-distributed host plants will not affect the distribution of their resources during the current season, and thus their movements will occur in what is essentially a static landscape. Thus, when movement occurs on a faster time scale than birth, death, and interaction terms, we can assume that population distribution will be at the redistribution equilibrium. If, however, the spatial distribution of organisms dynamically influences the landscape on a fast time scale (e.g., predators rapidly decimating patches of prey), then we will need the full time-dependent model.

Our goal in this section is to write down the formula for the residence index. The concept of the residence index was discussed in Section 4.2.5. Briefly, it summarizes the effects of environmental conditions on individual movements, and specifies how the relative density of organisms will change from region to region, because population density at equilibrium is proportional to the residence index:

$$\tilde{u}(x,y) \sim \rho\left(\epsilon(x,y)\right)$$

Here ϵ is the *environmental potential*, a variable that summarizes environmental conditions at the spatial point x, y. For example, ϵ could be the density of host plants. CRW parameters m_1, m_2, τ, and ψ are functions of ϵ.

To obtain the expression for ρ, we utilize the fact that at equilibrium the flux is zero:

$$\nabla(\mu u) - \chi \nabla(\gamma m_1)u = 0 \tag{4.39}$$

Next, using the chain rule, so that $\nabla(\gamma m_1) = (\gamma m_1)'\nabla\epsilon$ (prime denotes differentiation with respect to ϵ), we obtain

$$\frac{\nabla(\mu u)}{\mu u} = \frac{\chi}{\mu}(\gamma m_1)'\nabla\epsilon$$

Integrating, we have

$$u = \frac{\text{const}}{\mu}\exp\int_{\epsilon_0}^{\epsilon}\frac{\chi}{\mu}(\gamma m_1)'\,d\epsilon' \tag{4.40}$$

where ϵ' is the integration variable. Substituting μ and χ, we write the formula for the residence index:

$$\rho(\epsilon) = \frac{1}{\mu}\exp\int_{\epsilon_0}^{\epsilon}\frac{2(\ln\gamma m_1)'}{2 + \gamma(1-\psi)/\psi}\,d\epsilon' \tag{4.41}$$

Here ϵ_0 is some arbitrary reference point, for example, ϵ in areas where host density is zero, or an average ϵ.

It is possible to obtain a closed-form solution of Equation (4.41) in a reasonably simple form by making a simplifying assumption that the ratio $\gamma = m_2/m_1^2$ is approximately constant (although m_1 and m_2 may nevertheless vary with ϵ). This is not a very unreasonable assumption to make, since m_2 and m_1 are related as follows: $m_2 = m_1^2 + \sigma^2$, where σ^2 is the variance of move length distribution. The mean and the variance are often related to each other in such a way that σ is proportional to m_1 (this would be the case if the move length is determined by many independent factors acting in a multiplicative way, Sokal and Rohlf 1981). This, in turn, implies that $m_2 \sim m_1^2$, or that γ is constant. Formula 4.41, then, simplifies to

$$\rho(\epsilon) = \frac{\tau}{m_1^2} \exp \int_{\epsilon_0}^{\epsilon} \frac{2(\ln m_1)'}{2 + \gamma(1 - \psi)/\psi} \, d\epsilon' \tag{4.42}$$

Assuming that parameters m_1 and ψ vary piecewise linearly, we eventually obtain the following formula for the residence index (see Turchin 1991 for details):

$$\rho(\epsilon) = \tau(\epsilon)\varphi(\epsilon)^{\alpha} m_1(\epsilon)^{-\left(\frac{2-2\gamma}{2-\gamma} + \alpha\right)} \tag{4.43}$$

where $\varphi(\epsilon) = \gamma + (2 - \gamma)\psi(\epsilon)$, and

$$\alpha = \frac{2\gamma[m_1(\epsilon) - m_1(\epsilon_0)]}{(2 - \gamma)[\varphi(\epsilon_0)m_1(\epsilon) - \varphi(\epsilon)m_1(\epsilon_0)]}$$

Here $m_1(\epsilon_0)$ and $\psi(\epsilon_0)$ are simply the CRW parameters in patches characterized by the reference value of ϵ.

For the special case of $\gamma = 2$, which arises when the distribution of move lengths is exponential, the formula is (Turchin 1991):

$$\rho(\epsilon) = \tau(\epsilon)m_1(\epsilon)^{a-2} \exp \psi(\epsilon) \tag{4.44}$$

where

$$a = \frac{\psi(\epsilon_0)m_1(\epsilon) - \psi(\epsilon)m_1(\epsilon_0)}{m_1(\epsilon) - m_1(\epsilon_0)}$$

A further simplification is instructive. Suppose we keep $\gamma = 2$, and in addition let $\psi = \text{const}$. This assumption implies that organisms modify their move lengths and the frequency of turning when foraging in patches characterized by different ϵ, but do not vary the degree of directional persistence. In that case, the residence index is

$$\rho = \frac{\tau}{m_1^{2-\psi}}. \tag{4.45}$$

This formula reveals the effect of directional persistence on the functional form of the residence index. For uncorrelated random walk ($\psi = 0$), the exponent of m_1 becomes 2, and thus ρ is inversely related to the motility $\mu = m_2/2\tau = m_1^2/\tau$. We already know this, since the Patlak model is a generalization of Fokker-Planck diffusion. As the persistence in direction increases, $\psi \to 1$, and the exponent of m_1 approaches unity. Thus, the residence index is inversely related to the organism velocity $v = m_1/\tau$, which would make more sense than μ for linearly moving organisms. Once again, we see that the correlated random walk is in some sense an intermediate model between the uncorrelated random walk with infinitely wiggly paths and movement along straight-line paths.

4.4.4   External directional bias

External directional bias is present when the probability distribution of the absolute direction in which an organism is moving is not uniform. Directional bias may be constant (for example, when organisms always have a constant preference of moving east), or it may vary in space (for example, organisms may be attracted to certain features of terrain, in which case both bias direction and magnitude will depend on the spatial position of the moving individual in relation to the attractive focus). External bias is distinguished from (internal) directional persistence, which does not affect the long-term probability distribution of absolute directions.

Directional bias can affect movement in two ways. First, organisms may tend to increase speed or duration of a move (or both) when moving in a preferred direction. This would result in longer move lengths towards a center of attraction. Second, organisms may bias the direction of their movement towards attraction centers.

The first mechanism, bias in the move length, does not present a serious difficulty for constructing a diffusion approximation. As a first order approximation, we assume that the length of each move consists of the basic undirectional component with the mean m_1, and the directional components m_x and m_y. In other words, m_1 is the average distance the particle moves independently of direction, while m_x is the additional distance the particle moves on average in the x-direction, and m_y the additional average distance traveled in the y-direction (Patlak 1953a). If there is no persistence in direction, then the diffusion approximation of this random walk will be simply a Fokker-Planck equation (Patlak 1953a), similar to the ones we have discussed in Section 4.2.

The second mechanism (bias in move direction) can also be easily incorporated into a diffusion model, provided that we are dealing with an uncorrelated random walk. Persistence in direction, however, causes a difficulty. If both directional persistence and directional bias are operating, then the probability of moving in a certain direction after a turn, say α, is affected by both the direction of the previous move and the absolute direction (as well as the spatial and temporal coordinates). Patlak (1953a) assumed that these two influences are combined multiplicatively, so that the probability that an organism will turn in the direction α_2 at (x, y, t), given that it arrived at that point traveling in direction α_1, is:

$$A(\alpha_2|\alpha_1, x, y, t) = \frac{E(\alpha_2|x, y, t)I(\theta_2|x, y, t)}{\int_0^{2\pi} E(\alpha_2|x, y, t)I(\theta_2|x, y, t)\, d\alpha_2}.$$

where E is the probability of choosing the absolute direction α_2 (nonuniform due to directional bias), and I the probability of a turning angle $\theta_2 = \alpha_2 - \alpha_1$. The integral in the denominator is to make sure that the probabilities of all possible move directions after turning add up to one. Furthermore, Patlak assumed that external bias is not very strong, so that it could be expanded in a series of spherical harmonics, and only linear terms kept at first approximation:

$$E(\alpha_2|x, y, t) \approx \frac{\pi}{2}[1 + \phi_x(x, y, t)\cos\alpha_2 + \phi_y(x, y, t)\sin\alpha_2].$$

Thus, ϕ_x and ϕ_y are coefficients of external bias. As before, the directional persistence ψ is defined as the mean cosine of the distribution of turning angles I. Given these assumptions, the diffusion approximation of a random walk with persistence and external bias is (Patlak 1953a):

$$\frac{\partial u}{\partial t} = \frac{1}{2}\sum_{i=1}^{2}\frac{\partial}{\partial x_i}\left\{\frac{1 + \psi(2\frac{m_1^2}{m_2} - 1)}{1 - \psi}\frac{\partial}{\partial x_i}\left(\frac{m_2}{2\tau}u\right)\right.$$
$$\left. - \left[\frac{m_{x_i}}{\tau} + \frac{m_1(1 + \psi)\phi_{x_i}}{\tau} + \frac{\psi m_1^3}{\tau m_2(1 - \psi)}\frac{\partial}{\partial x_i}\left(\frac{m_2}{m_1}\right)\right]u\right\}$$

where $x_1 = x$ and $x_2 = y$.

Inclusion of the external bias into the CRW does not unduly complicate the resulting diffusion-approximation equation. Only the advection term is affected, which is now a sum of three components proportional to (1) the bias in move length (m_x, m_y), (2) the directionality bias (ϕ_x, ϕ_y), and (3) the gradient in m_2/m_1, which was present in the unbiased CRW formulation. However, this model comes short at the empirical end. The problem is that the parameters ψ, ϕ_x, and ϕ_y cannot be directly calculated by observing organism movement. Patlak (1953b:439) provides an indirect way of estimating these quantities. We shall see in Chapter 5 that there are certain difficulties associated with using his method.

It is possible that there is no general method of combining persistence with bias that would fit all applications. It may be necessary to make simplifying assumptions to tailor equations to each particular case study, or to assume specific mechanisms that are used by organisms to respond to variability of their environment. For example, Kareiva and Odell (1987) assumed that ladybug turning behavior was modulated by the fullness of their guts (Section 4.3.2). In this connection, it is worth mentioning another important paper on diffusion-approximation models of random walk with persistence and bias. Alt (1980) derived the expressions for turning frequency and turning angle distributions by assuming specific mechanisms used by chemotactic bacteria. Because of its emphasis on bacterial movements, Alt's (1981) work is somewhat outside the scope of this book. However, it is interesting that the diffusion equation derived by Alt (1980) appears to be very similar in form to the Patlak model:

$$\frac{\partial u}{\partial t} = \frac{1}{2} \nabla \cdot [\delta \nabla (vu) - \chi \nabla \epsilon u] \qquad (4.46)$$

Like the Patlak model, Alt's equation is a generalization of the Fokker-Planck diffusion. The advection term is proportional to the chemotactic sensitivity (χ), and the gradient of the environmental variable ϵ, which is the "chemotactic factor" in Alt's formulation. One interesting difference is that instead of motility $m_2/2\tau$ in the Patlak's diffusion term, Alt's diffusion term has the velocity $v = m_1/\tau$ inside the differentiation operator. This appears to be a result of a somewhat different random walk formulation.

A model that may turn out to be quite useful for quantifying movement with directional persistence and external bias was recently derived by Grünbaum (1998). The model assumes that organisms move with a constant velocity v, and that turning rate is modulated by two functions of resource density: $F(\epsilon)$ is the dependence of turning rate on local environmental potential ϵ, while $G(\epsilon)$ modulates sensitivity to the perceived rate of environmental change. In practice, these two functions can be measured by estimating the effect of environment on the nondirectional, $\tau_0(\epsilon)$, and the directional, $\tau_1(\epsilon)$, components of turning rate (see Grünbaum 1998 for details). Then, $F(\epsilon) = \tau_0^{-1}(\epsilon)$ and $G(\epsilon) = \tau_1(\epsilon)F^2(\epsilon)/v$. The diffusion-approximation model is

$$\frac{\partial u}{\partial t} = \nabla \left[\frac{v^2}{2(1-\psi)F(\epsilon)} \nabla u - \frac{v^2[F'(\epsilon) - G(\epsilon)F(\epsilon)]}{2F^2(\epsilon)} \nabla \epsilon u \right]$$

where ψ is the average cosine of the turning angle and $F'(\epsilon)$ is the derivative of F with respect to ϵ. The residence index for this model is

$$\rho(\epsilon) = \left\{ F(\epsilon) \exp \left[-\int_{\epsilon_0}^{\epsilon} G(\epsilon') \, d\epsilon' \right] \right\}^{1-\psi}$$

4.4.5 Synthesis

This is probably the most important section in this chapter. It discusses the Patlak model, which provides an extremely versatile and powerful tool for modeling movement with directional persistence. Although the section focuses on the 2D variant of the model, this is primarily done for the purpose of illustration and because it is applied to 2D examples. Mathematically, extension to 3D space is trivial.

I first consider the correlated random walk in 2D space unaffected by external directional biases. The Patlak model is compared to several other diffusion models and random walk formulas, and in most cases we find that other models are special cases of the Patlak model. Next I turn to the full Patlak model that includes the influences of external biases on individual movement. At this point the situation becomes very complex, and formulating viable schemes for establishing connections with data is conceptually more difficult. The primary issue is how to account for effects of both external bias and internal directional persistence on the direction of each move. I briefly consider two alternative models for biased CRW processes that may also be of use in practical applications.

4.5 Congregation

The models considered in this chapter can be loosely called aggregation models because they start by formulating random walks in heterogeneous landscapes, and attempt to predict where organisms will tend to accumulate. I define *aggregation* broadly as any movement process that results in formation of a nonuniform spatial distribution of organisms. Aggregation can result from organisms responding to a wide variety of stimuli, such as avoidance of harsh physical conditions, or attraction to patches of resources.

There is one kind of aggregation that has special features. I will call it *congregation*: aggregation as a result of behavioral responses of organisms to conspecifics (*congregate* is to gather *together*; as opposed to *aggregate*, which is to gather *at* some locality). Congregating organisms may respond directly to neighbors using visual, acoustic, or chemical (pheromones) stimuli, or indirectly to population density cues, such as feeding damage on a host plant.

The dynamics of animal grouping have been a subject of many theoretical studies (see Okubo 1986 for a review). However, the primary focus of these studies has been on the composition and social structure of animal groups. Because these models do not explicitly deal with the temporal and spatial changes in population density, they are not well suited for use in the context of population dynamics.

There is a pressing need for models of congregative movement, because, as I have argued elsewhere, gregarious movement can be a key factor in understanding population dynamics of many organisms (Turchin 1987, 1988b, 1989a, Turchin and Kareiva 1989). Modeling congregation, however, is not an easy task, because congregation involves a positive feedback loop between movement and population density, which leads, as we shall see, to nonlinear diffusion models. Congregation is important precisely because of the positive feedback implicit in it—it is capable of amplifying subtle gradients to create extreme variations in population density.

In fact, the inherent tendency of congregation to amplify gradients in population density causes some mathematical problems for the diffusion approach. We shall see that standard diffusion approximations, which have worked so well in previous sections, are inadequate for modeling congregation. I will discuss several modifications of diffusion approximation for congregative movement, and suggest that the one retaining higher spatial derivatives appears to be the simplest and most promising.

4.5.1 Random walk with attraction between individuals

I begin with a simple model of gregarious random walk (GRW), following the basic formulation of Section 4.2.1. The population is distributed along one-dimensional discrete space with the distance between spatial nodes equal to λ. Again, $p(x, t)$ is the probability of finding an organism at any spatial position x at time t. During the time interval τ any individual can make a step to the right with probability $R(x, t)$, to the left with probability $L(x, t)$, or make no move with probability $N(x, t)$. However, unlike the random walk in Section 4.2.1, individuals bias their movement towards each other. The movement of organisms is influenced by other individuals in the following way:

- When there are no other animals at adjacent positions, each animal moves randomly, i.e. the probabilities of moving left or right are the same.

- If there is a conspecific on an adjacent position, the animal moves there with conditional probability k (conditioned on the presence of the other animal), or ignores the neighbor with conditional probability $1 - k$.

When local population density is low, we can ignore the probability of having more than one conspecific in the immediate vicinity of each moving individual. These assumptions imply that at low density ($p << 1$),

$$R(x, t) \;=\; \frac{1}{2}r(x, t) + kp(x + \lambda, t)$$

$$L(x,t) = \frac{1}{2}r(x,t) + kp(x - \lambda, t) \qquad (4.47)$$

where $r(x,t)$ is the random component of movement

$$r(x,t) = 1 - N(x,t) - kp(x + \lambda, t) - kp(x - \lambda, t) \qquad (4.48)$$

When local density increases, for example as a result of congregation, Equations 4.47 will not strictly hold, since the probability that there are conspecifics both on the left and on the right can no longer be neglected. In addition, at high population densities the attraction between individuals can be greatly reduced, or even reversed, becoming repulsion. Instead of postulating any particular mechanism of behavioral interactions at high population densities, I simply assume that k is a decreasing function of $p(x,t)$. Turchin (1989a: Appendix I) showed that under certain circumstances k can be approximated by a linear function of p. I will assume that $k = k_0(1 - u/\omega)$, where k_0 is the maximum degree of congregative bias (as $u \to 0$), and ω is the critical density at which movement switches from congregative to repulsive.

Note that there is a constraint on the magnitude of $R(x,t)$ and $L(x,t)$: $r(x,t) + kp(x + \lambda, t) + kp(x - \lambda, t) + N(x,t)$ has to sum up to one. Thus, one should be careful that the products $kp(x + \lambda, t)$ and $kp(x - \lambda, t)$ do not become too large, otherwise $r(x,t)$ may inadvertently become negative (see Equation 4.48). The assumption of low probabilities p, ensures that this constraint will not be violated. Alternatively, we can assume that the probability of moving right (or left) is not a function of absolute density but of the difference between p at the current position and p on the right (or left) (Lewis 1994):

$$R(x,t) = \frac{1}{2}r(x,t) + k[p(x + \lambda, t) - p(x,t)]$$
$$L(x,t) = \frac{1}{2}r(x,t) + k[p(x - \lambda, t) - p(x,t)] \qquad (4.49)$$

This assumption leads to exactly the same diffusion approximation, but the constraint on the magnitudes of R and L can be satisfied by assuming that population density *gradient* is small.

The diffusion approximation for this type of random walk was already derived in Section 4.2.1 (Equation 4.4):

$$\frac{\partial u}{\partial t} = \frac{\partial^2}{\partial x^2}(\mu u) - \frac{\partial}{\partial x}(\beta u) \qquad (4.50)$$

where motility $\mu = \lambda^2(R + L)/2\tau$, and the bias $\beta = \lambda(R - L)/\tau$. To find the expression for the bias, we substitute $R(x,t)$ and $L(x,t)$ from Equation 4.47, and again expand in Taylor series:

$$
\begin{aligned}
R(x,t) - L(x,t) &= k[p(x+\lambda,t) - p(x-\lambda,t)] \\
&= 2k\lambda\frac{\partial p}{\partial x}(x,t) + O(\lambda^3)
\end{aligned}
\tag{4.51}
$$

Furthermore, substituting $k = k_0(1 - u/\omega)$ we find that

$$
\beta = \frac{\lambda^2}{\tau}2k_0\frac{\partial u}{\partial x}\left(1 - \frac{u}{\omega}\right) = 2\kappa\frac{\partial u}{\partial x}\left(1 - \frac{u}{\omega}\right)
\tag{4.52}
$$

where $\kappa = k_0\lambda^2/\tau$. The diffusion equation, thus, is

$$
\frac{\partial u}{\partial t} = \frac{\partial}{\partial x}\left[\frac{\partial}{\partial x}(\mu u) - 2\kappa\left(1 - \frac{u}{\omega}\right)\frac{\partial u}{\partial x}u\right]
\tag{4.53}
$$

The first term on the right hand side of Equation 4.53 represents diffusion (in the Fokker-Planck form), while the second term represents congregative advection. Note that the form of the advective term is similar to the chemotactic or preytactic terms we have encountered previously. The population density itself plays the role of the "chemotactic factor", and the quantity $\kappa(1 - u/\omega)$ is analogous to chemotactic sensitivity.

Repulsive movement can be modeled analogously by assuming that animals move away from conspecifics (i.e., effectively reversing the sign of k). Equation 4.53 with constant negative k is identical to the biased random motion model of Gurney and s (1975), Gurtin and McCamy (1977), Shigesada et al. (1979), and Shigesada (1980). These authors, however, derived their models by assuming that the probability of moving to an adjacent position was biased because animals preferred to move down a population gradient. By contrast, the dependence of the advection term on the population gradient in Equation 4.53 was derived as a consequence of the random walk set-up.

As a final step, in anticipation of the equilibrium analysis (deferred until Section 4.5.3) we bring all terms in Equation 4.53 within the diffusion operator:

$$
\frac{\partial u}{\partial t} = \frac{\partial^2}{\partial x^2}\left(\mu u - \kappa u^2 + \frac{2\kappa}{3\omega}u^3\right)
\tag{4.54}
$$

This equation is of the general form

$$
\frac{\partial u}{\partial t} = \frac{\partial^2}{\partial x^2}\Gamma(u)
\tag{4.55}
$$

where Γ is the dynamic level (Skellam 1973, see also Section A.3.2).

4.5.2 Congregation in a correlated random walk

The congregation-diffusion equation in the previous section was derived by using the approach in Section 4.2, which assumes no correlation between successive steps. As we know, an alternative (and in many ways more realistic) starting point for a diffusion approximation is the correlated random walk. The question is, will starting with a CRW process lead to a diffusion approximation similar to Equation 4.55?

I will explore this issue with a simple CRW formulation in which only one parameter will vary with population density. Let us assume that organisms move in homogeneous one- or two-dimensional space with constant speed v. The distribution of turning angles is also constant. The frequency of turning R and average move duration $\tau = R^{-1}$ are functions of u. Finally, the distribution of move durations, and therefore move distances is exponential.

To generate some hypotheses about the possible functional shapes of $\tau(u)$, let us consider a biological scenario where the model may apply. This scenario was inspired by "incidental congregations" of male butterflies *Euphydryas anicia* (Odendaal et al. 1988), although it is admittedly a great oversimplification of the actual field system. *Euphydryas anicia* is a hilltopping butterfly, but males in this species form congregations even in a topographically flat site. We suggested that these congregations arise as a side effect of male strategy to chase anything even remotely resembling a female conspecific (Odendaal et al. 1988). As a result, males tend to chase each other a lot, and according to the "incidental congregation" hypothesis, literally chase themselves into a congregation.

In the absence of objects to chase, males move along straightened out paths with relatively infrequent changes in direction. The more frequently males encounter a "chasable object," the higher is the frequency of reversals in direction, but at some point the ability or desire of males to chase is saturated. This suggests that the average move duration may be an S-shaped function. When u is near 0, it is at some high value, say τ_0; as u increases move duration declines. At high u move duration saturates at some lower value, say τ_∞ (Figure 4.6a). Note that u in this case refers only to male density, since it is the variable that dynamically affects itself. I assume that the density of other chasable objects, such as females and non-conspecific butterflies, is constant in space.

We already know that the diffusion approximation of CRW is the Patlak's equation (Section 4.4.1). Given the above assumptions, Patlak's equation in two-dimensional space simplifies to

$$\frac{\partial u}{\partial t} = \frac{v^2}{2(1-\psi)} \nabla \cdot [\nabla(\tau u) - \psi \nabla \tau u] \tag{4.56}$$

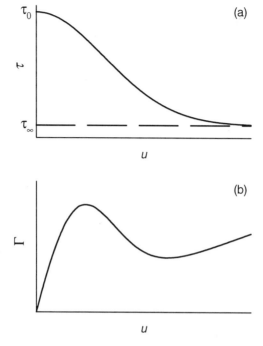

Figure 4.6: (a) A possible functional shape of $\tau(u)$. (b) The corresponding shape of the dynamic level $\Gamma(u)$.

Bringing both terms on the right hand side inside the gradient operator, we obtain

$$\frac{\partial u}{\partial t} = \frac{v^2}{2(1 - \psi)} \nabla \cdot [\tau^{-\psi} \nabla (\tau^{1-\psi} u)] \tag{4.57}$$

The dynamic level, therefore, is

$$\Gamma(u) = \tau^{1-\psi} u \tag{4.58}$$

We see that the CRW formulation results in a similar model to the one obtained by using the uncorrelated random walk model as a starting point. In both cases, the equilibrium distribution is affected by a nonlinear function $\Gamma(u)$. In the CRW case there is also a term $\tau^{-\psi}$ outside the gradient operator. This term, however, does not affect the equilibrium distribution, but only the speed of the approach to that distribution.

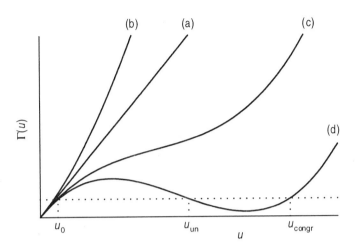

Figure 4.7: Effect of interactions between individuals on the shape of the dynamic level $\Gamma(u)$: (a) density-independent, (b) overdispersive, (c) weakly congregative, and (d) strongly congregative modes of movement.

4.5.3   Equilibrium analysis

The derivations of congregation-diffusion models in the previous two sections indicate that the dynamic level $\Gamma(u)$ can take a variety of functional forms. The qualitative nature of the population distribution at equilibrium, however, is determined by only a few basic shapes of $\Gamma(u)$ (Figure 4.7).

As we shall see in a moment, the congregation formation will be critically affected by the sign of the derivative of $\Gamma(u)$ with respect to u, $\Gamma'(u)$. Rewriting Equation 4.55 in the Fickian form

$$\frac{\partial u}{\partial t} = \frac{\partial}{\partial x}\left[\Gamma'(u)\frac{\partial u}{\partial x}\right] \tag{4.59}$$

we see that $\Gamma'(u)$ is equivalent to the Fickian diffusivity. For the model of CRW with congregation (Equation 4.57), the sign of the diffusivity will be determined by the sign of $\Gamma'(u)$.

The simplest case is when individuals move independently of each other, that is, according to the simple diffusion model. In that case $\Gamma(u) = Du$. In other words, $\Gamma(u)$ increases with u at a constant rate $\Gamma'(u) = D$ (Figure 4.7a). D in this case is simply the diffusion constant.

If interactions between moving individuals are repulsive then the rate of movement will increase with population density because at high densities organisms continuously come in contact and induce each other to disperse. In this case the diffusivity will increase with density, and $\Gamma(u)$ will have an accelerating shape shown in Figure 4.7b.

In the case of congregative movement, on the other hand, the diffusivity will initially decline as u increases, since organisms in low density localities will on average reduce their movement rate compared to organisms in denser areas. However, as discussed above, at very high densities movement of any real organisms has to be overdispersive, that is, Fickian diffusivity increases with density. Thus the shape of $\Gamma(u)$ for congregative movement is characterized by its rate of change first decreasing and then increasing again once a certain critical density is passed (Figure 4.7c,d). Case (d), "strong congregation", differs from case (c), "weak congregation", in that $\Gamma(u)$ has a maximum and a minimum, which implies that $\Gamma'(u)$ becomes negative for some region of population densities. As we shall, these two cases have very different consequences for the pattern formation in homogeneous space.

At equilibrium, $\Gamma(u) = \text{const.}$ More precisely, if we use the absorbing boundary condition $u(0,t) = u(L,t) = u_0$ (0 and L are the ends of the spatial domain), then all solutions at the equilibrium must satisfy the equation

$$\Gamma(u) = \Gamma(u_0) \tag{4.60}$$

In other words, population density at equilibrium can only have as many different values as there are roots to Equation 4.60. If there is only one root, u_0, then the equilibrium distribution $\tilde{u} = u_0$ anywhere within the spatial domain, that is, organisms are evenly distributed. Equation 4.60 can have only one root if movement is density-independent, overdispersive, or weakly congregative, since a line parallel to the abscissa can intersect the curve $\Gamma(u)$ at only one point (Figure 4.7). Any initial peaks of density in such populations will be eroded by diffusion.

In strongly congregating populations $\Gamma'(u)$ is negative for some range of densities, and for certain u_0 Equation 4.60 can have three roots (Figure 4.7). Therefore, any combination of flat pieces at heights corresponding to the three roots of (4.60) is a steady state, provided $\tilde{u}(0) = \tilde{u}(L) = u_0$. A stability analysis indicates that the smallest and the largest roots of Equation 4.60 correspond to stable equilibria, while the intermediate root corresponds to an unstable steady state (see Section 4.5.4). Thus, depending on initial conditions, some regions within the spatial domain will equilibrate at the lower steady state, while others will approach the upper steady state. The solutions never develop discontinuities at the "jump points," but instead approach the discontinuous steady state closer and closer with time (Figure 4.8).

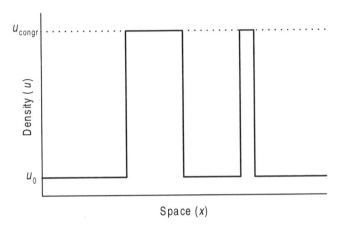

Figure 4.8: An example of the equilibrium distribution approached by a numerical solution of the congregation-diffusion equation.

Based on the results of this equilibrium analysis we can now state under what conditions movement with attraction to conspecifics will lead to formation of congregations. In a general nonlinear diffusion model (Equation 4.55), pattern formation in homogeneous space can occur only if $\Gamma'(u)$ is negative for some range of population density. For Equation 4.54 this condition translates into

$$\Gamma'(u) = \frac{2\kappa}{\omega}u^2 - 2\kappa u + \mu < 0 \tag{4.61}$$

for some u. Γ' is a parabola, and it will intersect the abscissa if the quadratic function above has real roots. This will occur only if its discriminant is greater than zero

$$4\kappa\left(\kappa - \frac{2\mu}{\omega}\right) > 0 \tag{4.62}$$

or if $\kappa\omega > 2\mu$, κ being positive. This condition indicates that whether congregations can form or not depends on the balance of the aggregative "force," measured by $\kappa\omega$, and the dispersive force due to random movement, measured by 2μ. If the aggregative tendency κ is weak, or the threshold density at which movement becomes repulsive, ω, is too low, then random movement dominates congregative response, and organisms will always tend to move down the population gradient.

For the model of CRW with congregation, the condition for strong congregation translates into

$$\frac{\tau_\infty}{\tau_0} < 1 - \frac{4(1-\psi)}{(2-\psi)^2} \tag{4.63}$$

Interestingly, this condition implies that the greater the persistence of movement direction, the easier it is to achieve strong congregation. In the extreme case of no persistence, $\psi = 0$, the left-hand side becomes zero, and the condition becomes impossible to fulfill. For example, for $\psi = 0.1$ τ_∞ has to be less than $0.003\tau_0$. By contrast, for $\psi = 0.9$ τ_∞ has to be less than $0.67\tau_0$.

Even if the basic conditions for strong congregation are fulfilled ($\Gamma'(u) < 0$ for some u), actual pattern formation in homogeneous space will depend on both boundary and initial conditions. If the value of population density at the boundary, u_0, is too low, then the horizontal line at height $\Gamma(u_0)$ will intersect the function $\Gamma(u)$ in only one place (Figure 4.7). Any initial clumps of organisms will eventually disappear due to the drain of individuals over the patch boundary.

Finally, whether congregations form and where they will form also depends on the initial population distribution $u(x, 0)$. For example, if organisms are distributed in such a way that u never exceeds the critical threshold where $\Gamma'(u) < 0$, then no congregations will arise. It is necessary to have an initial peak with u in the negative diffusivity region for it to grow and become a congregation.

4.5.4   The problem of ill-posedness

As we have seen, formation of congregations in a homogeneous space can occur within the nonlinear diffusion model only if the diffusivity is negative for some range of population density values. The problem is that diffusion models with negative diffusivity are not well-posed (Alt 1985, Aronson 1985, Turchin 1989a). The root of the problem is clearly revealed by a stability analysis of the congregation-diffusion equation

$$\frac{\partial u}{\partial t} = \frac{\partial^2}{\partial x^2} \Gamma(u) \tag{4.64}$$

Let us consider a spatially uniform state $u(x) = u_{eq}$, where u_{eq} is a root of the equation $\Gamma(u) = \Gamma(u_0)$. In the absence of perturbations, the solution $u(x) = u_{eq}$ will persist forever. To investigate whether this uniform equilibrium state is stable, we will consider small perturbations of the equilibrium state, $v(x, t)$, and determine the behavior of the perturbed solution

$$u = u_{eq} + v(x, t)$$

First, we need to rewrite the congregation-diffusion equation in terms of perturbations $v(x,t)$. The left hand side $\partial u/\partial t = \partial v/\partial t$. Expanding the right hand side in a Taylor series around $\Gamma(u_{eq})$, we obtain

$$\Gamma(u) = \Gamma(u_{eq}) + \left(\frac{\partial \Gamma}{\partial u}\right)_{u=u_{eq}} + \cdots$$

Since $v(x,t)$ is small, the higher-order terms can be ignored. We obtain the linearized equation for the congregation-diffusion:

$$\begin{aligned}
\frac{\partial v}{\partial t} &= \frac{\partial^2}{\partial x^2}\left[\Gamma(u_{eq}) + \Gamma'(u_{eq})v\right] \\
&= \Gamma'(u_{eq})\frac{\partial^2 v}{\partial x^2}
\end{aligned}$$

Next, we investigate the behavior of solutions for this linearized equation, using the standard sinusoidal form $v \sim \exp[\sigma t + iqx]$. Substituting it into the linearized equation, we obtain the dispersion relation between σ and q:

$$\sigma = -\Gamma'(u_{eq})q^2 \tag{4.65}$$

The perturbation will grow with time if $\sigma > 0$, and decay if $\sigma < 0$. We immediately see that perturbations will grow, and thus an equilibrium state will be unstable if $\Gamma'(u_{eq}) < 0$ (provided that $q \neq 0$). For the shape of $\Gamma(u)$ depicted in Figure 4.7 (strong congregation), there are three equilibria. The lower and higher ones are stable because the slope $\Gamma'(u)$ is positive at these two points, and the middle one is unstable since $\Gamma'(u) < 0$ in that region.

The spatial wavelength of the sinusoidal perturbation $\exp[\sigma t + iqx]$ is equal to $2\pi/q$. Since the rate of growth of sinusoidal perturbations increases with q^2, we conclude that the fastest growing wavelengths will be the smallest (high-frequency) ones. Any arbitrary disturbance can be decomposed into a sum of sinusoidal perturbations; the above result says that in the negative diffusivity regime, the high-frequency components of a disturbance will dominate.

Unlike simple diffusion, which smooths out any initial bumps and dips of the population density profile, negative diffusivity exaggerates such unevenness. In the negative diffusivity regime any tiny perturbation of the initial conditions will grow out of all proportion under the influence of congregation. As a result, depending on the initial distribution, the density profile at equilibrium can be broken into clumps of any size—from very wide to very narrow. Thus the model clearly fails when it predicts that very narrow "congregations" consisting of a fraction of an individual are possible. Another problem is the rectangular shape of clusters predicted for the equilibrium distribution.

The reason for such seemingly strange behavior of the model is that congregating populations are characterized by movement of organisms up the population gradient. The steeper the gradient, the stronger is the congregative bias, which in turn causes the gradient to become steeper. As congregation proceeds, the population gradient becomes more and more vertical, and, as a result, congregation clumps acquire rectangular shape.

4.5.5   Well-posed congregation models

The equilibrium stability analysis suggests what may be the root of the problem with the straightforward diffusion approximation of congregative movement. In the congregation-diffusion model, the perturbations of the smallest wavelength dominate the evolving spatial pattern. Thus, the process of population redistribution is extremely local—density change at point x is affected only by the density and the density gradient right at x, and it does not matter that nearby the gradient could be quite different. In reality, there always will be some minimal spatial scale imposed by the perception range of organisms, or by the mean of their step-length distribution. It follows that to make congregation models well-behaved we need to somehow impose such a realistic minimal scale.

There has been a number of modifications proposed that avoid the problems associated with the straightforward diffusion approximation (Alt 1985, Turchin 1989a, Lewis 1994). One of the simplest ones is to assume that the organisms do not use a local estimate of population density to guide their movements, but instead average density over some spatial interval. A simple model making this modification is

$$\frac{\partial u}{\partial t} = \frac{\partial^2}{\partial x^2}[\mu(\bar{u})u] \tag{4.66}$$

in which the motility is a function of the average density $\bar{u}$:

$$\bar{u}(x,t) = \int_{-\infty}^{\infty} H(s)u(x+s,t)\,ds$$

Numerical explorations of this model showed that such a nonlocal estimate of population density will both prevent arbitrarily small congregations from forming, and smooth out the rectangular edges of congregated pattern at equilibrium (Turchin 1988b).

A similar reasoning can be applied to modeling congregative bias (Turchin 1989a: Appendix I). Previously I have assumed that organisms react only to the presence of conspecifics at adjacent spatial positions λ spatial units away. An alternative assumption is to allow organisms to perceive conspecifics farther away. Let us say that the organisms assess the population density to the right and to the left, and bias their movements in the direction where they see more conspecifics. Let the probability that a conspecific s units away is perceived (and reacted to) be $kH(s)$, where $H(s)$ is normalized so that $\int_0^\infty H(s)\,ds = 1$. Then the number of conspecifics perceived on the right is the product of $kH(s)$ and the density of conspecifics s units away, $u(x + s,t)$, summed over all possible values of s. In other words

$$R(x,t) = k \int_0^\infty H(s)u(x + s,t)\,ds \tag{4.67}$$

Analogously

$$L(x,t) = k \int_0^\infty H(s)u(x - s,t)\,ds \tag{4.68}$$

The bias is

$$R(x,t) - L(x,t) = k\left[\int_0^\infty H(s)u(x + s,t)\,ds - \int_0^\infty H(s)u(x - s,t)\,ds\right] \tag{4.69}$$

A similar formulation was used by Kawasaki (1978), who obtained an analytical solution for the case when $H(s) = \text{const.}$, i.e., the probability of perception does not decline with distance. A more realistic assumption, however, is that $H(s)$ declines with distance to zero.

When the attraction range is small compared to the spatial domain, the diffusion equation with the integral bias given by Equation 4.69 can be approximated by a fourth-order parabolic equation (Alt 1985, Turchin 1989a, Lewis 1994). To obtain such an approximation, we expand $u(x + s,t)$ and $u(x - s,t)$ in Equation 4.69 in a Taylor series

$$
\begin{aligned}
R(x,t) - L(x,t) &= k\int_0^\infty H(s)[u(x + s,t) - u(x - s,t)]\,ds \\
&= 2k\frac{\partial u}{\partial x}\int_0^\infty H(s)s\,ds + \frac{k}{3}\frac{\partial^3}{\partial x^3}\int_0^\infty H(s)s^3\,ds \\
&\quad + \int_0^\infty H(s)O(s^5)\,ds
\end{aligned} \tag{4.70}
$$

All terms of even order cancel each other. To further simplify this expression, let us assume a particular functional shape for $H(s)$. For example, if $H(s)$ is a "half-Gaussian" curve

$$H(s) = \frac{2}{\sqrt{2\pi}\sigma}\exp\left(-\frac{s^2}{2\sigma^2}\right) \tag{4.71}$$

then Equation 4.70 simplifies to (Turchin 1989a: Appendix I)

$$R(x,t) - L(x,t) = \frac{2\sqrt{2}k\sigma}{\sqrt{\pi}} \left(\frac{\partial u}{\partial x} + \frac{\sigma^2}{3} \frac{\partial^3 u}{\partial x^3} \right) + O(\sigma^5) \qquad (4.72)$$

Neglecting the fifth order and higher terms, the bias β is (see Section 4.5.1):

$$\beta = \frac{\lambda}{\tau}[R(x,t) - L(x,t)] = \kappa \left(\frac{\partial u}{\partial x} + \frac{\sigma^2}{3} \frac{\partial^3 u}{\partial x^3} \right) \qquad (4.73)$$

where

$$\kappa = 2\sqrt{\frac{2}{\pi}} \frac{k\lambda\sigma}{\tau}$$

Finally, substituting this expression for bias into Equation 4.50, we obtain a fourth-order PDE:

$$\frac{\partial u}{\partial t} = \frac{\partial}{\partial x} \left[\frac{\partial(\mu u)}{\partial x} - \kappa u \left(\frac{\partial u}{\partial x} + \frac{\sigma^2}{3} \frac{\partial^3 u}{\partial x^3} \right) \right] \qquad (4.74)$$

Equation 4.74 is a generalization of the congregation-diffusion equation derived in Section 4.5.1. It has three parameters. The motility μ and the congregative sensitivity κ have the same interpretation as before. The new parameter σ^2 is the variance of the distribution of perception distance $H(s)$. Alternatively, σ can be thought of as the *perception range*—the spatial scale at which organisms perceive and react to conspecifics. In deriving Equation 4.74 we assumed that σ is much smaller than the spatial domain within which congregation occurs. Thus, the magnitude of the fourth-order term $\partial/\partial x(u\partial^3 u/\partial x^3)$ is small compared to other terms, because it has a multiplier σ^2 in front of it. We could neglect it (as we in effect did in Section 4.5.1). If we further assume that the perception range is of the same magnitude as the movement step, $\sigma \sim \lambda$, then the congregation sensitivity $\kappa \sim k\sigma\lambda/\tau \sim k\lambda^2/\tau$, which makes it the same (apart from a constant factor $2\sqrt{2/\pi}$) as the congregation sensitivity in the diffusion approximation of random walk with attraction in Section 4.5.1. Thus, by neglecting the fourth-order terms, we would recover the congregation-diffusion equation, although that would defeat our purpose of making congregation a well-posed model.

A model similar to Equation 4.74 was derived by Lewis (1994). Like the derivation above, the starting point of his model was the uncorrelated random walk with fixed step length. Lewis (1994) also assumed that organism movement was affected by a weighted spatial average of the surrounding population density. The congregation bias, however, was defined by Lewis in a somewhat different way. Let the average population density perceived by an organism be

$$A(x,t) = \int_{-\infty}^{\infty} H(s)u(x+s,t)\,ds \qquad (4.75)$$

where the weighting kernel $H(s)$ is normalized so that $\int_{-\infty}^{\infty} H(s)\,ds = 1$. The net increase in $A(x,t)$ achieved by moving from point x_0 to point x_1 is

$$A(x_1,t) - A(x_0,t) = \int_{-\infty}^{\infty} H(s)[u(x_1+s,t) - u(x_0+s,t)]\,ds \qquad (4.76)$$

Lewis assumed that organisms bias their movements towards the regions of increasing $A(x,t)$. Thus

$$R(x,t) = \frac{1}{2}r(x,t) + k\sum_{j=-\infty}^{\infty} w(j,\lambda)[p(x+(j+1)\lambda,t) - p(x+j\lambda,t)] \qquad (4.77)$$

$L(x,t)$ is defined analogously. All the variables have been defined before: $r(x,t)$ is the random component of motion, $p(x,t)$ is the probability of finding an individual at position x at time t, and k is the congregative sensitivity. Because this assumption requires that organisms be capable of estimating $A(x\pm\lambda,t)$ while themselves being at position x, and thus having the first-hand knowledge of only $A(x,t)$, it is biologically somewhat less realistic than the alternative formulation that I discussed first. This is not a serious limitation of the model, however, because it still leads to practically the same model as Equation 4.74, suggesting that such details do not affect the form of the resulting PDE approximation.

Employing the diffusion approximation in a usual way, Lewis (1994) obtained the following integro-differential equation:

$$\frac{\partial u}{\partial t} = \frac{\partial}{\partial x}\left[\mu\frac{\partial u}{\partial x} - \kappa u\int_{-\infty}^{\infty} H(s)\frac{\partial u}{\partial x}(x+s,t)\,ds\right] \qquad (4.78)$$

where $\mu = (\lambda^2/2\tau)r(x,t)$ and $\kappa = 2k\lambda^2/\tau$. This equation can be reduced to an alternative partial differential equation (PDE) with higher order derivatives:

$$\frac{\partial u}{\partial t} = \frac{\partial}{\partial x}\left[\mu\frac{\partial u}{\partial x} - \kappa u\sum_{j=1}^{\infty} h_j\frac{\partial^j u}{\partial x^j}\right] \qquad (4.79)$$

where

$$h_j = \frac{1}{j!}\int_{-\infty}^{\infty} s^j h(s)\,ds, \; j = 0, 1, 2, \ldots$$

Equation 4.79 is easier to study mathematically than the integro-differential model (Equation 4.78), particularly if it is truncated after a number of terms.

Lewis (1994) kept terms up to fourth order, in which case Equation 4.79 simplifies to

$$\frac{\partial u}{\partial t} = \frac{\partial}{\partial x}\left[\mu\frac{\partial u}{\partial x} - \kappa u\left(\frac{\partial u}{\partial x} + \frac{\sigma^2}{2}\frac{\partial^3 u}{\partial x^3}\right)\right] \tag{4.80}$$

where σ^2 is the variance of the kernel $H(s)$. The odd terms drop out because $H(s)$ is a symmetric function. This equation is very similar to Equation 4.74.

Lewis (1994) compared the predictions of the fourth-order PDE to those made by the full integro-differential equation using three different functional shapes for the kernel $H(s)$: normally distributed, linear, and "rectangular" [$H(s) = $ const. for $|s| < a$; zero otherwise]. The predictions of the truncated fourth-order model were approximately correct for all the three different kernels, suggesting that the result would hold true for most biologically relevant spatial averaging kernels.

STABILITY OF THE FOURTH-ORDER CONGREGATION MODEL   We still need to determine the effect of the fourth-order terms on the stability of the PDE congregation model. For simplicity, let us consider the case where the coefficients μ, κ, and σ^2 are constant:

$$\frac{\partial u}{\partial t} = \frac{\partial}{\partial x}\left[(\mu - \kappa u)\frac{\partial u}{\partial x} - \frac{1}{3}\kappa\sigma^2 u\frac{\partial^3 u}{\partial x^3}\right] \tag{4.81}$$

Again, we consider small perturbations of the spatially uniform state $u = u_{eq} + v(x,t)$. Linearizing Equation 4.81 we obtain

$$\frac{\partial v}{\partial x} = (\mu - \kappa u_{eq})\frac{\partial^2 v}{\partial x^2} - \frac{1}{3}\kappa\sigma^2 u_{eq}\frac{\partial^4 v}{\partial x^4} \tag{4.82}$$

We investigate the behavior of solutions for this linearized equation, using the standard sinusoidal form $v \sim \exp[rt + iqx]$. The dispersion relation between r and q is

$$r = (\kappa u_{eq} - \mu)q^2 - \frac{1}{3}\kappa\sigma^2 u_{eq}q^4 \tag{4.83}$$

The fundamental condition for $r > 0$, and thus pattern formation, is $\kappa u_{eq} > \mu$. This makes sense, because motility μ parameterizes the intensity of undirected, diffusive motion, and if μ is large compared to the congregative sensitivity κ, then the undirected component of motion will overwhelm the congregative "force." Moreover, increased average density u_{eq} makes congregation more likely. We have already observed an analogous effect in the congregation-diffusion model 4.53, where the condition for congregation formation took the form $\kappa\omega > 2\mu$.

In the absence of fourth-order terms Equation 4.74 becomes a special case of the congregation-diffusion model, and should be ill-posed. Indeed, the dispersion relation (Equation 4.83) indicates that if $\sigma^2 = 0$, then r would grow without bound as q^2 increases. The fourth-order term, however, causes r to reach maximum at

$$q_{max}^2 = \frac{3}{2} \frac{(1 - \mu/\kappa u_{eq})}{\sigma^2}$$

and then decrease, so that r becomes negative for $q^2 > 2q_{max}^2$. This means that (1) small wave lengths (characterized by high q) will not grow at all, and (2) the spatial pattern evolving after perturbation of a uniform unstable state will be dominated by the fastest-growing wave length $l_{max} = 2\pi/q_{max}$. Note that $l_{max} \sim \sigma$. This means that the spatial scale of congregation clumps is directly related to the spatial scale at which organisms perceive conspecifics (at least initially; other wave-lengths may dominate the spatial pattern of congregations when they evolve away from the uniform equilibrium).

In summary, the fourth-order terms in Equations 4.74 or 4.80 make congregation a well-posed mathematical problem by imposing a minimal spatial scale on congregation clumps that can evolve from an unstable uniform state. This minimal congregation scale is directly proportional to the perception range.

4.5.6 Synthesis

Congregation, movement with mutual attraction between individuals, is a biologically important, but mathematically little studied subject. Here I attempt to address this gap. I discuss derivation of a congregation-diffusion model, starting from both uncorrelated and correlated random walk formulations. Because congregation implies positive feedback and fluxes of organisms up population density gradients, simple-minded approaches to obtaining diffusion-approximation models run into mathematical difficulties. I discuss several alternatives to the diffusion framework—integro-differential equations and their partial differential approximations that retain fourth-order terms. These modifications appear to resolve the difficulties in a satisfactory way. In addition to approaches I reviewed above, readers should also consult the paper by Grünbaum (1994), who derives a partial integro-differential model for krill congregation, starting with a detailed Lagrangian description of individual motion. Finally, simple congregation-diffusion models appear to give correct predictions about the conditions under which congregations can arise. This observation suggests that the best approach to congregation may employ a mixed strategy in which diffusion models are employed to obtain general insights, while detailed individual-based simulations are used to (i) test the validity of diffusion results, and (ii) to make predictions of those aspects of the problem where the diffusion model fails.

Chapter 5

Analysis of Movement Paths

5.1 Introduction

Direct observation of individuals moving in the field, combined with recordings of their paths through time and space, is a very powerful empirical method for quantifying movement. It has several advantages over the mark-recapture approach (Section 2.1). For instance, following a representative sample of individuals ensures that our results are not biased towards individuals that are easier to recapture. Furthermore, since the actual movement path and the environment through which the track passes can be recorded, we can test mechanistic hypotheses about the environmental cues that affect movement. Finally, an intangible, but very real benefit of observing the actual behavior of a moving insect is that ideas about possible mechanisms of the observed patterns can be generated and rejected quickly, thus shortening the path to an understanding of why organisms behave in one way and not another. Thus, recording movement behaviors and paths of organisms is the most powerful and preferred approach to studying their movements—when it is possible. Unfortunately, it is usually the most labor-intensive method, and there are many organisms (possibly the majority) to which this method cannot be applied for a variety of reasons. Modern technology can extend our ability to follow moving organisms, but in many cases we have no recourse but a mark-recapture study.

Methods for recording movement behaviors and measuring movement paths have been already addressed in Chapter 2. I begin this chapter by discussing the first step in the analysis of these data—how to translate field observations into a form suitable for further analysis, the discrete representation of paths. The bulk of the chapter is organized around three major themes: (1) inferring the rate of population spread from individual-based data, (2) quantifying the effects of spatial heterogeneity on individual movements and population redistribution, and (3) measuring the effects of long-distance attraction.

5.2   Discrete Representation of Paths

5.2.1   Undersampled and oversampled paths

Moving animals trace continuous paths through space. However, in order to record and analyze the pattern of their movement the essential characteristics of an observed path have to be represented in a discrete form suitable for computer storage and analysis. A commonly used method for digitizing a curvilinear path is to approximate it with a series of straight lines. More complicated alternatives can be borrowed from the field of computer graphics, in which curvilinear lines are represented with splines and Bezier curves. (I am not aware of anybody using these methods, however, and they would probably be an overkill in behavioral and ecological applications.)

Note that this empirical approach to representing paths fits well with the theoretical framework of discrete random walks. Within the random walk framework, we imagine that an organism travels through the environment by a series of behavioral events, or *moves*. At the beginning of each move, the organism "makes a decision" as to the duration, speed (or distance), and direction of its next move. This decision can be influenced by the organism's past experience (in particular, the direction of its previous movement), the local conditions, the conditions at the point of destination (for example, direction and proximity toward a resource patch), and absolute direction (for example, wind direction). Typically (but not necessarily), there is a stochastic element involved in each decision.

Because random walks and the associated diffusion-approximation models provide a powerful analytic and modeling framework, it is desirable that the "data move" of a digitized path at least approximately correspond to the "theoretical move" of the random walk model. Paths of some organisms appear to conform very closely to this conceptual model. For example, the movement pattern of the bacterium *Escherichia coli* is characterized by bouts of almost straight movement that are periodically interrupted by reorientation or "tumbling" (Koshland 1980, Berg 1983; see Figure 3.1). We would feel relatively confident in applying random walk models to the analysis of bacterial paths.

Unfortunately, such clearcut movement patterns are rare. However, movement process in many organisms is punctuated with periodic stops. For example, flying butterflies periodically land on vegetation (Figure 4.5a), and we can approximate the butterfly's actual path by connecting the stop points with straight lines (Figure 4.5b). Although the actual trajectory between two landing points may be circuitous, in many cases straight-line moves appropriately summarize the realized displacements (Root and Kareiva 1984, Turchin 1991).

I have already used the terms "path" and "move" informally, and now it is time to define them more rigorously. A *path* is the complete spatio-temporal record of a followed organism, from the beginning to the end of observations. Each path is represented as a series of straight-line *moves*, where a move is defined as the displacement between two consecutive stopping points. As was discussed above, in the 2D case, each move is defined by three spatio-temporal coordinates. Treating moves as straight lines is an idealization. A *move* should be distinguished from a *step*, which is defined below.

A more complex problem is presented by paths of organisms that move continuously (e.g., many walking or crawling insects), and thus do not have convenient break-points that would help to define moves. The usual method for digitizing such paths is to record the spatial coordinates of the organism at regular time intervals and connect the successive positions with straight lines (e.g., Kareiva and Shigesada 1983). I will refer to such displacements during a regular time interval as *steps*. Treating each step automatically as a move should be avoided, as it results in a number of problems. For example, the biologically meaningful way of characterizing movement patterns by the turning frequency of organisms is negated by this methodology, since "turns" occur at arbitrarily defined regular intervals.

The problem is that artificial "moves" equated to steps do not correspond to actual behavioral events (where behavioral events are defined within the random walk framework discussed above), and we lose even rough correspondence between "data moves" and "theoretical moves." Either the time interval is too long, in which case several behavioral events will be lumped together, or the time interval is too short, and then some actual events will be artificially split into several "moves." This is a serious problem, alluded to in Kareiva and Shigesada (1983), and more recently discussed by Tourtellot et al. (1991), Bell (1991:293), and Turchin et al. (1991).

The general problem is not peculiar to behavioral ecology, and arises in many statistical applications (e.g., signal processing) where one needs to avoid the opposite extremes of either oversampling or undersampling a signal. The problem of undersampling data is obvious—if the organism path is sampled at a resolution that is too coarse, then important information is lost. For data collection, the solution is also clear: collect data at the highest resolution rate that is feasible. Caveat: If the cost of information increases sharply with the resolution, then it may be worthwhile to determine the optimum rate of sampling (see below) and avoid collecting data at a much higher resolution. Oversampled data sets can always be resampled at a lower resolution later.

Oversampling, however, presents problems at the analysis stage. The root of the problem is that a data point in an oversampled data set does not add much new information to information contained in the previous point, and the small signal it carries tends to be drowned out by noise. Thus, attempts to analyze tiny moves characterizing oversampled paths will run into the twin problem of high autocorrelation on one hand and high variability on the other.

5.2.2 Avoiding oversampling

At this time, there is no generally acceptable solution of how to deal with oversampling, and it is quite possible that different empirical systems and different questions will require different approaches. There are basically three approaches: (1) resample the path at a lower temporal or spatial resolution, (2) aggregate displacements detected at high resolution into moves of variable length, or (3) represent paths as sequences of discrete accelerations, rather than discrete moves.

RESAMPLING WITH FIXED MOVE LENGTH OR DURATION   Resampling the path can be accomplished by incrementing either the temporal or spatial scale. Because continuous paths are typically collected by noting an animal's position at regular time intervals, it is more natural to vary the temporal scale. A simple method for achieving coarser temporal resolution is to retain every other position, or every third position, etc. Resampling was recommended by Kareiva and Shigesada (1983). They suggested trying several different time intervals, and choosing an intermediate one at which move parameters most vividly reflect behavioral responses to varying ecological situations.

An example of this procedure is given by Bell (1991: Figures 17.6–17.7), using the sample path of a male cockroach engaged in a local search for a female. Figure 5.1 shows this path at three different resolutions. The path taken at 0.2-s resolution is clearly oversampled, while the path sampled at 2 s intervals is just as clearly undersampled. Bell (1991) suggests that the appropriate resolution scale for the analysis of these data should be between 0.2 and 0.5 s. On one hand, this resolution minimizes the "wobble"—a characteristic alternation in the cockroach orientation caused by the way in which extensions and retractions of the six legs bring about lateral translational movements of the body. On the other hand, the resampled path has not yet begun to deviate from the its real structure, so that the movement pattern of the animal is depicted realistically (that is, the movement pattern the investigator is focusing on).

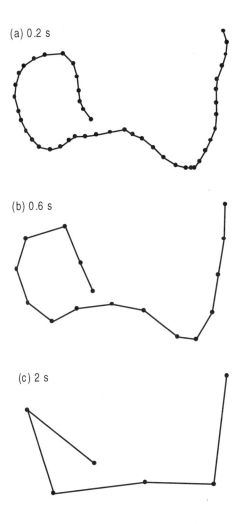

(a) 0.2 s

(b) 0.6 s

(c) 2 s

Figure 5.1: The path of a German cockroach (*Blatella germanica*) sampled at different resolutions. Time intervals used to "step off" the path: (a) 0.1, (b) 0.6, and (c) 2.0 s. (After Bell 1991.)

AGGREGATION OF STEPS INTO VARIABLE-LENGTH MOVES   The resampling procedure described above translates an oversampled "raw" path into a sequence of moves of equal durations. Such an approach is sufficient if we are primarily interested in the turning angles or the velocity of an animal as it moves under various environmental conditions. However, because all moves have fixed duration, we lose one useful way of characterizing movement patterns—by the frequency of turning. We know from the diffusion approximation of the correlated random walk (see Section 4.4) that turning behavior has at least two dimensions: the turning frequency (or average move duration) and the average cosine of the turning angle. Diffusion-approximation theory suggests that variation in these two parameters will have very different consequences for spatial distribution of organisms. For example, if the environment modulates only the average magnitude of the turning angle there will be no aggregation, while environmental modulation of turning frequency will result in aggregation (see Section 4.4). Thus, in situations where we wish to quantify the turning frequency (for example, in studies of area-restricted search), it is desirable to allow moves of variable duration.

The simplest approach is to use the processing power of the human brain, that is, to aggregate discrete-time steps into moves by eye (e.g., Berry and Holtzer 1990). Such a procedure is, obviously, subjective, and the end result may be affected by unconscious biases of the investigator. However, there are ways for getting around the investigator's biases (e.g., hiring an undergraduate student for this task who would be unaware of how the aggregated data will be analyzed). A more objective approach was suggested by Turchin et al. (1991): n steps are aggregated into one move if the $n-1$ intermediate spatial positions are no more than x cm away from the line connecting the beginning of the first step to the end of the last one (see Figure 5.2). The value of x must be selected iteratively by starting with a small value and then incrementing it until oversampling is minimized.

At what point do we deem that oversampling is not a problem any more? This depends on the questions we are asking. In the cockroach example, the wobble (high frequency alternation between right and left turns) was an artifact of the cockroach's gait that we were interested in tuning out. Wobble leads to a short-term (i.e., at small lags) negative autocorrelation in the turning angle, and one way of tuning it out would be to resample the path at the smallest resolution at which this autocorrelation disappears. Other hypothetical examples of how oversampling may result in either positive or negative high-order autocorrelation are given in Turchin et al. (1991). (I use the term "higher-order" autocorrelation here because the turning angle can be thought of as the first-order autocorrelation in the movement direction.)

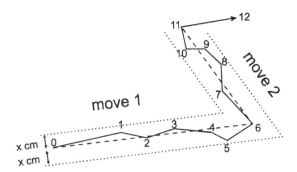

Figure 5.2: A method for the discrete representation of the path of a continuously moving organism that results in unequal move durations. Each of the numbers 0–12 indicates the spatial position of the organism at successive intervals of time.

These observations suggest that in order to avoid oversampling, we should choose a value of x for which the serial correlation in the turning angle vanishes. In practice it means that we start with a small value of x, for example, 1/10th of the average step length, convert the sequence of steps into moves, test for serial correlation, and iteratively increment x until serial correlation disappears. An added benefit of this procedure is that absence of serial correlations between moves greatly simplifies the statistical analysis of paths, as we shall see in subsequent sections.

I should issue a caveat here. The preceding discussion assumes that serial autocorrelations in the turning angle are not a quantity of interest, but rather some nuisance feature of movement that has to be tuned out. In some situations, however, higher-order autocorrelation may actually be the quantity of interest, and then, obviously, a different rule for avoiding oversampling would need to be selected.

DISCRETE ACCELERATIONS   At the most basic level, each path is a sequence of points characterized by their temporal and spatial coordinates. Representing a path as a collection of moves is equivalent to taking first differences since a move i is a vector defined by subtracting spatio-temporal coordinates of point $i - 1$ from point i. In some situations it is appropriate to take second differences and obtain a set of discrete accelerations. This will be discussed in Section 5.7. The kinematic approach simplifies the analysis in many ways. In particular, the question of oversampling can be resolved by choosing the scale at which autocorrelation in acceleration vanishes.

5.2.3   Synthesis

This section deals with the first step in the analysis of paths—representing a path as a sequence of discrete moves that will provide basic units for the subsequent analysis. In some situations, for example, a butterfly punctuating its flight with periodic stops to investigate a plant for oviposition, breaking a path into a set of discrete moves is straightforward. When an organism moves continuously, however, there may not be a biologically obvious way to discretize its path. Using the resolution at which the path was sampled is a bad idea because it may result in either undersampling or oversampling the path.

Undersampling occurs when individual positions are recorded too infrequently, and results in lost information. The remedy is to collect data at a higher frequency, if possible. Oversampling is a more subtle problem. When a path is oversampled, each subsequent position adds little information to the previous point, and useful information it carries may be drowned by noise. Furthermore, statistical analysis becomes difficult because of the high degree of autocorrelation in the data set.

The preferred methodology for minimizing oversampling depends on the goals of the analysis. When the primary variable of interest is the pattern and the magnitude of turning angles, resampling at increased step duration is indicated. To prepare the data for analysis based on the CRW approach, we need to aggregate many steps made at regular time intervals into moves of variable duration. For kinematic analysis of paths, our focus is on discrete accelerations, and the primary concern is that they are not autocorrelated. The general rule proposed here is to resample paths at an increasingly coarser spatial scale, until higher-order autocorrelations disappear. This approach, however, assumes that these autocorrelations are a "nuisance" factor to be eliminated. If the higher-order correlations are of biological interest, then a different approach is needed, although no guidelines exist at present as to what it should be.

5.3   Inferring the Rate of Population Spread

5.3.1   Analysis of movement as correlated random walk

Our main goal in this section is to develop methods for translating individual movement data into a measure of dispersal, or more precisely, population redistribution. The main tool I will employ to achieve this goal is the model of correlated random walk (CRW). In general, methods based on the random walk theory provide a very powerful approach to analyzing path data. Various random walk formulas can be used to test qualitative hypotheses about the mode of organism movement. More importantly, random walk methods can provide quantitative measures of movement that are useful for interspecific comparisons, and possibly for prediction (for example, inferring the rate of population spread of introduced organisms or alleles from individual-based information).

Correlated random walk was introduced in Section 4.4 (see also Figure 4.5). CRW is usually the simplest random walk formulation that can be used for analysis of paths, because paths are almost always characterized by some degree of directional persistence (correlation between subsequent move directions). A typical CRW-based approach starts with the move-level description of movement, then uses move characteristics to estimate various random walk parameters, and finally predicts some path-level features. In order for this analysis to yield meaningful results, *moves* have to be defined appropriately (see Section 5.2). In fact, a common mistake in analyzing continuous paths is to focus on fine-resolution *steps* as the basic unit of analysis, which leads to the problem of oversampling (see Section 5.2).

The *path* characteristic that is most often used in analysis is either net displacement or net squared displacement. *Net* refers to the total displacement, or the straight-line distance between the beginning and the end of a path. Net squared displacement is often the quantity of interest because in a variety of random walk formulations and associated diffusion approximations it is the squared displacement, rather than the linear displacement, that grows linearly with time (or with the number of moves). Thus, it is net squared displacement that provides us with a measure of spread on the population level.

5.3.2 Testing for serial correlations

The only way that the CRW model includes correlations between subsequent moves is by accounting for autocorrelation in the direction of movement. The interdependence of subsequent move directions is reflected in the distribution of the turning angle. Turning angles are typically concentrated around zero, indicating positive autocorrelation in move direction, or directional persistence (see Figure 5.5b). Less frequently, turning angles are grouped around $\pm 180°$ indicating negative autocorrelation, or tendency to reverse direction (Figure 5.3).

CRW formulation assumes that the move durations, speeds, and turning angles are not serially correlated, an assumption that should be tested statistically. In performing such tests it is important to factor out the dependence of movement parameters on local environmental conditions (Root and Kareiva 1984). Consider, for instance, the movement of a butterfly that makes short

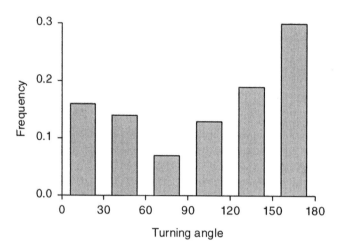

Figure 5.3: The frequency distribution of turning angles characterizing movement of *Euphydryas editha* males at a hilltop in Colorado. (After Turchin et al. 1991.)

moves when flying within a host patch, and long moves between host patches. In this case, the probability that its next move is a short one would appear to increase following a sequence of short moves. A run of short moves occurs, however, not because of a serial correlation, but because the butterfly has encountered a food patch. Thus, if path data collected within a resource patch and outside it are lumped together, then we would detect an autocorrelation, even if there is none. It is also important not to lump together organisms engaged in distinctly different behaviors (Root and Kareiva 1984), such as butterflies searching for hosts and those searching for nectar flowers.

Presence or absence of serial correlation in move parameters can be assessed by calculating autocorrelations. For example, the first-order correlation in move length l_i is the correlation coefficient between all pairs l_i and l_{i-1}. Higher-order autocorrelations can be investigated by estimating the autocorrelation function (ACF). ACF is constructed by plotting the autocorrelation between values separated by lag d against the lag. Alternatively, higher order correlations in, for example, move length, can be assessed by correlating l_i with an average of two or three preceeding move lengths, $l_{i-1}, l_{i-2}, l_{i-3}$ (Root and Kareiva 1984). Autocorrelations in move length can also be assessed by means of contingency tables using an approach similar to the one described below for turning angles (Smith 1974, Zalucki and Kitching 1982). In this approach, moves are classified into being either less, or greater than the mean move length. The problem, however, is that we throw out a lot of information when we classify a continuous variable into two discrete classes. An approach based on the autocorrelation function is, on the other hand, quantitative and easy to use (almost any statistical software package implements it). It is a standard statistical technique, and my recommendation is to use it in preference to contingency tables.

DIRECTIONAL AUTOCORRELATION   Because absolute directions and turning angles are circular quantities (the angle 180° is the same as the angle −180°), calculating autocorrelations for them requires some care (Cain 1989a). Cain (1989a) surveyed 22 articles published during the 1980s that report detailed descriptions of individual movements, and in 17 of them the turning (or branching) angles were analyzed incorrectly. The most common mistake is to calculate arithmetic means and standard deviations of angles as though they were usual (linear) quantities (see Batschelet 1981 and Cain 1989a for reasons why this leads to problems). For example, Bell (1991:287) incorrectly recommends that linear statistics should be employed when analyzing turning rate and turn bias measured on a ±180° scale. The mean and SD calculated in this way would be approximately correct only when angles do not deviate too far from 0°. If there are many direction reversals (turning angles greater than 90° or less than −90°), then the estimates of the means and variance will be seriously biased.

It would be desirable to have a quantitative measure of autocorrelation for turning angles analogous to the autocorrelation function for linear quantities. One possible measure for angular correlation is the average cosine of the difference between two angles (Batschelet 1981). Unfortunately, this statistic cannot be used in assessing turning angle autocorrelations, because it assumes that angles are uniformly distributed between −180° and 180° (or, equivalently, between 0° and 360°). Because turning angles are typically concentrated around zero, the difference between two successive turning angles is likely to be near zero, even if there is no autocorrelation. This would result in a significantly positive, but spurious angular correlation. (Note, however, that this is not a problem for measuring the autocorrelation in the *absolute* direction.)

Several quantitative approaches to measuring angular correlation are described by Fisher (1993). We can also use a qualitative test for turning angle autocorrelation. Two kinds of tests have been employed: runs tests (Cain 1989a, Crist and MacMahon 1991) and contingency tables (Zalucki and Kitching 1982, Cain 1989a). Turning angles are defined as right (R) or left (L) turns.

A runs test (Sokal and Rohlf 1981) can be applied to the sequence of R and L to test for nonrandomness. An alternative approach is to place sequences of pairs into contingency tables. For example, for the first-order test, the table has four entries: RR, RL, LR, and LL. Deviations from a random sequence can then be assessed by a χ^2 test with one degree of freedom. Often we are interested in not only first order correlations, but in lagged effects of turning history on the current turning angle. One approach is to use triplets instead of pairs. This results in a second-order test (Smith 1974, Zalucki and Kitching 1982). As we increase lag time, however, this approach quickly becomes unwieldy. An alternative is to construct pairs but to allow the lag between them to vary; in effect, constructing an analog of the autocorrelation function, but with discrete values (L or R) instead of continuous quantities. An example of this approach will be given in Section 5.3.5.

The final approach that should be mentioned here was recently proposed by Blanché et al. (1996). These authors focused on autocorrelation in the absolute direction, rather than the turning angle. The measure of the directional autocorrelation that they used was the average cosine of the angular difference between two move directions separated by a time lag. By plotting this measure against the time lag we obtain an estimate of the autocorrelation function. This could give us a way to distinguish between different hypotheses on the presence of higher-order autocorrelations in directionality. Thus, for a simple random walk, ACF should decline to zero at first lag. For a CRW process with only the first-order directional autocorrelation, the ACF should decline exponentially to zero. If higher-order correlations are present, then the ACF shape should deviate from the exponential decay, and it is possible that such deviations may be detected statistically. This appears to be a promising approach, but only the future will tell whether it can yield useful insights.

5.3.3   Net squared displacement

While tests of independence check whether any particular assumption of the CRW process is violated, comparing theoretical and actual displacement provides an overall test of appropriateness of the CRW model. A simple formula for net squared displacement, $\bar{R}_n^2$ (the bar indicates the expectation, or alternatively an average taken over several paths, and the subscript n indicates the number of moves) was developed by Skellam (1973), and extended to a more general case by Kareiva and Shigesada (1983) (see Box 5.1). In practice, one of the simplified variants of the formula is used. For example, in most applications we find that the frequency distribution of the turning angle is symmetric, that is, turns to the left are as likely as turns to the right. In this case, Formula 5.1 reduces to 5.2.

Box 5.1 Net squared displacement, $\bar{R}_n^2$, in CRW.

Define

$$m_1 = \frac{1}{k}\sum_{i=1}^{k} l_i \qquad \text{mean move length}$$

$$m_2 = \frac{1}{k}\sum_{i=1}^{k} l_i^2 \qquad \text{mean squared move length}$$

$$\psi = \frac{1}{k}\sum_{i=1}^{k}\cos\theta_i \qquad \text{average cosine of the turning angle}$$

$$s = \frac{1}{k}\sum_{i=1}^{k}\sin\theta_i \qquad \text{average sine of the turning angle}$$

Then, for the most general case:

$$\bar{R}_n^2 = nm_2 + 2m_1^2\left[\frac{(\psi - \psi^2 - s^2)n - \psi}{(1-\psi)^2 + s^2} + \frac{2s^2 + (\psi + s^2)^{\frac{n+1}{2}}}{[(1-\psi)^2 + s^2]^2}\gamma\right] \quad (5.1)$$

where

$$\gamma = [(1-\psi)^2 - s^2]\cos[(n+1)\alpha] - 2s(1-\psi)\sin[(n+1)\alpha]$$

$$\alpha = \arctan(s/\psi)$$

For the case of symmetric distribution of the turning angle ($s = 0$):

$$\bar{R}_n^2 = nm_2 + 2m_1^2\frac{\psi}{1-\psi}\left(n - \frac{1 - \psi^{(n-1)/2}}{1-\psi}\right) \quad (5.2)$$

Assuming that $n \gg 1$:

$$\bar{R}_n^2 \approx n\left(m_2 + 2m_1^2\frac{\psi}{1-\psi}\right) \quad (5.3)$$

Note that the frequency distributions of move lengths and turning angles are each summarized by only two parameters, for a total of four: the first two moments of the distribution of move lengths, and the averages of cosine and sine of the turning angle. However, there is no explicit dependence on time in these formulas; the number of moves n implicitly stands for the temporal component. After some moves, the net squared displacement grows linearly with n, which is expected since CRW at large spatio-temporal scales behaves like a diffusion process (see Section 4.3.1). Directional persistence affects the rate of spread through the ratio $\psi/(1-\psi)$, with small turning angles producing the largest $\psi/(1-\psi)$ ratios and largest displacements.

A test of CRW as a description of the movement process proceeds as follows. First, we use path data to calculate m_1, m_2, ψ, and s as the averages of the move length, move length squared, and cosine and sine of the turning angle, respectively. We check to make sure that $s \approx 0$. We then use Equation 5.2 (or Equation 5.1 if $s \neq 0$) to predict what $\bar{R}_n^2$ should be for all n up to the maximum number of moves observed. Finally, we compare the predictions with the observed $\bar{R}_n^2$ averaged over all paths (using the displacement after first n moves for each n).

5.3.4   Significance tests

Although the formula of Kareiva and Shigesada (1983) specifies what the *expected* net squared displacement should be, it does not provide a measure of variance around this expectation. In applications, observed $\bar{R}_n^2$ will always differ somewhat from the theoretical curve, and we need a way to determine whether the deviation is statistically significant.

RECIPE FOR BOOTSTRAPPING A SIGNIFICANCE TEST FOR CRW   The first step is to prepare the distributions of move lengths and turning angles. These are directly taken from data. Usually, one simply pools together different individuals. However, care should be taken not to mix paths occuring in different environments; it might also be useful to test for heterogeneity between different paths.

The second step is to simulate a large number of *pseudopaths*. To do this, we start an organism at an arbitrary coordinate such as $(x, y) = (0, 0)$, and give it a random initial direction, that should be an angle evenly distributed between $0°$ and $360°$. A move length is drawn from the empirical distribution, the coordinates are incremented using the move direction and length, and stored. Next we draw a turning angle from the empirical distribution of turning angles, and add it to the previous move direction to obtain the current one. We again draw a move length and increment the coordinates. These steps are repeated, until the maximum number of steps is reached (typically the maximum number of steps will be determined by the empirical data set). An important note: sampling in bootstrap is always done with *replacement*. In other words, once we have drawn a move length or a turning angle from their respective empirical distributions, we place them right back. Thus, the same move length may be drawn several times during construction of a single pseudopath.

Once we have a large number of pseudopaths (1,000 to 10,000), we go to the third step. Typically, path lengths in the actual data set will vary so that observed $\bar{R}_n^2$ for low n is an average taken over all paths, but as n increases fewer and fewer paths can be used. The consequence of this is greater error bars at higher n, and when bootstrapping the significance test we should take this into account. Let us define i_n as the number of paths that have at least n moves. In the third step, we choose n, and randomly draw (with replacement) i_n paths. We calculate the sample statistic $\bar{R}_n^2$ for this set (the net squared displacement after n moves averaged over the i_n paths). We repeat this procedure many times. To obtain a 95% confidence interval, we throw away the smallest 2.5% and the largest 2.5% of the values, and use the extremes of what is left as our confidence interval. A simple computer algorithm for doing this is to sort all 1,000 (for example) values in an ascending order, and then to take the 26th and the 975th values as the ends of the 95% confidence interval. Finally, we test step-by-step whether observed $\bar{R}_n^2$ is located within the confidence interval for each step n or not.

Confidence intervals at other levels of significance are constructed analogously. Tests of overall deviation, combining all steps, can also be designed using the bootstrap. A final note: the above bootstrap procedure assumed that there are no serial correlations in the move length and the turning angle (this was tested in Section 5.3.2). If serial correlations are present in the data (because, for example, they are of biological interest), then there are two ways to proceed. First, a moving block bootstrap can be used (Efron and Tibshirani 1993). Second, we can build the higher-order correlations in the model and use the model to generate pseudopaths.

OTHER APPROACHES   McCulloch and Cain (1989) developed an algorithm for calculating the variance of $\bar{R}_n^2$. Their procedure, however, is very complex, and I do not reproduce the algorithm here (see their Appendix). Another alternative approach was proposed by Cain (1989b). He pointed out that if we know the theoretical value of the net displacement $\bar{R}_n$ (not to be confused with the net *squared* displacement), then we can directly calculate its variance from the formula:

$$\sigma_n^2 = \bar{R}_n^2 - (\bar{R}_n)^2 \qquad (5.4)$$

where $\bar{R}_n^2$ is obtained by using the Kareiva and Shigesada (1983) formula. A theoretical formula for net displacement is not available, so it is necessary to obtain the predicted $\bar{R}_n$ by a form of bootstrap. A large number of CRW runs (say, 1000 or 10,000) is simulated on the computer, using the observed distributions of turning angles and move lengths (Cain 1989a,b, McCulloch and Cain 1989).

Instead of constructing an overall test for all n up to the maximum, Cain

(1989b) recommends using a standard Z-test on a move-by move basis:

$$Z_n = \frac{|\bar{R}_n - \mu_n|}{\sqrt{\sigma_n^2/i_n}} \qquad (5.5)$$

where i_n is the number of individuals that made at least n consecutive moves; $\bar{R}_n$ is the mean observed displacement (distance connecting the beginning of the path to the end of n-th move) averaged over the i_n individuals; μ_n is the predicted net displacement calculated by bootstrap; and σ_n^2 is the variance in the net displacement calculated by Equation 5.4. Z_n is distributed approximately as a normal distribution with mean zero, and variance one. On a move-by-move basis, the null hypothesis that observed displacements equal CRW-predicted displacements is rejected if $Z_n > C$, where the probability that Z_n is greater than C is equal to the desired significance level α. Cain (1989b) also discusses an overall test for all n based on Bonferroni critical values.

Tests based on the net displacement $\bar{R}_n$ are equivalent to tests based on the net squared displacement (Cain 1989b). However, net squared displacement is a more interesting theoretical quantity because it is related to the rate of population spread. It is not as biologically intuitive as net displacement because it is more difficult to think in terms of m^2 than m. If a linear measure of population spread is desired, however, we can take the square root of $\bar{R}_n^2$, the *root mean squared displacement*.

My recommendation is to use the recipe I gave above, using net squared displacement as the statistic of interest. It does not really take much time to code a computer algorithm that will bootstrap a significance test for $\bar{R}_n^2$. Additionally, the bootstrap does not make any assumptions about the distribution properties of the test statistic.

5.3.5   Examples: butterflies, ants, and beetles

Kareiva and Shigesada (1983) were the first to apply their formula to real data sets. In one case, *Pieris rapae* butterflies searching for oviposition plants in a collard garden, the correspondence between the predicted and observed $\bar{R}_n^2$ was very close. When nectar-feeding in linear arrays, however, the movement pattern of cabbage butterflies appeared to depart from the predicted one (Kareiva and Shigesada 1983: Figure 2B; this assessment was made by eye). The distribution of resources in linear arrays was not controlled by Root and Kareiva (1984), and they hypothesized that this departure may be due to inappropriate lumping together of several CRW processes. Applying their method to paths of crawling caterpillars of *Battus philenor* (data collected by Rausher 1979), Kareiva and Shigesada observed that the CRW model underpredicted

$\bar{R}_n^2$. They could not evaluate whether this departure was statistically significant, but reported that *Battus* larvae tended to alternate turning angles. One
possible explanation for this pattern, however, is that the movement of *Battus*
caterpillars was discretized using a fixed 2 min time interval (see Section 5.2).

Cain (1989b) reanalyzed two of the data sets from Kareiva and Shigesada
(1983). For *P. rapae* butterflies ovipositing in a collard garden, R_n values lay
well within the 90% confidence intervals, and thus there was no reason to reject
the CRW hypothesis. By contrast, net displacements of crawling *B. philenor*
caterpillars increased faster than the predicted R_n, and on moves seven and
eight lay outside the confidence intervals. Thus, the CRW null hypothesis is
rejected for these data, as would be expected given the observation of Kareiva
and Shigesada (1983) that there were higher-order autocorrelations in the
turning angle.

As part of an investigation of harvester ant foraging movements, Crist and
McMahon (1991) compared the expected and observed $\bar{R}_n^2$ in two situations:
ants running along trunk trails (Figure 5.4a), and ants searching for food
(Figure 5.4b). The observed $\bar{R}_n^2$ exceeded the expected, indicating that paths
of running ants are more directed than would be suggested by CRW. This
is not surprising, since the ants were not engaging in a random walk, but
ran along linear trails. For searching ants, results were more complex. In
6 out of 20 time steps a Z-test of McCulloch and Cain (1989) indicated a
significant departure from the expected $\bar{R}_n^2$ (Crist and McMahon 1991), but
this departure came around moves 5–10, and after that the mean $\bar{R}_n^2$ converged
to the expected curve.

Wallin and Ekbom (1988) used a portable harmonic radar to trace movements of four species of carabid beetles. Beetle positions were recorded at 15
min intervals. Like many others they found that for some beetles under some
conditions the CRW null model was not rejected (3 out of 6 cases in their Figures 1-4), while in other cases (the remaining 3) the observed $\bar{R}_n^2$ exceeded the
expected one. However, they did not analyze the autocorrelation structure in
their data, and thus we cannot interpret the significance of their findings. An
additional problem is that a 15 min interval was used to define moves in paths
of all four species. However, the scale of movement varied markedly between
species (by an order of magnitude) and thus it is likely that for some species
paths were oversampled.

5.3.6   Spread of goldenrod clones

Patterns of vegetative spread influence many aspects of the biology of clonal
plants: the likelihood of outbreeding, the rate of expansion into a new habitat,
the efficiency of substrate utilization, and the probability that near-neighbor

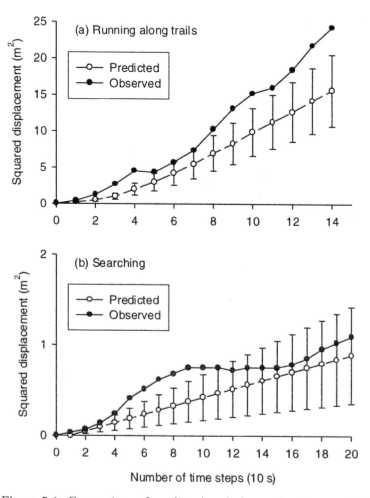

Figure 5.4: Comparison of predicted and observed net squared displacement: *Pogonomyrmex occidentalis* ants (a) running along a trail, and (b) in localized search. Error bars are one SE. (After Crist and MacMahon 1991.)

interactions are interspecific, intraspecific, or intraclonal (Cain 1990). In Section 3.5.2 I discussed how the CRW model can be modified to fit the growth pattern of clonal plants. Cain (1990) used a very similar approach to analyze the rate of spatial spread in clones of the goldenrod *Solidago altissima*. Goldenrod ramets (equivalent to nodes in Section 3.5.2) initiate one or more daughter rhizomes, each producing a daughter ramet next year. Thus, a rhizome connecting a mother to a daughter ramet is equivalent to a *move* in the CRW formulation.

Cain (1990) measured clonal growth parameters (rhizome lengths, branching angles, and the number of daughter rhizomes) by excavating clonal fragments and tracing rhizome connections between ramets. As a first step in the analysis, Cain employed several statistical methods to test for the assumptions of the CRW model: (1) autocorrelation coefficients for rhizome length and branching angles, and cross-correlations between these two aspects of clonal growth; (2) two-way χ^2 contingency tests for independence between successive branching angles as well as three-way tests ($\text{year}_i/\text{year}_{i+1}/\text{year}_{i+2}$); and (3) runs tests of signs of the first difference in rhizome lengths. None of the tests indicated significant correlations. Branching angles were clustered around $0°$, indicating a strong persistence in the direction of rhizome growth across years, and frequencies of right and left turns were very similar (Figure 5.5). Finally, Cain checked on how well a straight line between two successive nodes approximated the actual rhizome length, and found that the difference was no more than 5%. All these results suggest that goldenrod clonal growth fits the assumptions of the CRW model with a remarkable degree of accuracy.

An overall test of the CRW model also found that the observed net squared displacements were very similar to $\bar{R}_n^2$ predicted by the model (Figure 5.5). In summary, this study showed that the pattern of clonal growth in the goldenrod is described by the CRW model very well. The results also emphasize that the pattern of growth is stochastic—there is no fixed rhizome length or branching angle; rather, these components of a clonal growth "move" are characterized by a probability distribution. Thus, a deterministic model of clonal growth, for example, that of Smith and Palmer (1976) in which clones spread through space along a hexagonal grid, would be inappropriate for the goldenrod plants studied by Cain (1990). A final observation: despite the intrinsic stochasticity of clonal growth at the level of individual rhizomes, the rate of expansion at the level of many clones is highly predictable (Figure 5.5c), illustrating once again the principle that stochasticity at one level may translate into determinism at another.

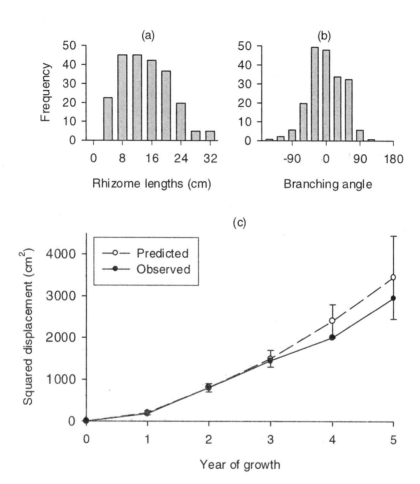

Figure 5.5: Patterns of clonal growth of goldenrod ramets: (a) frequency distribution of rhizome lengths, (b) frequency distribution of the branching angle, and (c) comparison between the predicted and observed net squared displacement. (After Cain 1990.)

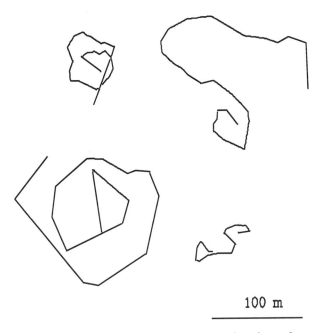

Figure 5.6: Examples of Mexican bean beetle paths.

5.3.7 Spiral paths in Mexican bean beetle

In most cases when the CRW null model is rejected, the observed $\bar{R}_n^2$ exceeds the predicted. The primary reason appears to be the negative autocorrelation in turning angles that leads to a more straightened-out pattern of movement than is predicted by CRW. An interesting data set which shows an opposite pattern was collected by W. S. Blau working at North Carolina State University. The study organism, Mexican bean beetle (*Epilachna varivestis*), is a phytophagous coccinellid that feeds on a variety of legumes. Blau released individuals in the middle of a large field that contained no host plants. Beetles moved by making discrete flights, punctuated by landings on vegetation. The data set consists of a total of 26 paths.

Although there were no significant barriers to beetle movement within the field, the majority did not follow straightened paths that would take them rapidly away. While a few paths were straight, and some "random-looking," most paths appeared to have a spiraling component in them (Figure 5.6). A general impression is that beetles tend to make several turns in a row in the same direction (left or right). This spiraling pattern was not due to an interaction with field boundaries (the field within which beetle movement was observed was very large, and very few beetles reached its boundaries) or any other obvious features of terrain. Despite the impression of spiraling, however, there was no overall tendency to favor left or right turns. Different beetles were characterized by different turning biases, and even the same beetle would often switch between a left and a right turning bias (Figure 5.6). Thus, it appears that instead of having either a left, or a right turning bias, beetles tended to positively autocorrelate the direction of their turns.

A spiraling pattern of movement is a very efficient mode of searching (Bell 1991), but are beetles really engaging in such a strategy, or could the patterns in their paths be produced by chance? Methods described in this chapter should be able to answer this question.

The first step is to test for sequential independence of move lengths and turning angles. I calculated the autocorrelation function for move lengths and found no significant autocorrelations. A contingency table for turning angles found a slight preponderance of subsequent turns in the same direction (LL = 137, and RR = 146, while LR = 120 and RL = 124). However, a G-test indicated only a marginal statistical significance to this pattern ($G = 2.87$, $0.10 > P > 0.05$). Thus, the first round of analysis of individual move attributes does not yield strong insights.

I next performed an overall test of the CRW model, following the bootstrap methodology described at the end of Section 5.3.4 (Figure 5.7). The $\bar{R}_n^2$-test results are quite dramatic. The observed net squared displacement significantly departs from the predicted after the 5th move. Note how the 95% confidence limits flare out at high n. This is a result of very few (3-4) paths that are longer than 30 moves.

More interestingly, the observed $\bar{R}_n^2$ does not grow monotonically with n. Instead, there is a decrease at about $n = 20$, followed by another increase at $n = 30$. This result suggests that the tendency to spiral is real. Since the peak of root mean square displacement is approximately 100 m, the spatial scale at which spiraling occurs is measured in hundreds of meters.

Why are the implications of the move-level and path-level analyses at variance with each other? One clue is that the cycle at the path level is fairly long—about 20 moves. The independence test on turning angles that I performed above, however, was limited to a lag of one move. I advanced in Section 5.3.2 an idea for testing higher-order autocorrelations in the turning angle. We can pursue this idea in the following way. For each lag d, all possible pairs of turning angles separated by d are placed into one of two categories: (1) S turns in the same direction (LL or RR), and (2) O opposite turns (LR and RL). A measure of autocorrelation is the ratio of $(S - O)/(S + O)$. This quan-

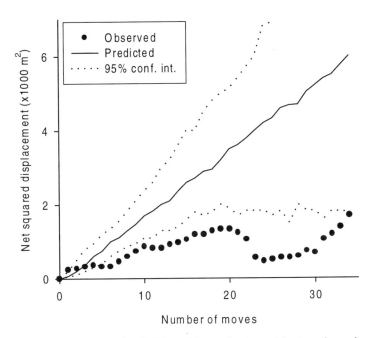

Figure 5.7: Testing the CRW null hypothesis on Mexican bean beetle data. Predicted $\bar{R}_n^2$ and 95% confidence interval were obtained by simulations.

tity is scaled from -1 (when all turns separated by lag d are in the opposite direction) to 1 (when all turns are in the same direction).

Using this definition, I calculated an autocorrelation function ACF[d] up to lag $d = 6$ for each path. Taking each path as a replicate, I then calculated average autocorrelations and their standard errors at each lag (Table 5.1). The first thing to notice is that all autocorrelations are positive. However, ACF[1] and ACF[2] (autocorrelations at lags one and two) are less than two standard errors away from zero (that is, not significantly different from zero), although ACF[1] comes close to significance (in agreement with the result of the G-test above). However, it is ACF[3] and especially ACF[4] that are most positive, and significantly different from zero. At lags 5 and 6, the ACF decays to zero. This pattern suggests that, indeed, there are positive autocorrelations in the turning angle, and that beetles tend to turn in the same direction for several

Table 5.1: Autocorrelation in the direction of the turning angle in Mexican beetle paths.

Lag	1	2	3	4	5	6
Mean	0.091	0.000	0.103	0.152	0.044	0.012
SE	0.053	0.061	0.048	0.053	0.054	0.081

moves. The lag, or memory, however, is rather long-term, with the third and, especially, fourth move exerting the most influence. To conclude, this example shows how multiple analyses of the same problem from different perspectives can supplement each other, with one line of approach suggesting ideas that can be tested using the other.

5.3.8   Synthesis

The recommended procedure for analysis consists of the following steps.

1. Test for autocorrelations that are not explicitly modeled by the CRW model (that is, everything except the correlation in the move direction, which is modeled by assuming a nonuniform distribution of the turning angle). If no autocorrelations are detected, proceed to the next step. Otherwise, either resample paths at a coarser resolution (see Section 5.2), or proceed anyway but with a plan to explicitly model higher-order autocorrelations at a later stage.

2. Use the appropriate CRW formula to predict the net squared displacement ($\bar{R}_n^2$). Compare the predicted $\bar{R}_n^2$ to the observed one, using the bootstrap test suggested in Section 5.3.4.

3. If all the tests support the CRW model, fine and well. Otherwise, it is time to start constructing an individual-based simulation model to explore various alternatives to the CRW model. Use examples and your biological intuition as the source of ideas.

The real-data examples in this section show that following these steps can be quite productive. Most interesting insights occur when the CRW null model is rejected, since in this case we learn something new about the pattern of individual movement characterizing the study organism.

It is important to remember, however, that a major limitation of the CRW-based methods covered in this section is that they assume homogeneous space at the spatial scale extending from a typical move length to a typical path length. Spatial heterogeneity at the scale smaller than move length is averaged over, while heterogeneity above the scale of the path has to be dealt with by separate analyses of paths collected under different environmental conditions.

Several recommendations for improving CRW analyses suggest themselves. The overall test of the CRW null model using $\bar{R}_n^2$ should always be complemented by specific tests of independence in move lengths and turning angles, without forgetting the potential importance of long-term autocorrelations. When both types of tests agree, their results reinforce each other. If the overall test rejects the CRW null hypothesis, but specific tests do not, the pattern of deviation in the observed net squared displacement from the predicted may suggest refinements in specific tests. Sometimes the opposite will occur—an overall test will fail to reject the CRW hypothesis, while specific tests will indicate significant deviations. In such situations, we may conclude that specific assumptions that were violated did not exert a very strong influence on the rate of population spread, and thus we may conclude that the CRW model is a reasonable approximation.

Another strong recommendation is to avoid seriously oversampled paths, because biologically uninteresting autocorrelations will cause rejection of the CRW null model without a significant insight into the movement pattern of the studied organisms. I also advocate the use of simulation and resampling (bootstrap) methods for significance tests. These methods are relatively simple to implement on the computer, and they result in nonparametric tests that can be tailored very specifically to the hypotheses entertained by the investigator.

Simulation is also useful in pursuing the insights yielded by analyses. If we find that some specific CRW assumption is violated, we can modify this assumption in the simulation to bring it in accord with the data. Comparison of $\bar{R}_n^2$ generated by the modified simulation with the observed pattern is a strong test for the hypothesis that the violation of this specific assumption caused the rejection of the CRW null hypothesis.

5.4 Effects of Spatial Heterogeneity

5.4.1 Diffusion-approximation approach

The primary focus of the previous section was on the rate of dispersal characterizing individuals moving in homogeneous environments (at the very least, we ignored any heterogeneity that might have been present). In the process of the analysis, we also probed the fine structure of movement behavior and its spatio-temporal record, a path. If we are interested in influences of spatial heterogeneity on spatial population dynamics, we can obtain predictions by simulation. However, a more general and powerful approach is to use diffusion-approximation models, as argued in Chapter 4 (which can, and should, always be supplemented by carefully chosen simulations).

Methods based on diffusion-approximation models are more appropriate to coarser spatio-temporal scales than CRW methods. The temporal scale of interest typically would be long enough so that population redistribution would approach some kind of an equilibrium (although predictions for shorter time scales can be obtained by numerical solving of equations, or by simulating a population of individuals on the computer). The spatial scale of population heterogeneity has to be somewhat larger than an average move length (this is one of the assumptions under which a diffusion-approximation model is derived from the discrete random walk).

I introduced in Section 4.4 the diffusion model of Patlak (1953a) that approximates population redistribution of organisms moving according to CRW in a heterogeneous environment. I also derived a formula for *the residence index* $\rho(\epsilon)$ of an area or a patch. The residence index is expressed in terms of random-walk parameters characterizing individual movement of organisms in a patch. Thus the residence index summarizes the effects of environmental conditions in an area on individual movements. The pattern of variation in the residence index within the whole habitat can be used to predict the spatial distribution of organisms that results from their movements. Low residence index indicates that organisms are passing quickly through the region, either because they increase their speed or because they follow "straightened-out" paths (or both). In consequence, average residence time, that is, time spent between entering and leaving a unit area, is low. By contrast, high residence index within an area implies that organisms linger there because the speed of their movement is low and they make frequent turns. If organisms can freely move across boundaries between adjacent areas, then the long-term population distribution will reflect the variation in ρ from area to area—organisms will be sparse in areas where ρ is low, but will accumulate in areas where ρ is high. In this way, the residence index provides a link between the pattern of individual movement and the spatial population distribution.

5.4.2   Estimation of the residence index

In order for the residence index analysis to be useful, we need to have data collected in two or more areas (patches) that differ in their characteristics. I assume that the path data has been first analyzed using the methods of Section 5.3 (each area separately), and that the appropriateness of CRW assumptions has been tested.

Given that the movement patterns do not violate the CRW assumptions,

Box 5.2 Residence index, $\rho(\epsilon_j)$.

For each area indexed by ϵ_j calculate the movement parameters:

$$m_1(\epsilon_j) = \frac{1}{k_j} \sum_{i=1}^{k_j} l_i \qquad \text{mean move length}$$

$$m_2(\epsilon_j) = \frac{1}{k_j} \sum_{i=1}^{k_j} l_i^2 \qquad \text{mean squared move length}$$

$$\psi(\epsilon_j) = \frac{1}{k_j} \sum_{i=1}^{k_j} \cos\theta_i \qquad \text{average cosine of the turning angle}$$

$$\tau(\epsilon_j) = \frac{1}{k_j} \sum_{i=1}^{k_j} t_i \qquad \text{mean move duration}$$

Next, calculate

$$\gamma = m_2/m_1^2$$

and average it for all the regions. Third, calculate

$$\varphi(\epsilon_j) = \gamma + (2 - \gamma)\psi(\epsilon_j)$$

and the exponent

$$\alpha_j = \frac{2\gamma[m_1(\epsilon_j) - m_1(\epsilon_0)]}{(2 - \gamma)[\varphi(\epsilon_0)m_1(\epsilon_j) - \varphi(\epsilon_j)m_1(\epsilon_0)]}$$

Finally, the residence index is

$$\rho(\epsilon_j) = \tau(\epsilon_j)\varphi(\epsilon_j)^{\alpha_j} m_1(\epsilon_j)^{-\left(\frac{2-2\gamma}{2-\gamma} + \alpha_j\right)}$$

we proceed as follows. Each area is indexed by its value of ϵ_j ($j = 0, 1, 2, \ldots$). One area is selected as the "reference" region, characterized by ϵ_0 that is set to some arbitrary number, most simply $\rho(\epsilon_0) = 1$ (remember that $\rho(\epsilon)$ is defined to a constant of proportionality).

The next step is to estimate the movement parameters for each area. All paths are separated into groups corresponding to each region of interest. Paths that cross from one region to the other should be broken into portions that are completely contained within a single region. We need estimates of the same parameters that we used in the CRW analysis: the mean move length, the mean squared move length, the mean move duration, and the mean cosine of the turning angle for each group (region) separately.

Box 5.2 lists the formulas for calculating the residence index for each area.

The predicted ratio of population densities between a region characterized by ϵ_j and the reference region is given by

$$\frac{\tilde{u}(\epsilon_j)}{\tilde{u}(\epsilon_0)} = \frac{\rho(\epsilon_j)}{\rho(\epsilon_0)}$$

5.4.3   Example: checkerspot butterflies searching for hosts

The most complete example of applying the above procedure is based on the data in Odendaal et al. (1989). In this project, we studied behavioral mechanisms that influence the spatial distribution of *Euphydryas anicia* females searching for larval host plants on a flat plain in Colorado. We followed mated females in two areas: within a host patch (host density ~100 plants/100 m²), and in an area that was essentially host-free (less than 1 plant/100 m²). A team of two investigators followed each female, one recording behavioral events with a hand-held computer, and the other marking landing sites with numbered flags. The distance and direction of each move (a move was defined as displacement between two consecutively numbered flags) were measured with a meter tape and a compass. Move durations were automatically recorded by the computer.

The female movement was affected by the density of host plants, and also by the presence of males. Harassment by males induced females to increase the rate of their movement, which could lead to their emigration from the host patch. The distribution of males was correlated with the distribution of host plants, so instead of attempting to separate the influences of males and hosts on female movement, I will simply compare their overall movement pattern within the host patch (where there were more males) to that outside the host patch (where there were fewer males).

INDIVIDUAL MOVEMENT   Within the host patch, movement of females was characterized by more frequent, and tighter turns (Table 5.2). Although the move distance decreased substantially from low-host to high-host areas, most of this decrease is due to the variation in move duration τ (so that speed decreased only by 38%). Note that despite a substantial shift in the movement pattern between the two areas, γ was practically unchanged.

COMPARISON OF PREDICTED AND OBSERVED DISTRIBUTIONS   We measured the spatial distribution of females by walking a set of parallel transects (200 m from each other), and recording the numbers of females observed per 100 m of transect (I will only use the 1986 data since that is when movement observations were done; for a discussion of other years see Odendaal et al.

Table 5.2: Estimated CRW parameters of *Euphydryas* females

	m_1	τ	ψ	γ	$\bar{\gamma}$
Host patch	2.80 m	3.83 s	0.43	3.54	
Outside patch	7.18 m	6.06 s	0.74	3.49	3.52

1989). The distribution of host plants was measured by placing 5×5 m quadrates along transects at 25 m intervals, and counting all host plants within each quadrat. I classified all areas with >10 plants/100 m² as high-host areas (average host density: 77 plants/100 m²), and areas with < 3 plants/100 m² as low-host area (average density: 0.6 plants/100 m²). Due to a sharp transition between the high-host and low-host areas, there were no areas of intermediate density (see Odendaal et al. 1989: Fig. 2b).

The model correctly predicted the spatial distribution of females in relation to host plants. The observed ratio of residence indices between patch and outside was $\rho(\epsilon_1)/\rho(\epsilon_0) = 3.3$, that is, the density of females flying within the host patch was more than three times higher than the female density outside the patch. The predicted ratio was 2.8, underpredicting the observed ratio by only 16%.

5.4.4 Other examples: ladybugs, butterflies

In addition to the data set on *Euphydryas* females, I have located three more case studies for testing the CRW diffusion-approximation model (Turchin 1991). Unfortunately, unlike the *Euphydryas* data set, the other case studies all had some minor problem that precluded a complete and rigorous test of the framework. Nevertheless, application of the framework to these studies showed that it could be useful in a variety of situations, and yielded some interesting results. I briefly review the results below (for more details see Turchin 1991).

The first case study was by Kareiva and Odell (1987) on ladybugs, *Coccinella septempunctata*, aggregating to aphid clusters. I have already discussed this study in Section 4.3.2. Kareiva and Odell (1987) restricted movement of their ladybugs to one-dimensional spatial arrays, and thus we do not need the full power of the Patlak model (it is much simpler to deal with CRW in one-dimensional space, see Section 4.3). Nevertheless, a test of the model is instructive. The model predicted a ladybug residence index of 8 and 200 in the low-density and high-density aphid clumps, respectively (taking the areas outside patches as reference points, ϵ_0). The observed ratios were 6.25 and 28. We see that the model predicted the aggregation of ladybugs in the low-density patch reasonably accurately, while appearing to substantially overpredict the aggregation in high-density patches. The latter discrepancy is more apparent than real, because both the theoretical prediction and the observations agreed that there would be practically no ladybugs outside the resource patch: the theoretical prediction of about 0.03 beetles/m, and the actual observation of about 0.25 beetles/m. Kareiva and Odell released only 20 beetles into the 10-m experimental arrays, and noted that "it is peculiar even to think of 1-3 ladybugs per meter in terms of a continuum population model"! Nevertheless, even under such extreme conditions, when a continuum model is used to predict the distribution of a few dozens of beetles, both the model of Kareiva and Odell, and Patlak's diffusion approximation generated predictions in good quantitative agreement with the data. I think that continuum models can be "pushed" quite far before they begin breaking down.

The other case study used the data collected by Root and Kareiva (1984), on movement and spatial distribution of cabbage white butterflies within two kinds of patches: collard monocultures (collards are host plants), and collard-potato dicultures. The results were not very interesting because both the movement patterns (as measured by move length and turning angle distributions) and the population densities (as measured by the number of eggs laid by females) were practically identical in both areas. Thus, the correct prediction of the CRW diffusion-approximation model that the ratio of the two residence indices will be approximately one is not particularly surprising.

The last case study used the data collected by Zalucki and Kitching (1982) on *Danaus plexippus* flying within patches of milkweeds (hostplants). Two predicted residence indices for males and females in high-density patches turned out to be close to the observed ratios (25% error and 7% error, respectively). However, the predicted residence index of females in the low-density patch was less than half of the observed ratio. This is interesting, because females flying in the low-density patch were the only group that had a significant turning bias, as measured by the direction of the mean vector (Turchin 1991). A tendency to make turns preferentially in one direction (to the left, in this case) would cause butterflies to circle, which should decrease their diffusion coefficient, and therefore increase the residence index. Thus, a turning bias could explain some, if not all the difference between the predicted and observed residence index.

5.4.5 Synthesis

What have we learned from applying the diffusion-approximation model to real data? Because the majority of predictions were close to the actual spatial distribution of foraging insects, we can tentatively conclude that the CRW model for heterogeneous environments provides a reasonably accurate description of the mechanisms by which these insects aggregated (or did not aggregate, in the case of cabbage butterflies) in response to patchily distributed resources. Remember that CRW postulates quite a specific model for the mechanism of aggregation—aggregation occurs by environmental factors modulating the frequency distributions of move durations, speeds, and turning angles. In behavioral literature, this mechanism is usually called kinesis, since no responses to directional cues are assumed. CRW assumes no long-distance attraction, no recognition or response to patch boundaries, no sensory habituation, to name just a few of alternative mechanisms by which organisms may aggregate to food patches. To the extent that the predictions of the CRW-based diffusion model correspond to the data, the postulated mechanisms are either supported or rejected.

As in analyses of net squared displacement, the deviations from predictions of the Patlak model can suggest a particular mechanism that organisms may employ in aggregation, but that is not part of the CRW model. In particular, serious deviations between the predicted and observed $\rho(\epsilon)$ for female *D. plexippus* in the low-density patch was strengthened by an observation that these females tended to make left-biased turns. A particularly interesting application of the CRW-based diffusion model will be in cases where there is a suspicion of non-trivial behavior of organisms at patch boundaries. For example, organisms encountering a patch boundary may bias their movements towards the patch interior (e.g., Sorensen and Bell 1986). In such a case, one would expect a substantial underprediction by the CRW model of the aggregation response. The residence index analyses could be supplemented by detailed analysis of moves at, or near, the patch boundary. Other complex search and aggregation strategies could be investigated using a similar logic. As far as I know, however, no such studies have yet been published.

5.5 An Alternative Approach: Fractal Analysis

How to meaningfully extrapolate ecological information across spatial scales is one of the central issues in landscape ecology (Gardner et al. 1989, Turner and Gardner 1991). Ecologists face problems that require understanding and predicting processes that occur at landscape, continental, or even global scales (Turner and Gardner 1991), while most experimental data are collected at much smaller spatial scales (Kareiva and Andersen 1988). Movement is the glue of spatial population dynamics, but movement studies and measuring paths are typically done at small spatial scales. Fractal analysis of paths extends the hope that by identifying scale-independent properties of movement processes we will be able to use the path data collected at patch or within-habitat scale to gain insights into the spatial population dynamics at the landscape level.

Fractal analysis of paths is based on the premise that the fractal dimension can serve as a scale-independent descriptor of organism movements. The logic of the approach is developed as follows (e.g., Milne 1991). If an organism moves along a completely linear path, then the actual distance traveled, l, equals the displacement between the start and the finish, R. The relationship between these two variables is linear. In other words if we assume a power law relating l to R, $l^d = R$, then the exponent $d = 1$. If the path is curvy, however, then the exponent will be greater than one. In the extreme, for the case of Brownian motion, $d = 2$ (the notion that paths of Brownian particles are fractal is discussed in Section A.1.1). It appears that d provides a measure of the path "sinuosity" or "tortuosity," with the extreme cases delineated by linear and Brownian movement, respectively, and real-life cases expected to fall within these extremes. The key assumption, to which I will return later, is that d is a *scale-independent* parameter. That is, if we measure d for paths of some organism walking in a particular environment that are several cm long, it will be the same as d for paths measured on the scale of meters or hundreds of meters.

ESTIMATING THE FRACTAL DIMENSION   Practical approaches to measuring d using real data have not been standardized yet. Some investigators plot net squared displacement as a function of time (Johnson et al. 1992), a practice that has a firm basis in the random walk theory (see Section 5.3). Others construct plots of the apparent path length versus the ruler length (With 1994). Here I will follow the logic of the second approach.

Let us suppose that we have a path consisting of coordinate fixes recorded at even time intervals. We will divide the path into n equal time segments of duration T. T is the temporal scale at which we want to measure path length. Let the expected displacement during time T be $\Delta_T l$, which is the length scale corresponding to the time scale T. The expected total length of the path measured at scale T, l_T, will simply be the sum of n expected displacements: $l_T = n\Delta_T l$. We now make a key assumption that

$$(\Delta_T l)^d \sim T \tag{5.6}$$

arguing by analogy with linear and Brownian motions, for which d is equal to

1 and 2, respectively. Since nT equals the total duration of a path, a constant, we can write $n \sim T^{-1} \sim (\Delta_T l)^{-d}$. It follows, then, that

$$l_T = n\Delta_T l \sim (\Delta_T l)^{-d}\Delta_T l = (\Delta_T l)^{1-d}$$

We now have a theoretical relationship between the length scale $\Delta_T l$ and the total path length l_T measured at this scale. When analyzing real paths, we systematically decrease T until we get to the lowest resolution at which the path was measured, calculate the average displacement $\Delta_T l$ and the sum of these displacements l_T, and plot them against each other on the double-log graph. The fitted slope of the relationship is $1 - d$, which gives us an estimate of the fractal dimension.

Recently there has appeared a number of empirical applications of the fractal analysis of paths (Crist et al. 1992, Fourcassie et al. 1992, Johnson et al. 1992a,b, Wiens et al. 1993a,b, 1995, With 1994). Some analyses found that estimated fractal dimensions were similar across different (but related) species and different habitats, even though net displacement increased markedly with beetle size and decreased with habitat complexity (e.g., the analysis of Crist et al. (1992) on three species of *Eleodes* beetles). On the basis of this result, Crist et al. (1992) argued that the three species interacted with the heterogeneous landscape in essentially similar ways, despite differences in the overall scale of dispersal. In other analyses, the fractal dimension varied between different species. For example, With (1994) found that movement patterns of two smaller grasshopper species were characterized by higher fractal dimensions, as compared to the larger species. With (1994) suggested that the smaller species were interacting with patch structure at a finer scale of resolution than the large species.

Johnson et al. (1992) were interested in investigating the conditions under which the fractal dimension could change, leading to piecewise linear relationships in the log path length–log ruler length plots (instead of a linear one postulated when fractal dimension is constant for all spatial scales). These authors simulated random walks in uniform and fragmented environments, and observed apparently abrupt changes in the fractal dimension, suggesting that the redistribution process shifts from one discrete pattern to another as spatial scale is increased. Johnson et al. (1992) also applied these ideas to an analysis of *Eleodes* beetle paths, although, in my opinion, they failed to convincingly establish the reality of the "crossover" from one movement pattern to another as spatial scale is increased.

IS THE FRACTAL DIMENSION SCALE-INDEPENDENT? I now address the key issue on which the validity of the fractal analysis is based (see also Turchin

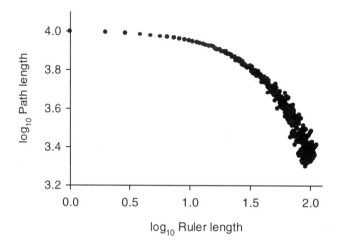

Figure 5.8: Calculating the fractal dimension of a simulated path of 10,000 steps resulting from a correlated random walk (assuming speed = 1, and the distribution of turning angle a circular normal with a standard deviation of 20°). (After Turchin 1996.)

1996). In order to extrapolate ecological information across spatial scales using the fractal dimension, one has to demonstrate that paths are characterized by self-similarity, in other words, that there is a scale-independent fractal dimension. In practical terms, this means that we have to show that the data patterns on various double-log plots are linear, and that the slope does not change with scale. The analyses of Crist et al. (1992) and With (1994) have implicitly made this linearity assumption, while Johnson et al. (1992) assumed that patterns are piece-wise linear, with breaks corresponding to some biologically-meaningful scales.

Random walk theory tells us to expect a constant dimension $d = 2$ only for infinitely wriggly, infinitely long Brownian paths, which is a rather extreme idealization of real organism tracks (Section A.1.1). For organisms moving according to CRW, we expect d to converge to 2 at very large spatial scales, and to 1 at very small spatial scales, with smooth variation in between (Figure 5.8).

A close examination of many log-log plots (see, for example Figure 1 in Turchin 1996) suggests that paths of real organisms are characterized by a similar pattern—in many species there is a noticeable curvature down, in the direction predicted by the random walk theory. At smaller ruler lengths the slope is very close to zero, and at highest ruler lengths it begins to curve down. That the slope never approaches –1 is probably a reflection of practical limitations on the length of observed paths. Thus, in my opinion, some of the differences in estimated fractal dimension observed by various authors may be not a reflection of how different species interact with a fragmented landscape, but rather an artifact of the scale on which the investigator happened to collect path data, and where that scale fits within the spectrum of d from 1 to 2 for each species.

Synthesis

Fractal analysis attempts to identify scale-independent properties of spatial patterns that could be used in translating information gathered at smaller spatial scales to make inferences about larger-scale phenomena. However, so far it has not been shown that this is possible to do. In fact, currently available results from fractal analyses of paths indicate that various estimated slopes and inferred fractal dimensions are scale dependent. The nature of scale dependence appears to be species specific and thus an interesting subject for study. In my opinion, however, such a study is better approached from a firmer foundation of random walk theory (see Section 5.4)

5.6 Measuring Attraction: Random Walk Approach

5.6.1 Biased correlated random walks

Section 4.4.4 discussed the difficulties associated with including directional bias into the CRW process. The problem is that the frequency distribution of a move direction is affected both by the previous move direction, and by the absolute (compass) direction. Because directions are circular quantities they are less amenable to intuition than linear quantities. Furthermore, if we allow both the directional bias and the directional persistence to depend on space, we are left with a very complicated process to model. Complex models usually result in unwieldy and complex methods of analysis. As a result, current approaches to analyzing directional influences on animal tracks usually focus on either external bias or directional persistence, but not both (e.g., Marsh and Jones 1988, Morris 1993, Casas and Aluja 1997).

Analysis is greatly simplified when there is no directional persistence in movement, and we can, therefore, use the biased, but uncorrelated random walk model. Methods for analyzing uncorrelated random walks will be covered in Chapter 7. Another possible simplification is to assume that the external bias is constant in space. In this case, we can sidestep the issue of directional persistence and analyze each path as a whole (see Section 5.6.2). Alternatively, we can use theoretical random walk formulas to test various hypotheses about external biases (see Section 5.6.3). In the most complex case of spatially variable biases, we may be able to use the trick of *dimension reduction*—a very useful approach, since it is conceptually much easier to deal with correlated random walks in 1D space (see Section 5.6.4).

5.6.2   Beeline headings and net displacement vectors

A simple method for avoiding the complications arising from directional persistence is to analyze the *beeline heading* of a path, defined as the direction of the vector connecting the beginning of the path with its end (the length of this vector being an already familiar quantity—the net displacement).

The null hypothesis is simply that beeline headings are distributed uniformly on the interval from 0° to 360°. It can be tested by classifying all beeline heading angles into several discrete groups (for example, 0°-60°, 60°-120°, and so on), and testing deviation from uniformity by a χ^2 test. An example of testing this hypothesis is given by Zalucki and Kitching (1982). They found that the frequency distribution of monarch butterfly (*Danaus plexippus*) headings did not significantly depart from the uniform (see their Figure 5a). A more quantitative test would calculate the mean-vector statistic for beeline headings (Batschelet 1981), and use Rayleigh's test to determine if its length is significantly different from zero (Batschelet 1981).

Another example of the same approach is Harrison's (1989) test of whether checkerspot butterflies can orient toward a habitat patch from distance. She released butterflies at 0.2, 0.5, and 1 km from the target patch (an isolated habitat patch more than 10 km distant from all other known checkerspot habitats), and observed the direction of their flight until they disappeared, recording the quadrant where they were last seen. She then tested whether the proportion of butterflies flying towards the target patch was different from the 25% expected under no-orientation hypothesis. There was no significant orientation towards habitat at any distance from the target patch.

An example of movement with significant directionality is described by Turchin et al. (1991). In that study, we were interested in elucidating the mechanisms of hilltopping in a checkerspot butterfly *Euphydryas editha*. We released a number of males on the slopes of a hill and followed their movements. To test for a directional component, we classified the beeline headings of all paths into four categories (each 90° wide): uphill, downhill, cross-hill right, and cross-hill left. We found that the number of paths directed uphill

(10) and in all other directions combined (4) were significantly different from the expected 25% and 75% (G-test, $P < 0.001$). Thus, we concluded that butterflies significantly biased the direction of their movement uphill.

When focusing on bias in the direction of movement, one should not forget that external bias can also affect speed or move length. This suggests testing whether or not absolute direction affects net displacement. In fact, an even better overall test for the presence of external bias is to look at the 2D vector of total displacement for each path. The null hypothesis of no bias implies that the expected displacement in both Cartesian coordinates (e.g., x and y) is zero. A simple t-test should suffice in determining if either the abscissa or the ordinate is significantly different from zero. This overall test should be performed as a first step in the analysis before examining more specific hypotheses.

5.6.3 Employing random walk formulas

The popularity enjoyed by the formula of Kareiva and Shigesada (1983) for unbiased CRW suggests that their approach may be fruitfully extended for an investigation of paths affected by an external bias. External bias can affect the frequency distribution of any of the three move components—move length (or speed), move duration (or turning frequency), and move direction (or turning angle). The form of random walk and resulting formulas will also be affected by whether there is directional persistence. In the theoretical literature a variety of models have been developed for biased random walk formulations (with or without persistence). Application of these formulas to data, however, has lagged behind.

The most basic comparison is between the correlated random walk (CRW) and the uncorrelated random walk in which bias affects move direction. Both these random walk models are characterized by "directional" movement. However, in the biased random walk the directionality is external, since move direction is influenced by the absolute (compass) direction; in CRW the directionality is internal, since the current move direction is influenced by the previous move direction. Two approaches that distinguish between these two alternatives were developed by Marsh and Jones (1988). First, one can compare the observed pattern in $\bar{R}_n^2$ to the expected ones under the two rival models. Net squared displacement in the biased random walk is described by the following formula (Marsh and Jones 1988):

$$\bar{R}_n^2 = nm_2 + n(n-1)m_1^2\phi^2 \tag{5.7}$$

where ϕ is the mean cosine of move direction (absolute direction, *not* turning angle). Net squared displacement in the CRW is given in Box 5.1.

Box 5.3 A test for correlated versus biased random walk (Marsh and Jones 1988.)

Calculate the statistic Δ for the data set:

$$\Delta = \frac{1}{n^2}\left[\left(\sum \cos \alpha_j\right)^2 + \left(\sum \sin \alpha_j\right)^2\right]$$
$$- \frac{1}{(n-1)^2}\left[\left(\sum \cos \theta_j\right)^2 + \left(\sum \sin \theta_j\right)^2\right] \tag{5.8}$$

where α_j and θ_j are the direction and the turning angle of move j. The expected value of Δ for the biased random walk is

$$\bar{\Delta} = -\frac{1}{n(n-1)} + \left(1 - \frac{1}{n}\right)\phi^2 - \frac{2(n-2)}{(n-1)^2}\phi^2\phi_2 - \frac{(n-2)(n-3)}{(n-1)^2}\phi^4$$

where ϕ_2 is the expectation of $\cos 2\alpha$.
For the CRW model it is:

$$\bar{\Delta} = -\frac{1}{n(n-1)} + \frac{s\psi}{n(1-\psi)}\left(\frac{\psi^n}{n} - \psi + 1 - \frac{1}{n}\right) - \left(1 - \frac{1}{n-1}\right)\psi^2$$

The second approach is to construct a statistic that attempts to capitalize on the difference in mechanisms that determine directionality of movement (see Box 5.3). The first term in square brackets in Equation 5.8 reflects the contribution of the external bias. If there is no bias, then its expected value is zero. Similarly, the second term reflects the directional persistence, so that if there is none, its expectation is zero. Thus, a positive Δ implies external bias, while a negative Δ suggests directional persistence.

A serious limitation of the test proposed by Marsh and Jones (1988) is that it limits the alternative hypotheses to either external directional bias or directional persistence. However, it is quite likely that most organisms will not completely lose directional persistence, even when moving under the influence of external bias. Thus, we usually need to be able to distinguish between the biased correlated random walk (BCRW) and the alternative of no bias, that is, directional persistence alone.

In the case of CRW, the expected position of individuals does not shift with time, while BCRW implies a constant drift of the expected position in the direction in which movement is biased. Thus, one potential approach for investigating bias is to measure this tendency to drift. There are two formulas for the expected net displacement in BCRW models of which I am aware (Nossal and Weiss 1974, Othmer et al. 1988; see Box 5.4).

Box 5.4 Displacement in a BCRW model (Othmer et al. 1988).

Assuming that the x-axis is aligned with the direction of bias, the expectation and the variance of the location of organisms along the x-axis are:

$$\bar{X}(t) = v\chi \left[t - \tau_0 \left(1 - e^{-t/\tau_0} \right) \right]$$

$$\sigma_X^2(t) = 2v^2\tau_0[(1-\chi^2)t - 2\chi^2 t e^{-t/\tau_0} + \tau_0(2\chi^2 - 1)(1 - e^{-t/\tau_0})$$
$$+\tau_0\chi^2(1 - e^{-t/\tau_0})^2/2]$$

where

$$\tau_0 = \frac{\tau}{1 - \psi}$$

$$\chi = \frac{\phi}{1 - \psi}$$

5.6.4 Analysis of move attributes

I have already stressed in Section 5.3.8 that comparisons of predicted to observed displacements should always be accomplished by an analysis of move attributes—distance, duration, and direction. Such an analysis may be especially important in situations for which we do not have random walk formulas, for example, random walks with a spatially variable bias. In this section I will discuss the approaches and potential problems associated with the analysis of move attributes.

The analysis of move distance and duration in BCRW does not usually pose special problems, because autocorrelations in these move parameters are often weak or absent. Thus, a simple approach is to regress the move length on the cosine of the angle between the move direction and the direction of possible bias. If the bias is spatially variable (for example, it varies with distance from the attraction source), then the location may be included as a covariate in the analysis.

The greatest difficulty lies in analyzing the influence of external bias on move direction. A naive approach of directly relating move direction to the direction of the possible bias can produce misleading results. I will illustrate this problem with a concrete example. The data set in question documents movements of caterpillars in the genus *Hyles* collected by G. Simmons, L. Goncharoff, and myself. We observed the behavior of caterpillars at a site within the eruption zone of Mt. St. Helens, in a mosaic of patches of host

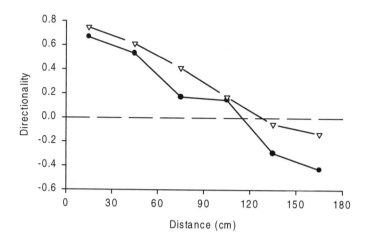

Figure 5.9: The influence of patch on move direction. (1) The average cosine of the angle between move direction and the direction to the attractive source (the host patch) plotted as a function of distance to the source ($\triangledown$). (2) Directionality measured by classifying all moves as either toward or away from the patch ($\bullet$).

plants (the fireweed *Epilobium angustifolium*) and pumice- and ash-covered ground between the patches. Caterpillars were released at various distances and directions from a patch of host plants, and their movements recorded at 2-min intervals until they found the host patch, or left the observation area. The observation area (approximately 5 m in radius) was devoid of all host patches, except for the one target patch located in its center.

To quantify the overall influence of patch on the move direction of caterpillars, we calculate the correlation coefficient between the move direction and the direction towards the patch. This correlation coefficient is simply the average cosine of the angle between these two directions (Batschelet 1981). Obviously, the distance between the moving caterpillar and the patch is an important factor, since we expect the bias to decrease to zero when caterpillars are far away from the patch. To deal with this distance-dependence, I classified all moves into 30-cm bins, and calculated the mean cosine of the move angle in relation to the direction to the patch for each bin separately (Figure 5.9). As we expected, the directional bias is highest near the patch. However, why does it become negative at distances greater than 120 cm? Is the patch repelling caterpillars? This seems unlikely. In fact, a more likely explanation is that we have been mislead because we did not include the influence of directional persistence into our analysis. Indeed, consider those caterpillars that "miss" the host plant. If they initially moved away from the patch, they will continue to move in the same general direction for a while as a result of directional persistence. Even if they initially moved in the general direction of the patch, or at right angles to it, and still missed it, their progress may continue to move them away from the patch. Therefore, whatever their initial direction, eventually caterpillars will tend to move away from the patch. When they are far away from the patch, the attraction is absent, but persistence of motion will ensure that most of them will continue moving away from the patch. Thus, even though there is no bias, we would expect a negative correlation between the direction of movement and direction to the patch. A similar reasoning indicates that close to the patch directional persistence will inflate the apparent bias.

There is a way to test this explanation of the pattern in Figure 5.9, and simultaneously to get around the problem of confounded directional persistence and external bias. Let us assume that the strength of attraction to the patch is influenced only by distance from the patch (we have already made this assumption implicitly in Figure 5.9). Thus, the random walk process is symmetric around the coordinate origin where the patch is, and we can collapse it to a one-dimensional random walk, with the distance to the patch as the only spatial coordinate. Things are much simpler in 1D space. In particular, we need to keep track of only two directions—toward the center and away from it. First, let us check that in this reformulation of the problem we still have apparent repelling by patch. Classifying all moves as either in the positive (away from the patch) or negative (towards the patch) direction, a measure of directionality is given by $(P_- - P_+)/(P_- + P_+)$. This measure varies from 1 when all moves are towards the patch, to –1 when all moves are away from the patch. Plotting this measure of directionality against distance we observe the same qualitative pattern as before (but quantitatively even more extreme). The next step is to take into account the autocorrelation between move directions. To do this, I classified all pairs of subsequent moves in four categories: $(-,-)$; $(-,+)$; $(+,-)$; $(+,+)$; where the first sign indicates the direction of the previous move, and the second sign the direction of the next move. We are primarily interested in the proportions of move direction reversal $P[-,+]$ and $P[+,-]$ (the two other proportions follow directly, since $P[-,-]+P[-,+] = 1$ and $P[+,-] + P[+,+] = 1$). Plotting $P[-,+]$ and $P[+,-]$ against distance (Figure 5.10), we observe that (1) the probability of reversing and moving toward the patch is greatest in the vicinity of the patch (0–90 cm), then rapidly

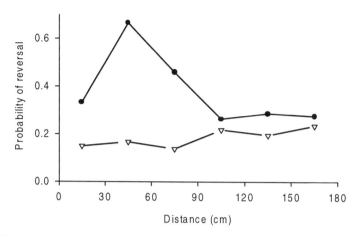

Figure 5.10: The estimated probabilities of reversing direction to move towards the patch $P[-,+]$ (●) and away from the patch $P[+,-]$ (▽).

declines to some constant value. The probability of reversing to move away from the patch slowly increases with distance. (2) *The two lines approach each other very closely, but never cross as the distance from patch increases.* This pattern is consistent with strong attraction near the patch (a large difference between $P[+,-]$ and $P[-,+]$) and no attraction far from the patch (the difference between the two probabilities of reversal goes to zero). There is no evidence of repulsion at large distances. Thus, I conclude that the patterns in Figure 5.9 are an artifact of directional persistence.

5.6.5   Synthesis

Quantitative analysis of external bias in path data is still in its infancy, and few empirical examples are available in the ecological literature. I have reviewed three approaches, which ideally should be used to complement each other. One is to analyze the influence of directionality on move attributes, such as distances and directions. Extra care should be taken to correct for autocorrelations. The problem of disentangling directional persistence from directional bias is especially thorny, but the example in Section 5.6.4 shows that it can be handled, even in rather complex situations (e.g., spatially varying bias) by dimension reduction.

Another approach is to use theoretical random walk formulas for average location and net squared displacement. I have listed such relationships for some biased random walk formulations. These formulas can be used to distinguish between alternative mechanisms of how external bias may affect move parameters. The final approach is to use theoretical formulas for fitting data. This allows an estimate of the influence of bias on movement in an indirect way.

5.7 Measuring Attraction: Kinematic Analysis

5.7.1 Discrete accelerations

Various incarnations of the random walk provided the dominant paradigm for quantitative analysis of paths in the literature, as well as in this chapter. While random walk is a very powerful and flexible framework, it has limitations. To put the approach in perspective, let us first consider that the basic data for the analysis comes as a set of 2D or 3D spatial coordinates with an associated temporal coordinate that we call a sample path, $\{X(t)\}$. Here each $X(t)$ is a vector of spatial coordinates occupied by the followed organisms at time t. The path specification in terms of its coordinates can be called the zero-order description. By taking first differences, we obtain a first-order description in terms of moves or steps. Each move is a vector characterized by its length, duration, and direction. For continuous paths sampled at regular time intervals, say τ, it may be more intuitive to express the first-order path description in terms of discrete velocities $V(t) = [X(t) - X(t - \tau)]/\tau$. The discrete velocity description is equivalent to the description in terms of moves, in the same way that the description in terms of Cartesian coordinates is equivalent to polar coordinates. The first-order description is the domain of random walks, since the primary focus is on a move or displacement, rather than on the actual coordinate. Although the subsequent coordinates are autocorrelated, subsequent moves are completely independent of each other (in uncorrelated random walks), making it more convenient mathematically to focus on moves. In a correlated random walk, one first-order attribute, move direction, is no longer independent of the previous history. Hence we focus on a second-order quantity, the turning angle, which is the difference between the subsequent move directions (it is second-order because it is a difference of a difference). However, move distances can also be autocorrelated, so we may have to difference them. An alternative approach is to go directly to the first difference in velocity, or the second difference in position, the discrete acceleration:

$$A(t) = \frac{X(t + \tau) - 2X(t) + X(t - \tau)}{\tau^2} \qquad (5.9)$$

The analysis of paths or trajectories that focuses on discrete accelerations is called *kinematic* (Okubo and Chiang 1974), because kinematics is the branch of dynamics that is exclusively concerned with trajectories, velocities, and accelerations, rather than the forces that cause accelerations. The second-order representation in terms of discrete accelerations will often make more intuitive sense than a representation as a correlated random walk for such cases as continuously sampled paths and trajectories in 3D space (the spherical coordinate system can be very confusing). Which approach to take in practice will be determined by the nature of the data, and the particular questions asked.

The problem of oversampling versus undersampling is as relevant for the description in terms of accelerations as it is for random walk approaches. As before, undersampling can be avoided by measuring the path at the highest rate feasible. Oversampling, on the other hand, will cause autocorrelations in the acceleration, so the path can be resampled at a lower rate until the autocorrelation structure disappears.

5.7.2   Example: midge swarming

I will review two examples of kinematic analysis based on discrete accelerations. These examples illustrate how the kinematic approach can be conceptually more simple than an approach based on the biased correlated random walk, especially in complex situations where bias is spatially variable.

In a pioneering study, Okubo and coworkers (Okubo and Chiang 1974, Okubo et al. 1977) filmed and analyzed 3D trajectories of midges, *Anarete pritchardii*, swarming under field conditions. They analyzed two 1-s sections of a roll of 16 mm film taken at rates between 48 and 64 frames per second. They focused on the projections of movements onto a horizontal plane, and calculated the x and y components of the discrete acceleration using the time interval τ defined by the interval between frames. They noted that these accelerations did not represent the instantaneous values, but rather averages over the time interval. They estimated the error with which acceleration was measured to be between 0.17 and 0.3 G (where $G = 0.98$ m/s^2, the acceleration due to gravity). The calculations of Okubo and Chiang showed that accelerations of 2 G were not uncommon, and one midge achieved an acceleration of 5 G. This occurred when the midge suddenly changed its course in order to avoid collision with another midge.

The next step was to estimate the mean acceleration field within the swarm. This was done by plotting each component of acceleration, $A_x(t)$ and $A_y(t)$ against the corresponding (x or y) coordinate of the insect relative to the center of mass of the swarm [Figure 5.11 shows an example for one swarm

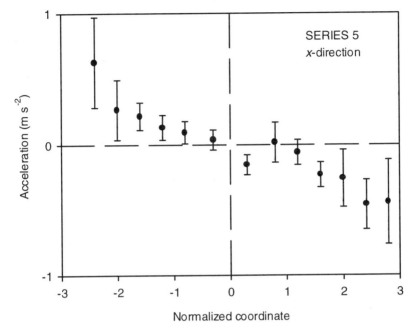

Figure 5.11: Mean acceleration field within a swarm of midges. The normalized coordinate is centered at the swarm center of mass with one unit equal to one standard deviation of midge positions. Error bars indicate 90% confidence intervals.

and one dimension (x)]. These graphs are very revealing. We see that in the positive x and y directions, the acceleration components are negative, and vice versa. This indicates that on the average midges were accelerating towards the center of the swarm. Moreover, at the origin mean accelerations are very close to zero, suggesting that in this region midges were flying virtually randomly with respect to the swarm center. The strongest accelerations towards the center are observed right at the edge of the swarm. The presence of this inward-oriented force plays a crucial role in maintaining the cohesion of the swarm against a general tendency of spreading by the randomness in motion. Okubo et al. (1977) also note that an inward orientation of peripheral insects was observed by still photography in swarms of desert locusts, although no quantitative analysis of acceleration was carried out.

5.7.3   Example: fish schooling

The second example comes from the analysis of individual trajectories of schooling fish by Parrish and Turchin (1997). The data comes from laboratory observations of fish behavior, but the analytical approach is general and can be applied to either lab or field situations.

Juvenile blacksmith (*Chromis punctipinnis*) typically feed in loose, nonpolarized congregations of tens to hundreds of individuals. They are not a schooling species in the strict sense, but are capable of assuming a packed, ordered arrangement when threatened by a predator. Fish movements were observed in a 1 m^3 tank using three video cameras placed along each of three orthogonal axes. Video tapes were digitized in 10 s clips at the recording rate of 15 frames/s. 3D coordinates of the centroid of each fish were used to define trajectories. At the start of each experiment, 5, 10, or 15 individuals were released in the tank. There was a 1 h acclimatization period before recordings were started. Altogether we analyzed 6, 5, and 3 replicates of group sizes 5, 10, and 15 fish, respectively.

Our first step in the analysis of these data was to check the appropriateness of the sampling rate. To do this we calculated the autocorrelation functions (ACF) in each of the three x, y, and z components of discrete accelerations for each fish for all group sizes and replicates. There were no systematic differences between the different axes or group sizes, so we focused on the grand average of all ACF. The accelerations defined by the highest resolution at which the trajectories were recorded ($\tau = 1/15$ s) showed a very clear autocorrelation pattern. There was a strong positive correlation of about 0.5 at first lag, and an almost as strong negative correlation of about 0.3 at lag 4. Both these autocorrelations were highly significant. It appears that it takes two frames on the average for a fish to accelerate (since the ACF is positive for the first two lags). On the other hand, negative ACF at lags 4 ± 1 suggests that this is the temporal scale at which fish "brake" to correct the initial acceleration and adopt a new course.

Whatever the locomotory mechanisms underlying the observed ACF pattern, the paths recorded at 1/15 s are clearly oversampled. Next, we resampled the paths by taking every second, third, fourth, and fifth frame and calculated the average ACF for each resampling rate. The autocorrelations completely disappear by the time we resample the path by taking every fourth frame. However, we decided that using every fourth frame would cause us to leave out too much data, and that the best balance between the twin problems of oversampling and undersampling would be achieved by using every third frame, which corresponds to $\tau = 0.2$ s. When sampling at this rate, the most important first-lag autocorrelation was already zero, and all other autocorrelations were very close to zero, apart from a small "blip" at the second lag.

After settling on the sampling rate, the next step was to use discrete accelerations to quantify the nature of fish-fish interactions within the school. $A(t)$ is a 3D vector, but we are only interested in the directional component to some "behavioral focus," such as a neighbor, a group of neighbors, or the entire school. Accordingly, our subsequent analysis focused on the projection of the acceleration vector on the direction towards such foci. A positive projection of $A(t)$ implies acceleration towards the focus, while a negative projection implies acceleration away from it. This approach is akin to Okubo and Chiang (1974) looking separately at the x and y components of acceleration, except in their case the location of the focus (swarm center) was fixed, while in our case the focus is moving around.

What are the foci to which fish react? To answer this question we tested a range of foci, starting with the simplest subset—the individual's nearest neighbor, and incrementing the subset by adding the next nearest neighbor, and so on, until the focus eventually became synonymous with the entire school. For each subset, we calculated the centroid position of all fish in this subset, and used it as a potential focus. Then we regressed the component of each individual's acceleration in the direction of the focus on the distance between the focus and the individual. We found that individual movements were most strongly influenced by the extremes of the continuum, that is, fish appear to be paying most attention to their nearest neighbor and the school as a whole unit.

The nature of interactions between these two kinds of foci, however, is different. At close range, nearest neighbors are always avoided, as evidenced by a strongly negative acceleration component at distances less than approximately 10 cm, regardless of group size (Figure 5.12). Interestingly, the strength of this close-range negative response appears to increase with school size, possibly because in bigger schools a larger proportion of individuals will find themselves in the interior. The movements of such fish will be more restricted, because they are surrounded by other fish on all sides, and they will find themselves frequently accelerating to avoid collisions. As the distance increases, the individuals begin to be attracted to nearest neighbors. However, this pattern may be a result not of being attracted to the nearest neighbor *per se* but rather of being attracted to the school (when a fish is outside the school, the direction toward the nearest neighbor and toward the school center will be strongly correlated).

Attraction towards the school centroid is always positive, and gradually increases in strength with distance to the centroid. This pattern is quite similar to the one observed by Okubo and Chiang (1974). In the central

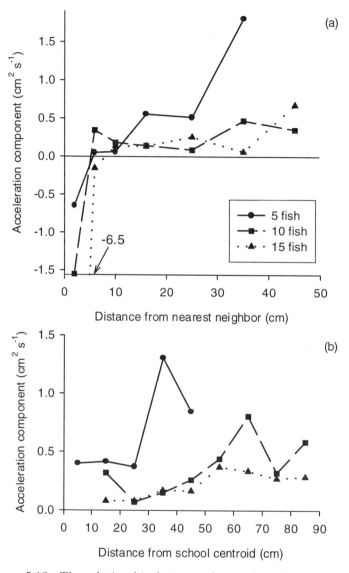

Figure 5.12: The relationship between the acceleration component in the direction of a focus and the distance from fish to that focus. Positive values indicate acceleration toward a focus, while negative values indicate acceleration away from the focus, or repulsion. The foci are: (a) nearest neighbor, and (b) the school centroid.

region of the school, the attraction is weak or largely absent, and fish move around largely at random. At the edges of the school the attraction becomes very strong.

5.7.4 Synthesis

The kinematic analysis appears to provide a viable alternative to the random-walk based paradigm, as the two empirical examples show. This is a quintessential Lagrangian approach, since we are focusing directly on individual trajectories, velocities, and accelerations. It appears to be particularly useful in situations where the questions to be answered are primarily behavioral, rather than ecological. Thus, the kinematic approach may not be quite as useful for issues in spatial ecology as the random walk approach proved to be. Nevertheless, nothing prevents us from implementing an individual-based simulation model, based on results from kinematic analysis, and obtaining a prediction of population redistribution by simulation.

Chapter 6

Mass Mark-Recapture

6.1 Introduction

While following individual organisms can provide very detailed information about their movement behavior (see Chapter 5), such studies are not always possible to conduct because most organisms are difficult or even impossible to follow. In addition, studies based on following individuals are typically limited in their spatial extent, temporal duration, and the number of organisms for which paths can be obtained. For instance, it is usually impractical to follow individuals of a species characterized by a slow rate of movement, since long observation periods yield little data. Furthermore, we may not require the detailed information collected by following individuals, being, instead, interested in population-level redistribution processes. This is where mass mark-recapture (MMR) studies excel.

One of the most widely used forms of MMR is to mark a large number of organisms, release them at a particular point in space (a *point release*), and recapture individuals later, after they have had an opportunity to move around. There are many variations on this basic theme. Organisms may be recaptured at a particular instant (or instants) in time—this provides a measure of population density in areas where marked organisms were recaptured. Alternatively, traps can be used to integrate the population density over time. Traps can be situated on a regular spatial grid, or haphazardly spread around the release point. In addition to the point release, there are other forms of MMR. For example, organisms can be released at a constant spatial density within a particular area and allowed to diffuse into the surrounding terrain (*area release*). It may not even be necessary to mark organisms if there is only a single source of them in an area. The most basic requirement of MMR methods is that we measure population density at no fewer than two points in time—the initial distribution in space, and the spatial distribution after some time has passed. The unifying feature of the MMR methods that I review in this chapter is the analysis of data using Eulerian methods. In other words, we fit the data with models whose basic variable is spatio-temporal population density (or its integral) rather than positions of individuals in space and time. Often, but not always, we use a partial differential equation model, such as diffusion.

The structure of this chapter is similar to that of Chapters 5 and 7. The chapter is organized around three themes: (1) estimating the rate of population spread, (2) quantifying the effects of spatial heterogeneity, and (3) measuring the effects of long-distance attraction.

6.2   Estimating the Rate of Dispersal

6.2.1   Analysis of density-distance curves

The end product of a MMR study is a data set containing measurements of organism density (usually, but not necessarily, marked; see Section 2.3.1) at various points in space and, sometimes, in time. Such data are often referred to as *density-distance* data because they document how the density of marked organisms falls off with distance from the release point. Although the emphasis is often on the effects of distance, density-distance relationships can also be affected by the direction from release to recapture, the time after release, and the spatial heterogeneity of the environment. When these factors are shown to be important, they generally can be included in the analysis, and their effects estimated.

The most common approach to the quantitative analysis of density-distance data is to fit them with some functional relationships, *density-distance curves*, either phenomenological or derived from mechanistic models. Such an approach often works well, provided that we can assume the environment to be approximately homogeneous (or, at least *quasihomogeneous*—when the spatial scale of heterogeneity is much smaller than the scale of dispersal, so that we are measuring the rate of spread averaged over the fine-grained environmental variation). If we need to quantify the effects of spatial heterogeneity, an alternative approach is usually needed, for example, direct fitting of dynamical models to data (see Section 6.4).

In Section 3.3 I argued that density-distance data should be fitted with mechanistic models rather than with phenomenological relationships. This is because results of purely phenomenological curve fitting are at best difficult to interpret and at worst meaningless. However, sometimes a phenomenological curve will have to be used to quantitatively describe data if no theoretical

curve is available, or if the empirical function provides a clearly superior fit and is not logically flawed (see Section 3.3).

In this section I will review a number of mechanistically based formulas that can be applied to most common experimental set-ups. Most of these formulas are based on the diffusion theory but not necessarily the simple diffusion equation. Thus, their application is not limited to organisms that are assumed to be moving "randomly" (see Section 3.4.2). Conversely, when simple diffusion provides a good fit to a data set, it cannot be inferred that the animals' movement is random.

Fitting mechanistically derived formulas should be approached with a great deal of thought. The following questions should be addressed:

- Exactly what does the model assume about the mode of organism movement? Is it a simple random walk, a correlated random walk, or some other, more realistic formulation? In this book, I attempt to be very explicit about these assumptions (see Chapter 4 and Appendix A). If you are using a formula from the literature, however, carefully read the model set-up and at least skim through the derivation. The latter is important since in many papers additional assumptions are often introduced in the course of derivation.

- What are the initial and boundary conditions of the model used to derive the formula? Which theoretical conditions best approximate the design of your movement study? Sometimes this is unknown—for example, you may not know whether the boundary in your study was reflecting or absorbing, in which case both formulas may be tried. In other cases, it may make sense to use a simpler model, even though it violates the study set-up. For example, even though the study may have used area release rather than point release, if the area of release is small compared to the dispersal range this effect can be safely ignored.

- What variable was measured? The major distinction here is between instantaneous density of marked organisms at a specific point of time versus time-integrated density, such as a trap catch.

Applying a wrong formula to data will obviously lead to erroneous results. For example, the Gaussian curve is often employed in the analysis of density-distance curves as a null model for "random movement" (see Section 3.4.2 for the discussion of why this is a misnomer). Indeed, the Gaussian curve is a particular solution of the simple diffusion equation. However, it describes the instantaneous density-distribution in space resulting from a point-release of marked organisms. I have already referred to an inappropriate use of fitting with the Gaussian curve when data are *time-integrated* (see Section 3.3).

Similarly, fitting a population distribution resulting from a time-distributed source of migrants with the Gaussian curve (e.g., Taylor 1978) is guaranteed to fail because the expected distribution will be very leptokurtic. For example, a continuous point-source in two-dimensional space will produce a Bessel distribution of population density (see Section A.3.5 in the Appendix).

I begin with a review of methods suitable for analyzing instantaneous densities and then move to the analysis of time-integrated densities.

6.2.2   Instantaneous density data

It is difficult, if not impossible, to measure the density distribution of marked organisms in a single instant of time. Thus, the important factor to consider is whether the finite time period during which density is measured is small compared to the temporal rate of population density change. Typically, instantaneous density data is obtained by direct sampling of population density of marked organisms. For example, one may visually count the number of marked organisms in each designated quadrat around a release point, or take a suction sample of marked insects from each host plant in a spatial array. Trapping data is typically more suitable for analysis using time-integrated formulas (see Section 6.2.5). However, if the spatial distribution of marked organisms changes slowly during the interval between trap collections, then instantaneous methods can be employed.

INSTANTANEOUS POINT RELEASE   The most common design for studying dispersal is the instantaneous point release, in which marked organisms are released instantaneously (at one point in time) at a single point in space. The general approach of the analysis is to fit the Gaussian curve (normal distribution) to the data. This density-distance curve is a solution of the simple diffusion equation with the boundary and initial conditions appropriate to the instantaneous point release design (see Section A.2 in the Appendix). Remember that this equation is a null model for movement. If we find that it fits well, then we can conclude that the movement pattern of the study organism is well approximated by simple diffusion in a homogeneous environment (or that the heterogeneity is fine-scaled compared to the spatial scale of dispersal) and that there is no need to assume more complex features. The estimated diffusion coefficient provides a measure of the rate of spatial population spread. If the simple diffusion model does not fit the data well, then we need to test more complex alternatives.

TESTING FOR DRIFT   Before fitting the Gaussian distribution, one should always check for the presence of significant drift. Drift is the population-level

---

Box 6.1 Gaussian formula for simple diffusion.

If we release N_0 marked organisms at location $x, y = 0$ at time $t = 0$, then the simple diffusion equation predicts that their spatio-temporal density will be described by the following formula:

$$u(x, y, t) = \frac{N_0}{4\pi Dt} \exp\left[-\frac{x^2 + y^2}{4Dt}\right] = \frac{N_0}{4\pi Dt} \exp\left[-\frac{r^2}{4Dt}\right] \qquad (6.1)$$

where D is the diffusion rate, and $r = \sqrt{x^2 + y^2}$ is the distance from the release point. Solutions for more complex cases are discussed in the Appendix; see Section A.2.

---

manifestation of directional (external) bias in the individual movements of organisms. It is easily detected by calculating the mean and the variance of the spatial positions at which each marked individual was recaptured. Assuming that there is no drift, and that organisms were recaptured (or resighted) using a symmetric array of spatial locations, the expected mean displacement is zero. The hypothesis of no drift, then, is tested by determining whether the mean x- and y-coordinates are significantly different from zero, using for example a t-statistic. If there is a significant average displacement in either direction, its potential causes should be investigated. However, sometimes the test gives a significant result, but the magnitude of the departure is not very large compared to the spatial scale of dispersal (e.g., the mean displacement is less than 10% of the root mean square of the dispersal distances). It may be best to ignore such small effects rather than complicate the model. If the drift is too large to ignore, it is estimated as the velocity with which mean displacement grows with time. Thus, the x-component of the drift is estimated to be $\hat{\beta}_x = (\sum x_i/n)/t$, that is, the average of x-coordinates (x_i) of n recaptured organisms, divided by the time between release and recapture, t. As usual, this formula assumes that organisms were released at $x = 0$. The y-component is estimated in the same manner.

TESTING THE HYPOTHESIS OF SIMPLE DIFFUSION   Several approaches have been proposed to use the Gaussian formula for data analysis. Dobzhansky and Wright (1943) calculated the kurtosis of the observed density distribution and determined whether it differed significantly from the expected for a normal distribution. Another approach is to regress the density of organisms on distance from the release point, using Formula 6.1 (Ito and Miyashita 1965). These approaches, however, do not fully utilize the available data to test the null model of simple diffusion. A comprehensive approach to testing the simple diffusion was proposed by Kareiva (1982, 1983).

Assuming that there is no drift:

1. Estimate the diffusion coefficient, $\hat{D}(t) = \bar{R}^2(t)/4t$, where $\bar{R}^2(t)$ is the mean square displacement of released individuals at time when their density was measured.

2. If the distribution of marked individuals is sampled repeatedly, estimate $\bar{D}_i(t_i)$ separately for each sampling period, t_i. Calculate the mean diffusion coefficient $\hat{D}$, and use Formula 6.1 to generate the predicted density of recaptures at each time t_i.

3. Compare the predicted to the actual spatial distributions of marked individuals using the nonparametric Kolmogorov-Smirnov test.

Note that this procedure constitutes a stronger test of the simple diffusion model than simply testing for normality. This is because the null hypothesis will be rejected not only when the distribution of marked organisms is non-normal, but also when the diffusion rate changes with time. Additional points to keep in mind:

- If there is drift, then instead of calculating the variance of the spatial distribution around 0, $\bar{R}^2(t)$, calculate it around the estimated drift $\hat{\beta}t$. The predicted spatial distribution of recaptures should also be centered at $\hat{\beta}t$, not at 0.

- If a substantial proportion of individuals reaches the ends of the recapture array (more than 10–15%), then a modified formula for the truncated normal distribution of Kareiva (1982) should be used to estimate D.

- The approach described above assumes that you have measured absolute densities, that is, the number of individuals per unit of area. If your data consists of relative measures of density (that is, density multiplied by an unknown constant of proportionality; such measures typically arise when organisms are recaptured with traps), then you need to scale both the predictions and the observed numbers in a way that will make them comparable. For example, you can compare probability distributions by dividing the predicted density distribution by N_0, and the observed distribution by the total number of organisms recaptured at time t_i.

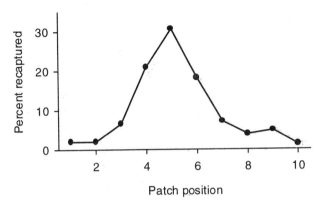

Figure 6.1: Recapture distribution of *Phyllotreta striolata* in a linear array with 6 m between patches (only one replicate is shown). (After Kareiva 1982.)

6.2.3   Example: diffusion in insects

Kareiva (1983) used his method to analyze the local dispersal of twelve species of herbivorous insects (Figure 6.1). He found that in 8 of 12 species the null hypothesis of simple diffusion was more often accepted than rejected. The typical deviation from the predicted distribution was about 10%. Only in two species were deviations consistently greater than 20%. Kareiva (1983) ascribed the success of simple diffusion at describing movement patterns of real insects to the simple environments in which dispersal was studied (such as golf courses, crops, and uniform meadows).

Typical departures from the pattern predicted by the simple diffusion model included a variation in D and deviations from the normal distribution. A frequently observed pattern in point-release studies is that D decreases with time. This could be due to agitation dispersal following the release, population heterogeneity for dispersal ability, or density dependence. Direct evidence for density dependence in D was provided by a case study involving *Trirhabda sericotrachyla* in which D increased from 0.19 m²/day (when 25 beetles per brush were released) to 0.43 m²/day (when 75 beetles per brush were released). Movement rate was also affected by the habitat within which releases took place, as indicated by a variation in D (*Nezara viridula*, both *Phyllotreta* species, and *Aporea crataegi*; see Kareiva 1983: Table 1).

Deviations from the Gaussian distribution in insect dispersal data occur most frequently in the direction of leptokurtosis (Okubo 1980, Kareiva 1983). This could be due to heterogeneous dispersal ability within the population of released organisms (see Okubo 1980:95-98). Another possibility is that dispersers become sedentary at a certain rate. Settlement of individuals violates the assumption of the simple diffusion model that individuals move continuously. It is interesting that one of the two cases showing the strongest departures from the normal distribution was the membracid *Publilia concava*, whose movement is characterized by its eventual settling on a particular goldenrod stem. Thus we expect and find a strongly leptokurtic recapture distribution for this species (Kareiva 1983).

6.2.4   Beyond the Gaussian distribution

Analyses of density-distance data almost always fit the data to the solution of the standard model, that is, simple diffusion from an instantaneous point release. The Gaussian curve provides an adequate fit in many situations, even if the assumptions of the standard model are violated to some degree. However, when the Gaussian fails, it should not be the end of the analysis. It is not very satisfactory to reject a model without an explicit alternative that works better. In Appendix A I have collected a number of solutions of the diffusion equation for various initial and boundary conditions, as well as for extensions of the simple diffusion model. Here I will consider some formulas that may prove useful in the analysis of data; and I hope that future analysts will find applications for other, more esoteric formulas that are listed in the Appendix.

Sometimes the release of all marked organisms at one point in space may cause problems, since this method causes overcrowding and may affect the initial dispersal (see Section 2.3.3). An alternative initial condition to the instantaneous point release is the instantaneous *area release*, in which a uniform density of organisms is established within the release area (e.g., Elkinton and Cardé 1980, see also Section 6.6.4). If the release area is approximately round, then the resulting density-distance curves can be fitted using Formula A.19. This formula does not give the solution in a closed form, however, and therefore has to be evaluated by a nonlinear least squares minimization algorithm. In one-dimensional diffusion the solution is much simpler (see Equation A.18).

Other possible deviations from the standard model may include different boundary conditions. Alternatives to the standard model's *zero at infinity* boundary conditions (Section A.2.1) include absorbing and reflecting boundary conditions. A number of solutions for the one-dimensional advection-diffusion model assuming an instantaneous point release and various combinations of boundary conditions are listed in Goel and Richter-Dyn (1974: Table 3.4).

Still other modifications may involve both initial and boundary conditions. The instantaneous point release involves an initial "pulse" of diffusing organisms. An alternative is to supply a steady "pressure" of organisms. For example, an area initially devoid of organisms may be located next to an area where organism density is constant. As organisms diffuse from the source patch into the empty patch, a population density gradient will become established in the direction perpendicular to the boundary dividing the two patches. This gradient will become more shallow with time as organisms fill the empty patch. The formula describing this gradient is given in Section A.2.2 (Equation A.17). An interesting example of the application of this formula to real data was developed by Thomas et al. (1990). They sprayed one part of a field of winter wheat with a pesticide, reducing the density of spiders in the sprayed part by 80–90%. Subsequent to spraying, Thomas et al. (1990) followed the spatio-temporal course of diffusion of spiders from the unsprayed part, using a grid of pitfall traps. The data were fitted with Equation A.17 using the NLIN procedure of SAS. Their data exhibited a steady convergence of the spider density in the sprayed part of the field to that in the unsprayed (source) part, and appeared to be well described by the simple diffusion model.

The next step after exploring the effects of the initial and the boundary conditions involves fitting solutions of various extensions of the simple diffusion equation. This stage of the analysis may reveal interesting, nontrivial features of the movement biology of the target organism. I have already indicated how to test for the advection (drift) term, and estimate its magnitude. Another realistic feature to add to the diffusion equation is a disappearance term. Disappearance from the population of marked organisms can be due to death or large-scale emigration from the experimental area. Disappearance rate does not affect the shape of the spatial distribution of marked organisms, but only their total number. For example, Equation A.50 in Section A.3.5 assumes that organisms disappear at a constant rate δ. When the disappearance rate is included, population density is multiplied by a term $\exp[-\delta t]$ which reflects the exponential decrease in the number of organisms (see Formula A.51).

When the spatial distribution of marked animals is significantly platykurtic, and there are no obvious barriers to their dispersal that would produce such a pattern, a possible explanation may be density-dependent dispersal. This possibility can be quantitatively explored by fitting the Okubo's density-dependent model (Equation A.30).

Finally, one of the most ubiquitous sources of deviation from simple diffusion is the effect of spatial heterogeneity on diffusion parameters. Quantifying spatially variable diffusion is not a trivial task, however. There are few analytical results (see Section A.2.4), but, speaking generally, fitting density-distance curves to data is not well suited to answering this question. I will take up this topic again in Section 6.4.

TESTING FOR HETEROGENEITY IN DISPERSAL ABILITY   Kareiva's (1983) method provides a rather blunt tool for investigating the deviations from the simple diffusion. If we find that the assumption of normality is rejected, then all we can say is that distribution is either platykurtic or leptokurtic. Leptokurtic distribution may arise when two or more subpopulations of moving organisms with different diffusion rates are summed together. Thus, if we observe significant leptokurtosis, instead of fitting the simple diffusion model with a common diffusion rate, we may instead attempt to estimate three parameters: diffusion rates of the two subpopulations D_1 and D_2, and p, the proportion of individuals belonging to subpopulation 1. This task is equivalent to estimating the variances and the mixing proportion in a mixture of two normal distributions (e.g., James 1978).

Another approach, proposed by Inoue (1978), may also be of help in such situations. Let $F(r)$ be the proportion of marked individuals that are enclosed by a circle of radius r. Inoue showed that log-transformed $1 - F$ (that is, the proportion of organisms traveling *beyond* radius r) is linearly related to r^2, assuming simple diffusion from the instantaneous source:

$$\ln(1 - F) = -r^2/(4Dt) \tag{6.2}$$

Furthermore, if the population of marked organisms consists of two subpopulations, slow movers characterized by a low diffusion rate D_s, and fast movers with high D_f, then the relationship between $\ln(1 - F)$ and r^2 will be approximately piecewise linear. Near the origin (small r^2) the slope will be determined by D_s, and far from the origin the slope of the curve will be dominated by D_f. The abscissa of the intersection point r_0 is given by

$$r_0^2 = 4t\frac{D_s D_f}{D_s - D_f}\ln q \tag{6.3}$$

where q is the proportion of fast-moving organisms. Inoue (1978) proposed that this compound curve be fitted with two straight lines. In this way the diffusion rates of each subpopulation can be extracted from the data. Using the estimated diffusion rates and the location of the intersection point, we can calculate q, the proportion of individuals moving with the diffusion rate D_f. Inoue (1978) applied this technique to a number of insect data sets and found that in some cases the relationship between $\ln(1 - F)$ and r^2 was indeed linear, while in other cases there appeared a more or less distinct breakpoint, separating two quasilinear pieces.

6.2.5 Time-integrated density data

Time-integrated density data can arise in a number of ways. They are actually the most commonly encountered type of data in dispersal studies. Most typically, time-integrated data comes from studies in which organisms are recaptured with traps. A trap integrates population density over time, since organisms captured early during the trapping period are added to the organisms captured late. A trap also performs some integration of density over space (see Section 6.6.3), however, we customarily ignore this effect because we assume that the effective sampling area is significantly less than the extent of spatial dispersal (if this assumption is seriously violated, then trap data becomes useless for quantifying dispersal). Second, time-integrated data can also result from indirect measures of organism density, for example, when the density distribution of eggs or host plant damage is used to infer presence of organisms. Third, organisms that have a tendency to settle down should be analyzed using time-integrated methods. For example, if organisms have a constant probability of terminating movement (per unit of time), then the number of organisms settling in any particular locality will be proportional to an integral of density of moving organisms. Finally, organisms may be released continuously rather than at a single point in time. Even though the distribution of organisms that started movement at the same time may be Gaussian, the total distribution will include both organisms that started recently and those that started long ago. Such data should also be analyzed using time-integrated methods, since population density at any given point in time is the sum of all dispersers, both early- and late-starters.

Sometimes the data are intermediate between the two extremes, for example, when traps are emptied repeatedly at regular time intervals. If the spatial distribution of marked organisms changes slowly during the interval between trap collections, then instantaneous methods can be employed. If the collection interval is too long with respect to population density change, then all collections for the same trap can be added together and the data analyzed with time-averaged methods. Alternatively, if one does not want to lose information by adding recaptures at the same trap together, then it will be necessary to write an explicit integral model, and fit its parameters using nonlinear fitting techniques.

An interesting distinction between instantaneous and time-integrated methods is that for the former we can often ignore the loss of marked organisms in the analysis, while in the latter it is often necessary to include the loss term explicitly. There are several reasons for this. Most importantly, a time-integrated solution of a diffusion equation is derived under the assumption that we integrate over a long period of time (formally, $t \to \infty$). It is unrealistic to assume that all marked organisms will be present during the whole time period. Some of them will die, others may be lost due to long-range emigration (e.g., insects flying above the boundary layer and carried away by weather systems). Yet other organisms may lose their mark, and some will leave the diffusing population by settling down, or burrowing into the substrate. The simplest way of modeling this is to assume that organisms are lost to the dispersing population at a constant rate per unit of time. The loss rate summarizes the effects all of the above processes (and maybe others), since it is usually impractical to separate their individual contributions. The assumption of constant loss rate implies exponential decrease in the number of marked organisms with time. This appears to be a reasonable first approximation, and the solutions for diffusion with more realistic loss functions have typically to be obtained numerically.

Models of diffusion with loss and their solutions are reviewed in Section A.3.5 in the Appendix. The parameters D and δ are the rates of spatial spread (diffusion) and of disappearance (e.g., death). When organisms are recaptured with traps, we need another parameter α, the *effective sampling rate* of traps (Schneider 1998). This parameter is the constant of proportionality between density of organisms in the vicinity of a trap, $u(x, y, t)$, and trap catch, $c(x, y, t)$, such that $c(x, y, t) = \alpha u(x, y, t)$. If δ is the rate with which organisms settle (leave the moving population) and we are interested in the spatial distribution of settled organisms, then $\alpha = \delta$. Formulas for the total number of animals captured in a trap over the course of the whole experiment (that is, waiting until all the marked animals have died off) are given in the Box 6.2, both for 1D and 2D spatial domains.

Note that Formula 6.4 is the same as the negative exponential curve, $C(x) = a \exp[-bx]$, that is frequently used in empirical analyses of density-distance relationships (see Section 3.3). Unlike the phenomenological negative exponential curve, however, the parameters in Equation 6.4 have a biological interpretation as combinations of D, δ, α, and N_0. If two quantities out of four are known, then the other two can be estimated by fitting the density-distance curve to data. For example, if we know the number of released animals and the effective sampling rate, we can estimate the diffusion and the loss rates.

The solution for the 2D case resembles the negative exponential curve, but with an additional multiplier $r^{-1/2}$. This multiplier reflects the area-dilution effect of symmetric diffusion in two-dimensional space (see Section A.1.5). The inverse square root of r varies with r at a much slower rate than an exponential, and thus the density-distance curve at larger r will be completely dominated by the negative exponential part. This similarity in functional form explains why fitting density-distance data with the negative exponential curve often produces adequate results. However, fitting the data with the Bessel curve (Formula 6.5) or its approximation (Formula 6.6) can yield estimates of biologically meaningful parameters, as I pointed out above.

Several useful quantities can be extracted from the fitted diffusion coefficients, including the median dispersal distance, or the radius of a circle enclosing 50% of dispersal end points, $r_{0.5}$ (Turchin and Thoeny 1993). Similarly, we can calculate $r_{0.95}$ or $r_{0.99}$, the radii enclosing 95% or 99% of dispersal distances, respectively. These numbers provide readily interpretable statistics describing the spatial scale of dispersal. The mean and variance of dispersal distances can be calculated directly: $E[R] = 0.5\pi B$; and $\text{Var}(R) = 4B^2(1 - \pi^2/16)$ (Curry and Feldman 1987:147).

Box 6.2 Formulas for time-integrated data.

For 1D space, define the total catch in a trap (as $t \to \infty$) as $C(x) = \int_0^\infty c(x,t)\,dt = \alpha \int_0^\infty u(x,t)\,dt$. Then,

$$C(x) = \frac{\alpha N_0}{2\sqrt{D\delta}} \exp\left[-\sqrt{\frac{\delta}{D}}\,|x|\right] \qquad (6.4)$$

where D is the diffusion rate, δ is the disappearance rate, α is the trap effective sampling rate, N_0 is the total number of organisms released, and x is the distance from the release point.

For 2D space, total trap catch is defined in the same way, but it is now a function of $r = \sqrt{x^2 + y^2}$, the distance from the release point in 2D space:

$$C(r) = \frac{\alpha N_0}{2\pi D} K_0\left(\sqrt{\frac{\delta}{D}}\,r\right) \qquad (6.5)$$

Here $K_0(z)$ is a modified Bessel function of the second kind. This formula can be further approximated as follows:

$$C(r) = Ar^{-\frac{1}{2}} \exp\left[-\frac{r}{B}\right] \qquad (6.6)$$

where $A = \alpha N_0 (8\pi)^{-\frac{1}{2}} (D^3\delta)^{-\frac{1}{4}}$ and $B = \sqrt{D/\delta}$.

EXTENSIONS OF THE DIFFUSION WITH LOSS MODEL   There are two extensions of the basic diffusion with loss model that may prove helpful in the analysis of some data sets. Awerbuch et al. (1979) provide a solution of the model for more realistic initial and boundary conditions. They assumed that the initial release of particles is evenly distributed in a circle of radius a, and that the boundary condition at $r = R$ is of the reflecting kind. Furthermore, their solution specifies the number of particles captured at any given point in space during a finite period of time (between $t = T_1$ and $t = T_2$). Thus, if traps are collected several times during the course of a MMR study then their solution can be used to analyze each trapping collection episode separately. However, their formula involves infinite sums (see Awerbuch et al. 1979: Equation 7), so one has to determine iteratively how many terms to retain.

The second extension should prove very useful for analyzing dispersal with drift. For example, dispersal may be affected by the wind or absolute direction. To account for such directional effects, Curry and Feldman (1987) added an advection term (with the drift parameter β) to the diffusion with loss model. Their solution for the instantaneous point release and zero-at-infinity boundary condition is given by Equation A.61.

APPLICATIONS   The Bessel function has been applied in several mark-recapture studies of insect dispersal such as the tobacco budworm (Schneider et al. 1989, Schneider 1997) and the southern pine beetle (Turchin and Thoeny 1993). An example of translating fitted parameters A and B into the mechanistic parameters D, δ, and α will be discussed in Section 6.7.1.

6.2.6 Synthesis

The main issue addressed by this section is the estimation of the rate of dispersal using mass mark-recapture data. Essentially, the approach is to fit the density-distance curve predicted by a mechanistic model of movement to the observed densities of marked organisms. It is important to keep in mind that we are not directly estimating the distribution of dispersal distances. However, we can estimate it indirectly by first fitting a model to density data, and then using the model with fitted parameters to infer the distribution of dispersal distances. As a result of adopting this approach, we do not need to worry about recapturing a large proportion of organisms (although we want to recapture enough so that we obtain reasonable estimates of density, especially at locations far from the release point). The corollary is that points at which the density of marked organisms is measured should be placed in a way that will maximize the amount of information for fitting models. In particular, since distance from release is one of the most important variables, marked organisms should be sampled at as many different distances as is practical (see Section 2.3.5).

The specific formulas used in the analysis are derived from a variety of diffusion models, starting with simple diffusion from a point release, and then considering such realistic features of movement as directional biases in movement (drift), death or settlement rate, effects of various kinds of boundary conditions, and the influence of different ways to release organisms. I stress that instantaneous and time-integrated data should be treated very differently, and I present two separate series of formulas for each of these cases. The approach is to use "canned" formulas, which works as long as we can assume that the environment is *quasihomogeneous*. In other words, spatial heterogeneity must be sufficiently fine-scaled so we can average over it. Analysis of dispersal in heterogeneous environments, or of attraction (spatially-varying biases in movement), has to employ approaches different from the ones discussed in this Section (see Sections 6.4 and 6.6).

6.3 Population Spread and Dispersal "Tails"

Population spread is probably the best-studied example of spatio-temporal dynamics in ecology. General models of population spread have been used in many areas of ecology, ranging in scale from the dynamics of focus expansion in plant epidemics (on the spatial scale of meters) to geographic invasions and range expansions (on the scale of thousands of kilometers). Models of population spread also have many important applications in such fields as pest control, biological conservation, and human epidemiology.

The purpose of this section is not to review the voluminous literature on population spread, which has been well covered by others (e.g., Kornberg and Williamson 1986, Hengeveld 1989, Okubo et al. 1989, Andow et al. 1990, Shigesada et al. 1995, Kot et al. 1996). Of the two mechanisms underlying population spread, local population growth and spatial redistribution of organisms or propagules, only the second one is relevant to the subject matter of this book. Not surprisingly, however, movement behaviors of organisms are of key importance in understanding and predicting the qualitative and quantitative patterns of population spread. My goal here, therefore, is to review approaches to quantifying dispersal with the purpose of understanding and predicting population spread. I begin with a review of some relevant theory in order to explain why, when studying spread, we need to focus on one particular aspect of movement—the behavior of the tail of the probability distribution of dispersal distances.

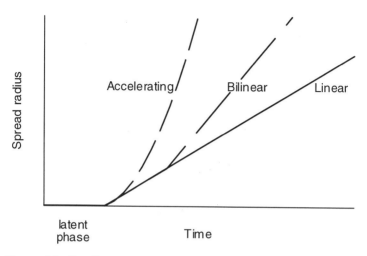

Figure 6.2: Qualitative types of population spread. Spread radius is calculated as a square root of the total area occupied by the species, divided by $\sqrt{\pi}$. (modified from Shigesada 1995.)

6.3.1 Movement patterns and qualitative types of spread

Most biological invasions go through an initial phase of no apparent expansion, either because it may take some time for population density to increase above the detection threshold, or because the invading species needs to undergo a period of adaptation to local conditions before its numbers can increase. After this initial "latent phase," a spectrum of qualitative behaviors may occur, ranging from the *linear* type of spread, characterized by a constant rate of radius expansion, to the *accelerating* pattern, in which the rate of spread continuously increases with time (Figure 6.2). A variety of intermediate patterns are also possible. The *bilinear* pattern shown in Figure 6.2 is characterized by an initially slow range increase followed by an abrupt change to a faster constant rate of increase. An accelerating type of spread may be further subclassified into a rapid exponential (or even faster than exponential) range increase ("explosive acceleration"), or slower parabolic one. Finally, there may be more than one change in the expansion rate, leading to a piece-wise linear pattern. Many empirical examples of different patterns of range expansion are found in Hengeveld (1989) and Shigesada et al. (1995). Connections between

Table 6.1: Theoretical predictions relating different qualitative types of spread to assumptions about dispersal in models.

Spread type	Model, dispersal tail	Reference
Linear	Reaction-diffusion models	Fisher 1937, Skellam 1951
Linear	Spatial contact model, exponentially-bounded tails	Mollison 1972
Linear	Integro-difference model, exponentially-bounded tails	Kot et al. 1996
Linear	Stratified dispersal model, constant colonization rate	Shigesada et al. 1995
Bilinear	Stratified dispersal model, linear colonization rate	Shigesada et al. 1995
Accelerating	Stratified dispersal model, quadratic colonization rate	Shigesada et al. 1995
Accelerating (parabolic)	Integro-difference model, exponentially-unbounded tails, finite variance	Kot et al. 1996
Accelerating (explosive)	Spatial contact model, exponentially-unbounded tails, infinite variance	Mollison 1972
Accelerating (explosive)	Integro-difference model, exponentially-unbounded tails, infinite variance	Kot et al. 1996

various models and qualitative types of spread are mapped in Table 6.1.

Determining which of the qualitative patterns characterizes a particular instance of population spread is of great importance in predicting the rate of range expansion. Expansion rate can be predicted empirically by observing the pattern of past spread and then extrapolating it in the future. However, this approach is unsatisfactory for two reasons. First, a population expanding linearly may not continue to do so in the future—it may be just about to undergo a shift to a faster expansion velocity. Second, observing a spread process for a long time may not be an option if predictions are needed immediately. Additionally, if we wait until the pattern of spread is established, the invading species may run out of free space to expand into. Thus, the question arises, Can we predict the pattern and rate of a population spread process by quantifying the mechanisms underlying it?

The theory reviewed in Section A.4 suggests that the details of population growth will primarily have quantitative effects on the rate of population spread. For example, if population redistribution is governed by diffusion (alternatively referred to as "local," "neighborhood," or "step-by-step" diffusion in the biological invasions literature), then the pattern of spread will resemble a steadily advancing front. The rate of spread will be given by $2\sqrt{\alpha D}$, where D is the diffusion coefficient and α is the rate of population growth at low population density. In other words, we should observe a linear pattern of spread. For more complex population growth terms than the logistic (e.g., Allee effects, or population interactions with competitors and predators), α has to be reinterpreted appropriately (see Section A.4). However, as long as dispersal is local (well described by diffusion) the qualitative pattern of spread will be unchanged.

When there is the possibility of long-distance dispersal (in other words, when diffusion provides a poor description of movement process), patterns other than linear may occur. The key aspect of dispersal, determining the qualitative pattern of spread, is the tail of the dispersal kernel (*dispersal kernel* is the functional form describing the probability distribution of dispersal distances, see Section A.4.3). The most important special case is the *exponential tail* in which the probability of long-distance dispersal is described by the formula $V(r) = a\exp[-br]$, where r is distance from the source of dispersers (since we are concerned with the tail, we assume that $r >> 0$) and a and b are constants. When plotted on the graph of log-transformed density against the *untransformed* distance, exponential tails look like straight lines (Figure 6.3). If the probability of moving to r (or, equivalently, the density of dispersers at r) drops off exponentially with distance or faster (for example the Gaussian tail that is predicted by simple diffusion; see Figure 6.3), then the results from diffusion theory hold and we should observe linear spread. If the probability of moving to r declines slower than exponentially (e.g., the power tail in Figure 6.3), two further possibilities need to be distinguished. (1) If the probability distribution of dispersal distances is characterized by a finite variance, then rate of spread will increase until reaching some asymptotic value. (2) If the variance is infinite, then the rate of spread will continue to increase with time. The general pattern of spread will be characterized by "great leaps forward" in which some propagules will get established far ahead of the population front, soon becoming sources of more propagules for more spread and for further leaps forward covering even more ground ("explosive" spread).

To summarize, in many spatial ecological applications other than spread we can safely ignore events of low probability. When studying population

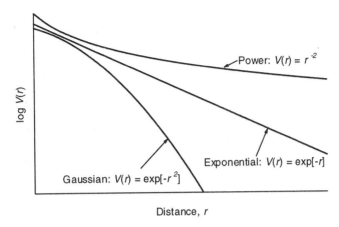

Figure 6.3: Dispersal tails: exponential; Gaussian, declining faster than exponential; and power, declining more slowly than exponential.

spread, however, the presence of rare long-distance dispersers may have profound influence on both its qualitative pattern and its quantitative rate. If the tails of the dispersal distance distribution decline exponentially or faster, then we can apply the well-developed reaction-diffusion framework to quantify the rate of population spread. This is the approach taken by the majority of authors, and I review several such studies in Section 6.3.2. A much more difficult job is predicting spread when dispersal distribution is characterized by non-exponential tails. The few approaches that have been proposed up to date will be discussed in Sections 6.3.3–6.3.4.

6.3.2 Diffusion-based approaches

Predictions of reaction-diffusion models regarding population spread can be tested at two levels of detail. The first, cruder, approach is to test the qualitative prediction that the rate of spread should be linear. This was the approach taken by Skellam (1951) who applied a diffusion model to data on the spread of muskrats in Europe, and later by Lubina and Levin (1988) on reinvasion by the California sea otter. More examples can be found in Hengeveld (1989) and Andow et al. (1990: Table 1).

The second approach, which provides a much more comprehensive test, is to estimate the parameters of population growth and redistribution (α and D)

from microscale data, and then to compare diffusion model predictions with observed quantitative features of spread (Andow et al. 1990). This approach, or similar ones, was employed in several case studies (although not always carried through to the point of comparing microscale-based predictions to macroscale observations). Examples include the spread of farming in neolithic Europe (Ammerman and Cavalli-Sforza 1973), the spread of rabies among foxes (Murray et al. 1986), the invasion of collared doves in Europe (Hengeveld 1989: Chapter 8), the prediction of the velocity of advance of foot and mouth disease in feral pigs (Pech and McIlroy 1990), and the spread of an insect pathogen (Dwyer 1992). A good illustration of this approach is provided by Andow et al. (1990).

Andow et al. examined the population spread in the muskrat, the cereal leaf beetle, and the small cabbage white butterfly. They estimated α either by constructing life tables or by calculating the slope of $\log N(t)$ versus time curves for populations growing approximately exponentially (before being limited by density-dependent feedbacks). They then estimated D from mark-recapture data, using the methods similar to those described in Section 6.2. This procedure yielded the predicted velocity of range expansion using the formula $c^* = 2\sqrt{\alpha D}$.

Their next step was to calculate the observed radius of the area occupied by each invading species. For those species invading relatively homogeneous environments they estimated the radius by dividing the range into eight sectors, measuring the radius of spread in each sector separately, and then calculating the root mean square radius (since the appropriate quantities to be averaged are areas, rather than radii) for successive points in time. For invasions that occurred in conspicuously heterogeneous regions Andow et al. divided the spread records into sectors whose boundaries reflected major irregularities (rivers, mountain ranges, etc). An average radius for each sector was calculated as the root mean square of the maximum and minimum radial distances of the pertinent sector.

Comparing the predicted and observed rates of spread (Table 6.2), we see that in two cases (the cabbage whites and the muskrat) the agreement between theory and data is good, while in one case (the cereal leaf beetle) the diffusion model predictions are off by two orders of magnitude. Andow et al. (1990) speculated that population spread in the cereal leaf beetle may be governed by processes not observable on the microscale at which their movements were quantified, for example, long-range movement on air currents or hitchhiking on human transport. One further observation to note is that although the theoretical and observed rates of spread for cabbage butterflies were reasonably similar, the qualitative pattern of spread significantly deviated from that

Table 6.2: Comparison of observed rates of spread to the rates predicted by the diffusion model. (From Andow et al. 1990.)

Invading species	α (y^{-1})	D (km^2 y^{-1})	Rate of spread (km y^{-1}) predicted	observed
Cereal leaf beetle	1.6–1.9	0.4	1.6–1.7	26–89
Small cabbage white	9–32	4.8	13–127	15–170
Muskrat	0.2–1.1	51–230	6.4–32	0.9–25

predicted by diffusion (Andow et al. 1990: Table 1). In fact, cabbage white appears to exhibit an accelerating pattern of spread. To summarize, only the muskrat case study conformed to both the qualitative and quantitative predictions of the diffusion model. The small cabbage white exhibited a nonlinear pattern of spread, while the rate of spread predicted for the cereal leaf beetle was much lower than observed.

Even though we may expect the diffusion-based approach to fail in any particular application, it is still a valuable first step in a mechanistic analysis of population spread. The diffusion model and its prediction $c^* = \sqrt{\alpha D}$ provides a null hypothesis. When the null hypothesis is not rejected, we have a working mechanistic model for range expansion. When it is rejected, the pattern of deviation between the predictions and observations will often suggest why the model failed. If the deviation is quantitative and not too extreme, then we may attempt to develop a better model within the reaction-diffusion framework. For example, we may attempt to fit a generalized diffusion model with spatially-varying coefficients, or include a drift term. It is also possible that the representation of birth/death processes in the model can be improved by including an Allee effect or by accounting for interactions with competitors or predators. Many potentially useful reaction-diffusion models are reviewed in Section A.4.

However, tinkering within the reaction-diffusion framework is likely to be of limited value. The currently prevailing paradigm is that the diffusion equation provides a poor framework for quantifying population spread (e.g., Kot et al. 1996). When considered on the intergenerational time scale, which is the one relevant to population spread, dispersal kernels are rarely well described by diffusion, and typically have fat (flatter than exponential) tails (with all the consequences for the pattern and rate of spread). Thus, my recommendation is to always go beyond diffusion methods.

Presently, we have two alternatives to the standard (local, neighborhood, step-by-step) diffusion models for dispersal. One approach is to use a stratified dispersal model; the other approach is based on spatial contact models and their relatives. The stratified dispersal (also known as hierarchical or stratified diffusion) approach assumes that there are two (or more) spatial scales at which dispersal occurs: local diffusion resulting in a steady front advance, and long-distance dispersal events resulting in establishment of new colonies far in advance of the front. One example of such a two-phase approach is the model of Rvachev and Longini (1985) that combines within-city and inter-city modes of influenza spread. Another example is the model of stratified dispersal developed by Shigesada et al. (1995). A stratified dispersal model is particularly appropriate when dispersal is a result of two completely distinct mechanisms characterized by extremely different distributions of dispersal lengths. For example, in the gypsy moth, small larvae disperse tens or hundreds of meters by ballooning, while an occasional eggcase attached to a recreational vehicle may be moved hundreds or thousands of kilometers. Similarly, most acorns fall very near the parent tree, but a few are cached by animals hundreds of meters away. In such cases, estimating the parameters of the stratified dispersal model is straightforward—we simply do it twice for data resulting from each different dispersal mechanism, and then combine the two processes using a model like the one developed by Shigesada et al. (1995).

In many situations, however, we cannot make an assumption that dispersal is a result of two distinct mechanisms. The distribution of the dispersal distance is continuous but is characterized by a fat tail. Theory tells us that if the tail is sufficiently fat, then the pattern of population spread will resemble that postulated by stratified diffusion. How can we approach the analysis of such cases? The problem is difficult but some promising approaches have been recently developed, such as the R&D kernel model reviewed in the next section.

6.3.3   The R&D kernel framework

The mathematical theory underlying the redistribution-and-dispersal (R&D) kernel models (van den Bosch 1988a,b,c, 1990a,b, 1992) is reviewed in Section A.4.4. The main advantage of the R&D kernel model over diffusion is that it explicitly addresses the effect of non-Gaussian dispersal kernels. In particular, van den Bosch and coworkers derived an approximate formula (Equation A.81) that relates the asymptotic velocity of population spread to net reproduction rate, the mean and the variance of the age at reproduction, the variance and the kurtosis of the dispersal kernel, and a measure of the interaction between reproduction and dispersal.

Van den Bosch and coworkers applied their analytic machinery to a number

Table 6.3: Comparison of observed velocity of population expansion, c_{obs}, the rate predicted by the diffusion model, c_{diff}, and the rate predicted by the R&D kernel model, $c_{R\&D}$. Percentages of deviation from the observed velocity, $100\% \times (PRED - OBS)/OBS$, are indicated in the parentheses. (Modified from van den Bosch et al. 1992.)

| | Rate of spread, km y^{-1} | | | | |
Species	c_{obs}	c_{diff}		$c_{R\&D}$	
Collared dove	43.7	56.3	(+29)	65.6	(+50)
Muskrat, 1900-30	10.9	4.8	(−56)	7.0	(−36)
Muskrat, 1930-60	5.1	3.3	(−35)	3.9	(−24)
Starling	91.6	46.3	(−50)	77.9	(−15)
Cattle egret	106.2	91.4	(−14)	135.2	(+27)
House sparrow, USA	16.8	6.0	(−64)	10.2	(−39)
House sparrow, Europe	27.9	8.2	(−71)	23.0	(−18)
Average			−37%		−8%

of case-studies, ranging in spatial scale from centimeters to hundreds of kilometers. At the lower end of the scale, van den Bosch et al. (1988c) predicted the rate of focus expansion in plant disease (striped rust in winter wheat). They fitted the reproduction data using a gamma probability distribution and the dispersal kernel using Bessel density. The rate of spread predicted by their formula based on these fitted relationships was 8.0 ± 1.5 cm day^{-1}, which compares well with the observed rate of 9.4 ± 0.8 cm day^{-1}.

In a subsequent paper, van den Bosch et al. (1992) compared the predictions of the diffusion versus R&D kernel approaches regarding range expansion in four bird and one mammal species (which was the ubiquitous muskrat). As we would expect from the review of general theory (see Section 6.3.1), the diffusion model generally underpredicted the rate of spread, with 4 out of 7 cases underpredicted by a factor of two or worse (Table 6.3). The predictions of the R&D kernel model were, in general closer to the observed rates of spread (Table 6.3). In particular, the overall bias in the R&D kernel predictions was only −8%, compared to the diffusion model bias of −37%.

Most recently, Metz and van den Bosch (1995) gathered together ten comparisons between the R&D kernel predictions and the observed rates of spread, in case studies spanning spatial scales over four orders of magnitude. In general, the approach did a very good job in predicting data, with all predictions within 50% of the observed rates (Metz and Van den Bosch 1995).

6.3.4   Quantifying dispersal tails

While the approach of van den Bosch and coworkers works quite well for many data sets, we should expect it to fail in some extreme cases (for example, I doubt R&D kernel model would accurately predict the rate of spread in the cereal leaf beetle; see Table 6.2). The approach may fail either because there is an additional mechanism of long-distance dispersal that is not captured by the available movement data (that is, we are dealing with stratified dispersal), or because the distribution of dispersal distances does not conform to the assumptions of the formulas of van den Bosch et al. (1992). These formulas assume that the tail of the dispersal kernel is well-behaved; in particular, that certain moments of the distribution, such as variance, are finite. The consequence of this assumption is that the rate of spread eventually approaches the asymptote c^*. Yet it is conceivable that the distribution of dispersal distances may have such a "fat tail" that the variance is infinite, and we know of some examples of biological invasions in which the rate of spread accelerates explosively until all available space is occupied (e.g., geographical expansion of cheat grass in western North America; Mack 1981). What is worrisome is that the method of van den Bosch et al. does not check whether the dispersal tail is well-behaved or not.

What we need is a method to directly probe the structure of the tail of the dispersal kernel. This is a difficult task. First, we may not have the appropriate data, lacking an empirical approach for detecting a sufficient number of rare events of long-distance dispersal. Second, assuming we can collect such data, we will then need statistical methods for making inferences about the shape of the dispersal tail. Of the several approaches to this issue of which I am aware, none appears to be satisfactory. Of the two approaches mentioned above, the R&D kernel model of van den Bosch and coworkers and the stratified dispersal model of Shigesada et al. (1995), neither directly addresses the question of what shape the dispersal tail is. The first focuses on approximations using higher moments, while the second summarizes the whole tail with a fixed dispersal distance (parameter L in Shigesada et al. 1995) that is set equal to the approximate mean of observed long-distance dispersal events.

An interesting approach was developed by Portnoy and Wilson (1993), who argued that the tail of the dispersal kernel in a wide range of stochastic dispersal processes could be approximated by the following relationship:

$$V(r) = a r^{-\phi} \exp[-b r^{\theta}] \qquad (6.7)$$

where r is the distance from the seed source. We have already encountered this formula under the guise of the empirical model X (Table 3.1). This functional form includes many mechanistic and phenomenological dispersal-distance curves as special cases: the familiar negative exponential (if $\phi = 0$ and $\theta = 1$), the Gaussian ($\phi = 0$ and $\theta = 2$), and the Bessel distribution, whose tail is characterized by $\phi = 1/2$ and $\theta = 1$. Additionally, for $\theta = 1$, Formula 6.7 is the same as the probability density function of the Gamma distribution.

Portnoy and Wilson (1993) developed a statistical approach to determine which model describes the data best (and most parsimoniously): the full model (Equation 6.7), its power submodel (that is, setting $\theta = 0$), or its exponential submodel (setting $\phi = 0$). There are many important ideas in this paper, but the actual method that Portnoy and Wilson used suffered from several limitations (see their discussion). Furthermore, I disagree with the statistical philosophy guiding their approach, which was based on testing each model against an unspecified alternative (that is, making a decision whether to accept or to reject a model). For instance, Portnoy and Wilson used a modified χ^2 statistic to accept or reject each of the three possible models (the algebraic, the exponential, or the full model). The consequence of this approach is that all models can be rejected, leaving us with no conclusion—something that it is especially likely to happen when we have abundant and detailed data! This is in fact what happened in the Portnoy and Wilson analysis—all models were rejected for several case-studies that had extremely large sample sizes. A much better approach is to explicitly contrast rival models to each other and select the best alternative among them. It would probably be a good idea to add a null model, for example, that the tail is flat. (This is a biologically nonsensical result, so if none of the other alternatives fits the data significantly better than this null hypothesis, we should conclude that the data are too poor to permit making any conclusions.)

In another useful article, Kot et al. (1996) give a very clear exposition of how different dispersal kernels in integrodifference models lead to various qualitative patterns of spread. These authors also illustrate their ideas on the Dobzhansky and Wright data on *Drosophila* dispersal. Their specific approach was to fit several phenomenological models to the *Drosophila* data (models I, II, V, VI, and VIII in Table 3.1), and to deduce the pattern of population spread implied by each of the fitted models. Again, there are several important ideas in this paper, but the specific approach used to quantify dispersal tails is, in my opinion, unsatisfactory. In particular, I do not think that fitting dispersal data with a multitude of purely phenomenological curves is a good approach (see Section 3.3). Second, Kot et al. fitted the whole data set, although we are primarily interested in the tail. The best fitting curve may fit the points near the origin and fare poorly in the tail. Third, judging by Figure 1 in Kot et al. (1996) (unfortunately, the authors did not explain how fits were obtained), the curves were fitted by minimizing least-squared deviations between *untransformed* data and model predictions. This procedure, again, gives the most weight to points near origin, where population densities were highest.

Combining ideas from several sources, I advance the following (tentative) proposal on how to investigate the shape of dispersal tails. The data can be organized in two ways. One is to count the number of dispersers or propagules falling within certain distance intervals. The approach to analyzing such data is essentially the same as fitting density-distance curves (see Section 6.2), but with several twists. The key issue that we need to resolve is whether the tail decreases with distance exponentially (or faster), or whether the tail is fat. In other words, we want to know whether the relationship between $\ln u(r)$ and r is linear [where $u(r)$ is the density of dispersers at distance r from the source], or whether it curves up or down. Therefore, the first step in the analysis is simply to plot $\ln u$ versus r. Next, we wish to statistically assess the degree of support for or against a fat tail. Several approaches are possible. One is to fit a model with $\ln u$ as the dependent variable and r and r^2 as independent variables, and determine whether the coefficient associated with r^2 is significantly greater than zero. Another approach is to fit log-transformed density, $\ln u$, against power-transformed distance, r^θ. The dispersal kernel underlying this model is

$$V(r) = A \exp\left[\left(\frac{x}{B}\right)^\theta\right] \tag{6.8}$$

(let us call it the *θ-exponential kernel*, for lack of better name). In this model, we would test whether $\theta > 1$. In both cases, we would need to worry about the distribution of residuals. However, it is often the case with these kinds of data that log-transforming u tends to also stabilize the variance, so we can usually employ regular least squares regression (linear when testing for the presence of the quadratic term, nonlinear when testing for $\theta > 1$). Another important question is where does the tail begin, or what is the optimal cut-off value. This will depend on the specific application and the quantity of the data (log-transformation requires no zero counts for any distance interval), but the general rule of thumb is that we should be at least 2-3 standard deviations away from 0. Finally, we should worry about any potential censoring of data, which may occur when the probability of detecting a disperser declines with distance.

The second way to organize the data is to focus on the behavior of the largest observed dispersal distances (extreme values). As Portnoy and Wilson

(1993) suggest, this is potentially a much more powerful approach as compared to fitting density-distance curves. A number of statistical approaches are available, in fact, there is a well-developed statistical literature on analyzing the tails of empirical distributions (Smith 1987, Dekkers et al. 1989). For example, Smith (1987) describes methods for estimating the parameters of the generalized Pareto distribution, which apparently provides a good approximation to tails of a variety of probability distributions (both fat- and thin-tailed). Another approach, suggested by Portnoy and Wilson (1993), is to focus on the largest 30–40 actual distance measurements, and analyze the differences between successive extreme differences. Here is a proposal further developing that idea. Rank extreme distances in the order from smallest (r_1) to largest (r_n) and calculate differences $d_i = r_{i+1} - r_i$. Since these distances should be proportional to the inverse of density, for the case of the exponential tail, log-transformed d_i should increase linearly with r_i. As in the analysis of categorized counts, we are looking for curvilinearities of the rate direction to suggest fat tails. The difference, however, is that we are using each extreme dispersal event as a data point, which results in a more efficient utilization of data. Additionally, we do not have the problem of zero counts that cannot be log-transformed. This is just a sketch of the idea for the analysis. Clearly, better methods for characterizing tails are desperately needed.

Once we have determined whether we are dealing with a fat tail, or not, we can proceed by using the methodology of Section 6.2 to fit the mechanistic model we have developed for the organism's dispersal. However, we need to make sure that our mechanistic model is congruent with the qualitative type of the dispersal kernel. Thus, if statistical evidence strongly favors a fat tail, then Gaussian and Bessel curves are ruled out. On the other hand, models for dispersal of winged seeds that are characterized by power tails (Portnoy and Wilson 1993) would be inconsistent with exponential tails. In case we do not have a reasonable mechanism-based model for dispersal, but are nevertheless interested in exploring the consequences of the estimated tail for population spread, I suggest using the θ-exponential kernel as the best of the phenomenological alternatives. Even though it is not based on any particular mechanism, its advantage is that it is closely tied to the theoretical predictions on how the tail's shape affects the qualitative pattern of spread.

6.3.5 Inverse approach

An especially striking example of mismatch between microscale predictions and actual patterns of spread is "Reid's paradox" (Clark et al. 1998a). Using radiocarbon-dated pollen sequences from lakes, paleoecologists estimate that average rates of spread in many common tree species can be very rapid. For

example, tree migration rates following last ice age typically exceed 0.1 km
per year (e.g., Davis 1976, see Clark et al. 1998a for review). By contrast,
average dispersal distances measured in the field are less than 0.1 km *per
generation*. Thus, the rates of spread predicted from microscale data are at
least two orders of magnitude less than the rates of spread observed in the
paleorecord (for detailed predictions incorporating species-specific dispersal
and reproduction rates see Clark 1998: Table 1 and Figure 1). Clark et al.
(1998a) termed this discrepancy "Reid's Paradox" in honor of the Clement
Reid's calculations of seemingly impossible seed dispersal distances required
to spread oaks into great Britain at the end of Pleistocene.

One possible approach to resolving Reid's Paradox is to argue that seed
dispersal kernels characterizing common tree species have fat tails. Thus,
measuring the distance that an "average seed" moves tells us little about the
possibility of rare long-distance dispersal events that drive geographic spread
of the population. Unfortunately, a direct test of this explanation, along the
lines suggested in the previous section, is not possible because we do not have
the appropriate data on seed dispersal.

Clark and coworkers (Clark et al. 1998a,b, Clark 1998) pointed out that
this explanation of Reid's Paradox may be tested by inverting the problem.
For example, Clark (1998) proposed an analysis sequence consisting of three
steps. First, he established the extent to which seed dispersal data for several
tree species admitted a fat tail. To do this, he fitted the data with a model
that mixed two kinds of dispersal, (i) local dispersal characterized by thin
tails, and (ii) less frequent long-distance dispersal characterized by a non-
exponentially bound tail. Second, Clark constructed a numerical simulation
model of tree spread, based on parameters derived from the first step, to assess
characteristics of the tail (such as its shape and the fraction of dispersal events
in it) needed to match the rate of spread inferred from the paleorecord. Third,
he asked whether dispersal kernels consistent with the rate of spread in the
paleorecord are compatible with microscale dispersal data.

Clark found that the dispersal model with mixed local–long-distance dispersal fitted the data better than a model with purely local dispersal. Although data were not sufficient to resolve the shape of the tail (the parameter
θ in the θ-exponential kernel, see Equation 6.8), they were compatible with
the possibility that the tail contains more than 5% of seed rain for all the studied taxa. This small amount is sufficient to ensure rapid rate of geographic
spread, provided that the tail is fat. For example, assuming $\theta = 0.5$ (a non-
exponentially bound tail) in the θ-exponential kernel generates rates of spread
of 0.1–1 km y^{-1} (Clark 1998). In summary, Reid's Paradox can be resolved
using a model that makes realistic life history assumptions and, in particular,

postulates seed dispersal patterns that are consistent with field measurements. Such a model predicts rates of tree spread similar to those observed in the early Holocene.

6.3.6 Synthesis

The question motivating this section is: can we use microscale data on individual reproduction and dispersal to understand (and hopefully even predict) the pattern and the rate of population spread? The principal difficulty to address is how to quantify those rare long-distance dispersal events that may have a disproportionately important effect on population spread. The sequence of analyses that I advocate proceeds from simple to increasingly more complex approaches.

1. Estimate the parameters of the Fisher-Skellam model, α and D, from individual-based data and predict the population rate of spread using the relationship $c^* = 2\sqrt{\alpha D}$.

2. Determine whether somewhat more elaborate formulas based on the R&D kernel model would yield a substantially different answer. If so, then use the R&D model.

3. Investigate the shape of the dispersal tail to the limits imposed by the availability and quality of data on long-distance dispersal events.

4. Compare the predictions based on reproduction-dispersal models to the observed population spread. Unless the pattern of spread is linear and its rate was accurately predicted, check the predictions from analytical formulas by simulation. The formulas give the asymptotic rate of spread that may not even be achieved by the time the invading population runs out of space to invade into. Obtaining predictions on the "transient" aspects of spread is especially important when the spread is of bilinear type. In such cases, we would also like to predict when the rate of spread will approach the asymptotic value.

5. If there is a substantial mismatch between predicted and observed rates of spread, then it is possible that the dispersal tail was incorrectly estimated (most likely, the probability of very long-distance dispersal is underestimated). To investigate this possibility use an inverse approach that starts with the pattern of spread and then asks whether the life histories and dispersal kernels required by a model of that pattern are compatible with the data.

6. If the population spread rate is inconsistent with the dispersal data, then
   it is very likely that there is a qualitatively different dispersal mechanism
   that needs to be discovered and quantified. In such case, a model of
   stratified dispersal (e.g., Shigesada et al. 1995) can be employed to obtain
   predictions.

Spread of exotic species is an area of great interest, and I expect much
progress in this area in the near future. On the mathematical front, we need
progress along two fronts. First, we should stop focusing on a single best
number to characterize population spread (such as c^*). Population spread is
usually a complex spatio-temporal phenomenon. We need predictions on the
transient behavior of the velocity of spread and better ways to characterize and
predict the spatial aspect of spread (e.g., a solid advancing front versus advance
colonies leaping forward and eventually coalescing together). Second, we need
better statistical methods for analyzing the few precious data on long-distance
dispersal that we may have. Empiricists, on the other hand, need to develop
new clever methods for measuring the frequency of long-distance movements.
We also need to build a database of case-studies in which reproduction and
dispersal parameters are measured using microscale data, and compared to
macroscale patterns of population spread. Although the results of Andow et
al. (1990) and Metz and van den Bosch (1995) suggest that we can accurately
predict the rate of spread in some real-life cases, we are nowhere near being
able to make broad generalizations on how frequently reproduction-dispersal
models can predict population spread.

6.4   Quantifying Effects of Spatial Heterogeneity

6.4.1   Spatio-temporal models as the analysis tool

Analysis of dispersal data using theoretical density-distance curves is relatively
straightforward (unless we need to worry about the shape of dispersal tails).
It is true that one may need to employ esoteric functional forms like the
error or Bessel functions, and occasionally the formulas involve integrals or
infinite sums, but many advanced statistical packages can handle this kind of
nonlinear model fitting. There comes a point in the analysis of some data sets,
however, when canned formulas are not enough. This occurs when either the
systematic deviations between the fitted curve and the data suggest that some
variable needs to be included in the analysis, or when we are interested in
some variable on *a priori* grounds and wish to estimate its effect. The canned
formulas most often fail just when we wish to analyze biologically interesting
features of movement, such as the spatial, temporal, and density variation in

movement parameters; or when we need to include population growth and interaction terms in the analysis.

Any approach to such higher-level analysis has to begin with formulating a specific model. Next, the model typically has to be implemented on the computer and solved numerically (if we can obtain analytical solutions, then we revert to fitting density-distance curves). Finally, we have to confront the model predictions with the data in some way, and draw statistical inferences.

6.4.2 Fitting by nonlinear least squares

Banks, Kareiva, and their associates have published a series of papers on parameter estimation techniques for population interaction and redistribution models (Banks and Kareiva 1983, Banks 1985, Banks et al. 1987, 1988, Banks and Fitzpatrick 1990). Their approach can be summarized as follows (Banks et al. 1987):

1. Approximate the partial differential equations (PDE) with a system of ordinary differential equations (ODE).

2. Make initial guesses of the numerical values of the parameters to be estimated.

3. Numerically solve the system of ODE using standard software. For example, Banks et al. (1987) recommend DGEAR from the International Mathematical and Scientific Library (IMSL) of software.

4. Compare the solutions to the data by calculating some measure of best fit. Banks and Kareiva usually attempt to minimize the sum of squared deviations between the data and the prediction for a particular combination of parameters.

5. Use an optimization algorithm to adjust parameters of the original PDE model until a best-fit is found. Banks and Kareiva recommend Levenberg-Marquardt algorithms, such as the IMSL routine called ZXSSQ.

6. Repeat the procedure for other model formulations, if desired. Use the statistical tests in Banks and Fitzpatrick (1990) for comparing the performance of different models to each other.

The mathematical development of the methodology can be found in Banks (1981, 1985), and Banks and Kunisch (1989).

Model fitting with nonlinear minimization routines should be approached very cautiously. The major problem is that such "inverse problems" are in general ill-posed, so that solutions need not be unique, and solutions may not

depend continuously on the data (Banks et al. 1987). There is no guarantee
that there exists only one set of parameters that provide the "best fit." The
minimization software searches for a local minimum in the sum of squares. For
example, the sum of squares as a function of two unknown (to be estimated)
parameters can be imagined as a surface in 3D space. The routine will attempt
to find a local minimum, just like a ball rolling to the lowest place in a hilly
landscape. The problem is that complicated problems with a large number of
parameters and strong nonlinearities in functional forms will have many local
minima. The more topographically complex the hilly landscape the more likely
it is that the ball will get trapped in one of the multiple valleys, never reaching
the absolute lowest place (the global minimum). The remedy in such cases is
to start the solution in many different places and observe whether the solutions
will converge to the same combination of parameters—if they do, then one can
be reasonably sure that the global minimum was found.

The approach described above will attempt to find the combination of
a finite number of parameters that provide the best fit between a model
and the data. But what if we need to estimate a function, such as density-
dependent growth? Banks et al. (1987) describe two approaches. One is to
select an *a priori* functional shape, for example, logistic population growth
$f(N) = \alpha N(1 - N/K)$. We have now reduced the problem of estimating the
population growth term to a simpler problem of estimating two parameters,
α and K. However, if the actual functional form is very different from the one
we assumed, then we will not obtain satisfactory results. In cases when little
is known about functional shapes, one can adopt an alternative approach of
function approximation, for example, approximation with cubic splines.

FLEA BEETLE DISPERSAL   Banks and Kareiva applied their methodology to
several data sets. The simplest problem concerned dispersal of flea beetles
(Kareiva 1982, see Figure 6.1). The data set, $\{N_{x,t}\}$, consists of numbers
of marked beetles found at each location x of a linear array of host plants,
censused on days 1, 2, and 3 after release (instantaneous point release into
the center of the array). In a first attempt, Banks and Kareiva (1983) fitted
the data with a diffusion model with spatially varying coefficients with poor
success. A later analysis by Banks et al. (1985) used a more general model

$$\frac{\partial u}{\partial t} = \frac{\partial}{\partial x}\left(D(x,t)\frac{\partial u}{\partial x}\right) - \frac{\partial}{\partial x}(\beta(x,t)u) - \delta(t)u \qquad (6.9)$$

This is a diffusion-advection with loss model in which parameters are allowed
to vary in space and time. Fitting this model to the data, led Banks et
al. (1987) to conclude that there was no evidence for (1) advection, and (2)
spatial variation in the diffusion rate. By contrast, temporal dependence in

some form was pronounced and consistent. Since the functional shape of time dependence in $D(t)$ and $\delta(t)$ was not known *a priori*, Banks et al. (1985) employed cubic splines approximations. They found that an excellent fit was achieved when only δ (the disappearance rate) was assumed to vary with time (with the coefficient of determination ranging from 0.70 to 0.98). Allowing D to vary with time yielded only marginal improvements. Furthermore, δ was very high during the first day after the release, and then declined almost to zero. Apparently, beetle emigration rate was very high right after the release, due to agitation dispersal, and then declined to more natural levels as time went on.

Considered on its own merits, this analysis is a clear case of overkill because the dispersal process of flea beetles in one-dimensional experimental arrays is very simple. As discussed in Section A.2.4, making parameters of the diffusion equation vary in time does not present any problems for obtaining analytical solutions. Thus, the same result could have been achieved by fitting a series of Gaussian distributions to each time-slice of data, directly calculating the diffusion and loss rates, and plotting them against time. In defense of the approach, on the other hand, one must point out that (1) this was one of the first tests of the methodology, and (2) testing spatial dependence in the data could not be done with analytical formulas, and it was not known *a priori* that there was no spatial dependence in diffusion rate.

SPATIAL INTERACTION BETWEEN LADYBIRDS AND APHIDS   The second case (Banks et al. 1987) concerns a much more difficult problem. I have already described the empirical study and a mechanistic model of the system in Section 4.3.2. The data set to be analyzed represents the densities of two interacting species in space and time. The spatial domain of the study consisted of 17×1 m strips of goldenrod. The first species is the aphid *Uroleucon nigrotuberculatum*. Its initial densities were manipulated to create a clump in the center of the goldenrod strip. The second species is the aphid predator, ladybird *Coccinella septempunctata*. Ladybirds were released into the goldenrod strip at a uniform initial density of 3 beetles/m^2. Both aphids and ladybirds were censused at 8 equidistant locations for times = 0, 1/4, 1/2, 1, and 2 days.

Banks et al. (1987) fitted the following model to these spatio-temporal data:

$$\frac{\partial A}{\partial t} = D_A \frac{\partial^2 A}{\partial x^2} + \alpha(A) - Lf(A)$$

$$\frac{\partial L}{\partial t} = D_L \frac{\partial^2 L}{\partial x^2} + i - Le(A)$$

where A and L are spatio-temporal densities of aphids and ladybirds, respectively, D_A and D_L are their diffusion coefficients, $\alpha(A)$ is the population growth of aphids in the absence of predators, $f(A)$ is ladybird functional response (consumption rate of aphids by one ladybird), i is ladybird immigration rate, and $e(A)$ is the emigration rate. Banks et al. investigated several specific functional forms for $\alpha(A)$, $f(A)$, and $e(A)$.

Banks et al. found several combinations of specific functional forms that yielded comparably good fits to data. One common thread was that logistic population growth consistently provided the best description of aphid population growth. Another thread was that in all the best models ladybird emigration rate rapidly declined with aphid density. Finally, predator functional response was almost always Type I. The match between model predictions and data was remarkably good, with models explaining 76–92% of variation in the data.

Both models and data showed a rapid aggregation of ladybirds at peaks of aphid abundance. However, as Banks et al. note, it is unlikely that this rapid aggregation is solely a result of aphid-dependent emigration and constant immigration of ladybirds since, as Kareiva and Odell (1987) showed, the primary mechanism behind ladybird aggregation is their preytaxis. Unfortunately, the computer algorithm used by Banks et al. (1987) was not capable of handling such cross-species advection terms. The caveat here is that obtaining a good or even excellent match between model predictions and the data is not a guarantee that the model is "correct," since a different model may fit the data as well, or even better.

6.4.3   Direct fitting with discrete derivatives

The nonlinear fitting approaches considered above are very powerful and flexible. However, the data are fitted indirectly and iteratively using very complex and often opaque algorithms. As a result, it is sometimes difficult to generate intuitive insights into the data set that is analyzed. An alternative approach is to analyze the observed temporal change in density. It is direct and fast, but may not be as general and rigorous as methods based on nonlinear optimization algorithms. This approach has not been used much, and when used it has not yielded spectacular results. Nevertheless, I believe that it has great potential, especially in exploratory analyses of data.

Suppose we have a data set documenting spatio-temporal changes in population density of some organism (to make presentation of ideas more understandable I will first assume that space is one-dimensional, and then later will generalize the approach to two dimensions). We will need data in the form of a matrix of population densities at each of spatial points x ($x = 0, 1, 2, \cdots, L$) and at all times t ($t = 0, 1, 2, \cdots, T$), or $\{N_{x,t}\}$. I will assume that both spatial and temporal sampling points are spaced regularly.

As an illustration, first suppose we wish to fit the simple diffusion model to this data set. The discrete approximation of the first temporal and the second spatial derivatives are:

$$\frac{\partial u}{\partial t}(x,t) = \frac{u(x,t+\tau) - u(x,t)}{\tau}$$
$$\frac{\partial^2 u}{\partial x^2}(x,t) = \frac{u(x-\lambda,t) - 2u(x,t) + u(x+\lambda,t)}{\lambda^2} \quad (6.10)$$

Let us set the temporal and spatial time steps (τ and λ) equal to the intervals at which the data were collected (scaled to 1, without loss of generality). Substituting the observed values $N_{x,t}$ instead of the theoretical $u(x,t)$ into the simple diffusion equation, and employing Equations (6.10), we obtain

$$N_{x,t+1} = N_{x,t} + D(N_{x-1,t} - 2N_{x,t} + N_{x+1,t}) + \epsilon_t \quad (6.11)$$

Because in real data the relationship will not be exact, I have added an explicit error term (ϵ_t). Note that the deterministic part of Equation 6.11 is the same as the equation for temporal change of population density in the simple (unbiased) random walk, with $D = (R + L)/2$ (see Section 4.2.1).

It is very simple to use Equation 6.11 as a regression model, and estimate the value of D. We need at least two temporal snapshots of population density (the first, $t = 0$, serves as the initial condition for the next), and we can use the spatial boundary points ($x = 0$ and $x = L$) only as predictors (on the right side of Equation 6.11). In other words, we can fit $N_{x,t}$ for all $t > 0$ and $x = 1, \ldots, L-1$.

So far, we have not done anything very useful, since there are many other established methods for estimating D in the simple diffusion equation. The interesting part comes when we add other terms to the simple diffusion and make the parameters spatially and temporally variable. For example, we can explore the effects of spatial heterogeneity by making D a function of space. An even better, more mechanistic, approach is to characterize space in terms of biological variables, assume a functional relationship, and fit the parameters of this relationship. For example, space may be characterized by presence or absence of host plants, and we expect D to vary accordingly.

If we are interested in investigating the effects of drift, then we add the drift term to the right side of Equation 6.11, using the approximation ($N_{t,x+1} - N_{t,x-1})/2$ for the first spatial derivative. The birth/death terms can also be added to the model, for example, a constant death term, $-\delta N_{t,x}$. Spatial and temporal dependence of all model parameters can be investigated by regression, subject to limitations imposed by degrees of freedom in the data set.

In two dimensions, the diffusion operator can be approximated as the sum of the x and y second derivatives:

$$\frac{\partial^2 N}{\partial x^2} \approx N_{x-1,y,t} + N_{x,y-1,t} - 4N_{x,y,t} + N_{x+1,y,t} + N_{x,y+1,t} \qquad (6.12)$$

This operator can be visualized with the following table:

	$x-1$	x	$x+1$
$y-1$		$+1$	
y	$+1$	-4	$+1$
$y+1$		$+1$	

where numbers for each combination of the x and y coordinates correspond to the weights associated with population density. We see that this approximation, Equation 6.12, uses the information on the observed population density in only the four orthogonally adjacent points to the central point x, y.

In real-world applications we have to deal with the fact that many values of $N_{x,y,t}$ are measured with error. Thus, it may be useful to base the estimate of the diffusion operator on all neighboring values, including the corners. J. G. Skellam (in Dempster 1957) derived an indirect approximation for the diffusion operator that uses all 8 orthogonal and diagonal neighbor cells. He assumed that $N_{x,t}$ and its 8 nearest neighbors are fitted with a second degree polynomial in x and y. The approximation of the diffusion operator is then obtained by taking the second derivatives of the fitted surface. It is not actually necessary to fit the polynomial, since Skellam calculated what the numerical weights would be for N in each neighboring cell. This discrete approximation of the two-dimensional diffusion operator is

	$x-1$	x	$x+1$
$y-1$	$+\frac{2}{3}$	$-\frac{1}{3}$	$+\frac{2}{3}$
y	$-\frac{1}{3}$	$-\frac{4}{3}$	$-\frac{1}{3}$
$y+1$	$+\frac{2}{3}$	$-\frac{1}{3}$	$+\frac{2}{3}$

or, algebraically

$$\begin{aligned}
\frac{\partial^2 N}{\partial x^2} \approx {}& \frac{1}{3}(2N_{x-1,y-1,t} - N_{x-1,y,t} + 2N_{x-1,y+1,t} - N_{x,y-1,t} - 4N_{x,y,t} \\
& - N_{x,y+1,t} + 2N_{x+1,y-1,t} - N_{x+1,y,t} + 2N_{x+1,y+1,t}) \qquad (6.13)
\end{aligned}$$

ESTIMATION OF LOCUST MOVEMENT AND MORTALITY   During a study of population dynamics of the Moroccan locust (*Dociostaurus maroccanus*) Dempster (1957) obtained a data set consisting of estimated numbers of hoppers entering each instar in each of 18 adjacent quadrats (Figure 6.4). The main quantity of interest was the mortality rate suffered by each hopper instar. However, the temporal change in population density in each quadrat is a result of both mortality and inter-quadrat movement, thus we need a method for separating the effects of these two processes. Dempster (1957) assumed

	A	B	C
1	44,230 14,600	45,650 16,145	6,478 5,840
2	47,370 22,580	50,500 26,475	16,650 6,623
3	50,720 30,015	103,900 52,680	89,160 57,860
4	52,060 28,560	85,200 20,675	70,950 32,330
5	48,060 36,760	35,065 17,570	32,260 33,100
6	87,200 74,990	124,100 27,070	44,040 33,630

Figure 6.4: The estimated numbers of locusts entering the first (upper numbers) and second (lower numbers) instars in each quadrat of the Mia Milea site in 1953. Each quadrat is approximately 30 × 30 m. (After Dempster 1957.)

Table 6.4: The estimated mortality and diffusion rates of locust nymphs at Mia Milea in 1953-1955. The time units are per instar duration. (After Dempster 1957.)

	1953		1954		1955	
Instar	$\hat{\delta}$	$\hat{D}$	$\hat{\delta}$	$\hat{D}$	$\hat{\delta}$	$\hat{D}$
I	0.59	−0.003	0.26	0.02	0.57	−0.06
II	0.34	0.02	0.16	0.15	0.33	0.04
III	0.43	0.10	0.20	0.12	0.12	0.16
VI	0.58	0.33	0.28	0.05	0.20	0.32
V	0.60	0.28	0.61	0.08	0.50	0.13

that movement occurs by simple diffusion and that the death rate within each instar is constant. In other words, he used the diffusion-loss model that has already made numerous appearances in this book:

$$\frac{\partial u}{\partial t} = D \left(\frac{\partial^2 u}{\partial x^2} + \frac{\partial^2 u}{\partial y^2} \right) - \delta u \qquad (6.14)$$

Substituting the change in numbers (in each quadrat) from instar i to the next one, $i+1$, for the temporal derivative, and using Equation 6.13 for the diffusion operator, Dempster obtained a discrete equation involving two unknowns, D and δ. These two parameters were estimated by linear regression, using each of the four central quadrats as a data point (Figure 6.4). The results are shown in Table 6.4. Apart from the two negative D values, which are probably a result of estimation errors (Dempster 1957), the method appears to give reasonable results. Note that the diffusion rate tends to increase with instar, reflecting greater mobility of late-instar hoppers. The estimated mortality rate is high for both early and late instars, and lowest for the middle instars. This result, however, should be interpreted with some caution, because there is one source of error that is difficult to overcome. The diffusion rate D characterizes only local movements of hoppers. Thus, the magnitude of δ in Equation 6.14 reflects not only the mortality rate but also long-distance emigration from the site. When such emigration events occur, morality will be overestimated and diffusion underestimated (Dempster 1957). This may account for the high estimated mortality of late instars, and also for the apparent decline in D in the fourth instar in 1954 and fifth instar in 1955. Another source of potential error could be hopper congregation (Dempster 1957). Given more data, however, such biologically interesting features could be explored by regression analysis (that is, making D density dependent).

SPATIAL DYNAMICS OF THE MOUNTAIN PINE BEETLE   Another study that used the discrete derivatives approach was done by Polymenopoulos and Long (1990). Their data set consisted of "outbreak maps" of the mountain pine beetle (*Dendroctonus ponderosae*) for the years 1981–1984. Maps were sampled on a 200×200 m grid, and each spatial point was characterized by the number of lodgepole pines killed by the beetle per ha ($N_{x,y,t}$), volume of living pines per ha ($R_{x,y,t}$), and the average phloem thickness of live pines ($E_{x,y,t}$).

Polymenopoulos and Long (1990) wished to analyze their data while taking into account such realistic effects as beetle attraction to areas characterized by thick phloem, and the effects of lagged density-dependence on population growth. Unfortunately, the model that they used, or at least the equation they published, appears to be incorrect. This is probably not important because, in addition to the complex advection model, Polymenopoulos and Long also fitted the simple diffusion model to their data. Comparing the predictive abilities of the models, they found that the simpler diffusion model did best, judged both by visual comparisons of the predicted to the actual spatial distributions of beetle-killed pines, and by more sophisticated spatial analysis methods. Their interpretation of this result was that including terms for resource availability did not improve the precision of forecasts.

6.4.4   Synthesis

This section reviews some approaches to fitting dynamic spatio-temporal model to data. This approach is potentially very powerful because theoretically one can fit data with a model of arbitrary complexity, incorporating any features of movement process that are deemed important. In practice, things are much more complex. The best approach developed to date is the one of Banks and coworkers. However, it is difficult to imagine that this approach will be used by empirical ecologists any time soon. First, numerical solution of partial differential equations is a highly technical field, full of traps for the unwary. Second, nonlinear minimization is another difficult and highly technical field. Finally, even if we master the methodology, our data may not be good enough to resolve all the realistic processes that characterize individual movements we may need to include in the model.

Given this pessimistic assessment, why bother to include this section in the book? First, quantification of how spatial heterogeneity affects movement is a truly fundamental issue that must be addressed. Second, even though empirical ecologists may not be able to use these techniques on their own, collaborative teams consisting of an ecologist and a mathematician can do it. In such a case, the ecologist on the team needs to understand the logic of the approach, if not all the details. Third, any model of spatio-temporal population dynamics can be used in this approach, not just a diffusion equation. Thus, the difficulties associated with numerical solving of partial differential equations may be avoided by constructing a simulation model. Fourth, software for nonlinear fitting is becoming easier to use, and ecologists are becoming more familiar with these methods (e.g., Hilborn and Mangel 1997). In fact, there has been several successful applications of basically the same approach to individual mark-recapture data (this will be discussed in Section 7.8).

The discrete-derivatives approach is another way to avoid some of the technical complexities discussed above. It has potential as a technique for exploratory data analysis similar to the uses of the partial autocorrelation function in time-series analysis (Box and Jenkins 1976). What I am proposing here is essentially a generalization of the autoregressive modeling of time-series data, something like "spatio-temporal autoregressive" (STAR) modeling approach. The discrete diffusion terms are a way of including biological mechanisms in what otherwise would be a purely phenomenological approach.

The simplest model, and a starting point of the analysis, is simple diffusion with a density-independent growth term (the Skellam model). After fitting data with this model, one notes how well it mimics qualitative features of the data, and what percent of variance it explains quantitatively. The next step might be to add various features to the model—density-dependent growth, advection, spatially and temporally varying coefficients—and continue evaluating the model's performance. Since this procedure is essentially stepwise regression, regular statistical methods are available for evaluating the statistical significance of each added term. Additionally, unlike nonlinear least squares, each model can be fitted rapidly and without straining computing resources, so many different formulations can be tried quickly. It is important, however, not to forget that this is an exploratory approach. For example, estimates of the model parameters are likely to be biased. Thus, once the form of the model is determined, it may still be necessary to estimate the parameters by nonlinear optimization routines.

6.5   Seed and Pollen Dispersal in Plants

A number of different approaches to studying plant dispersal is possible. Some adopt the Lagrangian point of view, most notably studies of the vegetative spread of clonal plants (see Sections 3.5.2 and 5.3.6). However, the majority of the quantitative studies of plant dispersal employ the Eulerian framework.

It is natural to use an Eulerian approach, like a diffusion model, for plant dispersal since seeds and pollen are typically mass-produced, and released from a point source (actually, tree crowns are not point sources, but this approximation is reasonable when the scale of dispersal is much greater than the crown diameter). Plant propagules are then moved around by various kinds of media (air, water, animals), and eventually deposited at some distance from the source plant. The quantity of interest is the density of settling propagules as a function of distance from the source. Because the spatial distribution of propagules is a result of two processes, movement and deposition, we should expect that it will be characterized by some degree of leptokurtosis (just as the combination of diffusion and settlement results in a Bessel distribution, which is more leptokurtic than the Gaussian).

In addition to two Eulerian approaches that I will review in this section—parameterizing mechanistic models and fitting empirical curves—I should mention two other approaches to plant dispersal. First, one may attempt to infer rates of movement between a pair of populations from measures of genetic distance between them (e.g., Godt and Hamrick 1993). I am skeptical that this approach can actually provide solid information on dispersal because it is based on rather restrictive assumptions. Most notably, Wright's (1931) equation for the number of migrants per generation assumes that genetic differentiation is a result of limited gene flow rather than different selection regimes. Yet, it is possible that genetic differentiation may be maintained by strong selection despite substantial gene flow.

The second, and very different, approach is to characterize spatial and spatio-temporal autocorrelations in plant or plant disease distributions (e.g., Brodie et al. 1995, Gottwald 1995, Herben et al. 1995, Nelson 1995). While this approach has a lot of potential, it has not yet been directly tied to estimates of movement rates. It is my hope that such approaches will eventually employ more mechanistic models of spatio-temporal population dynamics, possibly along the lines suggested in Section 6.4.

6.5.1 Parameterizing mechanistic models

The most rigorous approach is the one based on explicit modeling of mechanisms, such as the characteristics of carrier motion and details of seed or pollen deposition. A series of papers by Greene and Johnson (1989, 1992a,b, 1995) provides a good example of this approach.

Greene and Johnson (1989) began by developing a micrometeorological model of seed dispersal released from a point source (this model was mentioned in Section 3.6.1; see also Equation 3.5). The model was based on mechanistic, measurable parameters: height at which seeds are released, mean and variance of the terminal velocity of seeds, and mean and variance of wind velocity. These parameters were measured in a series of experiments using seeds of several tree species. The model was then used to predict the dispersal curves resulting from experimentally releasing seeds from a meteorological tower. In addition, Greene and Johnson (1989) applied their model to data on seeds naturally released from solitary trees.

Model predictions were generally in good agreement with the density-distance curves observed in experimental releases from the tower. However, the model underpredicted the median and modal dispersal distance in natural releases. Greene and Johnson (1989) thought that the most likely explanation of this pattern is that seeds may not detach randomly with respect to wind speed. If seeds detach only when wind speed exceeds some minimal velocity then their dispersal distance will be enhanced. In a subsequent paper, Greene and Johnson (1992a) found that seeds were indeed preferentially abscising at higher wind speeds. Thus, the process of seed detachment needs to be explicitly included in the model (see Greene and Johnson 1995).

The most sophisticated model of long-distance wind dispersal of tree seeds was developed by Greene and Johnson (1995). The predictions of this model were within 5-fold of the observed seed deposition densities, which is a respectable accuracy given the complexity of the process and the large number of assumptions underlying the model. It is troubling, however, that the model tended to underpredict the tail of the observed dispersal curve. In other words, the models consistently predict dispersal curves that are less leptokurtic than the observed ones. Thus, my assessment of the state of art in the mechanistic modeling of wind dispersal of seeds must echo the rather gloomy statement in the introduction by Greene and Johnson: "there is at present no tested argument for deposited seed density as a function of distance, source-strength, and vector characteristics."

Other examples of mechanistic approaches to plant dispersal can be found in the literature on pollen dispersal (e.g., Waddington and Heinrich 1981, Morris 1993). These studies focus on characterizing the movements of pollinators by utilizing individual-centered approaches very similar to those discussed in Chapter 5. For example, Morris (1993) used field observations to quantify the processes of pollinator movement and pollen deposition, built those processes into an empirically-based model, and then successfully predicted the resulting pollen dispersal curves. In a subsequent paper, Morris et al. (1995) re-examined the process of pollen deposition in greater detail. They fitted several mechanistic deposition models to data using likelihood methods, and found that the model that fitted data best was more leptokurtic than the standard exponential model usually assumed for deposition rate. As a result, the best-fit function, when combined with the advection-diffusion model for pollinator movements (Morris 1993), predicted a mean pollen dispersal distance more than three times greater than the exponential model.

An interesting message arising from the studies by Greene and Johnson (1989) and Morris et al. (1995) is that including greater degrees of realism in mechanistic models of dispersal can result in dispersal curves characterized by greater leptokurtosis than would be predicted by simple models. This may well be a general theoretical result (see also Section 6.2.3 on effects of heterogeneity in dispersal ability) that is also in agreement with the empirical observation that distributions of dispersal distances measured in the field are typically leptokurtic.

6.5.2 Fitting empirical models

Although mechanistic models tested with independently collected data may be the most rigorous approach to studying dispersal, such studies are rare. The majority of studies of plant dispersal (this is true for other taxons as well) take the approach of fitting density-distance curves, most frequently using empirical functional relationships (see Section 3.3). Some examples of this approach to seed dispersal include Stork (1984), Welch et al. (1990), and Masaki et al. (1994). Sometimes authors simply calculate various moments of the frequency distribution of observed dispersal distances, such as the mean and the variance in the dispersal distance (e.g., Horvitz and Shemske 1994).

An interesting approach to estimating seedling recruitment functions was developed by Ribbens et al. (1994) (see also Clark et al. 1998b). The basic idea was to measure the spatial distribution of seedlings along transects run through the forest, and then to relate it to locations of adult trees of the same species. Ribbens et al. (1994) assumed that the expected number of recruits produced by a single tree is given by

$$u(x) = Ad^\phi \exp\left[-Bx^\theta\right] \tag{6.15}$$

where d is the tree size (measured as diameter at breast height) and x is the distance from the tree. This model assumes that the total number of seedlings produced by a tree is proportional to power-transformed d, while the distribution of dispersal distances is described by the θ-exponential dispersal kernel. Parameters A, B, ϕ, and θ are unknowns that need to be estimated.

The total number of seedlings expected to be found at a particular quadrat will be the sum of contributions from all trees in the vicinity of the transect (Figure 6.5). Dotted lines in Figure 6.5 indicate seedling shadows of each individual tree (assuming the exponential model with $\theta = 1$ for the purpose of

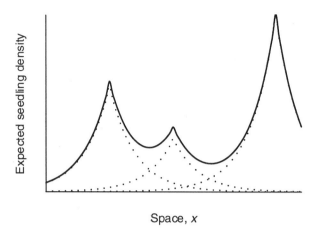

Figure 6.5: Expected distribution of seedlings resulting from three seed sources within a spatial transect.

illustration). The solid line is the sum of individual tree shadows, and is the expected seedling density that can be measured by counting seedlings along the transect.

The parameters of the model were estimated by Ribbens et al. using the maximum likelihood method (this is similar to the least-squares method encountered in Section 6.4.2; see also the general discussion in Section 7.8.1). However, maximizing the likelihood surface for all four parameters simultaneously proved to be difficult, because the parameters A and ϕ tended to trade off with each other, as did B and θ. To overcome this problem, Ribbens et al. first performed a maximum likelihood analysis for a grid of integer values of ϕ and θ, and found that $\phi = 2$ and $\theta = 3$ tended to produce models with highest likelihoods. Fixing ϕ and θ at these values, they next estimated parameters A and B for each tree species separately.

6.5.3 Synthesis

My impression, from an admittedly inadequate knowledge of the plant dispersal literature, is that the progress in this field is constrained as much by a lack of good empirical methods for quantifying seed dispersal as by an embryonic development of analytical approaches. Clearly, more work is needed to develop practical and effective markers for seed dispersal. An important strength of the method developed by Ribbens et al. (1994), therefore, is its ability to deal with situations where marking propagules is impossible. An additional advantage is that dispersal is quantified in the natural setting of a forest. By contrast, quantifying seedling shadows around isolated trees (a popular alternative when marking is impractical) is suspect, since dispersal curves in a pasture or a clearcut may be very different from those under the forest conditions. I am bothered, however, by the practice of using the same θ for all tree species [Clark et al. (1998b) also fixed θ, but unlike Ribbens et al. (1994), they assumed $\theta = 2$]. The exponent θ provides a necessary degree of flexibility in the phenomenological θ-exponential model, since it is very likely that different species will differ not only in the spatial *scale* of dispersal (quantified by B), but also in the *shape* of the dispersal function (quantified by θ). On the other hand, the statistical difficulties associated with the simultaneous estimation of both shape and scale are very real, as Ribbens et al. pointed out.

I think the solution of this conundrum may be to fit data with theoretically derived functions that take into account what is known about the seed properties of the species for which dispersal parameters are estimated. For example, Okubo and Levin (1989) discuss how such properties of seeds as mass may affect the shape of the dispersal curve. Unfortunately, as we saw in Section 6.5.1, the art of mechanistic modeling of seed dispersal is not as advanced as one might wish. Additionally, as far as I know, there have been no systematic attempts to map seed characteristics onto functional forms that can be used in fitting data. Thus, the only recourse for the present might be to fit several alternative functional forms that have been published (see also Section 3.6.1) and to choose the best fitting one, using an appropriate statistical criterion to control for the number of parameters.

The method of Ribbens et al. (1994) has one serious disadvantage in studies of range expansion in plants. In order to accurately predict the qualitative pattern and quantitative rate of spread, we need to be able to measure the shape of the dispersal tail (see Section 6.3). As Figure 6.5 makes abundantly clear, however, the method of Ribbens et al. can only make inferences on how fast the seedling density drops off in the neighborhood of the parent tree; the dispersal tails are masked by seedlings produced by other conspecific trees. Thus, unless adult trees are exceedingly rare, we will not be able to quantify the shape of dispersal tails, and should avoid making predictions about potential rates of spread on the basis of these data (however, the inverse approach discussed in Section 6.3.5 appears to be a legitimate method for making *indirect* inferences in such situations).

6.6   Measuring Attraction

6.6.1   Fitting spatio-temporal models

Quantifying long-distance attraction is always a difficult task (see also sections on attraction in Chapters 5 and 7). Perhaps it is most difficult in the context of a MMR study because we have access only to population-level data. Essentially, we have to rely on inverse methods—postulating some behavioral mechanism for attraction, constructing a model based on this mechanism, and then estimating the model parameters by fitting the model to the data (typically, using some nonlinear minimization algorithm). The conceptual framework for such an analysis has already been described in Section 6.4.

An illustration of how this approach may be applied to real data is the analysis by Banks et al. (1988) of Hawkes (1972) data on a cabbage root fly MMR study. Hawkes (1972) released marked flies outside a cabbage patch. The data represent captures of marked flies during the first and the second 7 hour period after release. Traps were arranged on a rectangular grid outside and inside the cabbage patch. Banks et al. (1988) postulated the following diffusion equation describing fly redistribution:

$$\frac{\partial u}{\partial t} = D \left(\frac{\partial^2 u}{\partial x^2} + \frac{\partial^2 u}{\partial y^2} \right) - \beta_x \frac{\partial u}{\partial x} - \beta_y \frac{\partial u}{\partial y} - \delta u \qquad (6.16)$$

where u is fly density, D is the diffusion coefficient, β_x and β_y are the x- and y-components of advection rate, and δ is the disappearance rate. As in other applications (see Section 6.4.2), Banks et al. attempted to fit a variety of models, ranging from a simple diffusion-disappearance model with constant D and δ (setting advection terms to zero) to the full model with spatially and temporally varying coefficients D, β_x, β_y, and δ (Equation 6.16). When all model parameters were held constant in time and space, the model did more poorly than the hypothesis of random variation. Allowing temporal variation in parameters resulted in a better fit. In particular, the model with constant D but time-varying β_x, β_y, and δ explained 35% of variance in the data. Notably, this model included a substantial advection vector, the direction of which was in almost perfect opposition to the wind. This is precisely the pattern expected if cabbage root flies travel upwind when presented with host odors. Moreover, the magnitude of the advection vector decreased with time. This result is most probably a consequence of most flies finding, and moving into the cabbage patch as time from release increased.

Banks et al. (1988) also fitted the data with a model including spatially varying advection terms. This is a realistic modification because we expect advection to be strongest near the host patch and to diminish with increasing distance from patch. Indeed, the model explained a larger proportion of variance (44%). However, the model with spatio-temporally varying coefficients employed 29 parameters, and, as the authors were careful to point out, the data were most likely not sufficient to support the analysis of this very complex model.

6.6.2   A flux-based approach

Although the bulk of this chapter focuses on quantifying spatio-temporal changes in the population density of organisms, an alternative and complementary approach is to focus on population fluxes. *Flux* is the net number of "particles" crossing a unit length of boundary per unit of time. Thus, if 10 organisms crossed the boundary moving to the right, while 15 crossed to the left, then the net movement rate, or flux, is -5 organisms (assuming that right represents the positive flux direction). In Section A.1.3 I show how a diffusion equation can be written in terms of population fluxes. Flux-based approaches to quantifying movement adopt an Eulerian framework, just as density-based methods do.

Fagan (1997) gives an example of how one can estimate diffusion rate by measuring fluxes of organisms at a boundary. A flux-based approach can be particularly useful in situations where we need to measure attractive biases in the movements of organisms. By measuring fluxes in addition to densities of organisms, we obtain a richer description of the population redistribution process, and thus can better resolve the parameters of their movement.

Let us suppose that we can measure the rate at which organisms cross a unit of length (if movement is in 2D space) or area (if movement is in 3D space), going in both directions. For example, we may employ a drift fence with pitfall traps on both sides, and then count every day the number of organisms caught on either side. An example of quantifying fluxes in 3D space will be described in Section 6.7. Let us define J_x^+ as the number of organisms crossing the boundary while going towards an attractive focus, while J_x^- is the number of organisms moving in the opposite direction, away from the attractive focus. The net movement rate, or flux, therefore is $J_x = J_x^+ - J_x^-$. The subscript x reminds us that we are actually measuring only one component of the flux with respect to the direction towards an attractive focus (arbitrarily given the x coordinate).

The question is, how can we use these flux data to estimate the aggregative bias in organism movement? Let us suppose that movement of organisms around an attractive focus can be described by the following generalized diffusion equation with a spatially-varying bias term:

$$\frac{\partial u}{\partial t} = -\frac{\partial}{\partial x}(\beta u) + \frac{\partial^2}{\partial x^2}(\mu u) \qquad (6.17)$$

Here β is the attractive bias, defined as the difference between the probabilities of going toward the focus versus going away; and μ is the Fokker-Planck motility defined in the usual way (see Section 4.2.1). If this model is correct, then the flux should have two components: the directional component due to the attractive bias towards the focus, and the random component, or net flow of organisms down the population density gradient. Since the density of organisms will tend to increase in the vicinity of the focus (as a result of the attractive bias), the random component of flux will generally work against the directed component. Turchin and Simmons (1997) derive an approximate formula relating the two diffusion parameters (μ and β) to flux data J_x^+ and J_x^-. Assuming that the motility does not change with space and time, while the bias is a function of distance to the focus

$$\frac{\beta(x)}{\mu} = \frac{J_x}{S_x} + \frac{1}{2}\frac{\partial(\ln S_x)}{\partial x} \qquad (6.18)$$

where $S_x = J_x^+ + J_x^-$. The quantity β/μ is the *relative attractive bias*; that is, the difference between the probabilities of going toward the focus versus going away, given that some displacement with respect to the focus occurred. It is scaled from -1 (perfect repulsion) to 1 (perfect attraction), and $\beta/\mu = 0$ indicates no attraction.

Note that a naive estimator of the relative bias would be J_x/S_x—the difference between organism numbers crossing a unit area toward versus away from the focus, scaled by the total number crossing in any direction. Although this quantity resembles the definition of the relative attractive bias given above, it would yield a biased estimate because random movements by organisms will result in a net flow down the gradient of population density. The second term on the right side of Equation 6.18 corrects for this random flow.

Equation 6.18 is the key result that allows us to use observable quantities J_x and S_x to estimate the ratio β/μ. The formula is applicable to the situation where attraction can be anisotropic, that is, vary with respect to direction towards the focus. Thus, by measuring organism fluxes at various distances and directions from the source, and using Equation 6.18, we can map the relative attractive biases, or an *attraction field* around a focus. If we can estimate μ independently, then we can translate relative biases into β. An example of the application of this approach to southern pine beetles congregating around mass attacked trees will be discussed in Section 6.7.2.

6.6.3 Application: attraction to pheromone traps

The pheromone trap is becoming one of the most widely used recapture devices in studies of insect dispersal. Natural or synthetic pheromones are known for many insects (674 species of arthropods according to Klassen et al. 1982) especially those of economic importance. The popularity of pheromone traps is based on their ability to sample very sparse insect populations. An added advantage is their specificity—only the target species (and sometimes its close relatives, or principal natural enemies) are attracted. Thus, the impact on non-target populations is minimized, and there is no need to sort through massive amounts of non-target insect material. However, because pheromone traps work by actively attracting insects they cannot directly tell us the absolute population density (numbers per unit of area). For some kinds of analyses, this does not present a problem. For example, analysis of density-distance curves (Section 6.2) is often performed on relative population density estimates.

In other analyses, however, it is necessary to translate pheromone trap catches into absolute estimates of population density. I will refer to this translation coefficient as the trap's *effective sampling area* (ESA). Suppose that insects are distributed at uniform density u in the area within which a trap is situated. Furthermore, the number of insects captured in the trap, C, is proportional to insect density: $C = \alpha u$. Because the units of C are insect numbers, and those of u are numbers per unit of area, α is measured in units of area. That is why I refer to α as the effective sampling *area* of a trap; it is the area by which we need to divide the trap catch, to obtain an estimate of population density, $\hat{u} = C/\alpha$.

It is worth emphasizing that ESA is a logical construct—a parameter, rather than an actual "piece of real estate." The attraction field of a pheromone trap does not have a definite boundary. It could be filamentous in nature, and it typically shifts around the trap in response to changes in wind speed and direction. It is probably best to think about it as a probability vector field. ESA is a single number summarizing how the mean probability of being captured in a trap attenuates with distance (and direction) from the trap.

Estimation of ESA is an important step in many dispersal studies employing pheromone traps (see Section 6.2). The analytical techniques involved in ESA estimation are also closely connected to other kinds of quantitative analyses of movement because the ESA depends very much on the mode of movement of the target species (for example, the more widely an insect ranges, the higher is the probability that it will approach a trap close enough to be attracted and captured). I will cover this topic in detail, concentrating on one well-studied case: attraction of male gypsy moths to traps baited with synthetic sex pheromone (another example dealing with bark beetles will be

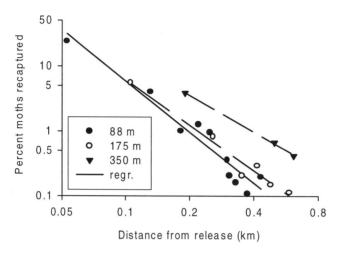

Figure 6.6: Percent recapture of male gypsy moths in traps at various distances from the release point. (After Schwalbe 1981.)

discussed in Section 6.7.3).

6.6.4   Example: gypsy moth traps

Attractive traps have been used in gypsy moth (*Lymantria dispar*) population research since the end of last century (Schwalbe 1981). At first traps were baited with live females or extracts of female abdominal tips. In the 1970s the synthetic sex pheromone disparlure became available. Disparlure-baited traps have been used in annual surveys conducted over most of the gypsy moth range in the U.S. since 1972. Because of the economic importance of gypsy moths, and the massive effort involved in the pheromone survey (about 100,000 traps placed every year during the 1970s; see Schwalbe 1981), it became imperative to be able to translate pheromone trap catches into absolute numbers of gypsy moths.

The first attempt to estimate ESA of the pheromone trap involved point releases of male moths within regular arrays of pheromone traps (Schwalbe 1981). These studies yielded two important conclusions. First, as expected, the closer traps were to the release point, the greater proportion of released population they captured (Figure 6.6). Second, total recovery of released insects increased as intertrap distance decreased (again, as expected). However,

individual traps in denser arrays (intertrap distance 88 m and 175 m) captured fewer insects than traps in the sparse array (350 m) (Figure 6.6). This
suggests that traps in dense arrays were interfering with each other. In other
words, their sampling areas were overlapping (more on this below).

It would not be easy to use the data from this study to estimate the translation coefficient between the absolute male density and the number of males
captured in a trap. As Schwalbe (1981) noted, if the insects were released
uniformly within trap arrays, then the recovery rate would be higher because
many insects would be released closer to individual traps. Theoretically, these
data could be interpreted using a model of gypsy moth movement and attraction to traps that would be parameterized using the density-distance relationships in Figure 6.6. However, this would be a difficult task and it was never
attempted. (One difficulty, for example, is that traps near the release point
captured up to 25% of released insects, thus depleting the numbers available
for other traps—see discussion of this problem in Section 2.3.4.)

Instead, the basic approach of Schwalbe (1981) was redesigned by Elkinton
and Cardé (1980). They released male moths in a uniform release, instead of
using a point release. Males were released in equal numbers at 100 points
within a 800 × 800 m block, and recaptured with traps located at nodes of a
800 × 800 m rectangular grid.

The elegant design of this study gets directly at the translation coefficient
between absolute population density and trap catch, or ESA. As I defined
it above, ESA is a translation coefficient between spatially uniform population density, and the trap catch. The most direct (albeit unrealistic) way to
measure ESA is to release insects uniformly in an infinitely large area, and recapture them with a regularly spaced trap array, also of infinite extent (making
sure that traps are far enough so that their attraction areas are not impinging
on each other). Suppose we release M insects in each square of area A (800 ×
800 m^2 in the Elkinton and Cardé study) of such an infinite regular array. The
population density is $N = M/A$. We then recapture p proportion of released
insects ($p = C/M$, where C is the total number recaptured). Thus, in terms
of p and A, $\alpha = C/N = (C/M)A = pA$.

It is not necessary, however, to set up an infinitely wide array of traps, and
to release males at constant density throughout it; it is sufficient to do so in
only one square. This can be seen by imagining that males were released not
only in the central 800 × 800 m square but also in an adjacent square. In this
case, the same proportion p of those males as the males in the actual release
would be recaptured. We can continue adding imaginary release squares and
continue getting the same recapture rate p. Thus, releasing males uniformly
within one square is equivalent, for our purposes, to releasing them uniformly

within an area of an infinite extent.

The mean recapture rate (average of 11 releases) in the study by Elkinton and Cardé (1980) was $p = 4\%$. Since trap density was one per 800×800 m^2 area, the effective attraction area of each trap can be estimated as $\alpha = pA = 0.04 \times 800 \times 800 = 25600$ m^2 or 2.56 ha. I should note that Elkinton and Cardé used Pherocon 1C sticky traps in their 1980 study, which have been superseded by "milk carton" traps in early 1980s. Because Elkinton and Childs (1983) showed that milk carton traps captured a bit less than half as many males compared to Pherocon 1C traps, we can estimate the ESA of a milk carton trap as approximately 1.2 ha. This corresponds to an effective sampling radius of just over 60 m (assuming circular attractive space).

Elkinton and Cardé (1980) also released males (marked with a different color) in a point release to compare the effects of the two release strategies on the estimated trap efficiency. They found that only 0.9% (as opposed to 4%) of point-released males were recaptured. This result further demonstrates that point releases cannot be directly used in estimating trap efficiency, particularly if the mean dispersal distance is much less than the spacing between traps (in Section 6.7.3 I will discuss how point releases can be used to estimate ESA indirectly). Elkinton and Cardé concluded their paper with a number of caveats: (1) the results only apply as long the trap capacity is not a factor, (2) the effect of female moth density on the proportion of males captured in traps is unknown, (3) the study assumes that laboratory-reared males are behaviorally equivalent to their wild counterparts, and (4) trap density may affect trap efficiency.

In a follow-up paper, Elkinton and Cardé (1988) addressed the last caveat. They established a 6×6 grid of pheromone traps spaced every 80 m, and monitored the numbers of wild males (naturally occurring population) captured in these traps. They found that periphery traps were capturing more males than traps in the center of the array, suggesting that at 80 m spacing the attraction areas ("active spaces") of traps were overlapping. This result is in agreement with their earlier findings that male moths are attracted to pheromone traps from at least 80 m (Elkinton et al. 1984), and the calculation above that the effective attraction radius of these traps is about 60 m (assuming circular attractive area; in actuality, the attractive area is likely to be elongated and to extend downwind, see Elkinton et al. 1984). To summarize, the efficiency of gypsy moth traps decreases with decreased intertrap distance, most likely as a result of the overlap of individual traps' attraction areas.

It also turns out that the efficiency of the gypsy moth trap depends on male density. Taylor et al. (1991) compared the number of male gypsy moths captured in milk-carton traps with the aerial density of flying males, deter-

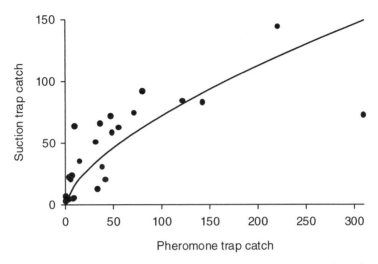

Figure 6.7: Relationship between a pheromone trap catch and the absolute aerial density of male gypsy moths, as measured by a suction trap. (After Taylor et al. 1991.)

mined by using a suction trap of known absolute efficiency (because the suction trap samples a known volume of air per unit of time). If the efficiency of a milk-carton trap does not depend on population density, then numbers of males captured in a pheromone trap and numbers captured by the suction trap should be linearly related. Taylor et al. (1991), however, found that this was not the case (Figure 6.7). They fitted a power relationship to these data, using the aerial density as the independent variable, and pheromone trap catch as the dependent variable. Because the estimated exponent associated with aerial density was significantly less than one, it appears that the efficiency of the pheromone trap decreases at high population densities.

A possible explanation for this loss of efficiency could be interference between males (Taylor et al. 1991). When two males approach the same female, they compete with each other, with one abandoning suit (Doane and Cardé 1973). At higher male densities, competitive interactions near the pheromone trap will induce a high proportion of males to leave the area, leading to lower trap efficiency.

6.6.5   Synthesis

In general MMR methods are not well suited to an investigation of long-distance attraction. Since we do not have information about movement tracks of individuals, the only viable approach is to investigate attraction indirectly, by fitting models to data. This approach has a reasonable chance of working if we have a good understanding of mechanisms employed by individuals to locate and approach attractive foci; in other words, if we have a good model for the movement process and the only task is to estimate the parameters of the model. By contrast, distinguishing between two or more alternative attraction mechanisms using only the MMR data is difficult, and may even be impossible. The study of Banks et al. (see Section 6.6.1) is a good illustration of this point. The results of fitting a variety of diffusion models to the data strongly indicated that long-distance attraction to host plants is present. However, the best-fitting model assumed a spatially constant and temporally varying advection coefficient, most likely getting the mechanism wrong (it is more probable that the strength of attraction varies with the distance from hosts, and its apparent decline with time was due to insects moving into the host patch).

Flux-based methods are better suited to quantifying attraction than methods relying solely on population density, because flux data contain directional information. Nevertheless, we cannot use flux data to directly infer directional influences on organism movements, and it is still necessary to use inverse methods, that is, to fit models to data.

The success of an MMR investigation into attraction, thus, appears to depend on two conditions. First, it is important to use simple, detail-free models. One should not expect to be able to resolve intricate details of how individuals bias their movements towards attractive foci based on MMR data only. Second, one should approach the problem from several directions, and collect data sets addressing different aspects of the movement process. The gypsy moth example is a nice illustration of this idea. Any one of the studies of the many described in Section 6.6.4 would not be capable of yielding a definitive answer. Taken all together, however, they provide an excellent model for working out details of pheromone trap attraction, and for estimating the effective attraction area and various factors that may affect it. Although ESA can be strongly affected by several factors, including trap interference and behavioral interactions among males, the situation is not hopeless. We can use the estimated quantitative relationships between environmental factors and trap efficiency to appropriately adjust the ESA of male gypsy moths, in order to translate trap catches into absolute population densities.

6.7 A Worked Example: Population Redistribution in a Bark Beetle

The southern pine beetle (*Dendroctonus frontalis*) is the most destructive insect pest of pine forests in the southern United States. For example, during 1995, at the peak of the last outbreak, estimated timber loss exceeded $300 million (Cronin et al. 1998). Pine trees protect themselves from insects and fungi by exuding resin. The southern pine beetle (SPB) has evolved a remarkable strategy to overcome such defenses. Pioneering beetles (individuals initiating attack) emit a congregation pheromone, frontalin, that attracts other conspecific beetles. As more beetles bore into the tree they release more pheromone to attract additional beetles, resulting in a positive-feedback process known as *mass attack*. As beetles congregate on the tree, they literally drain it of its resin resources, nullifying the tree's ability to defend itself (Hodges et al. 1979). It may take 2,000–4,000 beetles to overcome the defenses of a healthy pine tree (Goyer and Hayes 1991). As the mass attack progresses, and the larval resource—inner bark of the tree—starts to fill up with beetles, they begin to release a repelling pheromone that eventually inhibits congregation at the tree (Payne 1980) and shifts the attack focus to adjacent hosts.

Despite the high economic impact of this insect, little quantitative information was available on its movement in the late 1980s when we started a systematic exploration of the processes governing SPB population redistribution, combining data and modeling approaches. (I take this opportunity to acknowledge the help and support from my colleagues at the bark beetle project RWU-4501, Southern Forest Experiment Station, USDA Forest Service; the research was additionally supported by two grants from the USDA Competitive Grants Program.) We separated population redistribution in this beetle into two conceptual phases: dispersive movements when beetles fly far away from sources of congregation pheromone and other attractive volatiles, and congregative movements in the vicinity of mass-attacked trees. This distinction, although to a large degree artificial, allowed us to reduce the daunting task of quantifying SPB movement to manageable chunks. Accordingly, I begin by describing our efforts to quantify the SPB dispersal (Section 6.7.1), next address congregation (Section 6.7.2), and finally discuss the estimation of the effective sampling area of the SPB pheromone traps (Section 6.7.3).

The most serious difficulty we encountered in studying SPB movement was our inability to obtain any data on movements of individual beetles flying under natural conditions. This presented particularly great problems in studying SPB congregation. In fact, in our first, unsuccessful, attempts at quantifying beetle movements around mass-attacked trees we tried to use an individual-based approach. However, we were not able to consistently follow flying beetles. Some beetles were lost because they flew upwards (passive trap data suggest that the mean height at which beetles fly under natural conditions is about 5 m above ground). Even when they remained low, beetles were quickly lost against the forest background because they are small, dark colored, and follow erratic flight paths. In short, our understanding of SPB movement in the field had to be developed using exclusively Eulerian approaches (although we did use some data from a laboratory study employing flight mills; see below). This limitation makes the SPB movement project a good example for the chapter on MMR methods, but in many ways it was a frustrating experience. Lack of individual-based data forced us to make many simplifying assumptions and to abandon overly ambitious plans to measure fine details of SPB movement behavior.

6.7.1   Intraforest dispersal

We studied the dispersal of the southern pine beetle using mark-recapture methods (see Turchin and Thoeny 1993 for details). The dispersive nature of beetle movements was enforced in the experiment by releasing marked beetles outside of active congregations and by removing all incipient congregations (host trees in initial stages of mass attack) from the study area. Beetles were self-marked when they crawled on the outside of bolts cut from brood trees and coated with fluorescent powder (see Section 2.3.1). Beetles were recaptured with a circular array of pheromone-baited traps (Figure 2.2).

The interval between trap collections in this study (2–4 days) was too long to allow the use of instantaneous methods. In addition, beetles emerged from the brood bolts continuously throughout each replicate release. Thus, the appropriate method of analysis was to sum recaptures at each trap over the whole course of a replicate release and to fit these data with one of the time-integrated formulas. A check of directionality in the spatial pattern of recaptures did not reveal the presence of a biologically significant advection term (see Turchin and Thoeny 1993), indicating that Formula 6.6 is the appropriate one for the analysis of these data. Because we discovered that the variance in the data increased almost linearly with the mean, we log-tranformed the observed numbers of recaptures. This also served to linearize the fitting equation

$$\log C(r) = \log A - \frac{1}{2}\log r - \frac{r}{B} \tag{6.19}$$

(see Box 6.2 for the definitions of all quantities). This formula was fitted by a simple regression of $Y = \log C(r) + 1/2 \log r$ on r.

The theoretical curve provided an adequate fit to the data in the majority of replicate releases. Figure 6.8 shows the data and fitted curves in the three replicate releases for which we have enough information to translate fitted parameters A and B into mechanistic parameters D, δ and α (see below). The coefficients of determination for regressions were generally in the neighborhood of 0.8–0.9 (Turchin and Thoeny 1993: Table 1). Interestingly, fitting the same data with the negative exponential curve (the two functional relationships are comparable in that they both have two free parameters) revealed that the Bessel approximation fit the data significantly better ($P > 0.02$). This result provides support for the hypothesis that the diffusion model gives a good overall description of beetle dispersal. It does not, however, imply that all the assumptions of the model hold true for the system. For example, the model assumes a homogeneous environment, but by studying the residuals we found a significant effect of local host density on recaptures in a trap. The good overall fit of the model suggests that we can treat the environment as *quasihomogeneous* at the scale of SPB dispersal. In addition to varying in space, the dispersal rate also changed with season. For instance, the estimated median dispersal distance was 0.92 km in the releases conducted during fall months, and 0.45 km during the summer (Turchin and Thoeny 1993).

The quantitative information about SPB dispersal resulting from these analyses can be employed in two ways: (1) to estimate the dispersal kernel or (2) to estimate the diffusion rate D. A direct estimate of the SPB dispersal kernel is provided by the suitably scaled spatial distribution of recaptured beetles (see Turchin and Thoeny 1993). Thus, if our goal is to model SPB dynamics at the temporal scale of beetle generations (one month in summer) and the spatial scale of kilometers, the above analysis suggests that we can represent its dispersal with the Bessel dispersal kernel, $V(r) = aK_0(r/B)$. Here B is the parameter representing the spatial scale of dispersal that we estimated above and a is the scaling parameter to ensure that $V(r)$ integrates to one (since it is a probability distribution). The estimation of the dispersal kernel would be a satisfactory end point of a study of movement in many empirical systems. The problem with the SPB, however, is that its movement is strongly affected by the presence of congregation foci. Thus, the realized rate of dispersal could be much less than the one we measured if there is a high density of SPB infestations in the area (in fact, that is precisely what happened in one of the replicate releases; see Turchin and Thoeny 1993). This means that we need to integrate the dispersal and the congregation phases of SPB movement within the same modeling framework. Congregative movements occur on a much smaller spatio-temporal scale than months and kilometers (roughly speaking, on the scale of minutes and meters), and we need a measure of dispersal expressed in the same units. In other words, we need to translate

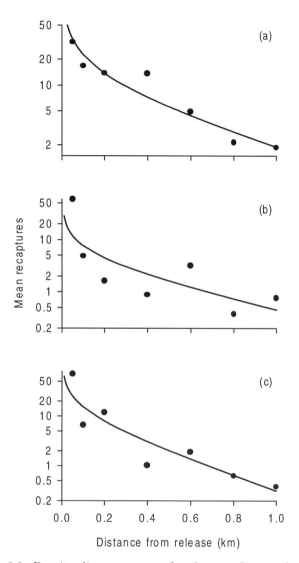

Figure 6.8: Density-distance curves for three replicate releases in a mark-recapture study of southern pine beetle dispersal. The data points are total recaptures per trap averaged over all traps at the same distance from the release point. The solid lines are results of fitting the data with Formula 6.19. (After Turchin and Thoeny 1993.)

fitted quantities A and B into movement parameters D, δ, and α.

The problem is that we have three unknowns (D, δ, and α) but only two equations to resolve them. Fortunately, we have some external information that allows us to approximate δ. Recall that δ is the disappearance rate, so that $1/\delta$ is the mean duration that a beetle would spend within the dispersing population. Beetles stop being dispersers because they attack trees, fly above the forest and get carried away by wind, or simply "run out of steam"—exhaust the lipid reserves that fuel their flight. We can discount the first possibility because congregation foci were removed within mark-recapture grids. Additionally, deploying sticky traps from a radio tower erected near a SPB infestation indicated that few beetles fly as high as tree tops (P. Turchin, unpublished data), suggesting that losses to "vertical emigration" of beetles (which could then be dispersed over long distances by weather systems) should be minimal. To estimate the distribution of flight durations we turn to the study of Kinn and Parresol (1998) who measured SPB flight potential by flying beetles to exhaustion on a flight mill. It would be better to estimate this parameter for beetles flying under natural conditions, but that option, unfortunately, was not available to us (see the comment above about our inability to obtain individual-based data on SPB movements).

The distribution of total flight durations measured by Kinn and Parresol was not very different from the exponential one, thus complying with the assumption of constant rate of loss in the diffusion-disappearance model. The mean flight duration (averaging over the both sexes) was 190 min. The distribution of total flight distances had a similar shape, with the mean distance of 3.5 km. Thus, the average speed of SPB flight is about 20 m/min. This may be an underestimate due to the drag imposed by the rotor arm of the flight mill. On the other hand, the flight duration measured in the laboratory may be an overestimate of that under field conditions where beetles are susceptible to predation and inclement weather. We will proceed with calculations assuming that the laboratory data give us the right order of magnitude for the parameter δ. Since disappearance rate is the inverse of the mean flight duration, our estimate is $\hat{\delta} = 1/190$ min^{-1}. This estimate, in turn, allows us to estimate $D = B^2\delta$ (see Box 6.2). The mean and SE of the D estimates from the three releases shown in Figure 6.8 are 1500 ± 500 m^2/min. The variance of this estimate is not too bad, considering that the diffusion rate is the rate of growth of *squared* distance. Finally, using the formula for A in Box 6.2 we estimate the effective sampling rate as 0.19 ± 0.07 m^2/min.

Can we interpret this estimate of D in terms of parameters of SPB individual movement? In particular, what does the estimate tell us about the "wiggliness" of beetle paths? We can answer this question by an application

of the Patlak model (see Section 4.4.1). Let us assume that beetles fly through
the forest with constant speed $v = 20$ m/min and that we sample their positions at regular intervals, say $\tau = 1$ min. This assumption implies that the
first two moments of move length distribution are $m_1 = v\tau$ and $m_2 = v^2\tau^2$.
Substituting these relationships in Equation 4.27 for 2D space, and assuming
spatial homogeneity, we obtain the following formula for D:

$$D = \frac{v^2\tau}{4}\frac{1 + \psi}{1 - \psi} \tag{6.20}$$

This formula and the estimated values of D and v imply that the average
cosine of the tuning angle $\psi = 0.88$. In other words, SPB movement measured
on the temporal scale of $\tau = 1$ min is characterized by a very high degree of
directional persistence (recollect that when ψ is close to one, turning angles
are concentrated near $0°$). Another indication of a high directional persistence
characterizing the SPB dispersive movements is the comparison between the
average distance flown on the flight mill, 3.5 km, and the estimated mean
displacement from the release point, 0.8 km (using Formula A.59). When the
ratio of the length of the actual track to the length of the straight-line displacement is only four or five, the pattern of movement must be characterized
by a very high degree of directional persistence, indeed.

6.7.2   Congregation dynamics

Studying congregation dynamics is a particularly challenging task when data
collection is limited to Eulerian approaches. The approach that we adopted
was to assume a very simple model for the SPB movement, and then estimate
its parameters by measuring fluxes of congregating beetles. The basic premise
of our study was that beetles flying in the vicinity of a mass-attacked tree
use chemical (pheromones and host volatiles) and visual (vertical shape of
tree bole) cues to bias their movements towards the tree (Gara and Coster
1968). This bias results in congregation that, in turn, fuels mass attack. The
attractive bias should be a function of the distance and direction from the
tree to the flying beetle. In addition, the bias is modified by the total number
of beetles already boring into the tree. At the beginning of mass attack, the
strength of the bias should increase with the number of attacking beetles,
since more beetles are congregating on the tree, releasing more congregation
pheromone. As the tree begins to fill up with beetles, the bias should decrease
in strength, possibly even becoming negative (repulsion).

The field procedure that we used to quantify the SPB congregation dynamics is described in Turchin and Simmons (1997). Briefly, a host tree (loblolly
pine) was selected as the focus for mass attack. At each of six distances from

the focal tree (ranging from 1.5 to 30 m), in each of the four cardinal directions, and at three different heights above ground (2, 5, and 7 m), we placed a 1 m by 1 m sticky screen. Next, we initiated attack on the focal tree by baiting it with the congregation pheromone and monitored the course of attack by recording the number of beetles landing on the tree as well as the cumulative number of successful attacks per dm^2 of bark. The three-dimensional structure of the SPB "swarm" that formed around the mass-attacked tree was mapped by recording once a day how many beetles were caught on each side of all 1 m × 1 m sticky screens. A similar experiment was conducted later in which beetle densities and fluxes were measured around a source of SPB population, a brood tree producing newly emerged beetles (see Cronin et al. 1998). The purpose of the second experiment was to measure parameters of beetle movement in the absence of congregation pheromone. Although the data collection was structured in a way that would allow us a full three-dimensional analysis, for simplicity I will focus on only one dimension, the dependence between the attractive bias and the distance to the congregation focus (results on how wind direction affects the attractive bias were presented in Turchin and Simmons 1997).

The model underlying data analysis is the diffusion approximation of the biased uncorrelated random walk developed in Section 4.2.1. The diffusion model has two parameters, the bias (attraction) coefficient β and the motility μ. The random walk model has two additional parameters: the move length λ and the interval between moves τ. I will assume that only β varies in space (we expect that it will decrease with distance from the attraction focus) and that μ is constant. What are the model's predictions about the data patterns? Our basic datum is the number of beetles hitting each side of a sticky trap per unit of time. For simplicity, let us align the x axis with the direction toward the attractive focus, and consider a sticky trap at x m from the source. Let J_+ be the number (per unit time) of beetles hitting the trap while going in the positive x direction. J_-, analogously, is the number trapped going in the opposite direction. Now consider the volume of space λ units long to the left of the trap, centered at $x - \lambda/2$. Assume that half of the beetles within this volume will move along the x axis and half will move along the y axis (I am assuming here that movement is confined to the two horizontal dimensions). Of the beetles moving along the x axis, some will move left with probability L and the rest will move right with probability R (the latter will be captured by the trap at x). The rate at which beetles will be captured, therefore, is the product of the number of beetles in the volume, $\lambda u(x - \lambda/2)$, and the probability of going right, $R(x - \lambda/2)$, divided by the time interval τ:

$$J_+ = \frac{1}{\tau} \lambda u \left(x - \frac{\lambda}{2} \right) R \left(x - \frac{\lambda}{2} \right) \tag{6.21}$$

The net flux along the x direction is $J = J_+ - J_-$. Expanding J_+ and J_- in a Taylor series (as in Section 4.2.1), we obtain an approximate equation for the flux

$$J = \frac{\lambda}{\tau}(R - L)u - \frac{\lambda^2}{4\tau} \frac{\partial u}{\partial x} = \beta u - \mu \frac{\partial u}{\partial x} \tag{6.22}$$

where $\beta = \lambda(R - L)/\tau$ and $\mu = \lambda^2/4\tau$. Using a similar argument, we can also calculate an approximate formula for the sum of beetles captured at both sides of a trap

$$S = J_+ + J_- \approx \frac{2\mu}{\lambda} u \tag{6.23}$$

Combining Equations 6.22 and 6.23 and solving for β we obtain

$$\beta = \frac{v}{2} \left[\frac{J}{S} + \frac{\lambda}{2} \frac{\partial (\ln S)}{\partial x} \right] \tag{6.24}$$

where $v = \lambda/\tau$ is the speed of beetle flight. The quantities J and S in Equation 6.24 are calculated from the data, and we already have an estimate of v (see Section 6.7.1). Unfortunately, we cannot yet estimate β because the right side of Equation 6.24 contains an unknown parameter λ. However, if $\beta = 0$ (that is, there is no congregation) then we can solve Equation 6.24 to express λ in terms of observable quantities J and S. Thus, a two-phase approach to estimating the attractive bias is suggested. First, measure J and S under conditions of no congregation and estimate λ. Second, use the λ estimate in Equation 6.24 to estimate β.

As I mentioned above, Cronin et al. (1998) measured SPB fluxes around source trees—previously attacked trees that were producing next generation beetles. I will focus here on the three replicates that were conducted within natural infestations. (The other replicates focused on infestations that were controlled with the cut-and-leave method, and it is possible that creating an opening in the forest changes the pattern of beetle movement rendering the data unsuitable for our purpose.) Because we are interested in movement of beetles unaffected by attractive bias I excluded the traps that were within 20 m of mass-attacked trees. Exploratory analysis suggested that the sum of recaptures, S, is well fitted by the Bessel approximation $S(x) = Ax^{-1/2} \exp[x/B]$. Fitting this relationship to the data, differentiating it with respect to x, and using the formula

$$\hat{\lambda} = -2 \frac{J}{\partial S/\partial x} \tag{6.25}$$

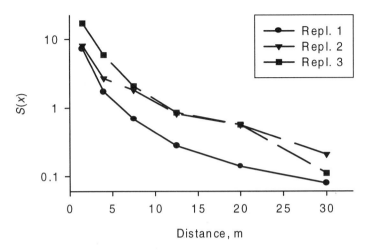

Figure 6.9: The density of SPB congregation "swarms" around mass-attacked trees measured by S, the number of beetles captured on both sides of a flux trap per day.

I obtained an estimate of $\lambda \approx 4.5$ m.

Having an estimate of λ in hand, we can now address the main question—the estimation of $\beta(x)$ using the data on the beetle fluxes measured around the mass-attacked trees. The temporal course of attack varied between the three replicates. The attack on the first tree developed slowly. As a result, the density of swarming beetles around the tree, as measured by $S(x)$, was lower than in the other two replicates (Figure 6.9). Despite this difference in the overall beetle density, the SPB density gradients were similar across the three replicates. In all cases $S(x)$ showed a sharp increase in the vicinity of the mass-attacked tree [note that $S(x)$ is plotted on a logarithmic scale in Figure 6.9]. Exploratory analysis indicated that log-transforming both $S(x)$ and x yields a linear relationship between these two variables; accordingly, I fitted the model $\ln S(x) = a + b \ln x$ to the data using linear least squares. Differentiating this model with respect to x we obtain $\partial(\ln S)/\partial x = \hat{b}/x$, where $\hat{b}$ is the estimated slope in the regression of $\ln S$ on $\ln x$. Finally, we substitute this estimate of $\partial(\ln S)/\partial x$, the previously obtained estimates of v and λ, and the measured J/S into Equation 6.24 to solve it for $\beta(x)$. Estimates of β were obtained separately for each replicate mass attack, for each distance x, and for different

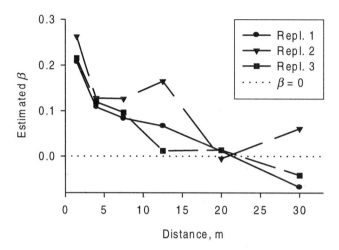

Figure 6.10: Estimated relationship between the attractive bias β and the distance from the mass-attacked tree x (during the peak attack stage).

stages of mass attack. Attack stages were defined as "early" (0–1.5 successful galleries per dm^2 of bark), "peak" (1.5–3.5 galleries dm^{-2}), and "late" (3.5–6 galleries dm^{-2}).

Despite differences in the course of attack between replicates, there was a surprising degree of agreement between the estimates of $\beta(x)$ (Figure 6.10). As expected, the relationship between β and x is a monotonically decreasing one. The spatial range of attraction (during the peak stage) appears to be around 10–15 m; there is no detectable bias at either 20 or 30 m from the attractive source. Estimates of $\beta(x)$ during early attack stages were similar to those shown in Figure 6.10. The pattern of attraction during the late stages, however, was substantially different (Figure 6.11). As expected, the magnitude of the attractive bias near the attack focus declines during the late stage of attack. What is puzzling is that the range of attraction appears to increase beyond 20 m. Our observations indicate, however, that as the experimental tree filled up with beetles, the focus of mass attack began shifting to other host trees nearby. Thus, the most likely explanation of the pattern in Figure 6.10 is that during the late attack stage we are measuring attraction not to a point source, but to a diffuse group of congregation foci.

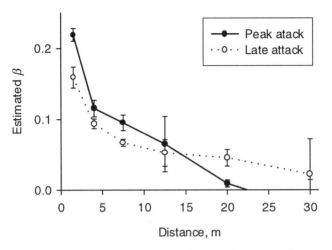

Figure 6.11: Comparing attractive biases during peak versus late attack (means and SE).

6.7.3 Effective sampling area of traps

In order to understand our conceptual approach to estimating ESA, imagine that the density of emerging beetles, B, is constant in space. Movement paths of individual beetles will be very complex because they will be responding to the constantly shifting, filamentous pheromone plume emanating from the trap. To estimate ESA, however, all we need to know is the average proportion of insects starting at the distance r from the trap that will be captured. Let this proportion be $P(r)$. The number of beetles emerging in an annulus centered on the pheromone trap of unit width and radius r is the product of beetle density and the area of the annulus, $B \times 2\pi r$. The number of beetles from this annulus that will be captured in the trap is $P(r) \times B \times 2\pi r$. Finally, the total number of beetles captured in the trap will be the sum of captured beetles originating from all annuli

$$T = \int_0^\infty 2\pi r P(r) B \, dr$$

Thus, if we know $P(r)$, ESA can be estimated by the following formula

$$\alpha = \frac{T}{B} = 2\pi \int_0^\infty r P(r) \, dr \qquad (6.26)$$

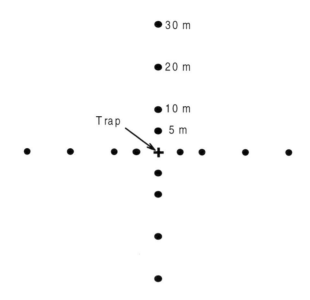

Figure 6.12: The multiple release/single trap design. Filled circles show positions of dusted bolts—sources of southern pine beetles.

Note that we are not assuming that all beetles at r are equally likely to be trapped. Clearly, there will be directional effects (e.g., beetles downwind should be more likely to be attracted to the trap than beetles starting upwind). The function $P(r)$ averages over all directional effects since it is the proportion of all beetles evenly distributed in the annulus of radius r that will be trapped. Also, our derivation is not affected if beetles are not distributed uniformly, provided that the trap is placed randomly with respect to any clumps (see the discussion in Elkinton and Cardé 1980).

Our empirical approach, therefore, was to estimate $P(r)$ in field studies, and then use Equation 6.26 to calculate the effective attraction area. There are two basic ways of doing this—a single release/multiple trap design, and a multiple release/single trap design (Figure 6.12). The first approach is more economical for studying long-distance recapture rates because probability of recapture is low (it is usually easier to employ 100 traps than to release 100 times as many beetles). Our first study, that quantified long-distance (up to 1 km) probabilities of recapture, therefore, used the single release/multiple trap design (see Section 6.7.1). The problem with this design, however, is that it is not well suited for examining short-distance recapture probabilities—if traps are placed too close to each other, then their attractive areas will overlap, and the probability of recaptures will be underestimated (Elkinton and Cardé 1988). In the long-distance attraction study no traps were placed closer than 50 m from the release point, and we only used two traps at 50 m, and four traps at 100 m (Figure 2.2). As we shall see later, this spacing was sufficient to reduce the interference effects since the recapture probability of a beetle originating 50 m from a trap was only about 1–2%.

The second study addressed the short-range (5–30 m) probabilities of recapture, employing a multiple release/single trap design (Figure 6.12). As in the dispersal study, self-marked beetles were self-released from SPB-infested pine bolts that were coated with a fluorescent pigment. All release bolts at the same distance from the trap were dusted with the same fluorescent color (we could use only four different distances, because we had only four dust colors that could be readily distinguished from each other).

Combining the results of the short-range study with data on SPB dispersal discussed in the previous section, we found that average recapture rate was about 10% in the close vicinity of a trap, and declined to less than 0.01% at distance of 1000 m (Figure 6.13). The quantitative nature of the relationship between the proportion recaptured $P(r)$ and distance was analyzed with regression. Our goal was to fit an empirical smooth curve rather than a theoretically motivated model. The most parsimonious model was

$$\log_{10} P(r) = -1.04 - 0.38(\log_{10} r)^2 \qquad (6.27)$$

This two-parameter model (which resulted from a log-log quadratic regression, see Turchin and Odendaal 1996 for rationale) explained 85% of variance in the data. Integrating, we obtain an estimate of the effective attraction area, $\hat{\alpha} = 1090$ m^2. Thus, ESA is estimated as approximately 0.1 ha.

Our results are reminiscent of those obtained by Elkinton, Cardé, and coworkers in their gypsy moth studies. For example, the efficiency of the SPB pheromone trap in recapturing beetles released at 5 m, about 10%, is on a par with the efficiency of the milk carton pheromone traps that only capture 9.6% of those males that approach within 2 m of them (Elkinton and Childs 1983). Nevertheless, the ESA of milk carton traps was an order of magnitude greater than the ESA of the SPB multi-funnel trap (1.2 ha versus 0.1 ha, respectively). This quantitative difference is probably due to a greater "active space" of gypsy moth traps. Indeed, while Elkinton et al. (1984) estimated that male moths are attracted to females from a distance of at least 80 m, our results in Section 6.7.2 suggest that the attractive range of SPB-attacked trees is only

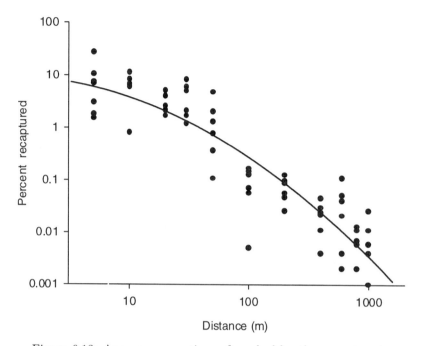

Figure 6.13: Average proportions of marked beetles recaptured as a function of distance between a beetle source and a trap. Data from the short-distance and long-distance studies combined. The curve is the fitted phenomenological model (Equation 6.27). (After Turchin and Odendaal 1996.)

10–15 m. It appears that male gypsy moths are much more sensitive to the sex pheromone than southern pine beetles are to the congregation pheromone.

6.7.4 Synthesis

The southern pine beetle example is a good illustration of both the potential and the limitations of mass mark-recapture methods. On one hand, we have obtained estimates for all the parameters of the SPB movement model. This was achieved by dividing the overall problem into several pieces, and designing a separate field study for each piece. On the other hand, we had to make several assumptions about the SPB movement that greatly oversimplify the actual process. For example, we assumed that we could use the distribution of flight durations measured in the lab to interpret the results of the field MMR study. Another severe oversimplification is our assumption that beetles in the vicinity of attractive sources move according to an uncorrelated random walk, although we know that this is not true. This is why it was so important to obtain a field measure of the parameter λ. This parameter, the "mean free path," is related to the wiggliness of the SPB flight trajectories (the higher is the degree of directional persistence, the larger λ should be).

Given the severe nature of the assumptions that we made to estimate the parameters describing SPB movement, the next critical step is to test the model's predictions using a novel data set that is independent of the data on which the parameter estimates are based. Such a test is currently in progress using the data of Cronin et al. (1998) on the numbers of marked SPB recaptured at a grid of trap trees serving as "mini-infestations." The data set presents a novel situation for the model because SPB population redistribution was a net result of both dispersal and congregation (recollect that the model parameters were estimated by considering dispersal and congregation separately).

It is well known that one cannot deduce mechanisms from observed patterns. Thus, any MMR study is limited in its ability to resolve between the possible behavioral mechanisms underlying movement. This limitation can be partially overcome by measuring more than one aspect of population redistribution patterns. In particular, the analysis of SPB congregation in Section 6.7.2 indicated that the flux approach can provide more information about the behavior of organisms than an approach limited to measuring population density near an attractive focus. Measuring population density only indicated that beetles were swarming densely around the attractive focus, suggesting that there was active congregation at the attacked pine tree. Analysis of population fluxes, on the other hand, provided more details about the SPB congregation and also yielded estimates of $\beta(x)$, the attractive bias as a function of distance to the attraction focus.

Chapter 7

Individual Mark-Recapture

7.1 Introduction

This chapter focuses on individual mark-recapture/resighting (IMR), an approach that occupies an intermediate position between analyses of individual paths (Chapter 5) and mass-mark recapture studies (Chapter 6). Superficially, individual mark-recapture is similar to mass mark-recapture because organisms are marked, released, and at a later time recaptured (or resighted) rather than followed continuously. The analytical approaches to IMR data, however, are more closely related to those used in the analysis of paths where emphasis is on individual displacements rather than population redistribution. In other words, the approaches in the analysis of paths and IMR data are Lagrangian, while the analysis of mass mark-recapture is Eulerian (see Section 3.1).

Quantitative IMR analyses are less frequently found in the literature than are mass mark-recapture or path analyses. This is surprising because, in my opinion, IMR is a very practical and potentially powerful approach. On one hand, IMR data can yield a more detailed understanding of movement and the factors affecting it, compared to mass mark-recapture. On the other hand, it is much easier to get periodic fixes on animal positions, the essence of IMR, than to follow organisms continuously. Additionally, following organisms continuously can be done for only a limited time, while IMR data can often be gathered until the end point of dispersal (e.g., settling down within a new territory, or dying). It is true that path analysis provides more detailed information about the behavior of the followed organisms and the actual locations visited. However, when analyzing path data we have to worry about autocorrelated moves, which greatly complicates the statistical analysis (see Section 5.6.1). Paradoxically, by leaving much of the detail out (whether intentionally, or because we have no choice), we may get a better understanding of biological factors affecting dispersal without getting bogged down in technical details.

IMR methods are of particular importance in conservation and natural resource management of animal populations. Methods are well developed for individually marking vertebrates and conspicuous invertebrates, such as butterflies (e.g., fish and bee tags, color-coded bird bands, and radiotransmitters; see Chapter 2) . Much dispersal data for these organisms has been collected, although few of these data sets have been properly analyzed. It is amazing that after spending innumerable hours of hard work many investigators simply report the mean dispersal distance or, even worse, just give the *P*-value for some test on the difference between two groups of animals (e.g., males versus females, or juveniles versus territory holders). Other studies use inappropriate methods of analysis, for example, calculating home range sizes for animals that are clearly nomadic. At the same time, many models employed for conservation purposes have no empirical basis for their movement parameters, although theory suggests that the mode and rate of dispersal are among the most critical parameters determining population persistence (see Section 7.4). Filling this gap between movement data and population models is the general goal of this book, and in this chapter I will pay a special attention to issues (and species) important for conservation biology.

The organization of this chapter follows the standard sequence. First, I discuss general approaches to measuring the rate of dispersal (Section 7.2) and some alternative approaches used by vertebrate ecologists (Section 7.3). Section 7.4 presents a detailed application of these methods to the dispersal of juvenile spotted owls. Second, I turn to the analysis of the effects of spatial heterogeneity (Section 7.5). One particular aspect of heterogeneity, movement corridors, is reviewed in Section 7.6. Third, I discuss the analysis of attraction, with a focus on density-dependent movement (Section 7.7). Finally, I review some very general approaches for fitting almost any kind of movement model to IMR data (Section 7.8).

7.2   Rate of Dispersal

7.2.1   Analysis of movement as a random walk

One of the strengths of the IMR approach lies in its power to examine the influences of various factors on individual movement. With the right kind of data, one can build increasingly more detailed and realistic models of movement within heterogeneous landscapes (Sections 7.5–7.8). In this section, however, we will be concerned with the less ambitious goal of measuring the rate of dispersal occurring within homogeneous or quasihomogeneous environments (the latter condition holds when the spatial scale of heterogeneity is less than the scale of dispersal).

Although it is possible to advance many different kinds of dispersal measures, I will focus on one, the diffusion rate. Measures more commonly used by field workers, such as the average dispersal distance, can be very misleading due to the very leptokurtic nature of most dispersal distance distributions. Median dispersal distance is a better measure of what the "average individual" does, but does not provide the information about the variance in dispersal distances that is of crucial importance in predicting population spread (see Section A.4). Median dispersal says nothing about the (often all-important) tail of the distribution. (In the extreme case when more than half of organisms do not disperse, the median dispersal is 0 no matter what the rest of individuals do.) Finally, measures solely derived from the distribution of dispersal distances lack an explicit temporal component.

The diffusion rate D has some theoretical support since it is a parameter in reaction-diffusion models. Additionally, D combines in a single measure the influences of both the mean and the variance in the dispersal distance. Finally, D explicitly incorporates the time element because it is the temporal rate of population spread. However, D should not be used to infer the rate of population redistribution and spread unless it is first shown that the mode of dispersal conforms, at least approximately, to the assumptions of the simple diffusion model (see Section 6.3.1). No single measure can be superior to others under all different circumstances. In practice this means that the most complete way of presenting one's results is to publish the whole frequency distribution of dispersal distances (as well as the time scale on which dispersal occurs), letting others calculate from these data whatever dispersal measure they prefer.

The main approach on which I will focus in this section is the analysis of IMR data as an uncorrelated random walk (no directional persistence, or any other kind of correlation between successive displacements). In this approach we equate each displacement between two successive fixes to a random walk *move*. The random walk process is characterized by the distribution of move lengths and durations (distance and time between two successive fixes). Equation 4.8 gives the formula for diffusion rate (or motility—these are the same in the absence of spatial heterogeneity) as a function of the first two moments of the move length distribution and the move frequency (the reciprocal of the first moment of the distribution of move durations). Before we apply this formula, however, we should test that the assumption of no correlation between subsequent moves is not violated by our data.

7.2.2   Independence between steps

I will assume that during an IMR program at least some animals have been recaptured or resighted more than once. In fact, the approaches described here are particularly useful when the same animal was resighted on numerous occasions. If this is not the case, then we lack the data needed to test for autocorrelation in the displacement between subsequent fixes (proceed to Section 7.2.4).

There are two general approaches: an overall test of independence between subsequent moves, and a battery of tests probing specific assumptions of independence between move lengths, directions, and so on. The overall test can be adapted from the procedure proposed by Swihart and Slade (1985) for testing for independence between subsequent positions of an animal within its home range. If an animal moves according to a random walk, clearly its subsequent positions will be autocorrelated. This is not a problem for the analysis, because we need to know whether subsequent *displacements* are autocorrelated or not. Thus, from the fix data x_i, y_i (the first number is the x-coordinate of fix i, and the second number is the y-coordinate), we first calculate the displacements $(X_i, Y_i) = (x_{i+1} - x_i, y_{i+1} - y_i)$, and then apply the Swihart and Slade test to subsequent displacements. Clearly, we need at least three spatial fixes for each marked animal (coordinates of the release point, and at least two recaptures) to construct a pair of subsequent displacements.

PROCEDURE FOR THE OVERALL TEST OF INDEPENDENCE   The test proceeds as follows. First, calculate the mean of the x and y components of displacements ($\bar{X}$ and $\bar{Y}$, respectively). Next, estimate the mean squared deviation (a measure of variance), s^2, and the mean square distance between successive displacements, d^2:

$$s^2 = \frac{1}{n-1} \sum_{i=1}^{n} [(X_i - \bar{X})^2 + (Y_i - \bar{Y})^2] \tag{7.1}$$

$$d^2 = \frac{1}{m} \sum_{i=1}^{m} [(X_{i+1} - X_i)^2 + (Y_{i+1} - Y_i)^2]$$

(m is the number of pairs of subsequent displacements). The test statistic is the ratio d^2/s^2. Values of this statistic significantly less than 2 imply positive autocorrelation between subsequent displacements, while values greater than 2 suggest negative autocorrelation. Swihart and Slade (1985) give the critical values of the ratio d^2/s^2 for several significance levels and a variety of eccentricity values (the latter measures the anisotropy in the diffusion along x and y directions under the null hypothesis). I recommend, however, a parametric bootstrap procedure for constructing a significance test. First, use the data to estimate the parameters of the uncorrelated random walk (the distribution of move distances and move durations). Next, implement the random walk as a computer simulation and generate a set of paths using the same number of paths and the same number of fixes per path as in the data set. Finally, for each pseudodata set, calculate the d^2/s^2 statistic. The whole procedure is repeated a large number of times (1,000 should be sufficient) to construct the frequency distribution of the statistic under the null hypothesis.

If significant autocorrelation is detected by this approach, the next step is to determine what attributes of movement contribute to this lack of independence. Additionally, it is a good approach to explore the fine structure of the movement process even if the overall test is not significant, because more narrowly focused tests may detect peculiarities in movement that were missed by the overall test. The logic of these tests is to estimate autocorrelation in various move attributes, such as length, direction, and duration, as well as dependence of these quantities on the age and sex of animals.

PROCEDURES FOR NARROWLY-FOCUSED INDEPENDENCE TESTS Testing for autocorrelations in the distances and durations of subsequent displacements is straightforward. It is accomplished by calculating the product-moment (Pearson's) correlation coefficients (Sokal and Rohlf 1981). The effects of individual, sex, and age on the average move distance and duration can be explored either by several separate one-way analyses of variance, or by an overall multifactorial ANOVA.

Move directions are circular quantities and thus the usual correlation coefficient cannot be used. The approach is, therefore, to calculate turning angles θ_i, and to test whether θ_i's are characterized by a significant degree of clustering. The degree of clustering in circular quantities is measured by the length of the mean vector (Batschelet 1981:10)

$$r = \frac{1}{n}\left[\left(\sum_{i=1}^{n}\cos\theta_i\right)^2 + \left(\sum_{i=1}^{n}\sin\theta_i\right)^2\right] \tag{7.2}$$

Statistical significance of r is tested by the Rayleigh test (Batschelet 1981:54). If the distribution of turning angles is symmetric, then the expected sine is zero, and we can simply use the average cosine as a measure of autocorrelation in the subsequent move directions.

In addition to calculating autocorrelations between subsequent moves, it is also a good idea to check how higher-order autocorrelations behave. This can be accomplished by examining the autocorrelation function (ACF). ACF for move length and duration is calculated in the usual fashion (e.g., Chatfield

1989). For ACF in the move direction, plot the average of $\cos(\alpha_i - \alpha_{i-\tau})$ against τ. Here α_i is the absolute direction of move i, and τ is the time lag separating moves i and $i - \tau$.

CAVEATS   Care should be taken not to mix together moves occurring within different kinds of habitats (this applies equally to the overall and the narrowly focused tests). For example, the same animal may be observed moving within a favorable habitat where it makes shorter steps, and within an unfavorable habitat where it makes lengthy moves. If displacements in both habitats are tested together for independence, the investigator will detect positive auto-correlation simply because several moves are needed to traverse each habitat. This may result in an erroneous rejection of the uncorrelated random walk model. The proper procedure is to analyze displacements in each habitat sep-arately. If no correlations are detected in both habitats, then the appropriate model to use is the uncorrelated random walk with spatially-dependent coeffi-cients. Similarly, it is important to distinguish between move autocorrelation and individual heterogeneity in move parameters. Individual variation in the mean of a move attribute may be factored out by using individual-specific means, instead of the population mean in Formula 7.1 and its equivalents.

A very important point to keep in mind is to not be carried away by a hypothesis testing mindset, and to always estimate the magnitude of effects that were shown to be statistically significant. Even a highly statistically significant effect may be of little biological importance, especially when large data sets are analyzed.

If we find significant deviations (both statistically and biologically) from the movement mode assumed by the random walk model, we have two choices. One is to use correlated random walk methods to analyze the data (see Chapter 5). The other approach is to decrease the spatio-temporal resolution of the data set by omitting some of the fixes until the temporal autocorrelations disappear (see the discussion of oversampling in Section 5.2.1). The decision should be based on the questions one wants to pose, and on the quantity of data available. For example, if tens or hundreds of fixes are available for each marked animal, but we are primarily interested in quantifying their large scale dispersal patterns, then subsampling is indicated.

EXAMPLES OF ANALYSIS   To illustrate the use of d^2/s^2 statistic as a test of null hypothesis for independence, Swihart and Slade (1985) radio-tracked a territorial female cotton rat. This example illustrates the use of the technique in estimating home range size, but is equally instructive for estimating the rate of dispersal (just substitute in the following text *locations* with *displace-*

ments). Locational readings were taken at 5–10 min intervals. Using all 302 successive pairs of fixes, the calculated value of $d^2/s^2 = 0.5$ was significantly less than 2, suggesting a high degree of positive autocorrelation between subsequent fixes. Next, Swihart and Slade asked the following question, what is the minimal time interval necessary to yield approximately independent pairs of observations? They calculated d^2/s^2 ratio for all locational records separated by a lag time varying from 5 to 455 min. Increasing lag time resulted in increased values of the statistic. It approached 2 and became statistically indistinguishable from it at a time lag of 270 min. What this result says is that sampling the cotton rat's positions at 5–10 min intervals results in a largely redundant, or oversampled, data set (see Section 5.2.1). A larger time interval of about 200 min would require much less work, while resulting in a minimal loss of information. This suggests that intensive samplings of animal positions, coupled with the autocorrelation analysis, could be particularly useful in establishing optimal rates of sampling during the early stages of designing an IMR program.

An example of probing the fine structure of the movement process with a battery of narrowly-focused tests comes from the work by Andow and Kiritani (1984) who observed individual movements of green rice leafhoppers within an array of rice plants. Andow and Kiritani (1984) determined that times between moves ("tenure times") and move distances were independent, as indicated by correlation analysis. However, there was a significant positive autocorrelation in the distance of subsequent moves. Andow and Kiritani then used an unbalanced one-way ANOVA to analyze individual differences in the movement distance, and found significant heterogeneity (which was not, however, related to either sex or age). This result prompted them to conclude that the autocorrelation in move distances was due to inter-individual differences. By contrast, tenure times and movement frequencies were not sequentially correlated, and there were no apparent individual differences in these attributes. Andow and Kiritani concluded that the simple random walk model was a reasonable first approximation of the movement process in the green rice leafhopper.

7.2.3 Net squared displacement

Analysis of net squared displacement, $\bar{R}_n^2$, was introduced in Section 5.3.3 as a way to test the applicability of the correlated random walk model. Calculating this quantity is also useful in the analysis of IMR data. For uncorrelated random walk, the formula relating $\bar{R}_n^2$ to move attributes is simply

$$\bar{R}_n^2 = nm_2 \tag{7.3}$$

where m_2 is the second moment of the distribution of move distances (the average squared distance), and n is the number of moves. In other words, under the assumption of no correlations between moves, $\bar{R}_n^2$ increases linearly with time. This provides a straightforward approach for the following test of the uncorrelated random walk model.

PROCEDURE   Plot $\bar{R}_n^2$ versus n and observe whether it increases linearly with n. If $\bar{R}_n^2$ increases faster than linearly (curves up), then one explanation is that there is significant directionality in movement. This could be a result of correlation between the direction of successive moves, or because there is a directional bias (either of the two mechanisms would lead net *unsquared* displacement to behave linearly with n). If net squared displacement curves down, then either dispersal rate is decreasing with time or there is some barrier to dispersal. An extreme example is movements within a home range, in which $\bar{R}_n^2$ should approach a constant asymptote.

   If the relationship between $\bar{R}_n^2$ and n appears to be approximately linear, then its slope can be predicted by calculating the average squared move length (m_2).

EXAMPLE OF ANALYSIS   Strong and Bancroft (1994) studied juvenile dispersal of radiotagged white-crowned pigeons. Because they reported the mean (m_1) and the standard deviation (σ) of displacements for each consecutive time interval in their Table 2, I could calculate the average net squared displacement as a function of time ($\bar{R}_n^2 = M_1^2 + \sigma^2$). $\bar{R}_n^2$ increased approximately linearly with time until day 15 (Figure 7.1), after which the curve apparently approached an asymptote. Two explanations are consistent with this pattern. One is that after 10–20 days of dispersal pigeons began settling down to permanent territories. The second explanation is that the dispersers reached the limits of the area within which they could disperse.

AUXILIARY ANALYSIS: RELATIONSHIP OF MOVE DISTANCE TO DURATION   Although not central to the goal of estimating dispersal rate, the analysis of the relationship between move distance and move duration can yield useful insights about the appropriate time scale on which to measure dispersal. The general idea of the analysis is a variation on the theme of how net displacement grows with time (or number of moves). Depending on the mode of dispersal of the studied animals and on how frequently their positions are determined, we can distinguish three possible extreme cases. First, the animal may move in a fairly directional manner, then spend some time resting or exploring the immediate locality before making another directional move.

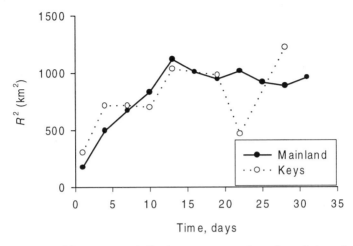

Figure 7.1: Mean squared displacement as a function of time during postfledging dispersal in white-crowned pigeons. (Data from Strong and Bancroft 1994: Table 2.)

In this case, the move distance should be linearly related to the time spent traveling. Second, the animal may wander in a haphazard manner through the landscape with many direction reversals during the interval between two successive fixes. Each fix provides information about an overall straight line displacement rather than the actual distance traveled, and the random walk theory predicts that the squared net displacement should increase linearly with time. Finally, an animal may leave its previous territory (or the territory of its parents) and undergo an intense period of dispersal terminated by settling in another permanent territory. If the dispersal period is short compared to the time between subsequent fixes, then we expect no relationship between the distance traveled and time between fixes. These three theoretical cases represent the possible extremes of the relationship between distance moved and time. Intermediate cases are also possible. For example, for small time intervals distance may increase linearly, but for large time intervals, it may be the squared distance that increases linearly (as in a correlated random walk process). Another example, is that distance may initially increase with time, reflecting travel between the natal and permanent territories, and then cease to increase when the animal settles down. All these possibilities may be in-

vestigated by plotting (and regressing) against time the displacement and the
squared displacement resulting from each move.

An interesting example of how movement may switch between different
modes was found in a checkerspot butterfly *Euphydryas anicia* by Odendaal
et al. (1988). The males of this butterfly form aggregations within a flat
high-altitude plain (Odendaal et al. 1988). We recorded the paths of male
butterflies and defined a "move" as the displacement between two consecutive landing points. Male movements outside aggregations was characterized
by highly directional flight. Within aggregations, however, males spent most
of their flying time chasing each other. As a result, their movement, when
involved in chases, was characterized by a high frequency of direction reversal. We separated all moves into "chases" and "non-chases," and plotted the
move distances against move durations (Figure 7.2). Next we investigated the
relationship between the move distance l_i and duration t_i by regression, and
found that for non-chase flights the model $l_i = at_i$ was characterized by a
higher coefficient of determination than the relationship suggested by random
walk, $l_i^2 = at_i$. For flights involving chases, the reverse was true (Figure 7.2).
This result supports the idea that non-chase flights in *E. anicia* males are
better described as linear movement, while flights involving chases are better
described as a random walk.

7.2.4   Estimating diffusion rate

The diffusion rate for an uncorrelated random walk in two-dimensional space
is

$$D = \frac{m_2}{4\tau} \tag{7.4}$$

where m_2 is the second moment of the distribution of move distances (the
average squared displacement between fixes), and τ is the first moment of the
distribution of move durations. Choosing the appropriate definition of move
duration requires some thought. For nomadic organisms, like many insects
that continuously move throughout their life, move duration can be defined as
time between two successive positional fixes, as long as subsequent moves are
not correlated (see Section 7.2.2). By contrast, territorial organisms, like many
birds and mammals, may disperse only once during their life time, as juveniles.
In such cases, the time between any two successive fixes is irrelevant and may
even be misleading. The appropriate temporal interval is, then, generation
time. The decision on which approach to use should be guided primarily by
what is known about the biology of the studied species. We can, however,
supplement the biological knowledge by analyzing the relationship between
the distance and time between successive fixes (see Section 7.2.3).

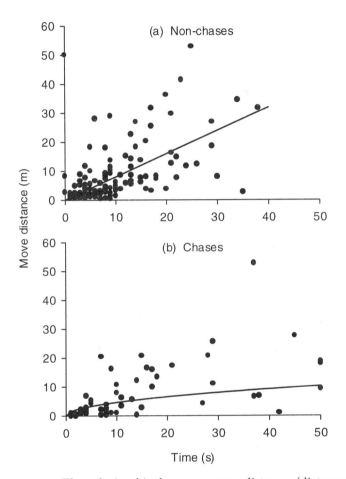

Figure 7.2: The relationship between move distance (distance between successive landing points) and move duration in male *Euphydryas anicia*. (a) Non-chases: the straight line is $l_i = 0.80t_i$. (b) Chases: the curve is $l_i^2 = 2.12t_i$. (After Odendaal et al. 1988.)

PROCEDURE FOR ESTIMATING DIFFUSION RATE   Once the appropriate temporal scale of movement has been determined, calculating the estimate of diffusion rate from n moves is straightforward:

$$\hat{D} = \frac{\sum_{i=1}^{n} l_i^2}{4 \sum_{i=1}^{n} t_i} \tag{7.5}$$

where l_i is the length of the i-th move (distance between fixes) and t_i is its duration. This formula assumes that move durations are the appropriate time scale. If the time scale is set by biological considerations, then the denominator of the formula becomes $4n\tau$ (for example, τ is one generation).

CAVEATS   The most serious problem plaguing estimates of the spatial extent of dispersal is that long-distance dispersal distances are often undersampled. Designs using spatial arrays of traps to recapture marked animals are particularly prone to this bias. Even radiotelemetry studies, which typically give us a much better understanding of long-distance dispersal, may be affected by this bias. For example, a radio-transmitter may fail before the animal carrying it settles down in a permanent territory.

We can attempt to correct for this bias by explicitly modeling the movement and detection processes, and then iteratively adjusting the parameters of the model until its output gives a good fit to the data. The general approach to this problem will be discussed in Section 7.8, and an example is given in Section 7.7.2.

7.2.5   Example: natal dispersal in birds and mammals

Speaking very broadly, we can distinguish two general classes of spatial behavior in animals. Some, like most insects, are nomadic—they shift their position continuously throughout their life, showing no attachment to any particular location. The variance in the spatial coordinates of nomadic animals increases throughout their life time. Others (e.g., most vertebrates) are territorial; they occupy a more or less well defined home range. In these species, the variance in the spatial position approaches an asymptote with time. Animals that hold a territory for part of a year and do not return to the same territory year after year occupy an intermediate position between the extremes of nomadism and a life-long territoriality.

Natal dispersal is the movement of prereproductive individuals from their place of birth (natal home range) to a new home range where they may attempt to breed (Wiggett and Boag 1989). Understanding and quantifying natal dispersal is of key importance to spatial population dynamics, evolution, and conservation of territorial animals (Lidicker 1975, 1995). Stimulated by a number of theoretical developments, particularly during the 1970s (e.g., Wright 1969, Gadgil 1971, Roff 1974a,b, 1975, Lidicker 1975, Hamilton and May 1977, Horn 1978), mammalian and avian ecologists directed a considerable amount of energy to studying dispersal. As a result, we now have a much better qualitative understanding of dispersal (for reviews, see Swingland and Greenwood 1983, Stenseth and Lidicker 1992a, Ims and Yoccoz 1997). However, although a large volume of dispersal data was collected during the last two decades, little of it has been summarized in quantitative form. In particular, I know of no broad comparisons of natal dispersal rates in different species. To initiate such comparisons, I performed an informal search of recent literature for studies that reported enough quantitative details on juvenile dispersal in birds and mammals to allow me to estimate the diffusion rate.

PROCEDURE   I used two methods for calculating natal dispersal rates. If the frequency distribution of net displacements resulting from juvenile dispersal was reported, I used Formula 7.5. Alternatively, if the distribution of dispersal distances was not reported, but both the mean and some measure of variance were, I estimated diffusion rate indirectly by first calculating the second moment of distribution of movement distances, m_2, and then using Formula 7.4. The second moment of distance distribution, or the mean average squared displacement is

$$m_2 = m_1^2 + \sigma^2$$

where m_1 and σ^2 are the mean and the variance of move distances, respectively. The variance was estimated as either the square of the reported standard deviation, or as the square of the reported standard error of the mean divided by the number of moves.

RESULTS AND CAVEATS   Tables 7.1 and 7.2 summarize the results of this exercise. Several caveats are in order. As I stressed earlier, no single number can truly summarize the complex process of dispersal, especially when we compare organisms characterized by very different modes of movement. With this in mind, I chose the diffusion rate as the most informative measure, because it incorporates both the mean and the variance of the distribution of dispersal distances.

Another caveat is that I have measured the temporal scale of natal dispersal in generation units. Strictly speaking, this is appropriate only to those species that disperse once in their lifetimes as juveniles. Thus, the rate of natal dispersal quoted in Tables 7.1 and 7.2 underestimates the true rate of population dispersal per generation for species that may shift their home ranges as adults.

Table 7.1: Natal dispersal rates in birds (the units of diffusion rate, D: m^2/gen).

Common name	D	Reference
Black-capped chickadee	$3.5\ 10^4$	Weise and Meyer 1979
Great tit		Greenwood et al. 1979
males	$2.0\ 10^5$	
females	$3.0\ 10^5$	
Great tit		Dhondt 1979
males	$0.9\ 10^5$	
females	$1.8\ 10^5$	
Willow warbler (males)		Foppen and Reijnen 1994
near highway	$5.9\ 10^4$	
away from highway	$0.8\ 10^4$	
House wren		Drilling and Thompson 1988
males	$1.9\ 10^5$	
females)	$3.0\ 10^5$	
White-crowned sparrow		Baker and Mewaldt 1978
males	$1.7\ 10^5$	
females	$1.5\ 10^5$	
Goldeneye (females)	$5.2\ 10^5$	Dow and Fredga 1983
White-crowned pigeon	$2.3\ 10^8$	Strong and Bancroft 1994
Eastern screech owl	$9.7\ 10^6$	Belthoff and Ritchison 1989
Tengmalm's owl	$1.6\ 10^9$	Korpimäki and Lagerström 1988
Sparrowhawk		Newton and Marquiss 1983
males, upland	$8.8\ 10^8$	
males, lowland	$3.6\ 10^8$	
females, upland	$9.8\ 10^8$	
females, lowland	$5.5\ 10^8$	
Swainson's hawk	$1.9\ 10^7$	Woodbridge et al. 1995
Spanish imperial eagle	$7.0\ 10^9$	Ferrer 1993

Table 7.2: Natal dispersal rates in mammals (m^2/gen).

Common name	D	Reference
Meadow vole	$3.2\ 10^1$	Boonstra et al. 1987
California mouse		Ribble 1992
females	$15\ 10^3$	
males	$3.5\ 10^3$	
Stephens' kangaroo rat		Price et al. 1994
females	$7.3\ 10^2$	
males	$4.3\ 10^2$	
Merriam's kangaroo rat		Jones 1989
females	$0.6\ 10^3$	
males	$3.0\ 10^3$	
Banner-tailed kangaroo rat		Jones 1987
females	$2.1\ 10^3$	
males	$0.7\ 10^3$	
Columbian ground squirrel		Wiggett and Boag 1989
females	$1.0\ 10^6$	
males	$2.0\ 10^6$	
Wolf	$5.5\ 10^6$	Mech 1987
Black-tailed deer		Brown 1961
females	$4.9\ 10^6$	
males	$6.7\ 10^6$	
Black-tailed deer		Bunnell and Harestad 1983
females	$1.3\ 10^7$	
males	$3.6\ 10^7$	

The final, and most important caveat is that the data on which diffusion rates in Tables 7.1 and 7.2 are based vary greatly in their quality, quantity, and the methodology with which they were collected. Of particular importance is whether the tail of the distribution of dispersal distances was well estimated or not. Because the diffusion rate averages over *squares* of distances moved, rare long-distance moves have a great deal of influence on the numerical value of D (as we have seen in Section 6.3, estimation of population rate of spread is even more sensitive to misestimation of the tail of dispersal distance distribution). Most of the studies listed in Tables 7.1 and 7.2 suffer from a spatially uneven sampling of dispersal distances, with highest detection probability concentrated near the release point. As I did not make any attempt to correct for this bias, most estimates of D in these tables are conservative with respect to estimating the spatial extent of dispersal.

Because of these caveats, these D estimates should be considered as tentative and very approximate, although they are probably accurate reflections of the order of magnitude of natal dispersal (10^x m^2/gen). Moreover, I did not bring the full power of the methods developed in this chapter to bear on the data sets on which the D estimates are based. It is my hope that, in the not too distant future, investigators themselves will refine these estimates by using analytical methods described in this chapter.

7.2.6 Synthesis

Calculating the rate of dispersal from IMR data is relatively straightforward. Probably the greatest danger is in assuming that the measured distribution of move lengths is an unbiased estimate of the true distribution. This is not true for most mark-recapture studies because long-distance moves are often less likely to be detected. Thus, it is imperative to adjust the observed distribution of move lengths to reflect this uneven sampling of space.

Another important point is that no single measure can summarize the dispersal rate in all different kind of organisms. Thus, we should not limit ourselves to calculating a single summary statistic, even one with good theoretical properties such as diffusion rate or $\bar{R}_n^2$. Data should be utilized fully, and some auxiliary analytical approaches are suggested in this section. One of the most useful ones is plotting square displacement against time, because qualitatively different movement patterns (such as straightened out movement, uncorrelated random walk, or territoriality) result in different expected curve shapes.

7.3 An Alternative Approach for Vertebrate Dispersal

7.3.1 Competition-driven dispersal

An interesting approach to understanding the processes that may determine the distribution of dispersal distances in territorial animals, such as many mammals and birds, has been advanced by Murray (1967) and further developed by Waser (1985, 1987). Their model is based on a simple mechanism—dispersing juveniles move no further than the first uncontested site (home range) that they can find. Murray (1967) assumed that juveniles move in a straight line using a randomly chosen direction until they find an empty territory, where they settle. This model assumes that juveniles posses no informa-

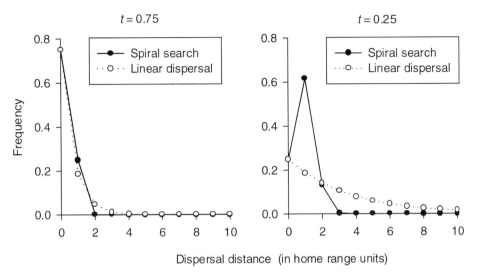

Figure 7.3: Distributions of movement distances predicted by two competition-driven dispersal models for two values of t (the probability that a site will be unoccupied).

tion about the status of a territory (occupied versus unoccupied) until they actually move there. Waser (1985), in addition, explored the consequences of systematic search, in which animals either have perfect information about the availability of all territories, or use a spiral searching pattern (checking all territories, starting with the ones adjacent to the natal site, and then in rings of progressively increasing radius). Spiral search is an extreme alternative to linear dispersal, because it assumes that juveniles will obtain perfect information about the status of all territories between their natal and breeding site. The consequence of this assumption for the dispersal distance distribution is that we will expect more short-distance moves, and many fewer long-distance ones (Figure 7.3).

Waser (1985) compared predictions of the completion-driven dispersal models to data and found a good fit of the data to one of the models (the linear dispersal) for prairie deermice, an intermediate data pattern between those predicted by the two models for white-crowned sparrows, and poor fit by either model for the big tit (Waser 1985: Figure 3). In the case of the poor fit (the big tit), there were significantly more middle-distance dispersal moves in the data than was predicted by either model, suggesting that processes other than competition for territories were responsible for the observed distribution of dispersal distances (Waser 1985).

An appealing feature of the models of competition-driven dispersal advanced by Waser is their simplicity. Only one parameter, the probability of a territory being empty (t) needs to be estimated. The estimation procedure is very simple, since t is taken to be equal to the proportion of dispersers staying in their natal ranges. The model is eminently testable. However, judging from Waser's results and subsequent tests (Buechner 1987, Miller and Carrol 1989, Rodgers and Klenner 1990, Porter and Dooley 1993), the models do not fit actual distributions of dispersal distances very well, with the spiral search variant failing to fit any data set. One good fit is between the linear dispersal model and the data for prairie deermice; but as Porter and Dooley (1993) pointed out, there are serious pitfalls in comparing model predictions to raw data on the distribution of dispersal distances (see Section 7.3.3), and it is not clear whether this problem affects the deermice data.

7.3.2   A geometric model of vertebrate dispersal

An even simpler, "geometric model" for vertebrate dispersal was advanced by Buechner (1987). Formally, her model has the same form as Waser's linear dispersal model, but instead of assuming that a disperser has a constant probability of settling (t), Buechner assumed that there is a constant probability of either settling or dying ($p = t + m$, where m is the probability of dying).

The distribution of movement distances (x) predicted by the model is $p(1 - p)^x$. Buechner outlined several methods of fitting the model to the data. One is to regress the log of the number of dispersers reaching x (the distance expressed in units of home range widths) on x. The other approach is to compare the mean and the variance of the distance distribution to those expected from the geometric, $(1 - p)/p$ and $(1 - p)/p^2$, respectively (Karlin and Taylor 1975: Table II). Comparing model predictions to a number of data sets, Buechner found that in several cases the geometric distribution fit the data better when the first distance class was excluded from the analysis.

Buechner (1987) argued that assumptions of her model were less restrictive than Waser's. However, the price is that the model is less mechanistic. Whereas Waser's model explicitly assumed that the only way that an animal could stop was to find an empty territory (thus, a mechanistic interpretation of the parameter t as the probability of a territory being empty), the geometric model assumes that a disperser can stop for any reason, including death. Thus, knowing only the best-fit estimate of p, it would be difficult to conclude anything about the mechanisms driving dispersal.

EXTENSIONS OF THE GEOMETRIC MODEL   Miller and Carroll (1989) argued that the geometric model has two important limitations: the requirement that stopping probabilities stay constant throughout the dispersal, and the inability of the model to incorporate the maximum dispersal distance. They proposed a modification of the geometric model in which the probability of stopping was modeled as a function of distance, $p = p(x)$. They used three different functions to represent the effect of distance on p: (1) a linear increase in p with distance, (2) an elliptical increase, first slow but then accelerating, and (3) an S-shaped increase, modeled by a sine function.

Miller and Carroll used simulation to estimate parameters of the three models. For each combination of model parameters, they used computer simulation to generate an expected distribution of dispersal distances. The best combination of parameters was selected by minimizing the statistic of the Kolmogorov-Smirnov test for goodness-of-fit. Miller and Carroll applied their technique to five sets of field dispersal data, and found that in several cases one of the modifications fit the data better than the geometric model.

7.3.3   Some problems

An attractive feature of the approaches considered in this section (at least, as they were first formulated) is that they connect an analysis of dispersal data to mechanisms that could drive dispersal in territorial animals. Unfortunately, the subsequent development of the approach took the more phenomenological route, probably because the initial mechanistic but too simplified models did not fit the data well. For example, the modifications of the geometric model proposed by Miller and Carroll (1989) are of the curve-fitting nature without an explicit mechanistic basis.

One serious problem with the approaches discussed in this section is that they are not spatially explicit. First, the Waser model assumed that occupied and unoccupied territories are distributed independently of each other. It is much more likely, however, that occupied territories will be clustered. Clustering implies that more territories near the dispersal origin will be occupied, and thus a disperser will have to move further away than would be expected under the assumption of no clustering.

Second, the analyses with competition and geometric models assume that dispersal end-points are sampled evenly over space, leading to an unbiased measure of the distribution of dispersal distances. Yet, as Porter and Dooley (1994) pointed out, the majority of data sets were obtained by methods that sampled dispersers unevenly over space. The most common problem is that dispersers leaving the study area are undetected, and thus long-distance movements are undersampled. Another, more subtle, problem is when the space is sampled unevenly. For example, the study area of Baker and Mewaldt (1978) was about 7 km long but only 1 km wide. In addition, within that general study area, some locations were sampled more thoroughly than others (see their Figure 1). Porter and Dooley (1994) showed by simulation that even in the extreme case of uniformly-distributed dispersal distances, the measured distribution will still resemble the geometric if dispersers are sampled unevenly over space.

If the distribution of sampling stations is known, the bias due to uneven sampling can be corrected (see Porter and Dooley 1994 for details). But even with this correction we quickly reach the limits of resolution imposed by the nature of data. After all, when trying to fit models to a single function (the distribution of dispersal distances), we can estimate at best three or four parameters (e.g., the intercept, the general slope, a measure of curvature, and possibly an inflection point, if one is present). This means that we can resolve, at best, 3–4 mechanistic parameters of the model. In other words, the distribution of dispersal distances is not a very informative data set on which to test various models. It does not incorporate the information on intermediate localities where animals were detected (as is the case in many IMR studies). In fact, by focusing solely on the distribution of dispersal distances we forego all the advantages that individual-based data have, and might as well analyze these data using the Eulerian methods of Chapter 6.

7.3.4   Synthesis

I see two directions in which the analysis of vertebrate dispersal can be advanced. One is to use unabashedly Eulerian methods (see Chapter 6). In line with the approaches described there, however, I recommend focusing not on the distribution of dispersal distances, but on the spatial density of detected dispersers. This approach avoids the difficulties imposed by uneven spatial sampling more gracefully than the approach described by Porter and Dooley (1994). In Chapter 6 I review a number of formulas based on random walks and diffusion, which can be used in the analysis of dispersal. I am aware that these are precisely the approaches that Buechner criticized as "complex and mathematically cumbersome analytical models." The geometric model that she advocates as an alternative to diffusion models is actually an instance of the use of an empirical model (see Section 3.3). In fact, the geometric distribution, $p(1-p)^x$, is simply a discrete version of the most popular empirical curve, the negative exponential, ae^{-bx} [with parameters $a \equiv p$, and $b \equiv -\ln(1-p)$]. To illustrate the points I discuss here, let's compare the geometric model to the Bessel function (the solution of the diffusion-disappearance model for time-integrated data; see Section 6.2.5). There is nothing inherently complex or cumbersome about this curve. In practice, we will be fitting the data with the formula $Ar^{-1/2}\exp[-r/B]$ (the approximation of the tail of the Bessel function; r is the distance from release). Numerically, or conceptually, it is as easy to fit this formula to the data (see Section 6.2.5) as the geometric distribution or the negative exponential curve. Fitting the Bessel function to the data, however, may allow us to distinguish between the losses due to dispersal versus death. Moreover, there are analytical formulas for certain extensions of the simple diffusion model, for example, when there is an externally imposed directionality on dispersal. Finally, the Bessel curve is based on a better mechanistic model, the random walk, than the model of linear movement underlying the geometric distribution. I doubt that there are any animals that disperse along straight lines (even approximately). On the other hand, the random walk framework describes well the movement patterns of a variety of animals, including dispersing vertebrates (e.g., see the analysis of dispersal in the juvenile spotted owl, Section 7.4).

The second approach that I advocate (and that can be used to complement the first approach) is to analyze not only the distribution of net dispersal distances, but the complete data set, including the known intermediate positions of dispersing animals. Such an approach would start with formulating an explicit model for the mechanisms responsible for dispersal, attempt to estimate the parameters of the model by analyzing the IMR data using the approaches described in this chapter, and then test the resulting model with data on population-level dispersal patterns (this could be the same distribution of distances between the natal and the permanent territory).

7.4 A Worked Example: Dispersal of Juvenile Spotted Owls

The northern spotted owl (*Strix occidentalis caurina*) is a famous bird. Its ecology and conservation are the topic of intense debate among foresters, wildlife ecologists, academics, politicians, social scientists, and economists (Gutiérrez et al. 1995). A key process, about which very little quantitative information exist, is dispersal of juvenile spotted owls (Gutiérrez et al. 1998). Dispersal is the mechanism by which new habitats or habitats made vacant by local extinction can be colonized. Dispersal can contribute to stabilization of local population fluctuations and to prevention of local extinctions—*rescue effect* (Gutiérrez and Harrison 1996). Spatial models used to predict success of the owl conservation strategies are extremely sensitive to assumptions about habitat geometry and, especially, juvenile dispersal behavior (Harrison et al. 1993). Yet dispersal is probably the least understood demographic process in spotted owl ecology (LaHaye et al. 1994, Gutiérrez and Harrison 1996).

Several groups of investigators studied dispersal of radio-collared juveniles (Forsman 1980, Gutiérrez et al. 1985, Laymon 1988, Miller 1989, Miller et al. 1997; see the summary in Thomas et al. 1990: Appendix P). Although these data were collected during the 1980s, they were never analyzed in detail (for example, Thomas et al. 1990: Table P1 simply presents the frequency distribution of maximum dispersal distances). In the absence of detailed information on dispersal, the spatially explicit models for spotted owl dynamics typically assume a wide range of dispersal coefficients (e.g., LaHaye et al. 1994, Lamberson et al. 1994).

I will apply the methods described in this chapter to analyze one data set on the movements of radio-collared juvenile owls, collected by R. Gutiérrez and coworkers.

EMPIRICAL METHODS   Gutiérrez et al. (1985, 1998) followed the dispersal of 23 juvenile owls outfitted with transmitters in two years: 1983 (11 individuals) and 1984 (12 individuals). Birds were followed from the natal nest (transmitters put on birds in August) until they either died or lost the transmitter, which typically happened during the following winter (November–March). Birds were monitored at least once per week, except during periods of inclement weather. Owlets lost during ground tracking or located in inaccessible areas were found and monitored using an aircraft. (Full details of the methods can be found in Gutiérrez et al. 1998.)

OVERALL DIRECTIONALITY   The first issue in the analysis is to determine if there is an overall directionality of dispersal. In 1983 the owls dispersed in a southerly direction (significantly differently from a uniform distribution; see Gutiérrez et al. 1985). However, there was no apparent directionality in 1984 (Figure 7.4). Thus, there is no consistent pattern in the data. A persistent directional bias operating over many years is doubtful, as it would result in a general migration of the owl population southwards, and there is no evidence that such a migration actually occurs. Keeping to my philosophy of using the simplest model in the absence of compelling reason to do otherwise, I chose to model dispersal as having no preferred direction.

DEFINING A DISPERSAL MOVE   We now are ready to probe the fine structure of recorded paths. Visual examination suggests that owl dispersal does not fit well the pattern of a usual random walk model (Figure 7.5a). The general impression, confirmed by what we know about owl biology (Gutiérrez et al. 1998), is that some fixes reflect the outcomes of a genuine dispersive move,

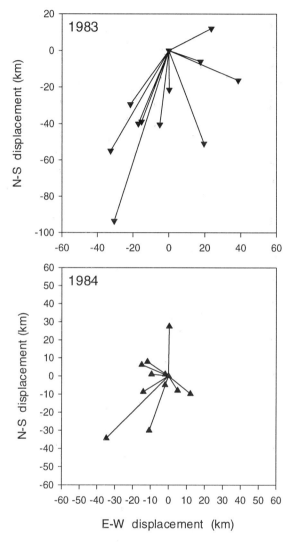

Figure 7.4: Net displacements of radio-tracked northern spotted owlets. The x-axis plots the magnitude of displacement from the starting point to the last fix along the East-West direction, while the y-axis plots the same along the North-South direction. (Data from Gutiérrez et al. 1998.)

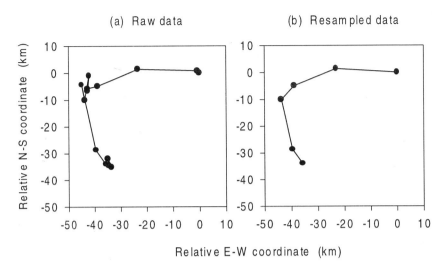

Figure 7.5: Resampling a path (owlet 'Bertha,' 1983). (a) Raw data: all fixes shown. (b) Resampled data: some fixes are combined together in a single move, using the algorithm described in the text.

while the majority of displacements between fixes are exploratory, with owls tending to return back to some temporary home range (THR). The territory of a northern spotted owl is typically somewhat less than 1,000 ha (Gutiérrez et al. 1995), corresponding to a territory diameter of about 3 km. Let us hypothesize that after a major dispersive move, owls explore the territory in which they find themselves, as well as neighboring territories. This should result in a pattern of exploratory forays of characteristic length, followed by a return to the THR. We can test this idea because moves resulting from exploratory forays should have one peculiarity—a higher than expected frequency of complete direction reversals, or turning angles grouped around ±180°. This prediction does not assume that all exploratory forays are recorded by fixes (since fixes were taken at fairly infrequent intervals, not all exploratory movements would be detected). Even when not all forays are detected, however, there still should be a preponderance of direction reversals. The pattern will be somewhat diluted, but still detectable.

I tested this idea by taking the cosines of turning angles and sorting them by move distance. Thus, the hypothesis is that there is a characteristic length of return moves that is associated with an unusual frequency of direction reversals. The results suggested that turning angles associated with moves

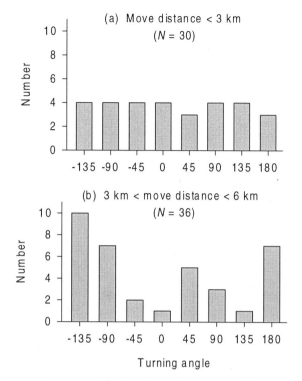

Figure 7.6: Frequency distributions of turning angles or radiocollared owls sorted by distance.

of less than 3 km in length were uniformly distributed (mean ±SE cosine $\psi = -0.03 \pm 0.13$, $N = 30$; see Figure 7.6a). By contrast, moves between 3 and 6 km in length had too many direction reversals to occur by chance alone ($\psi = -0.35 \pm 0.12$, $N = 36$; see Figure 7.6b). Turning angle distribution of moves of length greater than 6 km was not significantly different from the uniform ($\psi = -0.03 \pm 0.11$, $N = 51$). This result supports the hypothesis of exploratory moves of 3–6 km in length. It is interesting that this corresponds to moves of length between 1 and 2 home-range diameters. Thus, we tentatively conclude that moves less than 3 km in length represent displacements within a THR, while moves of length between 3 and 6 km represent exploratory trips to neighboring territories.

Our task now is to resample paths in such a way that non-dispersive (both exploratory and within THR) moves are "tuned out," and we are left with the

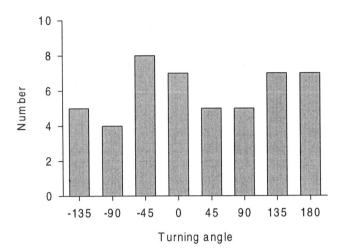

Figure 7.7: Frequency distributions of turning angles of resampled moves (radiocollared owls).

moves that correspond to actual dispersal events. One completely legitimate way to approach this task is to ask a highly experienced owl biologist to simply do it for us. Another approach is to use some objective rule to combine displacements between fixes into moves (see discussion of this problem in Section 5.2.2). The preceeding analysis of turning angles suggests that we should combine together short moves. To do this, I wrote a simple program that combined fixes less than d km apart together in one move, and subjected the resulting "resampled" paths to a test for overall independence between moves (using the Swihart-Slade formula in Section 7.2.2). I also combined together fixes less than two days apart, on the hypothesis that some long-distance moves could require more than a day to be accomplished. For d between 1 and 3 km, the test suggested a statistically significant nonindependence between subsequent moves. For $d = 4$ km and greater, the statistic was not significant. I decided to use a cut-off point of $d = 5$ km, as a compromise between this result and the cut-off distance of 6 km suggested above. When paths are resampled according to this algorithm, the resulting distribution of turning angles is very close to the uniform (Figure 7.7). An example of what a resampled path looks like is shown in Figure 7.5b.

MODELING OWL DISPERSAL   Remember that the goal of this analysis is to provide some empirically-based estimates of dispersal parameters for spatially-explicit models of owl population dynamics. We have already learned valuable information, that after each dispersing move owls appear to investigate an area of approximately two home range diameters in extent. (By the way, this suggests the spatial scale at which to quantify spatial heterogeneity in any analysis of effects of habitat characteristics on owl dispersal.) The next step is to try to describe the dispersal scale and pattern, using the resampled paths as data. Absence of directional persistence in resampled moves (Figure 7.7) suggests that we may be able to use the uncorrelated random walk as a framework for modeling owl dispersal. We also need to check the autocorrelations and the crosscorrelation in move distance and duration (duration is defined as time between two dispersal moves; this includes both the traveling time and the time spent exploring after the move is completed). None of the correlations turns out to be significant, so we assume that the uncorrelated random walk is indeed an appropriate model to use. The reason that there is no correlation between move distance and duration is probably because the actual traveling time occupies only a small proportion of move "duration," most time being spent by the owlet moving within its THR and exploring nearby territories.

Having reassured ourselves that there are no correlations between move attributes, we should also check that the stochastic process is stationary (that its parameters do not change with time). To do this, we plot both the move distance and duration against move number (Figure 7.8). The duration of the first move reflects the predispersal period (time between radio-collaring and the first dispersal move). Omitting this move, there is no statistically significant effect of move number on duration. The average time between dispersal events is 17.3 days, although there is a great amount of variation around the mean (SD = 18 days).

The mean move distance (±SD) was 16.5 (±12.5) km. Unlike move duration, however, average move distance tended to decrease with move number (Figure 7.8, regression significant at $P = 0.05$ level).

Based on these results, we can formulate the following empirically-based model for owl dispersal. In order not to assume any particular probability distributions for move attributes, we can randomly draw from the empirically observed distributions. Thus, to initiate dispersal, we randomly draw a date from the set of observed dates of first dispersal. The distance is randomly drawn from the observed distances of first moves, and the move direction is drawn from a uniform distribution of directions. Next, we draw a duration between dispersal moves using the distribution for all moves. The move distance is drawn from the observed distances of second moves, and the direction again

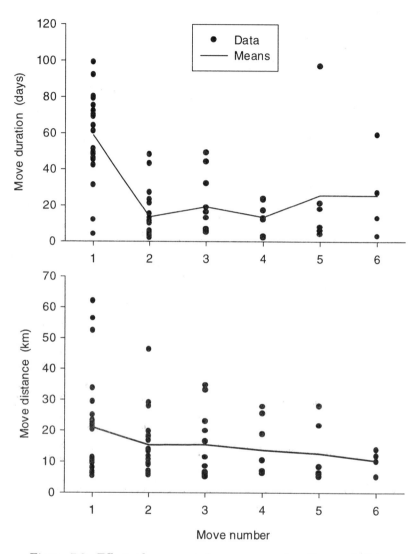

Figure 7.8: Effect of move number on move duration and distance (radiocollared owls).

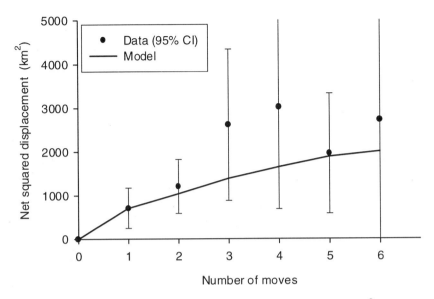

Figure 7.9: Comparison of the predicted and observed R_n^2 (radio-collared owls). Error bars indicate the 95% confidence interval.

is completely random. The whole process is repeated for a desired number of moves.

NET SQUARE DISPLACEMENT   The final step is to test the prediction of the random walk model on the population spread of juveniles. In the usual uncorrelated random walk model the net squared displacement R_n^2 grows linearly with the number of moves (n). The increment of R_n^2 with each move is the second moment of move length distribution. However, in juvenile owls move length decreases with time. To incorporate this effect, I constructed the prediction of the random walk model by incrementing R_n^2 with the actual mean of squared lengths for each move number separately. The predicted R_n^2 was within 95% confidence limits of the actual one (Figure 7.9), so the random walk model appears to give an adequate prediction of the spread process. There might be a hint of underpredicting R_n^2 at $n = 3$–4. Because it was not a significant difference, we will need more data to determine whether it is real or not.

Synthesis

The pattern of movement emerging from the preceding analysis is quite fascinating, and appears to agree with what we know about owl biology (Gutiérrez et al. 1998). Owl movements occur on two spatial scales. Local moves within THR (< 3 km) and forays to explore the THR vicinity (between 3 and 6 km in length) conform to the pattern of a central-place forager. Dispersive moves are long (16.5 ± 12.5 km), and fit well the assumptions of the uncorrelated random walk process. These moves take a dispersing owlet from one THR to another, and contribute to the growth of the variance in the owl spatial position (see the discussion of nomadic versus territorial movements in Section 7.2.5). However, as time progresses, owls make shorter dispersive moves and are more likely to settle.

Clearly characteristics of the environment within which owls find themselves should have an effect on the pattern of their dispersive moves and the probability of settlement (or death). In particular, whether a territory is occupied by another owl or not should have a profound effect on the length of stay in a location. It would also be interesting to analyze the effect of other factors, such as the quality and the spatial distribution of the habitat and prey availability, on the length of stay and the length of the next dispersive move. Finally, the nature of the terrain over which owls pass also may be taken into the account (although it is not certain that an owl can accurately assess the nature of the terrain it passes over). A general discussion of effects of spatial heterogeneity on movement, and approaches to quantifying these effects will be taken up in the next section.

7.5   Effects of Spatial Heterogeneity

7.5.1   General approach

One of the strengths of the IMR approach lies in its power to examine the influences of various factors on individual movement. With the right kind of data, one can build increasingly more detailed and realistic models of movement within heterogeneous landscapes. The basic idea of the analysis is to quantify the effects of environmental variables on movement parameters: the probability of moving, and the distance, direction, and duration of each move (remember that moves should be defined appropriately; see Section 5.2.1). Ideally, we should observe several consecutive moves for each marked individual. This allows us to investigate such movement attributes as turning angles between two subsequent moves, and to test for the effects of history on individual responses to variable environments.

Two general approaches to collecting data are possible: a manipulative experiment, in which animals are released in locations chosen to represent the range of environmental conditions of interest; and an observational study, in which animals choose themselves where they will go. A possible disadvantage of a manipulative approach is that the handling/release procedure may result in a nontypical movement behavior. On the other hand, simply following movements of marked individuals typically has a disadvantage in that animals will unevenly sample the range of environmental variation. As a consequence, there could be too few moves for statistical analysis for one or more kinds of patches. Thus, the best approach is, if possible, to do both controlled releases and observations of undisturbed individuals.

An important point to keep in mind is that in an IMR study, we typically know only the start and end points of each move. Even if one "biological" move combines together several consecutive fixes, we still do not know the actual path the organism took between fixes. The practical implication of this is that we cannot analyze the effect of fine-scale spatial variation on movement. Instead, we should focus on environmental variables that change slowly at the spatial scale of a single move. Ideally, for most moves in the data, both the start and the end point should be enclosed within the same patch (i.e., same kind of habitat). IMR data is simply not suitable for an investigation of microcues that may affect individual movements. This limitation of the IMR approach is not as restrictive as it sounds. Although we may not be able to investigate how an encounter with a particular tree would affect movements of a marked animal, given the right data, we may still be able to assess how the density of these trees may influence movement parameters.

PROCEDURE   If the environment is represented as a mosaic of discrete patches, then the general approach is to estimate the probability of initiating movement and the distributions of movement parameters separately for each qualitative class of spatial locations. Separate all moves into two or more groups, based on what spatial location they took place in. Ideally, both the start and the end point should be enclosed within the same locally homogeneous patch. An alternative approach is to classify moves according to the conditions at the start point (this assumes that animals do not gather information as they move, so that the direction and the rate of movement are determined by conditions at the starting point only). If some habitat classes end up with too few moves to estimate the distribution reliably, summarize each distribution with its moments (at the very least, the mean and the variance, and possibly the skewness and kurtosis).

Movement across patch boundaries poses a challenge for analysis. It is not a good idea to simply separate moves that crossed a boundary from moves that occurred within a patch. This procedure does not distinguish moves of animals that approached a boundary and turned back from moves within the patch unaffected by the proximity of the boundary. A better approach is to focus on all moves originating within a certain distance from the boundary (e.g., the largest distance from which there is a non-zero probability to cross the boundary). Then we can focus on whether such moves near the boundary tend to be unusual in their distance or direction (e.g., there could be a high probability of turning away from the boundary).

If the environment cannot be easily classified into a few qualitative types, then we can investigate the effect of environmental variables on movement using regression. There are three important points to keep in mind. First, do not be limited to linear regression; always test for nonlinearities. In some spatial variables, the magnitude (and even direction) of the effect depends on the level of the stimulus (e.g., Neary et al. 1994). Second, do not focus exclusively on the analysis of means of move attributes. For example, random walk theory suggests that the variation in the square of move length may have an even more profound effect on population redistribution as the variation in the mean length. Third, consider not only the level of an environmental variable but also its spatial gradient. Even if animals cannot measure the gradient directly, they may do so effectively by making exploratory forays in different directions from the start point, and then moving in the direction in which some variable is increasing. IMR data reflects only this resultant displacement, and even though we will not be able to detect the actual mechanism that animals use to move up a gradient, we can still model it by making the direction of their movement dependent on the gradient.

CAVEATS Define "moves" appropriately. Don't automatically use displacements between successive fixes (see Section 5.2 for what criteria to use to define "biological moves"). Be a lumper, not a splitter. It is fine to look at a number of different variables, or a large number of qualitative classes during the exploratory stage of the analysis, but you should zero in on a few important classes at the final analysis.

Be sure to collect and analyze data in such a way that the effects of spatial heterogeneity can be examined on all components of movement. In most terrestrial cases, we are primarily concerned with movement occurring within a two-dimensional space. Therefore, for a complete description of spatio-temporal coordinates of each position we need three numbers (two spatial and one temporal coordinate). During the analysis stage, the three spatio-temporal coordinates (fixes) may be translated into movement components in a number of ways. The most common approach is to translate fix coordinates into the distance, direction, and duration of each move. However, other representations may make more sense, depending on the biology of the studied animals. For example, speed may be used instead of distance (or, alternatively, duration), and turning angle may be more appropriate instead of the absolute (compass) direction (especially if we are analyzing movement using the correlated random walk framework; see Chapter 5). Do not limit analysis to only one or two components of movement. The effect of space on all three should be quantified. (If no statistically or biologically significant effect is found, then, of course, there is no need to include it in the model. The point is, do not do it by omission.)

7.5.2 Example: dispersal in a cricket metapopulation

Metapopulation dynamics (for review see Hanski and Gilpin 1997) is a powerful metaphor for conservation of endangered species living in fragmented habitats. Persistence in classical metapopulations (Harrison and Taylor 1997) depends critically on colonization, yet little is known about dispersal patterns in the metapopulation context. Wiens et al. (1993b) have argued that at such an early stage of development of the subject, it pays to focus on "experimental model systems"—small-scale systems occupying microlandscapes that are easy to manipulate and monitor. Examples of such experimental model systems include small mammals (for examples see Sections 7.6.3 and 7.6.4) and insects (which provide many examples in this book). A population of the bush cricket in southern Sweden is another example. Kindval and Ahlén (1992) showed that this system fits well the concept of metapopulation dynamics. Bush crickets live in dry grassland habitat patches surrounded and separated by pine forest. Local populations (especially those of small area) regularly go extinct and can be recolonized by movement from other patches (Kindval and Ahlén 1992). Understanding and modeling the dispersal process underlying colonization is thus key for understanding metapopulation dynamics in this system.

If the environment can unambiguously be divided into two classes, the preferred habitat and the nonhabitat matrix surrounding habitat patches, then to model dispersal process we need to quantify movement patterns in three spatial situations: (1) within the habitat patch, (2) within the matrix, and (3) on the habitat/matrix boundary. Accordingly, Kindvall (1996) released individually-marked crickets in all three situations, and observed their movements by daily resightings. Considering first the directionality of movement, the data suggested that movement of crickets can be modeled as an uncorrelated random walk because the frequency distribution of turning angles within the matrix was not significantly different from the uniform, and within the habitat the deviations from the uniform were minor. Moves within the forest matrix, however, were of much greater length than moves within the habitat. Summarizing Kindvall's data on the distribution of move lengths, I calculate the diffusion rate in the habitat versus matrix as 5.4 versus 841 m^2/day. Since the ratio of diffusion rates, and therefore, residence indices (see Section 4.2.5) is about 150, this result alone would suggest that cricket density in the matrix should be two orders of magnitude lower than the density within habitat patches. This differential in density is further exacerbated by cricket behavior on the patch edges. Typically, less than 10% of individuals released at boundaries emigrated from patches (compared to 50% expected under the null hypothesis of no edge effect).

On the basis of these results, Kindvall constructed a simulation model for cricket dispersal and colonization within the habitat-matrix landscapes. In its basic structure, the model was an (uncorrelated) random walk with spatially varying distributions of move lengths and semi-impermeable boundaries between habitat patches and the surrounding matrix. To test this model, Kindval conducted a separate study in which unmarked crickets were released in areas without naturally occurring crickets, and their spatial distribution was determined one month later. The model attempted to predict the distribution of movement distances for the released crickets given the spatial configurations of habitat patches and the matrix at each of the release sites. An excellent degree of agreement between the model and the data (especially since the model was tested with independent data) suggests that Kindval's model, although quite simple, captured the essential features of the dispersal process in the bush cricket (Figure 7.10).

7.5.3   Synthesis

Individual mark-recapture field methods combined with an analysis based on random-walk models can be a very powerful approach for quantifying and modeling effects of spatial heterogeneity on population redistribution. Compared to mass mark-recapture, the IMR approach provides a better insight into biological mechanisms that govern the responses of organisms to spatial heterogeneity. On the other hand, it does not require the detailed data and complicated statistical approaches characterizing analysis of individual paths (see Section 7.1). IMR methods can be particularly useful for quantifying the effects of habitat fragmentation (a kind of spatial heterogeneity) on movements of threatened or endangered species. The next section provides several examples of such applications in conservation biology.

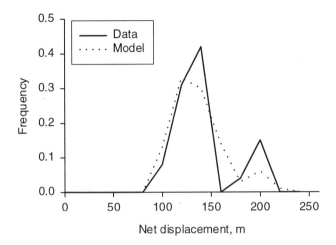

Figure 7.10: Comparison of observed distribution of movement distances to that predicted by the movement model of Kindvall (1996). Only one location (Ilstrop) is shown. (After Kindvall 1996.)

7.6 Applications: Movement Corridors for Conservation

The potential role of habitat corridors in facilitating movement of endangered species between wildlife refuges has been a topic of considerable controversy (Wilson and Willis 1975, Simberloff and Cox 1987, Noss 1987, Saunders and Hobbs 1991, Simberloff et al. 1992, Hobbs 1992, Mann and Plummer 1993). The original justification for corridors was based on the equilibrium theory of island biogeography (MacArthur and Wilson 1967). Arguing by analogy with archipelagoes of islands, Wilson and Willis (1975) suggested that any mechanism facilitating colonization would lead to a greater number of species present in a network of wildlife refuges. Critics charged that there is a paucity of data showing how corridors are used and whether their use by wildlife lessens the chance of extinction in refuge networks (Simberloff and Cox 1987, Simberloff et al. 1992). Nicholls and Margulis (1991) and Inglis and Underwood (1992) proposed designs for experiments that would test whether recolonization of fragmented habitats unconnected to a source of migrants would be slower than recolonization of habitats connected to a source by movement corridors.

Such experiments would be expensive, labor-intensive, and not practical under many circumstances, as Ingliss and Underwood (1992) acknowledge, and progress has been slow. While waiting for such studies to be funded and conducted, we can ask a less ambitious question: What is the effect of corridors on movements of individuals?

Although this question is less ambitious, it still requires development of new methods for data collection and analysis. The conceptual framework for answering this question was introduced in the previous section on general methods for studying the effects of spatial heterogeneity on movement. When dealing with movement corridors in a conservation setting, we have at least three kinds of "space": habitat islands (or patches), the nonhabitat matrix, and movement corridors connecting habitat islands. Each kind presents a separate set of difficulties for analysis. The critical question for movement within habitat islands is what is the behavior of individuals at the boundary between habitat and nonhabitat matrix. Is this boundary completely reflective, or does some proportion of individuals cross over? The second question is how individuals locate and enter movement corridors. The primary difficulty with the nonhabitat matrix is to determine how likely animals are to enter it, and what their pattern of movement is there. Typically, few animals are naturally found in the nonhabitat matrix, and, thus, the problem is to obtain enough numbers to do statistics. Finally, the difficulties associated with studying movement in corridors are, first, being able to quantify the differences in habitat quality between them and islands. One difficult parameter to measure is the effect of edges. Since corridors are narrow and long, the habitat in them is expected to be strongly affected by edge effects. Second, we need to understand the effect of the linear geometry of corridors on movement. The key question is whether corridors increase the directionality of movement, thus helping to channel dispersers to the next habitat island. Alternatively, being always in close proximity with a nonhabitat boundary may confuse dispersers, resulting in a high frequency of direction reversals. This tendency of wandering unproductively within the corridor (Soulé and Gilpin 1991) may slow, or even prevent the dispersers' progress towards the next habitat island.

Development of approaches to resolve these issues is still in its infancy. Because of high interest, and hype (Simberloff et al. 1992), in movement corridors, there have been several recent studies examining the effect of corridors on movement. The studies reviewed below are by no means definitive, but should be considered as first steps, illustrating both the difficulties, and innovative approaches to the analysis.

7.6.1 Dispersal of juvenile cougars

As in many other vertebrates, dispersal of juvenile cougars from their natal range plays a key role in their population dynamics, allowing cougars to expand their ranges and recolonize habitats where local extinction occurred (Beier 1995). The cougar population in the Santa Ana Mountain Range of Southern California, studied by Beier (1993, 1995), presents a fascinating (although depressing, as prospects for this population are bleak) case study for conservation in fragmented landscapes. The current population consists of about 20 adults on 2,000 km^2 of habitat, approximately 60% of which are protected from urban uses (Beier 1993). The critical importance of connectivity in this system was demonstrated by events at San Joaquin Hills. After this 75 km^2 area was isolated from the rest of population by urban development during the late 1970's, the cougar population in it went extinct (Beier 1993).

Two other habitat areas are situated near the Santa Ana Mountain Range, the Chino Hills and the Palomar Range (see Figure 1 in Beier 1995). These areas are connected to Santa Ana by corridors 1.5 and 4.0 km long. A third corridor, 6 km in length, provided an alternative route between the northern and southern parts of Santa Ana. The three passages were not designed as wildlife movement corridors, but were simply habitats made linear by urban growth (Beier 1995). The movement corridors, especially the critical links to the Chino Hills and the Palomar Range, were really obstacle courses more than clear avenues for dispersal, being interrupted in several places by roads (including a major freeway) and golf courses, and exposed to artifical outdoor lighting and urban noise.

To study the potential role of corridors in cougar dispersal, Beier (1995) tracked movements of nine radiocollared juvenile cougars. Only two juveniles were successful in obtaining territories. The other seven died as a result of a variety of causes: collision with a car (three cases; dispersing cougars also recovered from two other car accidents), killed by police (one case), intestinal disease (one case), and unknown, but apparently natural causes (two cases).

The pattern that emerges from these observations on the paths of radiocollared cougars is clear—they will thoroughly explore all possible avenues for dispersal, even when partly blocked by semi-impermeable wildland-urban interface. Except for one short-lived individual, all dispersers encountered at least three of four habitat edges. There were ten forays into habitat peninsulas surrounded by dense urban areas. On four such forays dispersers entered the urban area, with two being treed by dogs, captured, and released back into the wild, and two being killed (by police or by car).

All three corridors were successfully negotiated by at least one disperser. Two individuals successfully used the 1.5 km corridor to the Chino Hills, while a third was hit by a vehicle there. Of the three dispersers that encountered the 4 km corridor to the Palomar Range, one did not enter it and another traversed it in a single night. A third negotiated half its length, but then took a wrong fork, wandering into a habitat peninsula where it was captured. Three individuals successfully used the 6 km-long corridor (an alternative connection between the northern and southern parts of Santa Ana).

The remarkable result from this study is that despite the poor quality of habitat corridors they all were used by dispersers, and each was successfully used on at least one occasion. The behavior of the animals and the problems they encountered as they traversed the corridors suggested ways to improve their quality for cougar dispersal (see the recommendations in Beier 1995). For example, because dispersers oriented towards dark areas and away from light, it is critical that movement corridors were free of artificial light. On the other hand, bright artifical light can be used to deter dispersers from entering dead-end habitat peninsulas (Beier 1995).

Since only nine animals were followed, the results of this study are primarily qualitative. However, even such qualitative results are a great stride forward in designing a conservation program for cougars. Using a simulation model of cougar dynamics in refuges, Beier (1993) showed that for best estimates of parameters the Santa Ana population is facing a 3% risk of extinction in the next 100 years with the current 2,000 km^2 of habitat. Reducing the amount of habitat by 40% (which is a very likely scenario) would increase the probability of extinction to 33%. However, if only three males and one female manage to immigrate into Santa Ana per decade, the probability of extinction drops back to about 3% (see Figure 7 in Beier 1993). This is a clear case where limited but carefully collected data and a quantitative model work synergistically (which is not to say that we do not need additional data and better empirically-based models!). Beier notes that neither the field data, nor the model alone would be persuasive in the face of development pressure. Together, they stimulated interest in restoring and protecting critical corridors for this population (Beier 1993).

7.6.2   Corridors for bird dispersal

Studying the influence of corridors on the spatial dynamics of migratory bird populations is particularly interesting. It would be natural to expect that on the scale of up to tens of kilometers, there would be little benefit from corridors to these birds since they are capable of moving over distances of hundreds and thousand kilometers. The results of the study by Haas (1994), however, go against this common-sense expectation.

Haas (1994) studied the dispersal behavior of three common migratory birds (American robin, brown thrasher, and loggerhead shrike) that breed within wooded habitat islands scattered within the sea of treeless agricultural landscape in North Dakota. The wooded habitat in this area consists of shelterbelts (rows of trees planted as protection from wind) and naturally growing riparian woodlands and woody draws (the latter is a native woodland occurring where topographical features concentrate moisture). The focus of the study was on dispersal within and from shelterbelt sites (each composed of one to seven adjacent shelterbelts). Out of 16 sites within the area, two pairs of sites were connected by a corridor consisting of a woody draw.

Haas captured and banded birds during the breeding season over a period of four years. The locations by banded birds were determined by weekly resightings. Breeding dispersal was defined as movement between subsequent nests (which could occur either within a year or between years). Almost all dispersal of thrashers (98%) was within the same site; too few shrikes were banded for meaningful analysis.

Robins were less likely to stay within a site (76%), with 19% moving into a nearby woody draw and 5% switching sites. Of particular interest is that of those robins that switched sites, 56% moved between two sites connected by a draw. To assess the statistical significance of this result Haas focused on 12 pairs formed by each site with its closest neighbor. These nearest-neighbor pairs were separated by distances ranging from 0.65 to 2.5 km. The two pairs connected by draws were separated by similar distances (1.1 and 2.6 km). There were five dispersal events between the two connected pairs, but only two between 12 unconnected pairs, a statistically significant difference (Haas 1994).

The conclusion is that most breeding dispersal in these birds is very local. When robins move between wooded islands, they are more likely to disperse along wooded draws, suggesting that these linear habitats may function as stepping stones for dispersal. This conclusion should be qualified with several caveats. Haas (1994) did not design her study to explicitly address the role of corridors in dispersal of migratory birds. The presence of two pairs of connected patches was a serendipitous occurrence that made the comparison possible. Sample sizes were small, especially for all important dispersal events between different shelterwood sites. Corridors were not essential for dispersal, since some dispersal events took place between unconnected patches. The focus of the study was on breeding dispersal, although it is possible that natal dispersal by juveniles would have a much more important effect on species persistence. Finally, it is not understood why birds, capable of moving across hundreds of kilometers of unsuitable habitat during seasonal migrations to reach their breeding grounds, would be unable, or unwilling, to search for other suitable breeding habitat tens of kilometers away. Nevertheless, this study and similar results by Wegner and Merriam (1979) and Dmowski and Kozakiewicz (1990) suggest that further research into the influence of movement corridors on the spatial dynamics of bird populations is warranted.

7.6.3   Corridor use by chipmunks

One of the key practical issues in designing an effective network of refuges connected by movement corridors is identifying what features of corridors enhance dispersal rates between refuges. This was the question motivating Bennett et al. (1994), who chose the eastern chipmunk as a representative woodland animal for their study. Previous work (Wegner and Merriam 1979) showed that chipmunks are seldom found in, or moving through, grassy fields. Thus, linear habitats with wooded or shrubby vegetation are primary routes for dispersal of these animals between isolated woodlots.

Bennett et al. (1994) studied movements and population densities of chipmunks within a 2 km² area of farmland that included four woods connected by a network of fence rows. Chipmunks were captured, marked with an individual tag, and released at the point of capture. The relationship between the number of chipmunks and a variety of fence row variables was examined by correlation and forward stepwise multiple regression.

One of the most important insights to emerge from the analysis of the data was that elements of corridor quality varied depending on how the corridor was used by chipmunks. Bennett et al. classified all captured animals into two main and one intermediate group. (1) "Residents" were recorded in the same fence row during two or more trapping sessions (each session was 2 weeks long, and there were 2 weeks between consecutive sessions). (2) "Transients" were captured in a particular fence row only once. (3) "Temporary residents" were captured more than once in the same fence row during a single trapping session. The last category was used to ensure the clearest distinction between residents and transients (and not analyzed).

The primary factor affecting the numbers of residents living in a corridor was its woodland quality, since the only two explanatory factors included in the regression were the numbers of tall trees and tall vines (see Bennet et al. 1994: Table 7). Neither fence row width, nor linear continuity accounted for any additional variation in stepwise regression. By contrast, linear continuity was the most important variable explaining numbers of transients using a corridor (both percent of gaps in path and path length had a strong negative effect). Other two variables were related to the amount of cover (presence of litter and tall shrubs). An analysis of transients and residents as a single group would have obscured these differing responses (Bennett et al. 1994).

One of the implications for corridor design from the Bennett et al. study is that it is useful to distinguish two types of corridors: those that serve both as movement corridors and as habitat for resident animals, and those facilitating movement only. The first kind is likely to be more effective in promoting persistence at the landscape level. The critical issue for assessing the usefulness of the second kind (movement only) is measuring the effect of distance to be traveled on the effectiveness of the corridor, that is, the probability of an animal successfully traversing it. The study of Bennett et al. was not really designed to answer this question, yet it provides a clue, since the length of corridor between woods had a significantly negative effect on the densities of dispersing chipmunks (Bennett et al. 1994: Table 7). In addition, these authors observed a number of movement events from one trap grid to another, but did not analyze these data for the effects of distance and corridor quality on the probability of successful movement between various elements of the landscape. What I am saying is that, in order to intelligently design movement corridors for conservation, knowing what kinds of corridors are used by dispersing animals is not enough. We also have to measure (1) how far can animals move down a corridor and (2) what are animal movement patterns in corridors. In other words, future corridor studies should quantify the distribution of movement distances, movement speeds, and turning angles. The study reviewed next has made a great stride in this direction, albeit under simplified experimental conditions.

7.6.4   Effects of corridor characteristics on vole dispersal

Andreassen et al. (1996a,b) chose the root vole as their model animal (Wiens et al. 1993b). They created a 300 m-long grassy corridor (meadow vegetation is the preferred habitat by root voles) connecting two habitat patches, manipulated it in various ways, and tested the effect of manipulations by recording the movements of radio-collared voles released from the terminal habitat patches. Their first manipulation (Andreassen et al. 1996a) was to sequentially decrease the width of the corridor from 3 to 1 to 0.4 m. The striking result was that the intermediate width (1 m) corridor proved to be the best connection between the habitat patches (Figure 7.11). The explanation for this result is that voles were reluctant to enter the 0.4 m corridor, and those voles (27%) that entered the narrow corridor spent little time in it. By contrast, all or almost all voles in the 3 m and 1 m treatments entered the corridor. The linear progress of voles within the wide corridor, however, was slow due to an apparently high frequency of direction reversal and a resulting meandering path (as indicated by high ratio of edge to mid-runway footprint counts). It would be interesting to document the distribution of turning angles directly,

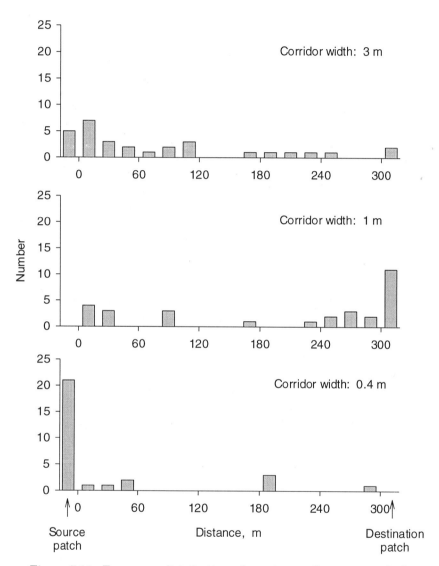

Figure 7.11: Frequency distribution of maximum distances reached by root voles from the release point for three corridor widths. (After Andreassen et al. 1996a.)

but the low temporal resolution of Andreassen et al. (1996a) data probably would not allow it (animal positions along the corridor were determined at 1 h intervals). Thus, the 1 m-wide corridor was the most effective conductor of dispersing voles because its width was sufficient so that voles felt comfortable entering it, but corridor edges were near enough to provide continuous cues as to the direction of travel. A similar result was observed by La Polla and Barrett (1993) working with meadow voles, although the corridors that they used were short (30 m) and should probably be considered as a connector for within home-range movements (Ims 1995).

The second experiment was to manipulate a linear continuity of corridors, which Andreassen et al. (1996b) did by creating gaps of variable width situated at 10 m intervals along the corridor. The authors increased the width of gaps from 0.25 to 4 m in a series of trials, and compared movements of animals within the experimental corridor to that in a continuous corridor. They found that the gap width had no effect of movement until it was increased to 4 m. The maximum distance moved along the corridor was reduced by a factor of about three for corridors interrupted with the widest gaps (see Figure 2 in Andreassen et al. 1996b). Interestingly, although voles crossed gaps by rapid, straight-lined movement this did not lead to faster progress along the corridor for intermediate gap widths (that were not a deterrent to corridor use). Thus, gaps of intermediate width did not increase movement rates by a *stepping stone effect* as was initially hypothesized by the investigators, apparently because rapid dashes across gaps were offset by stops in patches.

7.6.5 Synthesis

This section reviewed four studies that examined the role of dispersal corridors in facilitating movements of mammals and birds between habitat islands. The quantitative analysis of data collected in such studies is still in its infancy. When followed individuals are few and the observed patterns are clearcut (e.g., the cougar study) a complicated modeling analysis is unlikely to add much. In other cases, such as the chipmunk study, a more detailed analysis of the data using the machinery developed in this chapter would clearly be warranted. Dispersal corridors are not cheap and the main question is whether limited resources should be devoted to establishing corridors instead of other, perhaps more effective, conservation measures. Thus, it is important to show not only whether corridors enhance dispersal, but also to measure by how much. This means that future studies need to build models of movement within a network of habitat islands connected by corridors and to measure parameters of these models.

7.7   Attraction to Conspecifics

7.7.1   General approach

Measuring attraction in an IMR setting is conceptually similar to quantifying effects of spatial heterogeneity (see Section 7.5.1). However, instead of classifying moves by the kind of patch they occured in (or by the start point), we now focus on the conditions at the end of the move. Attraction often makes analysis of movement in heterogeneous landscapes complex since we need to keep track of the conditions both at the beginning of the move and at its end, which requires greater quantities of data. In an IMR setting, however, we typically do not need to worry about the effects of history, such as directional persistence.

Quantifying attraction to conspecifics, *congregation*, is similar to quantifying attraction to any other feature in the environment. The only added complexity is that the strength and direction of the attractive bias continuously changes as a result of changes in population density brought about by movements of individuals. This means that we must continuously readjust our representation of the environmental heterogeneity.

These thoughts suggest that while quantifying attraction to conspecifics is not a trivial task, it is certainly possible to do, provided that one designs the study appropriately. Three points should be kept in mind. First, the scale at which movement is measured (in particular, the time interval between fixes) should be carefully chosen. It should be long enough so that there are no autocorrelations between successive moves (otherwise we will be forced to either subsample position fixes or to use the methods of Chapter 5, leading to a more involved analysis), and, ideally, not much longer than that (so that we lose as little information as possible). Second, it is best to limit the number of environmental factors to be studied simultaneously. Ideally, we want to focus on congregation and possibly one additional environmental variable. Third, if possible, the initial distribution of conspecifics should be manipulated to create a wide range of local densities (see Section 7.5.1).

These are all the general comments I have about quantifying congregation. I now illustrate these points with an example drawn from my personal research. This study is interesting because it examined the interaction between herbivore congregation and the effects of spatial heterogeneity in the distribution of host plants (patch size and host density).

7.7.2   Congregation in Mexican bean beetle

My research on Mexican bean beetle (*Epilachna varivestis*) movements was motivated by the resource concentration hypothesis advanced by Root (1973).

This hypothesis suggests that the nonrandom distribution of insect herbivores in relation to spatial dispersion of their host plants is a result of their movement patterns, rather than spatial variation in their death rates, as postulated by the rival "natural enemies" hypothesis (Root 1973). Resource concentration hypothesis enjoyed some popularity during the 1980s, with a number of empirical studies showing that, indeed, movement patterns were the primary factor explaining variation in herbivore densities in response to spatial arrangement of host plants (Jones 1977, Bach 1980, Risch 1981, Root and Kareiva 1984, Kareiva 1985a, Turchin 1986, 1988a). During the 1990s, for an inexplicable reason, it has fallen out of vogue. For example, there is only a single mention of the resource concentration hypothesis in a recent book on population dynamics of herbivorous insects (Cappuccino and Price 1995). This is a pity, because much of the empirical work testing the resource concentration hypothesis was a forerunner to the current fascination with population dynamics in heterogeneous landscapes.

In my first study on bean beetle movements (Turchin 1986), I focused on one aspect of host-plant dispersion, the size (area) of the host-plant patch. I released individually marked beetles in the centers of hexagonal host patches of two sizes, 61 plants and 19 plants. In both patches, plants were spaced at 50 cm. The positions of beetles within a patch were determined at two hour intervals by checking all plants in the patch. These data were used to parameterize the following random walk model of beetle movement.

The random walk model was formulated as a discrete-time Markov chain. During a two hour period, beetles could do one of three things: stay on the plant with probability P_{stay}, initiate a "migratory" move with probability P_{migr}, or move in a "trivial" mode with probability P_{triv}. It was necessary to distinguish between the two modes of movement because they occur on very different spatial scales. When in the migratory mode, a beetle rapidly gains altitude and may fly 10–100 m before landing. The movements of Mexican bean beetles in a large field without host plants (analyzed in Section 5.3.7) occurred in the migratory mode. Migratory moves always took beetles out of the experimental patch. By contrast, beetles in the trivial mode fly slowly at low altitude (30–40 cm), and usually land either on another plant within patch or on vegetation just outside it (in the latter case, beetles immediately initiated another move that would almost always take them away from the patch). Trivial moves are characterized by a frequency distribution of lengths; their direction was assumed to be uniformly distributed.

An estimate of P_{stay} is simply the proportion of beetles who did not leave the plant during a two hour period. P_{migr} can be estimated by $1 - (P_{stay} + P_{triv})$. The estimation of P_{triv} and the distribution of trivial move distances,

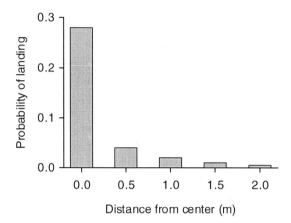

Figure 7.12: Probability that a beetle immigrating to a patch would land on a plant as a function of distance from the patch center. (After Turchin 1986.)

however, is complicated by the fact that some trivial moves result in emigration. Therefore I estimated these parameters by an iterative procedure. First, I equated the distribution of move distances to the observed frequency of moves of various lengths, and P_{triv} to the proportion of times that beetles moved within a patch. Then, I used the model to predict these two observables, and adjusted the parameters until the predictions of the model agreed with the observations. All the parameters were estimated using the data from large patches only, reserving small patches for testing the model. The parameterized model performed very well, since its predictions about the emigration rate of beetles were very similar to the observed emigration in both large and small experimental patches (Turchin 1986).

There was one peculiarity, however. Immigrants appearing in the patch tended to strongly bias their moves towards the central plant (Figure 7.12). Since the central plant was where the beetles were released, and where beetle density was high throughout the experiment, a logical explanation would be that immigrating beetles are somehow attracted to clumps of conspecifics. Therefore, in the second study focusing on the effect of host-plant density, instead of releasing all beetles on one plant, I placed them in clumps varying in size from one to nine beetles.

Analysis of beetle movements suggested that P_{stay} had a tendency to in-

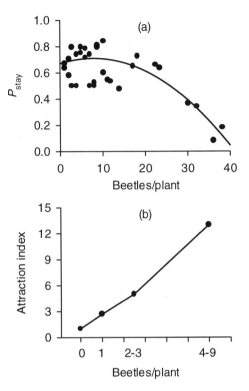

Figure 7.13: Density-dependence in movement parameters for Mexican bean beetles. (a) Probability of staying, P_{stay}. (b) Attraction index, $a(N)$. (After Turchin 1987.)

crease as N, the number of beetles on the plant, increased from 1 to 9, but this tendency was of only borderline significance ($0.05 < P < 0.1$, Turchin 1987: Table 1a). Interestingly, if we combine the data from both experiments, we see that P_{stay} has a nonlinear relationship with N, increasing slightly (and not statistically significantly) in the range of 1–5 beetles per plant and strongly decreasing for $N > 20$ (Figure 7.13a). In sum, the effect of beetle density on the probability of movement initiation was not the kind that would lead to congregation.

By contrast, the beetle density at the end of a move had a very strong attractive influence. I used the following simple model to quantify this attractive effect (see also Turchin 1987: Appendix I). First, consider beetles moving in the absence of congregative attraction, specifically, the number of beetles moving from plant j to plant k, w_{jk}. Of N_j beetles on plant j, $P_{triv}N_j$ will leave it during a two hour time interval. Of these beetles, $p(d_{jk})P_{triv}N_j$ will move a distance equal to the distance between plants j and k, d_{jk}, where $p(d)$ is the frequency distribution of trivial move distances. Since plants are arranged in a hexagonal array, and beetles will move in randomly chosen directions, only $1/6d_{jk}$th will end up on plant k. In other words

$$w_{jk} = \frac{1}{6d_{jk}}p(d_{jk})P_{triv}N_j \tag{7.6}$$

Next, consider the effect of attraction. Let $a(N)$ be a function quantifying how much more likely beetles are to end up on a plant with N beetles compared to a plant with $N = 0$ beetles. Because plants with beetles are more attractive, we need to weight w_{jk} by $a(N_k)$:

$$w_{jk} = c_j a(N_k)\frac{1}{6d_{jk}}p(d_{jk})P_{triv}N_j \tag{7.7}$$

The coefficient c_j ensures that after weighting, the probability of stopping at all possible nodes sums up to one

$$c_j = \left[\sum_k a(N_k)p(d_{jk})/(6d_{jk})\right]^{-1} \tag{7.8}$$

It is now a simple matter to calculate the attractive index , $a(N)$, by substituting into Equation 7.7 the observed values of w_{jk} and N_{jk}, and the estimates of $p(d)$ and P_{triv}. (The estimate can be further fine-tuned by taking the effect of $a(N)$ on estimates of the move length distribution and P_{triv} in an iterative fashion, until all estimates converge.) It is clear that the number of beetles on a plant has a very strong influence on its attractive index (Figure 7.13b).

7.7.3   Synthesis

This section illustrates how an IMR study can be used in quantifying attraction to conspecifics. In the example involving Mexican bean beetles, congregation turned out to be one of the most important factors influencing beetle movements. Moreover, congregation was the key to explaining why dense or large patches of host plants tend to have a higher number of beetles per plant. Thus, a model without congregation could not explain the magnitude of the effect, while the model with congregation was much closer to what was observed (Turchin 1987). A diffusion-approximation model for bean beetle congregative movements also predicted that congregations should arise only in the center of large patches (Turchin 1989a). This was indeed the case, as both the average and the variance in beetle numbers increased from patch edges to its center (Turchin 1989a: Figure 12).

7.8 Maximum Likelihood Estimation

7.8.1 General framework for analysis

There comes a point in a serious analysis of movement data when the canned formulas are just not enough. By a *serious* effort I mean the situation when data are of reasonable quality and quantity, the patterns of animal movements are more complex than assumed by simple movement models, and the analyst is ambitious enough to attempt to resolve the mechanisms underlying movement patterns using the data. This is the time to use the approach described in this section. It is not by chance that I review this approach at the end of the chapter. My philosophy of analysis is to first look at the data using simple and more intuitive, but also more limited, methods. (Simplicity, of course, is in the eye of the beholder—I am sure that many empirically-oriented ecologists will be appalled at the amount of math and statistics they will have to slog through to understand even the simpler approaches described in this book.) Simpler, more direct analyses may make unwarranted assumptions, but they are better at revealing important patterns in the data, and their results can suggest what variables and functional forms to use in the modeling of data. Eventually, however, direct methods of analysis get beyond the bounds of their competence. The general approach discussed in this section can in principle estimate parameters of any model, given infinite amounts of informative data and infinite computer power.

The basic approach is to construct a detailed simulation model (better even, a series of models) and fit it to the data using nonlinear estimation techniques. Jon Schnute colorfully describes a detailed simulation as a "stew" of calculations from which observable quantities (to be compared to the actual data) bubble up to the surface (quoted from Hilborn and Mangel 1997). Nonlinear estimation is the process of adjusting the parameters of the stew (adding more or less salt, increasing or decreasing temperature, etc.) until the stuff that bubbles up resembles the actual data the best. The crudest approach is to change parameters in the simulation by the method of trail and error and to compare the simulation results to data by eye. A more refined approach is to use some quantitative measure of goodness of fit and a nonlinear minimization routine to search for the best fit automatically. In principle, the general approach can be applied not only to IMR data, but to any kind of data (in fact, specific applications to the analysis of MMR data have already been discussed in Section 6.4.2).

PROCEDURE   The general method consists of four major components (see, e.g., Hilborn 1990):

1. A model of population dynamics and redistribution that describes how the number of marked individuals changes in each spatial location over time.

2. An observation model that describes how marked individuals are located and recaptured or resighted.

3. A likelihood function that specifies the likelihood of observing a specific number of recaptures in each spatial location during each time interval as a function of the number expected under the specific set of parameters of the model (including both biological and observation components).

4. A nonlinear function minimization computer algorithm.

   The first component, the biological model, is the least constrained. This is where a lot of creativity and previous experience will be required. The trick in constructing a good model is to balance what is known about the system with what is not known. It is not a good idea to fit a model with lots of free parameters; this is a good way to butt against the problem of unidentifiability (not being able to obtain an estimate of one or more parameters). In practice, this takes the form of either the nonlinear routine failing to converge, or different runs converging to wildly different values of parameters. It pays to build into the model what is known about the system, and to try to estimate only those parameters for which *a priori* information is absent. Generally speaking, it is a good idea to start with simple models and then proceed to models of greater complexity. Another consideration is to realize that some parameters may not be estimable given the data. For example, if there is little variation in population density between different strata (a *stratum* is a short-hand for "a particular location during a particular period of time") then it would be futile to try to estimate the density-dependence in the movement rate (or any other vital rates). The data are *noninformative* with respect to estimating density dependence.

   The second component, the observation model, should incorporate the details of experimental technique. It should reflect the spatial distribution of recapture stations (where traps are located, areas that are searched, localities with intensive fishing). Additionally, animals may differ in the probability of being captured. Finally, the observation process may distort the spatial distribution of dispersers, for example, by removing them from the population.

Usually, not every feature of the observation process will be known, and thus the observation model will have some parameters that will need to be estimated (e.g., the trappability of animals belonging to different classes, the attractive area of a trap, etc).

There is much guidance in the statistical literature that will aid specification of the third component, the statistical model. Three general approaches have been tried. Some authors fit models by nonlinear least squares, minimizing the sum of squared deviations between the model predictions and the data (for example, the approach of Banks and coworkers; see Section 6.4.2). This approach is equivalent to a likelihood approach if the data are distributed approximately normally (or can be normalized by an appropriate transformation). Due to the nature of population data, the numbers of recaptures almost always should be transformed, with the two most useful transformations being logarithmic and square-root. A variation on the theme is to use weighted least squares (e.g., Walters et al. 1993; although they ended up using the same weights because they found that variation in weights had a negligible impact on parameter estimates). The most rigorous approach is to assume that recaptures are distributed according to a multinomial distribution (since every individual is either recaptured with probability p, or not recaptured with probability $1 - p$). The final approach is to approximate the multinomial by the Poisson. This should work well in situations where the probability of recapture is small. Hilborn (1990) performed a number of Monte-Carlo experiments comparing the Poisson and multinomial approaches, and concluded that they produce essentially identical answers. In summary, one can follow either the exact multinomial approach, or one of two approximations: the Poisson if the probability of recapture in a particular spatio-temporal stratum is small; and least squares if the number of recaptures in a particular spatio-temporal stratum is large enough to be approximated by the Gaussian distribution. An example of the formula for the likelihood assuming the Poisson distribution will be given in Section 7.8.2. An example of fitting using least squares was discussed in Section 6.4.2.

There is no unanimity among various authors as to which nonlinear function minimization algorithm to use. At the risk of incurring censure from the practitioners of the art, I would recommend using whatever algorithm is most readily accessible. The standard reference for numerical analysis currently is Press et al. (1992: Chapter 10). It comes with a diskette containing canned routines written in either C, Pascal, or FORTRAN. I have had good experience with the Powell method, but others found it too slow (e.g., Walters et al. 1993).

These are general points about the nonlinear estimation approach. The devil, however, is in details. I now illustrate the approach with two examples dealing with the analysis of fish tags and bird bands (for an insect example, see Brooks and Butlin 1994).

7.8.2   Determining movement patterns from fish tag data

Some of the most sophisticated quantitative methods used in ecology have been developed by applied fisheries biologists. The explanation for this is clearly that "necessity is the mother of invention." On one hand, studying fish populations in the open oceans is a formidable task—it is next to impossible to observe fish behaviors (including movements), and is difficult to even estimate their abundances. On the other hand, there are intense economic and political pressures on fisheries biologists to come up with quantitative answers. (How many fish are there in the ocean? How many can we take out?)

Many commercial fish species are highly mobile. Fisheries managers and biologists need to know movement rates to assess the interactions between fisheries in different locations, and to define the discreteness of stocks (Hilborn 1990). Even estimating population numbers and mortality rates is impossible without an estimate of dispersal rate (Hampton 1991). The knowledge of fish movements comes primarily from tagging studies. How can we use these data to understand fish movement patterns? Originally, the most commonly used technique was for fisheries biologists to draw arrows from where fish were tagged to where they were recovered (Hilborn 1991). Little can be learned from such an analysis because no tags are recovered in areas without fishing effort. Thus, a quantitative analysis of tag returns must take into account the probability of capture between the time of release and the location of recovery. Such an approach was developed by Hilborn (1991) building on the previous work by Ishii (1979) and Sibert (1984).

The biological model assumed by Hilborn (1991) is very simple. It divides the total spatial domain into discrete areas and follows the survival of tagged fish in each area, as well as their movements between areas. The only source term in the model is the number of tagged fish introduced into each spatial compartment during each time interval. The fish disappear as a result of natural and fishing mortality, and can move to another area with a certain probability. The observation model assumes that the number of captured fish is proportional to the product of the number of fish in the area and the fishing effort there.

I will describe the statistical approach of Hilborn (1991) in some detail here, because it is very general and can be modified for almost any mark-recapture study. Let the actual number of recaptures from a tag group i in area x at time t be C_{ixt}. A tag group refers to all animals released together at the same time into the same spatial location. In mass mark-recapture experiments there will typically be only one such group. Together, all C_{ixt} are our data. Let $\hat{C}_{ixt}$ be the expected number of recaptures. This number is obtained by simulation, in which exactly the same number of organisms is released into the same areas using the same timing as in the actual experiment. The organisms in the simulation are recaptured using the same distribution of capture effort as in real life. Simulation is run repeatedly (at least 100 times) and $\hat{C}_{ixt}$ is estimated by taking an average over all 100 runs. It is important to realize that $\hat{C}_{ixt}$ is really a function of simulation parameters, since it will vary as we change parameters.

The Poisson distribution for an individual tag group, space, and time is (Hilborn 1991)

$$L(C_{ixt}|\hat{C}_{ixt}) = \frac{e^{-\hat{C}_{ixt}}\hat{C}_{ixt}^{C_{ixt}}}{C_{ixt}!} \qquad (7.9)$$

The total likelihood for all observed recoveries given the parameters of the biological and observational models, and the number of marked organisms released is the product of all individual group likelihoods:

$$L = \prod_i \prod_x \prod_t \frac{e^{-\hat{C}_{ixt}}\hat{C}_{ixt}^{C_{ixt}}}{C_{ixt}!} \qquad (7.10)$$

This is the function that we want to minimize using a nonlinear function minimizing routine. Two hints: take logs (that is, minimize a log-likelihood function), and ignore $C_{ixt}!$ in the denominator—this is a constant, which will not change as parameters of the simulation are varied, and thus will not affect the final result.

Hilborn (1991) applied this approach to the data on tag returns in the skipjack tuna fishery in the eastern tropical Pacific. First, he reanalyzed the data of Sibert (1984) for two spatial areas. Hilborn's analysis resulted in a somewhat different parameter estimates, possibly because he used the maximum likelihood estimator instead of nonlinear least squares. Hilborn then expanded his analysis to a larger geographical area consisting of seven fisheries. He found the estimates of the movement rates between different areas to be unconfounded. In other words, good statistical estimates for all rates in the model could be obtained. Hilborn ascribed this pleasing aspect of the data set to the fact that the experimental design was close to the ideal—fish were released and recaptured in all seven areas, providing a good informative data set with which to estimate movement rates. Hilborn concluded that it is possible to estimate movements from tagging data in a rigorous and reliable way. This optimistic conclusion is corroborated by generally successful efforts of other authors who fitted spatio-temporal models to southern bluefin tuna (Hampton 1991) and Western Australian rock lobster (Walters et al. 1993).

7.8.3   Analysis of Canada geese mark-resight data

The Hestbeck et al. (1990) analysis of data on resighting of banded geese is similar in spirit to the Hilborn (1991) analysis of fish tag data. These two studies illustrate how the same general approach can be applied to very different kinds of animals. The data analyzed by Hestbeck et al. consisted of resighting observations during 1984–86 of 28,849 Canada geese marked with coded neck bands. They divided the wintering area of geese into three localities: mid-Atlantic, Chesapeake, and Carolinas.

Hestbeck et al. developed two simple biological models for goose demography and movement. Both models assumed that each individual goose during a one year period (from winter to winter) could either die, winter in the same locality, or move to winter in another locality. In one, the first-order model, movement between the three localities was described as a first-order Markov chain—in other words, where a goose would winter depended only on the site it wintered in last year. The more general second-order model incorporated the effect of memory of previous wintering locations. Thus, the transition probability from one wintering site to another was affected not only by the site of the previous year, but also by where the bird was two years ago.

The observation model assumed that all birds within the same locality had the same probability of being resighted, but resighting probabilities differed between localities. Hestbeck et al. also assumed that the probability of losing the mark was negligibly small. The likelihood functions for the two models were written in terms of the multinomial distribution.

After fitting each model to data, Hestbeck et al. calculated a goodness-of-fit test. According to the test, the first-order model was rejected ($P < 0.001$) for all three years (1984–86). The second-order model was not rejected for the first two years, but was rejected for the third year ($P < 0.001$).

In my opinion this result is a good illustration of why goodness-of-fit tests without a specific alternative are a waste of time. If we take these results literally, then we should reject both models, in which case we have nothing to show for our pains. We will not, of course, be this foolish. Instead, we should ask which of the two models fit the data better and provisionally choose that model over the other one (until something even better comes along). We also need a measure of how accurately the better model fits the data, but the P-value of the goodness-of-fit test does not tell us that. We could also examine the way in which the model's predictions depart from the data, because this might suggest a way to better the model. But, again, the P-value does not give us this information. So why do we need to calculate it at all?

Hestbeck et al. (1990), actually, did not stop after performing goodness-of-fit tests (and, therefore, do not deserve to be the butt of my diatribe). Examining the observed and expected numbers of geese for each observation history, Hestbeck et al. discovered that only a few specific histories were responsible for the mismatch between the first-order model and data. The number of geese switching from location x to location y was greater than expected if they had wintered in location y two years ago. This observation suggests that there is an effect of memory postulated by the second-order model. Indeed, a likelihood ratio test suggested that the second-order model fit the data much better ($P < 0.001$ for all three years).

7.8.4 Synthesis

The approach discussed in this section should be used after simpler, but also more limited, direct avenues of analyses have been pushed against their limits. The main advantage of the nonlinear fitting approach is that it is not limited to standard movement models—in principle any model can be fitted to the data. The second strength is that the observation process can be (and should be) explicitly modeled. This gives us the likelihood function that specifies how probable the observed data are under the assumed model. Thus, nonlinear likelihood-based approaches are typically characterized by a high degree of statistical rigor.

Given infinite amounts of *informative* data and infinite computing power a model of arbitrary complexity can be fitted. In the real world, however, we have to make compromises. Thus, it pays to start with a simple model and increase its complexity in a stepwise fashion, keeping only those components that significantly increase the degree of fit. The end result of such a process is the simplest model that explains the data the best. "The best" may not be very good, but until we have a better alternative we should not abandon a model that provides at least a partial explanation of the empirical patterns.

Appendix A

Diffusion for Ecologists

A.1 Derivation of the Diffusion Equation

To most ecologists who have little experience with partial differential equations, diffusion is more intimidating than the more familiar Lotka-Volterra theory based on the framework of ordinary differential equations. Intuitively it is not obvious why there is a first temporal derivative on the left side of the equation, but a second spatial derivative on its right side. In this section, I will attempt to dispel some of the mystique surrounding diffusion by discussing two alternative ways of deriving it. The first one is based on the simplest possible formulation of a random walk process (e.g., Karlin and Taylor 1975:342). This derivation sets the stage for the more involved derivation in Chapter 4 that systematically explores various ways of including biological realism in random walk formulations, and the resulting diffusion approximations. The second way of deriving the diffusion equation comes from physics, and uses an argument based on fluxes. This alternative derivation gives a better intuitive feeling of why there is a second spatial derivative on the right hand side of the diffusion equation.

A.1.1 From a simple random walk to simple diffusion

Consider a bee foraging for nectar in a one-dimensional array of flowers. I will only consider the one-dimensional situation because the logic of the derivation for higher-dimensional cases is the same, but with a more complicated algebra. Let's assume that after leaving a flower the bee will move a fixed distance λ to either a flower on its left or one on its right, with the probability of either move equal to $1/2$. The direction of a current move is completely independent of the directions of previous moves. (A real bee, of course, would employ a better nectar-gathering strategy, but for the moment I will ignore such complications, as I am interested in formulating the simplest random walk process possible.) Let's also assume that the bee spends the same amount of time between moves from flower to flower. Let τ be the time between two consecutive moves.

The question is: given that the bee starts at the position $x = 0$ at time $t = 0$, what is the probability of finding the bee at any position x at later time t, $p(x, t)$? It is clear that the probability distribution of finding any individual at position x and time t translates directly into the spatial population density of an ensemble of individuals, if all individuals start in the same locality at $t = 0$, employ identical movement rules, and do not affect the movement of each other. Thus if we can derive a formula governing the time evolution of $p(x, t)$ then we will also know the spatio-temporal redistribution of the population. I start deriving this formula by writing down the recurrence relationship between $p(x, t + \tau)$ and $p(x, t)$. The probability that a bee will be at position x at time $t + \tau$ is directly related only to the probabilities of finding the bee at two neighboring positions before the last jump, since these are the only two places that the bee could come from in one step. Thus, finding a bee at x after the latest jump could occur if the bee was at the left neighboring position, $x - \lambda$, and moved right, or if the bee was at the right position, $x + \lambda$, and moved left. Translating this statement into probabilities, while remembering that both probability of moving right and left are $1/2$, yields

$$p(x, t + \tau) = \frac{1}{2}p(x - \lambda, t) + \frac{1}{2}p(x + \lambda, t) \qquad (A.1)$$

Subtracting $p(x, t)$ from both sides of the equation, dividing the left hand side by τ and the right hand side by λ^2, we have

$$p(x, t + \tau) - p(x, t) = \frac{1}{2}[p(x + \lambda, t) - 2p(x, t) + p(x - \lambda, t)]$$

$$\frac{p(x, t + \tau) - p(x, t)}{\tau} = \frac{\lambda^2}{2\tau}\left[\frac{p(x + \lambda, t) - 2p(x, t) + p(x - \lambda, t)}{\lambda^2}\right]$$

Notice the discrete version of the time derivative on the left, and on the right the second spatial derivative multiplied by the factor $\lambda^2/2\tau$. It may be easier to see the second derivative if the quantity in the square brackets is rearranged in the following way:

$$\frac{p(x + \lambda, t) - 2p(x, t) + p(x - \lambda, t)}{\lambda^2} = \frac{\frac{p(x+\lambda,t)-p(x,t)}{\lambda} - \frac{p(x,t)-p(x-\lambda,t)}{\lambda}}{\lambda}$$

If τ is small relative to the time scale over which we observe the bee, and λ is small relative to spatial extent of the flower array within which the bee forages, then approximately

$$\frac{\partial p(x,t)}{\partial t} \approx \frac{p(x,t+\tau) - p(x,t)}{\tau}$$

$$\frac{\partial^2 p(x,t)}{\partial x^2} \approx \frac{p(x+\lambda,t) - 2p(x,t) + p(x-\lambda,t)}{\lambda^2}$$

Defining $D \equiv \lambda^2/2\tau$ and substituting partial derivatives from above, I obtain the one-dimensional equation for passive diffusion

$$\frac{\partial p}{\partial t} = D\frac{\partial^2 p}{\partial x^2}$$

where p is a short-hand notation for $p(x,t)$. Here D is the diffusion rate, or *diffusivity*. When $D = $ const, we usually refer to it as the *diffusion coefficient*. Note that in making the transition from the random-walk recurrence equation to the diffusion equation, I have also substituted discrete variables t and x with their continuous counterparts. Thus, the space does not consist of discrete units anymore. In effect, flowers have been "smeared" along the spatial axis x, losing their discrete nature.

The logic of the above derivation explicitly acknowledges the fact that the diffusion equation is a continuum approximation of the discrete random walk process. An alternative, and more frequently used approach is the limiting argument (e.g., Okubo 1980:67-68). According to this argument, one imagines a series of processes in which bees make progressively smaller and more frequent steps. In other words, one considers the limit as the parameters τ and $\lambda \to 0$. However, the parameters must go to zero in a special way, so that λ^2 is of the same order of magnitude as τ. Then the diffusion rate is defined as $D \equiv \lim \lambda^2/2\tau$, the discrete versions of the derivatives converge to their continuous counterparts, and we obtain the same diffusion equation as above.

The limiting argument leading to the diffusion equation has several features that appear to be at variance with intuition. It is not clear why we must take limits in such a strange way, apart from the trivial observation that any other way of taking limits will not lead to a diffusion equation. Moreover, assuming that $\lim \lambda^2/\tau = D$, a constant, does not make much biological sense. Indeed, the speed of our hypothetical bee goes to infinity in the diffusion limit! Since the speed $v \equiv \lambda/\tau$

$$\lim_{\lambda,\tau \to 0} v = \lim_{\lambda,\tau \to 0} \lambda/\tau = \lim_{\lambda,\tau \to 0} \lambda^2/(\tau\lambda) = D\lim_{\lambda \to 0} 1/\lambda = \infty.$$

In addition, $\tau \to 0$ implies that the bee makes an infinite number of direction reversals during any finite period of time. Thus, according to the limiting argument the bee is tracing an infinitely rapid, infinitely wriggly trajectory through space.

The counterintuitive features of the diffusion limit are much easier to understand and accept in the context of the classical physical problem of Brownian motion (see Segel 1978:171 for a particularly helpful discussion). In Brownian motion, the finer the temporal scale τ at which we resolve the path, the greater will be the total path length and the apparent speed v (as long as each step is caused by a large number of collisions with water molecules). Similarly, the frequency of directional changes will also increase as we decrease τ (as long as each step is caused by a number of collisions with water molecules, the directions of each successive step will be uncorrelated).

Close examination of the nature of Brownian motion, thus, suggests that this process does not really have some fundamental characteristic speed. However, it can be shown that the squared displacement grows linearly with time (Segel 1978). Therefore, we adopt the mathematical convention that $v = \lambda/\tau \to \infty$ as $\tau \to 0$, while keeping $D = \lambda^2/\tau$ constant.

One consequence if the diffusion limit is that the path of a Brownian particle appears to be a fractal object, since its length depends on the scale at which it is measured (see also Section 5.5). Brownian path and the coast of England are alike in that the smaller our measuring stick is, the longer their apparent length. However, the *fractal dimension* of the path equals two, a whole number. The fact that the dimension of the Brownian path is the same as the dimension of the space within which the particle moves suggests that the path visits all points, not leaving any areas unfilled. This is not very counter-intuitive; since the path is of infinite length and is not attracted to any particular region, it should cover the whole 2D space evenly.

An important caveat is that the time scale τ that we choose to characterize Brownian motion is restricted from both above and below (Segel 1978). It cannot be too long, or our description of the problem would miss interesting features of the phenomena we study. I would also add that when τ is on the order of the time it takes a particle to cross a container, we no longer have an unrestricted random walk. The time scale cannot be too short, either, because τ has to be large compared to the time between successive molecule-particle collisions, typically 10^{-10} s (Segel 1978). Otherwise, successive steps will become correlated. Within these limits, the diffusion approximation of the Brownian motion will hold, and the fractal paths will have the property of self-similarity.

Returning to the consideration of biological motion, we observe that it has a strong similarity to Brownian motion (Segel 1978). A major contrast, however, is that the "actual" trajectory of a Brownian particle is impossible to observe, while the trajectory of an organism is readily observable. The organism's linear speed v is also readily measurable and finite, while no finite particle speed appears in the Brownian motion. In Sections 4.3 and 4.4 I consider more sophisticated approaches to diffusion approximation of random walks that start by assuming finite speeds and directional persistence. For the derivation at hand, however, we conclude that at the microscopic level appropriate for organisms we cannot really make $\tau \to \infty$. For this reason, rather than going through the limiting argument, I favor the alternative of explicitly acknowledging that any diffusion model is an idealized continuum representation of the inherently discrete world. This serves to remind us that the diffusion equation is an approximation, and that its accuracy will depend on the specifics of the biological system under study. Moreover, this approach gives us a way to assess the accuracy of the diffusion approximation. For example, in Chapter 4 we used the Taylor expansion to obtain diffusion models. In such cases, one can assess the accuracy of approximation by looking at the magnitude of the terms dropped during the derivation. Probably the most important advantage, given the focus of this book, is that the parameters of the diffusion model are expressed in quantities that can be directly measured by observing the behavior of individual organisms. For example, if we observe our hypothetical bee, we can measure its move lengths to estimate λ and the time between moves to estimate τ. This immediately gives us $D = \lambda^2/2\tau$, which we can use to predict the rate of spatial spread of a number of bees released at $x = 0$. Such a direct mechanistic connection between individual behavior and the population spread would not be available if we defined D as a limit of λ^2/τ as $\lambda, \tau \to 0$. In that case, our only recourse would be to estimate D statistically by observing the rate of spread of a population of bees.

A.1.2 Derivation for variable move lengths

We start with the recurrence relationship of Section 4.2.2:

$$p(x,t) = p(x,t-\tau)[1 - \pi(x,t-\tau)\tau]$$
$$+ \int_{-\infty}^{\infty} p(x-\lambda, t-\tau)\pi(x-\lambda, t-\tau)\tau M(\lambda, x-\lambda, t-\tau)\, d\lambda$$

The first term on the right side is simply the probability of a beetle being at position x at time $t - \tau$, multiplied by the probability of *not* moving during τ. The second term, the integral, is a continuous analog of the last two terms in Equation 4.1. Again we consider all the possible positions from which the beetle could move to x (see Figure 4.2). For example, if the beetle was at the position $x - \lambda$, then by moving λ spatial units (to the right if λ is positive, or to the left if it is negative) the beetle will arrive at the position x. Thus, the probability that the beetle will move to x is the product of the probability of being found at $x - \lambda$, the probability of moving from that position, and the probability of moving λ units; all these products summed over all possible positions from which the beetle could reach x.

Proceeding further in the now familiar manner, I expand all terms in a Taylor series. However, instead of expanding p, π, and M separately, let's expand their product (it will result in less complicated algebra)

$$\Gamma(\lambda, x, t) \equiv p(x, t)\pi(x, t)M(\lambda, x, t)$$

The recurrence equation becomes:

$$p(x, t) = p(x, t - \tau)[1 - \pi(x, t - \tau)\tau] + \int_{-\infty}^{\infty} \tau\Gamma(\lambda, x - \lambda, t - \tau) \, d\lambda \quad \text{(A.2)}$$

Expanding the terms and dividing by τ we obtain

$$\frac{\partial p}{\partial t} = -\pi p + \int_{-\infty}^{\infty} (\Gamma - \lambda\frac{\partial}{\partial x}\Gamma + \frac{\lambda^2}{2}\frac{\partial^2}{\partial x^2}\Gamma + \cdots) \, d\lambda + O(\tau^2)$$

Here I incorporated $\tau\Gamma_t$ into $O(\tau)$. We now can take a limit with $\tau \to 0$, so that $O(\tau) \to 0$. Note that this limiting procedure is straightforward, unlike the one discussed in Section A.1.1, since we do not need to make special assumptions about the relationship between the temporal and spatial scales (e.g., we do not assume that the width of the distribution of move lengths goes to zero). We thus have

$$\frac{\partial p}{\partial t} = -\pi p + \int_{-\infty}^{\infty} \Gamma \, d\lambda - \int_{-\infty}^{\infty} \lambda\frac{\partial}{\partial x}\Gamma \, d\lambda + \int_{-\infty}^{\infty} \frac{\lambda^2}{2}\frac{\partial^2}{\partial x^2}\Gamma \, d\lambda + \cdots$$

Using the definition of Γ and the formulas for M's moments, we obtain

$$\int_{-\infty}^{\infty} \Gamma \, d\lambda = \pi p \int_{-\infty}^{\infty} M \, d\lambda = \pi p$$

$$\int_{-\infty}^{\infty} \lambda\frac{\partial}{\partial x}\Gamma \, d\lambda = \frac{\partial}{\partial x}\left(\int_{-\infty}^{\infty} \lambda\pi p M \, d\lambda\right) = \frac{\partial}{\partial x}\left(\pi p \int_{-\infty}^{\infty} \lambda M \, d\lambda\right)$$

$$= \frac{\partial}{\partial x}(\pi m_1 p)$$

and so on. We have finally arrived at the partial-differential equation for the evolution of p

$$\frac{\partial p}{\partial t} = -\frac{\partial}{\partial x}(\pi m_1 p) + \frac{1}{2}\frac{\partial^2}{\partial x^2}(\pi m_2 p) + \cdots \quad \text{(A.3)}$$

A.1.3 Deriving the diffusion equation using flux considerations

The equation for physical diffusion (e.g., diffusion of dissolved molecules or particles; also heat conduction) is derived in two steps. First, one states the conservation equation that relates the change in spatial concentration of particles to their flux (and possibly to sources and sinks, if any are present). Second, one needs an empirical law connecting particle fluxes to their concentration gradients. More details on this procedure are available in the excellent textbook by Edelstein-Keshet (1988).

For simplicity, I will again assume that movement of particles occurs in a one-dimensional space (for example, a thin long tube). Selecting a section of the tube with its left end at the spatial coordinate x and right end at $x + \lambda$, let us consider how the concentration of particles can change with time. Assuming that particles do not die and new particles are not born, the total number of particles in the $(x, x + \lambda)$ section of the tube is affected only by flow into or out of the section at its ends. Thus, we can write the balance equation in terms of the number of particles

$$
\begin{array}{lcll}
\text{rate of change} \\
\text{of particle} \\
\text{number in} & = & \text{net (entry minus} & \text{net (entry minus} \\
(x, x + \lambda) & & \text{departure) at the} + & \text{departure) at the} \quad \text{(A.4)} \\
\text{per unit time} & & x \text{ end} & x + \lambda \text{ end}
\end{array}
$$

The total number of particles in $(x, x + \lambda)$ is the product of the concentration of particles, $u(x, t)$, and the length of the interval, λ (since we are dealing with a one-dimensional space, concentration is defined as the number of particles per unit length). The quantities on the right are called *fluxes*. Flux of particles at (x, t), $J(x, t)$, is the rate at which particles cross x in the positive direction (from left to right), minus the rate at which particles cross x in the negative direction. Thus flux is the *net* number of particles crossing x per unit of time. Rewriting Equation A.4 in terms of concentration and fluxes leads to

$$
\frac{\partial}{\partial t}[u(x, t)\lambda] = J(x, t) - J(x + \lambda, t) \tag{A.5}
$$

Writing $u(x, t)$ instead of $u(x + \lambda, t)$ does not affect the end result, since I am about to take the limit $\lambda \to 0$. Dividing both sides by λ and slightly rearranging the right side, I obtain

$$
\frac{\partial u}{\partial t} = -\frac{J(x + \lambda, t) - J(x, t)}{\lambda} \tag{A.6}
$$

Taking the limit as $\lambda \to 0$, I end up with the one-dimensional balance equation

(for the case of no sources or sinks of particles within the tube)

$$\frac{\partial u}{\partial t} = -\frac{\partial J(x,t)}{\partial x} \qquad (A.7)$$

The next step is to relate the flux to the spatial change of particle concentration. This is done by evoking an empirical relationship, known as Fick's law, which states that the flux due to the random motion of particles is approximately proportional to the local gradient in the particle concentration

$$J = -D\frac{\partial u}{\partial x} \qquad (A.8)$$

where D is the diffusivity. This relationship makes intuitive sense. If there is a concentration gradient with more particles right of x than left of x (that is, the sign of the gradient is positive), then on the average more particles will be crossing to the left, than to the right. In other words, the flux (net flow) will be in the negative direction—thus the negative sign on the left side in Equation A.8. There is no reason, however, to believe that the relationship must be linear, and indeed, at high concentrations, when interactions between particles become important, Fick's law is no longer accurate. However, assuming that Fick's law holds, I substitute Equation A.8 into Equation A.7 to obtain the diffusion equation:

$$\frac{\partial u(x,t)}{\partial t} = \frac{\partial}{\partial x}\left(D\frac{\partial u}{\partial x}\right) \qquad (A.9)$$

If $D = \text{const}$, then we have the simple diffusion equation

$$\frac{\partial u}{\partial t} = D\frac{\partial^2 u}{\partial x^2}$$

A.1.4   The second spatial derivative in diffusion

The first spatial derivative $\partial u/\partial x$ measures the magnitude of the linear gradient in u, while the second spatial derivative $\partial^2 u/\partial x^2$ quantifies the degree of curvature. Because the temporal derivative in u is proportional to the second spatial derivative, population density will grow or decline only in localities where spatial gradients in u are curved. To understand this better, let us go back to equation A.9 and emphasize the flux component in it

$$\frac{\partial u}{\partial t} = -\frac{\partial J}{\partial x} = -\frac{\partial}{\partial x}\left(-D\frac{\partial u}{\partial x}\right) \qquad (A.10)$$

We now see that the second derivative does not appear by magic, but because $\partial u/\partial t$ is affected by the spatial gradient in u indirectly, *via* the flux J.

This form of dependence suggests that diffusion operates not on spatial gradients, but on their curvatures. Consider what happens when the spatial profile of population density is linear. The fluxes J_1 and J_2, at x_1 and x_2 respectively, will be proportional to the rate of change in density u. Both fluxes will be positive because u declines in the direction of increasing x (remember that there is a negative sign in Equation A.8 because the direction of net flow is *down* the population gradient). Moreover, since $\partial u/\partial x$ is constant (because the gradient is linear), $J_1 = J_2$. This means that particles enter the region $[x_1, x_2]$ on the left at the same rate with which they leave it on the right, with no net increase within the region. In other words, a linear gradient implies $\partial u/\partial t = 0$.

A curved concave gradient is obtained when the second spatial derivative is positive. In this case, the gradient is more steep at x_1 than at x_2. In consequence, $J_1 > J_2$, and more particles enter the region $[x_1, x_2]$ on the left than leave on the right. The particles will accumulate in the region, and u will increase ($\partial u/\partial t > 0$). Where gradients are convex ($\partial^2 u/\partial x^2 > 0$), the opposite will hold: the flux of particles into the region will be less than the flux out of it, with a net decrease in u. Finally the regions with a local maximum (or minimum) in u are the easiest to understand because the flow of particles at both ends will be outwards (inwards). This squares with elementary intuition: simple diffusion erodes the "hills" in the spatial population distribution and fills in the "valleys". The key idea, however, is that for diffusion to operate (to change population density), the necessary condition is not the presence of hills and valleys, but only of nonlinearities in the spatial population gradients.

A.1.5 Radially symmetric diffusion in two dimensions

The two-dimensional simple diffusion is completely analogous to the one-dimensional case

$$\frac{\partial u}{\partial t} = D\left(\frac{\partial^2 u}{\partial x^2} + \frac{\partial^2 u}{\partial y^2}\right) \tag{A.11}$$

Here $u = u(x, y, t)$ is the spatio-temporal density of organisms, and x and y are Cartesian space coordinates. In polar coordinates r and θ, the two-dimensional simple diffusion equation becomes

$$\frac{\partial u}{\partial t} = \frac{1}{r}\left[\frac{\partial}{\partial r}\left(rD\frac{\partial u}{\partial r}\right) + \frac{\partial}{\partial \theta}\left(\frac{D}{r}\frac{\partial u}{\partial \theta}\right)\right] \tag{A.12}$$

If the initial population distribution is radially symmetric, then it will continue to be so, and the term involving $\partial u/\partial \theta$ will be zero. The equation then simplifies to

$$\frac{\partial u}{\partial t} = \frac{1}{r}\frac{\partial}{\partial r}\left(rD\frac{\partial u}{\partial r}\right) = D\frac{\partial^2 u}{\partial r^2} + \frac{D}{r}\frac{\partial u}{\partial r} \tag{A.13}$$

We see that the first term involving the second spatial derivative is identical to the one-dimensional case. The second term arises because of the dilution effect due to increased area at greater r. Equation A.13 can be also deduced *via* flux considerations (Edelstein-Keshet 1988:421).

A.2   Time-Dependent Solutions

A.2.1   Initial and boundary conditions

The diffusion equation by itself does not provide enough information to obtain a unique solution, that is, to specify the spatial population density at any given point in time. Because a first temporal and a second spatial derivative are involved in the equation, we need one initial condition and two boundary conditions to completely specify the problem. Boundary conditions (BC) commonly encountered in ecological problems can be of several kinds:

1. **Absorbing BC:** the population density at the boundary is set to zero. This condition is appropriate when the habitat outside the modeled spatial domain is so hostile, that any organisms crossing the boundary immediately perish. A possible variation is to set the density at the boundary to some non-zero constant: $u(0,t) = u_0$. Such a BC is useful when we want to model population redistribution within a habitat that is loosely connected to other habitats by a constant influx of immigrants. We are assuming that the population density at the boundary, u_0, is dominated by the rate of arrival of immigrants. In other words, organisms leaving the habitat effectively disappear and do not affect the density at the boundary.

2. **Reflecting BC:** the flux of organisms at the boundaries is set to zero, which implies that the gradient $\partial u(0,t)/\partial x = 0$. This means that there is no net movement of organisms across the boundary. One situation in which this BC is useful, is when organisms cannot cross the boundary—such as a population on an island, or in a cage. Another situation is when there is complete symmetry around some point, for example, $x = 0$. Then, we need to model only one half of the spatial domain, for example, to the right of $x = 0$. The BC at $x = 0$ is reflecting since, as a result of symmetry, the number of organisms crossing the boundary from left to right equals the number crossing from right to left, resulting in no net flow.

3. **Zero at infinity BC:** $u(\infty, t) = 0$. This BC is appropriate when the boundaries are so far from the point of interest, that we can ignore their

effects. For example, a population of marked organisms is released at some point in space (e.g., $x = 0$) in the center of a such large habitat that no organisms are expected to reach its boundaries.

4. **Periodic BC:** in a domain with its ends at $x = 0$ and $x = L$, $u(0,t) = u(L,t)$ and $\partial u/\partial x(0,t) = \partial u/\partial x(L,t)$. Effectively we have wrapped the domain around in a ring, connecting the point $x = 0$ to the point $x = L$. In two dimensions, wrapping the domain around results in a doughnut. This BC is not particularly useful in field applications, although it is convenient for theoretical investigations because it in effect removes boundaries.

Note that the two boundary conditions needed to completely specify a diffusion problem do not have to be of the same kind. For example, one may have a reflecting boundary condition at $x = 0$, and a zero-at-infinity condition at $x = \infty$.

Initial conditions (IC) also can be of several different kinds.

1. **Point release:** all organisms are released at one spatial point, usually $x = 0$. This is an idealization because it assumes that at $t = 0$ the density of organisms at the point of release is infinite. Mathematically, this IC is handled by means of the Dirac delta-function. It is a useful approximation in modeling mark-recapture releases. Even though marked organisms cannot be physically released into an infinitely small area, the approximation is not bad if the area is much smaller than the spatial domain within which released organisms will diffuse.

2. **Area release:** a more realistic IC, but one needs to specify the width of the region within which organisms are released, a. The density $u(x,0) = u_0$ for $-a/2 < x < a/2$, otherwise $u(x,0) = 0$.

3. **Arbitrary distribution:** a more general IC, in which $u(x,0) = f(x)$ some arbitrary function of space. This IC allows one to model irregular spatial profiles of initial population distribution.

A.2.2 Simple diffusion in infinite domains

A treatise on how to solve diffusion equations is well beyond the scope of this book. A good introduction to this topic can be found in Part III of the Edelstein-Keshet (1988) book *Mathematical Models in Biology*. Her exposition requires only the knowledge of basic calculus. A more thorough, but still readable guide to diffusion is Crank's (1975) *The Mathematics of Diffusion*.

Finally, many solutions for various combinations of initial and boundary conditions are given in Carslaw and Jaeger (1959). The *heat equation* of Carslaw and Jaeger (1959) is mathematically identical to the diffusion equation.

I will follow the "cookbook" approach here. I will focus on situations that are relevant to ecological problems, avoid any derivations or proofs, and simply give the solutions. The exposition in this section largely follows Crank (1975).

INSTANTANEOUS POINT RELEASE   The most familiar solution of diffusion equation to ecologists is the Gaussian curve. It arises when all organisms are released at one point in space and diffuse within an infinite spatial domain. The formal statement of the problem, complete with the initial (IC) and boundary (BC) conditions, is

$$\frac{\partial u}{\partial t} \;=\; D\frac{\partial^2 u}{\partial x^2} \qquad \text{Eqn:} \quad \text{simple diffusion}$$

$$
\begin{aligned}
u(x,0) &= N_0\delta(x) & \text{IC:} & \quad \text{single point release} \\
u(\pm\infty, t) &= 0 & \text{BC:} & \quad \text{zero at infinity}
\end{aligned}
$$

Here D is the diffusion constant, N_0 is the total number of released organisms, and $\delta(x)$ is the Dirac delta function (which essentially says that initial distribution of released organisms is concentrated within an infinitely small area—a single point in space). The solution of this initial-boundary value problem is (Crank 1975:12)

$$u(x,t) = \frac{N_0}{2\sqrt{\pi D t}} \exp\left[-\frac{x^2}{4Dt}\right] \tag{A.14}$$

In two-dimensional space (see Equation A.13) the solution is similar. Using the same initial and boundary conditions as in the 1D case, the solution is (Crank 1975:29)

$$u(x,y,t) = \frac{N_0}{4\pi D t} \exp\left[-\frac{(x^2+y^2)}{4Dt}\right] = \frac{N_0}{4\pi D t} \exp\left[-\frac{r^2}{4Dt}\right] \tag{A.15}$$

where r is the distance from the release point, $r = \sqrt{x^2 + y^2}$.

A line source in the plane results in the same spatio-temporal population distribution as a point source in one-dimensional space (Crank 1975:29)

$$u(x,y,t) = \frac{N_0}{2\sqrt{\pi D t}} \exp\left[-\frac{x^2}{4Dt}\right] \tag{A.16}$$

CONTINUOUS POINT RELEASE   Returning to one-dimensional diffusion, let us assume that organisms are released continously at $x = 0$ in such a way that their density is kept constant $u(0,t) = u_0$. This boundary condition may arise when there is a large reservoir of organisms to the left of $x = 0$, where their density is u_0, or as a result of an experimental manipulation. The other boundary condition is the same as before (zero at infinity), and the initial distribution $u(x,0) = 0$ (no organisms present). The solution is (Crank 1975:21)

$$u(x,t) = u_0 \left(1 - \text{erf} \left[\frac{x}{2\sqrt{Dt}} \right] \right) \tag{A.17}$$

The error function, erf$[z]$, is tabulated in many mathematics handbooks, for example, Abramowitz and Stegun (1964), and is also included in many mathematical or statistical computer software packages, such as *Mathematica* (Wolfram 1988).

The above solution also applies to the two-dimensional situation where the organism density is kept constant at the boundary perpendicular to the x-axis and crossing it at $x = 0$. Crank (1975:33-35) also provides solutions for the case when the density at the $x = 0$ boundary changes, either linearly or according to a power law, $u(0,t) = kt^{n/2}$. These cases may provide a useful first-order approximation for variable population densities in the reservoir.

INSTANTANEOUS AREA RELEASE   If organisms are released by initially confining them in the region $-h < x < h$, the solution is (Crank 1975:15)

$$u(x,t) = \frac{1}{2} u_0 \left(\text{erf} \left[\frac{h-x}{2\sqrt{Dt}} \right] + \text{erf} \left[\frac{h+x}{2\sqrt{Dt}} \right] \right) \tag{A.18}$$

Here u_0 is the initial density of organisms uniformly distributed in the spatial region $[-h, h]$.

Unfortunately, the solution of the corresponding problem in two dimensions involves an integral of a Bessel function of the second kind of order 0 (like erf$[z]$, another higher transcendental function), and thus has to be evaluated numerically (Crank 1975:29)

$$u = \frac{u_0}{2Dt} \exp \left[-\frac{r^2}{4Dt} \right] \int_0^h \exp \left[-\frac{r'^2}{4Dt} \right] I_0 \left[\frac{rr'}{2Dt} \right] r' \, dr' \tag{A.19}$$

However, at the origin, where $r = 0$ the expression simplifies to (Crank 1975:30)

$$u = u_0 \left(1 - \exp \left[-\frac{h^2}{4Dt} \right] \right) \tag{A.20}$$

As in the one-dimensional case, I have assumed that organisms have been rel ased at a uniform density u_0 within a disk of radius h.

A.2.3   Advection-diffusion: infinite and bounded domains

The advection-diffusion equation arises when organisms bias their movement in some preferred direction (see Section 4.2.1)

$$\frac{\partial u}{\partial t} = -\beta \frac{\partial u}{\partial x} + D \frac{\partial^2 u}{\partial x^2} \tag{A.21}$$

The first term reflects the directed flow of organisms (advection) due to the systematic bias in their movements, and the second term represents the undirected component (diffusion). Equation A.21 also arises in many other contexts. In particular, it has been used to model stochastic growth of populations (e.g., Goel and Richter-Dyn 1974). Goel and Richter-Dyn (1974) tabulated a number of solutions of Equation A.21 corresponding to various combinations of boundary conditions. Since the equation is the same, whether we are modeling population redistribution in 1D space or stochastic population growth, we can use many of the Goel and Richter-Dyn formulas. All subsequent models assume a point release and 1D space.

The simplest boundary conditions are zero-at-infinity (infinite spatial domain). Assuming that organisms are released at the origin ($x = 0$), the solution is very similar to Equation A.14

$$u(x,t) = \frac{N_0}{2\sqrt{\pi Dt}} \exp\left[-\frac{(x - \beta t)^2}{4Dt} \right] \tag{A.22}$$

but the squared term inside the exponential function is not x but $x - \beta t$. The implications of this formula are as follows. The variance of the distribution around the mean is unaffected by advection, and is still $2Dt$. However, the whole Gaussian distribution is drifting to the right (assuming $\beta > 0$) with speed β, and thus the mean of the distribution is at βt.

Formula (A.22) provides an alternative hypothesis to fitting the simple diffusion model to data, and allows a statistical test for the presence of systematic biases in movement. However, it assumes that the movement of organisms will be unrestricted by boundaries, which is not always going to be true. For example, suppose marked organisms are initially released in the vicinity of a resource patch in a habitat devoid of resources. Let the patch boundary be located at $x = 0$, and the release point at x_0. Furthermore, suppose that organisms will actively search for resources and that their movement will be biased towards the resource patch due to some long-distance attraction cues. Finally, let's assume that once organisms find the patch, they will not move back to where there are no resources. The last assumption implies an absorbing boundary condition at $x = 0$. The full initial-boundary value problem, therefore, is

$$\frac{\partial u}{\partial t} = -\beta \frac{\partial u}{\partial x} + D \frac{\partial^2 u}{\partial x^2} \qquad \text{Eqn: advection-diffusion}$$

$$
\begin{aligned}
u(x,0) &= N_0 \delta(x - x_0) & \text{IC:} &\quad \text{single point release at } x_0 \\
u(0,t) &= 0 & \text{BC 1:} &\quad \text{absorbing} \\
u(\infty,t) &= 0 & \text{BC 2:} &\quad \text{zero at infinity}
\end{aligned}
$$

The solution of this problem is (Goel and Richter-Dyn 1974)

$$u(x,t) = \frac{N_0}{2\sqrt{\pi D t}} \left\{ \exp\left[-\frac{(x - x_0 - \beta t)^2}{4Dt} \right] - \exp\left[-\frac{4\beta x_0 t - (x + x_0 - \beta t)^2}{4Dt} \right] \right\}$$

$$(A.23)$$

A.2.4 Variable diffusion coefficients

The preceeding sections have focused exclusively on problems in which the diffusivity D was constant. There are three fundamental variables in the diffusion equation (time, space, and population density), and each of these variables may affect D. Temporal variability may be expected as organisms age, or as the environment changes (e.g., diurnal periodicity, seasonality). Dependence of D on space will arise because of heterogeneity in the spatial distribution of various resources (food, mates, and shelter) and in features of the environment that affect locomotion (topography, nature of substrate, and boundaries). Finally, density-dependence could be a result of attraction or repulsion between conspecific organisms.

Obtaining solutions for diffusion models with time-dependent coefficients is easy. For example, the equation for one-dimensional diffusion becomes

$$\frac{\partial u}{\partial t} = D(t) \frac{\partial^2 u}{\partial x^2} \qquad (A.24)$$

Defining

$$T = \int_0^t D(t') \, dt' \qquad (A.25)$$

so that $dT = D(t)\, dt$, Equation A.24 reduces to (Crank 1975:105)

$$\frac{\partial u}{\partial T} = \frac{\partial^2 u}{\partial x^2} \qquad (A.26)$$

Next, the solution for constant diffusivity is obtained in terms of T and x, and T is converted to t using Equation A.25. If there is a simple functional relationship, then the integral can be evaluated explicitly; otherwise it may be approximated graphically or numerically. What we have essentially done is to adopt a different time scale, that sometimes moves faster than the clock, and sometimes slower, and thus recovered the simple diffusion equation. One important consequence of this result is that temporal dependence in D does not affect the shape of the spatial density profile at any particular point in time. Thus, a single-point release in an infinite domain will still result in a Gaussian distribution of organisms, but the variance of the distribution will grow nonlinearly, reflecting time-variation in D. Moreover, in certain situations we can completely ignore temporal variability. For example, D will often have a diurnal periodicity (e.g., a period of activity followed by a period of rest). The argument above indicates that the simple diffusion equation with daily-averaged D will generate the same spatial population densities taken at daily intervals as the more complicated equation with a time-dependent D.

Spatial and density effects on D present more difficulties. Most of the physical literature on spatially-dependent or concentration-dependent diffusion is not very helpful because physical and ecological diffusion in heterogeneous environments have different forms—Fickian versus Fokker-Planck (see Section 4.2.4). The spatial variation in diffusivity affects the spatial distribution of organisms in the two equations differently. Fickian diffusion, even with spatially varying diffusivity, eventually leads to linear density gradients. Fokker-Planck diffusion, by contrast, results in accumulation of organisms in areas where the motility is low, and particle "avoidance" of regions where motility is high.

In general, diffusion models with spatially varying or density-dependent coefficients have to be solved numerically. There are, however, analytical solutions for some simpler cases. Below I discuss two such models. Goel and Richter-Dyn (1974: Table 3.4) give some solutions for the Fokker-Planck equation, assuming particular functional forms of spatial dependence in the coefficients. One of these models, the diffusion equation for the Ornstein-Uhlenbeck process, has been used as a simple model for swarming insects (Okubo 1980:114).

LINEARLY VARYING ADVECTION   Let us suppose that a swarm is centered at $x = 0$. Because the swarm is a dynamic entity (unlike a crystal), members of the swarm will continuously redistribute themselves within it. We will assume that individuals undergo a random walk, but with attraction to the center of the swarm. Since individuals prefer being within the swarm, the attraction is strongest when they are outside it and are moving to rejoin the swarm. Inside the swarm attraction decreases, and near the center it is close to zero. Using a linear approximation, the bias term can be written as $\beta(x) = -\beta_0 x$. That is, when an organism is to the right of the attraction center, it is biasing its movement to the left, towards the center. An individual to the left of the center, by contrast, will be biasing its movement to the right. The strength of attraction increases with distance at the rate measured by β_0. The diffusion equation, then, is of the following form

$$\frac{\partial u}{\partial t} = -\frac{\partial}{\partial x}(-\beta_0 x u) + D\frac{\partial^2 u}{\partial x^2} \tag{A.27}$$

To fully specify the model, we now need to add boundary and initial conditions. Let us assume that there are no barriers in the vicinity of the swarm. Thus, the appropriate BC is zero-at-infinity. Furthermore, we are interested in the probability of an individual to be found at any given point in space at time t, assuming it starts at $x = x_0$ at $t = 0$ (point release IC). These assumptions lead to the following initial-boundary value problem

$$\frac{\partial u}{\partial t} = \beta_0\frac{\partial}{\partial x}(xu) + D\frac{\partial^2 u}{\partial x^2} \quad \text{Eqn:} \quad \text{Ornstein-Uhlenbeck}$$

$$u(x,0) = \delta(x - x_0) \quad \text{IC:} \quad \text{instantaneous point release}$$
$$u(\pm\infty, t) = 0 \quad \text{BC:} \quad \text{zero at infinity}$$

The solution is (Goel and Richter-Dyn 1974)

$$u = \frac{1}{\sqrt{2\pi}\sigma(t)} \exp\left[-\frac{[x - m(t)]^2}{2\sigma^2(t)}\right] \tag{A.28}$$

where $m(t) \equiv x_0 \exp[-\beta_0 t]$ and $\sigma^2(t) \equiv (D/\beta_0)(1 - \exp[-2\beta_0 t])$. We now see that the probability of finding an individual at position x at time t, given that it started at x_0 at $t = 0$, follows normal (Gaussian) distribution with mean $m(t)$ and variance $\sigma^2(t)$. As $t \to \infty$, the mean position converges to 0 (where the center of the swarm is), and the variance converges to $\sigma_\infty^2 = D/\beta_0$. Since all individuals are behaving identically, their density within the swarm will approach a stationary distribution when the flux outwards, due to diffusion, will be exactly counteracted by the flux inwards, due to attraction. It also makes intuitive sense that the width of the swarm, as measured by σ_∞, reflects the balance of the diffusion/attraction strengths.

CROWDING-INDUCED DIFFUSION   A simple model of density-dependent diffusion was discussed by Okubo (1980)

$$\frac{\partial u}{\partial t} = \frac{\partial}{\partial x}\left[D_0\left(\frac{u}{u_0}\right)^m \frac{\partial u}{\partial x}\right] \tag{A.29}$$

Here the diffusivity increases with population density according to the power law ($m > 0$). D_0 is the diffusivity at some reference density u_0. This model is similar to the porous medium equation (Aronson 1980). Okubo gives the solution

$$u = u_0 \ \left(\tfrac{t_0}{t}\right)^{2+\frac{1}{m}} \left(1 - \tfrac{x^2}{x_0^2}\right)^{\frac{1}{m}}, \quad |x| \leq x_0$$
$$= 0, \qquad\qquad\qquad\qquad\qquad |x| > x_0 \qquad (A.30)$$

with $x_0 = r_0(t/t_0)^{1/m+2}$, $r_0 = Q\Gamma(1/m + 3/2)/\pi^{1/2}u_0\Gamma(1/m + 1)$, and $t_0 = r_0^2 m/2D_0(m + 2)$. Q is the initial flux of individuals from the origin, and Γ is the gamma function.

This model confirms the intuitive suggestion that density-dependent dispersal should result in a platykurtic spatial distribution of dispersers (this was already touched on in Section 3.3). In fact, the distribution is so platykurtic that there are no tails at $x > x_1$.

Two observations. First, Equation A.29 is written down as Fickian diffusion, rather than in the Fokker-Planck form. Fortunately, however, making μ density-dependent according to the power law in the Fokker-Planck model leads to essentially the same equation

$$\frac{\partial u}{\partial t} = \frac{\partial^2}{\partial x^2}\left[\mu_0\left(\frac{u^m}{u_0}\right)u\right]$$
$$= \frac{\mu_0}{u_0^m}\frac{\partial^2}{\partial x^2}\left(u^{m+1}\right)$$
$$= \frac{\mu_0(m + 1)}{u_0^m}\frac{\partial}{\partial x}\left(u^m\frac{\partial u}{\partial x}\right)$$

Setting $\mu_0(m + 1) = D_0$ we obtain Equation A.29. Second, as a model for describing movements of real organisms, Equation A.29 has a flaw since as $u \to 0$, $D(u) \to 0$. In other words, movement comes to a complete stop as population density becomes very sparse. This is why, unlike simple diffusion, there are no organisms beyond x_0. Thus, this model may be applied to organisms that move only in response to overcrowding. Nevertheless, I think that its qualitative insights are relevant to the issue of density-dependent dispersal.

A.2.5   Traveling wave solutions

THE SKELLAM MODEL   Traveling waves is a class of solutions that arises in mathematical models of population spread (see Section A.4). The simplest model of population spread was analyzed by Skellam (1951):

$$\frac{\partial u}{\partial t} = D\frac{\partial^2 u}{\partial x^2} + \alpha u \qquad (A.31)$$

This model has two terms, one for simple diffusion (with the diffusion rate D), and one for exponential, or density-independent growth (with the intrinsic rate of natural increase α). In order to solve it, we need to add initial and boundary conditions. Assume that N_0 organisms are released at $x = 0$, and that the boundaries of the habitat are so far from the release point that they do not affect the population spread

$$\frac{\partial u}{\partial t} = D\frac{\partial^2 u}{\partial x^2} + \alpha u \quad \text{Eqn:} \quad \text{the Skellam model}$$

$$\begin{aligned} u(x,0) &= N_0\delta(x) & \text{IC:} & \quad \text{single point release} \\ u(\pm\infty,t) &= 0 & \text{BC:} & \quad \text{zero at infinity} \end{aligned}$$

The solution of this model is well known (e.g., Okubo 1980)

$$u(x,t) = \frac{N_0}{2\sqrt{\pi Dt}} \exp\left[\alpha t - \frac{x^2}{4Dt}\right] \tag{A.32}$$

The solution is a Gaussian distribution that is simultaneously growing (so that the total number of organisms increases exponentially) and spreading outwards. The precise definition of the rate of spread requires some thought. Clearly, some isolated individuals will be found far in advance of the population front. In fact, the simple diffusion equation predicts that there will be a non-zero density of organisms at any position, even far away from the release point ($x \to \infty$), immediately after the spread begins ($t > 0$). This unrealistic feature of the model arises because diffusion models are only approximations of discrete spatial processes (see discussion in Section A.1.1). However, this does not affect real-life applications since the predicted population density in advance of the front is extremely close to zero. In most practical applications, we are not interested in when the very first individuals get to any locality (since such pioneers are very difficult to detect), but in when population density exceeds some threshold of detection. Let $\hat{x}(t)$ be the position at which the threshold density is achieved at time t. The velocity of the front advance, then, can be defined as $c = \hat{x}(t)/t$. Asymptotically ($t \to \infty$), this velocity approaches

$$c^* = 2\sqrt{\alpha D} \tag{A.33}$$

(see Okubo 1980:172, for derivation). The asymptotic velocity of the front advance is achieved quickly (see Okubo 1980: Equation 10.12 for the full time-dependent formula). Thus, the ultimate rate of population spread is increased by both the reproductive and dispersive abilities of the invading organism, a result that agrees with the intuition.

THE FISHER MODEL   Replacing the assumption of exponential with logistic growth, we obtain the following model

$$\frac{\partial u}{\partial t} \;=\; D\frac{\partial^2 u}{\partial x^2} + \alpha u \left(1 - \frac{u}{K} \right) \quad \text{Eqn:} \quad \text{simple diff./logistic growth}$$

$$u(-\infty, t) \;=\; K \qquad\qquad \text{BC:} \quad K \text{ far behind the front}$$
$$u(+\infty, t) \;=\; 0 \qquad\qquad \text{BC:} \quad \text{zero far in advance}$$

The initial conditions are not specified because I assume that the population has been spreading from the "beachhead" for some time. Behind the advancing front, the population density has approached the carrying capacity (the first boundary condition), while far in advance of the front there are no organisms (the second BC).

This simple diffusion/logistic growth model was studied independently by Kolmogoroff, Petrovsky, and Piscounoff (1937) and Fisher (1937) in a population genetics context, and later by Skellam (1951) in an ecological context. It is variously known as Fisher, KPP-Fisher, or Fisher-Skellam model. I will refer to it simply as the *Fisher model.*

The mathematical analysis of the Fisher model is not very involved; a good exposition of the ideas can be found in Edelstein-Keshet (1988, Section 10.6). The main point of interest is that the model exhibits propagating wave solutions. The shape of the frontal wave is preserved as it translates forward with velocity c. Analysis of the Fisher model indicates that a variety of waves can arise, as long as their velocities are greater than the critical velocity c^*. In practice, however, all waves die out, except for the one propagating with the critical velocity. The asymptotic rate of spread is $c^* = 2\sqrt{\alpha D}$, exactly the same as the velocity of front expansion in the diffusion/exponential growth model, Equation A.33. The result that the rate of spread does not depend on K indicates that the advance of the front is influenced primarily by population growth at the front edge, where density-dependent factors are not yet exerting their influence. The population at carrying capacity behind the front exerts no influence on the rate of advance.

A.3   Time-Independent Solutions

A.3.1   Equilibrium solutions: homogeneous space

The logic for finding the equilibrium or steady-state solutions of diffusion equations is the same as with ordinary differential equations (ODE). A steady state implies that the temporal derivative of population density is equal to zero

$$\frac{\partial u}{\partial t} = 0 = D\frac{\partial^2 u}{\partial x^2} \tag{A.34}$$

Unlike the simpler ODE case, however, we still have to solve a differential equation

$$\frac{\partial^2 u}{\partial x^2} = 0 \tag{A.35}$$

Fortunately, this is a very simple equation. Integrating it twice with respect to space, we obtain

$$u = Ax + B \tag{A.36}$$

where A and B are constants to be determined by boundary conditions. If the diffusion occured in an infinite domain, and $u(\pm\infty, t) = 0$, then both A and B must be equal to zero. This, in turn, implies that the steady state for the instantaneous point release is zero population density everywhere. This steady state will be approached as $t \to \infty$ and all organisms are spread so far that their density eventually approaches zero.

For the boundary condition $u(0, t) = u_0$ and $u(L, t) = u_L$ the population density profile will be a straight line connecting these two boundary values

$$u = u_0 + \frac{u_L - u_0}{L}x \tag{A.37}$$

Finally, for reflecting boundary conditions, the population profile will be a level line, the height of which will be determined by the total number of organisms in the spatial domain at $t = 0$ (since there is no flux at the boundaries, no organisms are gained or lost).

In conclusion, the end result of simple diffusion in one dimension is always either level population density, or a linear density gradient. This should not be surprising, since diffusion works on curved gradients, as was discussed in Section A.1.4, filling concave ones and eroding convex ones.

In two dimensions, the equilibrium density gradients of organisms diffusing from a center will not be linear, due to the area-dilution effect. Recollect that the equation for 2D radially-symmetric diffusion is

$$\frac{\partial u}{\partial t} = \frac{1}{r}\frac{\partial}{\partial r}\left(rD\frac{\partial u}{\partial t}\right) \tag{A.38}$$

Setting $\partial u/\partial t = 0$ and integrating, we obtain a general solution of the form (Crank 1975:69)

$$u = A + B\ln r \tag{A.39}$$

where A and B are constants to be determined by boundary conditions. For example, assume the following biological scenario. The density of organisms within a circular patch of radius a is kept constant at u_1 by combined effects of birth and death. Organisms diffuse through the region bounded by $r = a$ on the inside, and by $r = b$ $(b > a)$ on the outside. At the $r = b$ boundary the population density is kept constant at u_2 by immigration pressure. What will the density profile be in the $a < r < b$ region? Clearly, we have absorbing boundary conditions: $u(a, t) = u_1$ and $u(b, t) = u_2$. The solution is (Crank 1975:69)

$$u = \frac{u_1 \ln(b/r) + u_2 \ln(r/a)}{\ln(b/a)} \tag{A.40}$$

A.3.2   Equilibrium solutions: heterogeneous space

Section 4.2.4 shows that the appropriate form of ecological diffusion for heterogeneous environments is the Fokker-Planck equation

$$\frac{\partial u}{\partial t} = \frac{\partial^2}{\partial x^2}(\mu u) \tag{A.41}$$

(for the moment assuming no advection). Here $\mu = \mu(x)$ is the spatially-dependent motility of organisms, which is analogous to, but not the same as the Fickian diffusivity D (Fokker-Planck motility is discussed in detail in Chapter 4). To obtain the equilibrium solution, we set the time derivative to zero, and integrate twice the resulting equation

$$\mu u = Ax + B \tag{A.42}$$

Using either the reflecting BC, or absorbing BC with the same density at both ends, eliminates the Ax term. Thus, in most situations, the solution will be of the form

$$\tilde{u}(x) = \frac{\text{const.}}{\mu(x)} \tag{A.43}$$

This result says that equilibrium population density will be high where the motility is low, and vice versa. In other words, organisms will tend to accumulate in localities where their rate of movement is slow, a conclusion in agreement with intuition.

A.3.3   Dynamic level and residence index

The equation (A.41) can be rewritten as

$$\frac{\partial u}{\partial t} = \frac{\partial^2}{\partial x^2} \Gamma \tag{A.44}$$

where $\Gamma(u, x) = \mu(x)u$. The quantity Γ has been called the *dynamic level* by Skellam (1973). If there is spatial variation in Γ, then animals diffuse from high to low dynamic levels, until at equilibrium $\Gamma = $ const. Thus, the end result of diffusion is to smooth nonhomogeneities in Γ.

The composition of Γ depends on the particular diffusion model. For simple diffusion, Γ simply equals u. The same holds for Fickian diffusion in heterogeneous environments

$$\frac{\partial u}{\partial t} = \frac{\partial}{\partial x}\left[D(x)\frac{\partial u}{\partial x}\right] \tag{A.45}$$

The Fokker-Planck diffusion with an advection term

$$\frac{\partial u}{\partial t} = \frac{\partial^2}{\partial x^2}(\mu u) - \frac{\partial}{\partial x}(\beta u) \tag{A.46}$$

can be rewritten as

$$\frac{\partial u}{\partial t} = \frac{\partial}{\partial x}\left[\phi\frac{\partial}{\partial x}\left(\frac{\mu u}{\phi}\right)\right] \tag{A.47}$$

where ϕ is defined by $\beta/\mu = \partial/\partial x(\log \phi)$. In other words,

$$\log \phi = \int \frac{\beta}{\mu}\,dx$$

For this model the dynamic level $\Gamma = \mu u/\phi$.

A related concept that will be of use later is the *residence index*. Unless movement is density-dependent (such as overdispersion or congregation, see Section 4.5), the dynamic level is a linear function of population density u, and can be written $\Gamma(u, x) = u/\rho(x)$, separating density-dependence and spatial dependence into two separate functions. At equilibrium

$$u(x) \sim \rho(x) \tag{A.48}$$

This equation says that the equilibrium population density at any given point in space is proportional to $\rho(x)$, the *residence index*. For example, in Equation A.41 above, the residence index $\rho = \mu^{-1}$. The residence index is a relative measure of the average time that an organism spends between entering and leaving a unit area that is characterized by the particular combination of movement parameters, such as $\mu(x)$. Clearly, the higher the motility within an area, the lower the residence index will be.

The residence index has an undefined but constant multiplier associated with it, so it is only used for comparative purposes. To obtain the actual equilibrium population density, we also need to know the total number of organisms within the modeled spatial domain, $\int_0^L u(x)\,dx$. Then,

$$u(x) = \frac{\rho(x)\int_0^L u(x)\,dx}{\int_0^L \rho(x)\,dx} \tag{A.49}$$

The residence index provides a connection between the individual movement patterns and population-level redistribution. On one hand, it is expressed in terms of individual movement parameters (for the Fokker-Planck equation it is simply the inverse of motility, but in other models it has a more complex form, see Section 4.4.3). On the other hand, it directly specifies the spatial distribution to which the population density will tend with time.

A.3.4   Stability of equilibrium solutions

Systematic exposition of the mathematical ideas and methods underlying stability analysis of partial differential equations is beyond the scope of this book. My primary goal in this section, therefore, is simply to indicate that such methods exist and can yield useful insights into biological problems.

Qualitative stability analysis is particularly useful when dealing with complex problems (involving spatially varying aggregation and bias coefficients, as well as nonlinear growth/death and interaction terms) for which time-dependent analytical solutions are difficult, or impossible to obtain. Rather than attempting to describe the solution precisely and quantitatively, we try to gain insight into what kind of solution or solutions the system is capable of producing, depending on various factors such as parameter values, or initial and boundary conditions. The simplest qualitative behavior of a spatial system is *homogeneous steady state*. *Steady state* indicates that no temporal change is occurring ($\partial u/\partial t = 0$), while *homogeneous* (sometimes also referred to as *spatially uniform*) refers to no variation of density across space ($\partial u/\partial x = 0$). Homogeneous steady state is the end result of simple diffusion. This state is stable because any perturbation would be smoothed out by simple diffusion—hills eroded, and valleys filled (see Section A.1.4). With more complex reaction-diffusion models, more complicated long-term patterns are possible. In particular, we would often like to know if introducing spatially nonuniform perturbations to a spatially homogeneous state will lead to the smoothing of the perturbations, like in simple diffusion, or whether it will lead to *spatial pattern formation*. To answer this question we need to determine the stability of the spatially homogeneous state. A classic example of this problem—initiation of slime mold aggregation—was investigated by Keller and Segel (1970) (for more readable accounts see Segel 1984: Chapter 6, and Edelstein-Keshet 1988: Chapter 11). The basic idea of the approach is to investigate the behavior of small nonuniform perturbations. For example, we introduce a "wiggle" having a sinusoidal shape to the steady state, and observe whether the amplitude of the disturbance decreases with time (implying stability) or increases with time (implying instability). Growth or decay of the disturbance can depend on its wavelength. In the slime mold aggregation example, the perturbations characterized by very small wavelengths decayed, while perturbations with the largest wavelength grew the fastest (Keller and Segel 1970).

In compounded perturbations each wavelength behaves independently, so that small-wavelength perturbations die out and the large-wavelength ones predominate. This gives us some indication of the spatial pattern away from the equilibrium, since the wavelengths that grow fastest will tend to dominate as time goes on. Another insight is the values of the parameters which permit the instability to develop.

A.3.5 Time-integrated solutions

Time-independent solutions can be obtained in two ways: we can either wait until the solution settles to some sort of an equilibrium and ceases to change, or we can integrate over time, obtaining an average of population density. The following example (Broadbent and Kendall 1953) illustrates the utility of time-integrated solutions.

Consider parasitic helminth eggs deposited at $x = 0$ in the excreta of their host (e.g., a sheep). The larvae that hatch from these eggs will wander around according to the simple random walk, until they climb a blade of grass, where they settle down to wait for ingestion by another host. Let us suppose that the probability of leaving the dispersing population and settling down is a constant, independent of time and space. We are interested in the distribution of larvae after they have settled down. To answer this question, we write the following equation for the evolution of the spatial distribution of moving larvae, u

$$\frac{\partial u}{\partial t} = D\frac{\partial^2 u}{\partial x^2} - \delta u \tag{A.50}$$

where D is the diffusion coefficient, and δ is the constant rate of transition from moving to settled larvae. The initial condition is a point release of N_0 individuals at $x = 0$, and the boundary conditions are zero-at-infinity. The solution of this problem is

$$u = \frac{N_0}{2\sqrt{\pi Dt}} \exp\left[-\frac{x^2}{4Dt} - \delta t\right] \tag{A.51}$$

We see that it is the solution of the simple diffusion equation multiplied by the factor $\exp[-\delta t]$ which is the proportion of organisms surviving to time t. However, we are not interested in the distribution of movers, but in that of settled larvae. At any given point in time, the rate at which larvae leave the moving population is proportional to the density of movers

$$\frac{\partial s}{\partial t} = \delta u \tag{A.52}$$

so that their distribution after all larvae stopped moving is proportional to the integral of u over time

$$s(\infty) = \delta \int_0^\infty u \, dt \tag{A.53}$$

Substituting u from Equation A.51 into the above equation, and integrating we obtain (Okubo 1980:101)

$$\tilde{s}(x) = \frac{\delta N_0}{2\sqrt{D\delta}} \exp\left[-\sqrt{\frac{\delta}{D}} \, |x|\right] \tag{A.54}$$

In two dimensions, we have radially symmetric diffusion equation

$$\frac{\partial u}{\partial t} = \frac{1}{r}\frac{\partial}{\partial r}\left(rD\frac{\partial u}{\partial t}\right) - \delta u \tag{A.55}$$

The solution, using initial and boundary conditions as before, is (Awerbuch et al. 1979)

$$\tilde{s}(r) = \frac{\delta N_0}{2\pi D} K_0\left(\sqrt{\frac{\delta}{D}}r\right) \tag{A.56}$$

$K_0(z)$ is a modified Bessel function. This equation can be approximated as follows (Turchin and Thoeny 1993)

$$\tilde{s}(r) \approx \delta N_0 (8\pi)^{-\frac{1}{2}} (D^3\delta)^{-\frac{1}{4}} r^{-\frac{1}{2}} \exp\left[-r/\sqrt{D/\delta}\right] \tag{A.57}$$

Equation A.56 turns out to be quite useful in a number of ecological applications. I have already mentioned how Broadbent and Kendall (1953) used it to model a random walk with settlement for helminth larvae. Williams (1961) applied the same model to calculate the distribution of larvae deposited by diffusing insects, while Okubo (1980) addressed essentially the same problem, although dealing with egg distribution. Finally, I used this equation to analyze the data of a mark-recapture experiment (Turchin and Thoeny 1993; see also Section 6.2.5).

Interestingly, Equation A.56 is unaffected if the insects are not released all at once but in several batches, or even continuously over a period of time. This is because the solution for the instantaneous release can be used to construct, by superposition, the solution for any arbitrary temporal pattern of release. This is intuitively clear, since Formula A.56 contains no reference to time, and thus distributing release over time should not make any difference.

We can also use Equation A.56 to calculate the mean and the variance of the move distance (a move here is the displacement between the origin and settling point). Integrating over all move directions, and dividing by N_0, we obtain the probability density function for the length of displacement r

$$\phi(r) = \frac{\delta}{D} r K_0 \left(\sqrt{\frac{\delta}{D}} r \right) \tag{A.58}$$

Curry and Feldman (1987) derived the formula for the moments of this probability distribution. In particular, the mean and the variance of the move distance are

$$E[r] = \frac{\pi}{2} \sqrt{\frac{D}{\delta}} \tag{A.59}$$

$$\mathrm{Var}[r] = \frac{D}{\delta} \left(4 - \frac{\pi^2}{4} \right) \tag{A.60}$$

Curry and Feldman (1987) also derived the formula for the distribution of settled organisms for the case when there is drift. They assumed, without loss of generality, that the drift of magnitude β occurs only in the positive x-direction. There is some inconsistency in the formulas following their Equation 7.9, but the correct result appears to be

$$\tilde{s}(r, \theta) = \frac{\delta N_0}{2\pi D} \exp\left[\frac{\beta \cos\theta}{2D} r \right] K_0 \left[\left(\frac{\delta}{D} + \frac{\beta^2}{4D^2} \right)^{\frac{1}{2}} r \right] \tag{A.61}$$

A.4 Population Spread

One of the first spatio-temporal ecological problems that engaged the interest of mathematicians was the dynamic patterns of population spread (Skellam 1951). Population spread is the closest thing we have to a mature theory in spatial ecology. This is due to several factors: the problem has been much studied since the 1930's (Fisher 1937, Kolmogoroff et al. 1937); it was approached with several different mathematical formalisms, and the field has been characterized by an unusual degree of cooperation between empiricists and mathematicians.

A.4.1   Spread in models with simple diffusion

LOGISTIC-LIKE POPULATION GROWTH   I begin by considering reaction-diffusion models with the redistribution process occurring *via* simple diffusion, e.g., models of the form

$$\frac{\partial u}{\partial t} = D\frac{\partial^2 u}{\partial x^2} + f(u) \qquad (A.62)$$

The starting point for the study of population spread is provided by the Skellam model discussed in Section A.2.5, in which $f(u) = \alpha u$. Because the Skellam model assumes exponential growth, population density at each locality grows without an upper bound, and the model's solution does not develop a true wavefront of invariant shape. However, the spatial point at which population density reaches a detection threshold moves away from the point of introduction with an asymptotically constant velocity

$$c^* = 2\sqrt{\alpha D} \qquad (A.63)$$

In two-dimensional space, the population will spread out radially, and the isoconcentration front will be a circle. In this situation, we define the front velocity as the square root of the area enclosed by the circle of threshold density, divided by t. The asymptotic front velocity in two-dimensions is also $c^* = 2\sqrt{\alpha D}$.

The assumption of exponential growth severely limits the usefulness of the Skellam model in ecological applications. We are interested in long-term (asymptotic) patterns of population spread, yet no real population would continue to grow exponentially indefinitely. Thus, an obvious modification of the Skellam model to investigate is to replace the exponential growth with a logistic term. The resulting equation is the Fisher model

$$\frac{\partial u}{\partial t} = D\frac{\partial^2 u}{\partial x^2} + \alpha u \left(1 - \frac{u}{K}\right) \qquad (A.64)$$

The Fisher model exhibits traveling wave solutions, characterized by a defined shape that is translated forward with velocity c (see Section A.2.5). If the area of the "beachhead" initially established by invading organisms is small compared to the area into which invaders are spreading, then the critical velocity is $c^* = 2\sqrt{\alpha D}$. Interestingly, this is exactly the same as the velocity of the front expansion in the Skellam model (see Equation A.63). The advance of the front is determined by population growth at the front edge, where density-dependent factors are not yet exerting their influence.

Even more interestingly, it turns out that minor variations in the shape of the logistic growth function have no influence on the velocity of population spread. As long as the maximum rate of per capita population growth occurs at $u = 0$, and population growth function $f(u)$ is positive for all $u < K$, the asymptotic rate of spread in Equation A.62 is

$$c^* = 2\sqrt{f'(0)D} \tag{A.65}$$

(Hadeler and Rothe 1975), where $f'(0)$ is the derivative of $f(u)$ with respect to u, evaluated at $u = 0$. In other words, $f'(0)$ is the intrinsic rate of population growth, and for logistic growth, where $f(u) = \alpha u(1 - u/K)$, $f'(0) = \alpha$, and we see that Equation A.63 is a special case of Equation A.65.

THE ALLEE EFFECT   There is one case of ecological importance for which the above conditions (the *logistic-like* growth) are not satisfied—when population growth is negative at low densities, or the Allee effect. The effect of Allee dynamics on the rate of spread was investigated by Fife and McLeod (1975), and more recently by Lewis and Kareiva (1993). Lewis and Kareiva (1993) assumed a cubic form for the population growth function

$$f(u) = ku(u - a)(1 - u) \tag{A.66}$$

Here u is population density expressed in units of carrying capacity (that is, $K = 1$), and a is the fraction of carrying capacity below which population growth is negative. If $a \le -1$, then population growth is in the logistic-like form. When $-1 < a \le 0$, then per capita rate of population increase exhibits a maximum not at $u = 0$ (as is the case for logistic-like functions), but at some point intermediate between 0 and 1. However, the growth function is positive within the interval $0 < u < 1$, and therefore there is no Allee effect. Allee effect is present when $0 < a < 1$.

Analysis of the diffusion equation with the cubic growth term (Equation A.66) indicates that traveling wave solutions are present, and that the asymptotic rate of spread is given by (Lewis and Kareiva 1993)

$$c^* = \begin{cases} 2\sqrt{-akD} & \text{for } a \le -1/2 \\ \sqrt{2kD}(1/2 - a) & \text{for } -1/2 \le a < 1/2 \end{cases} \tag{A.67}$$

We see that for logistic-like population growth ($a \le -1$) and even for part of the region where per capita rate of increase has a maximum ($-1 < a < 1/2$), the general result for logistic-like growth holds. That is, $c^* = 2\sqrt{f'(0)D}$, since $f'(0) = ak$. As the per capita rate of population growth becomes more nonlinear ($-1/2 < a \le 0$), and eventually of the Allee kind ($0 < a$), the velocity of the advancing wave slows down, and vanishes at $a = 1/2$.

Allee effect not only slows down the rate of spread, but also makes the establishment of the "beachhead" more difficult. In particular, the density and spatial distribution of the initial invading population are of critical importance to the success of the invasion. Clearly, if at $t = 0$ the population density is less then the threshold a, then the population growth will be negative and the invasion will fail. Moreover, Lewis and Kareiva (1993) showed that in two-dimensional space the founder population may fail even if its initial density is above the threshold. This occurs because the growth in population density may not be sufficient to counteract loss of individuals due to dispersal. Lewis and Kareiva considered a radially expanding wave in two dimensional space with radius $r(t)$. They showed that in order for the wave to expand, the initial radius of the beachhead, $r(0)$, has to be greater than

$$r_{\min} = \frac{\sqrt{D/2k}}{1/2 - a} \qquad (A.68)$$

Thus, larger diffusion coefficients D, or Allee thresholds a, will require larger initial beachheads.

We can draw the following conclusions from the Lewis and Kareiva analysis. First, the asymptotic rate of spread is reduced in proportion to the Allee effect. For very strong Allee effects $(a > 1/2)$, an invading population will not be able to expand. Second, the initial number of colonists must exceed the critical density a in order for the population to begin expanding. Third, the size of the area initially occupied by the founder population (the beachhead) has to be greater than a certain threshold; otherwise, the diffusive losses across the boundary of this area will overwhelm the reproduction within it. Lewis and Kareiva (1993) also point out that if the range of the founding population is slightly above the threshold size, the initial expansion will be very slow, and will gradually increase to the asymptotic rate of spread. This pattern is not predicted by the classic model of simple diffusion with logistic growth. Because most invasions start with a small number of individuals, it is important to consider how possible Allee effects may influence invasion dynamics.

A.4.2 Spread in generalized diffusion models

ADVECTION-DIFFUSION   The effect of constant drift on the spread of an invading species is very straightforward (e.g., van den Bosch et al. 1990a, Lewis and Kareiva 1993). The shape of the spatial distribution of population density is completely unaffected by drift, but the whole distribution is translated in the direction of drift with constant velocity (see van den Bosch et al. 1990a: Figure 1). If drift is strong in relation to diffusivity, the "advancing front" may actually be traveling backwards (see van den Bosch 1990a: Figure 2).

CROWDING-INDUCED DIFFUSION   A simple model for density-dependent dispersal, in which the diffusivity increases with population density according to the power law, is Equation A.29. Because organisms move only as a result of population pressure (since diffusivity approaches zero as $u \to 0$), I referred to this model as the *crowding-induced diffusion*.

Aronson (1980) investigated the spread dynamics of a population in which individuals move according to Equation (A.29), while the population growth is logistic

$$\frac{\partial u}{\partial t} = \frac{\partial^2 u^m}{\partial x^2} + u(1 - u) \qquad (A.69)$$

Note that this equation has only one parameter, m, because the density, time, and space have been scaled in such a way that K, α, and D are equal to 1. The case of $m = 1$ corresponds to the Fisher model, while $m > 1$ indicates crowding-induced dispersal. As Aronson and Weinberger (cited in Aronson 1980) showed, there exists a critical wave velocity c^* for Equation A.69, just like in the Fisher model. There are, however, two differences between the Fisher model and Equation A.69 with $m > 1$. First, the asymptotic rate of spread is slowed by density-dependent dispersal. For example, if $m = 2$ (that is, the diffusivity is a linearly increasing function of population density), then c^* is one-half the asymptotic velocity in the Fisher model. Second, the shape of the advancing front is different. In the Fisher model, the density ahead of the front decreases gradually to zero, while in the crowding-induced dispersal model there is a point beyond which $u(x,t) = 0$. We have already seen this effect when discussing this model without population growth terms (see Section A.2.4). It arises because of the assumption that individuals move only in response to crowding.

SPATIALLY-VARIABLE DIFFUSION   Shigesada et al. (1986) modified the Fisher model to include effects of spatial heterogeneity on the diffusivity and the intrinsic rate of population increase

$$\frac{\partial u}{\partial t} = \frac{\partial}{\partial x} \left(D(x) \frac{\partial u}{\partial x} \right) + [\alpha(x) - gu]u \qquad (A.70)$$

Note that dispersal is treated as Fickian diffusion (although the Fokker-Planck form would be preferable for ecological applications), and that the carrying capacity varies with space, since $K = \alpha(x)/g$ (this form assumes that the coefficient of intraspecific competition g is constant, which may be a reasonable first approximation). Shigesada et al. investigated the rate of wave advance in this model for a special kind of spatial heterogeneity, in which the environment consisted of two kinds of patches ("favorable" and "unfavorable"), each characterized by its diffusivity D_i and intrinsic rate of growth α_i. Each kind of patch had its own characteristic width, l_i, and patches were alternated along the spatial dimension. In other words, the environmental heterogeneity varied in a periodic manner, with a period of $l_1 + l_2$.

Obviously, population persistence requires that the intrinsic growth rate in favorable patches is positive. Moreover, the width of favorable patches has to be greater than a certain threshold value (Shigesada et al. 1986: Equation 14b). If this condition is satisfied, then founder population will grow and eventually evolve into a distribution propagating away from the invasion point. The frontal waves exhibited by Equation A.70 differ, however, from the traveling waves in the Fisher model because of periodic spatial variation in model parameters. Shigesada et al. refer to these propagating solutions as *traveling periodic waves*. Numerical solution of Equation A.70 showed that the velocity of traveling waves always converge to a critical velocity c^*.

Shigesada et al. (1986) derived an implicit formula for c^* in terms of parameter combinations α_2/α_1, D_2/D_1, $\sqrt{\alpha_1/D_1}l_1$, and $\sqrt{\alpha_1/D_1}l_2$ (Shigesada et al. 1986: Figure 6). The following broad conclusions can be drawn from their results:

1. The asymptotic rate of spread is a decreasing function of α_2/α_1. That is, the more hostile is the unfavorable environment, the slower will be the rate of spread.

2. The width of unfavorable patches l_2 also has a negative influence on c^*. If the unfavorable patches are too wide and sufficiently hostile, the population will not be able to spread at all.

3. The effect of the diffusivities ratio D_2/D_1 on c^* is complex. If the unfavorable patch size l_2 is below a certain threshold, then increased diffusivity in unfavorable patches (D_2) promotes faster rate of spread, apparently by speeding organism travel through the unfavorable habitat. However, if l_2 is sufficiently large, than the effect is reversed: increased D_2 *reduces* the overall rate of spread. This happens because individuals in favorable patches rapidly diffuse into unfavorable patches, and a large proportion of them die out before reaching the next favorable patch. This complex result illustrates once again the value of a quantitative model, since qualitative reasoning and intuition in this case would lead one astray.

Finally, Shigesada et al. (1986) derived an approximate formula for c^* when the scale of patchiness is small compared to the overall diffusion rate through the environment. In this case

$$c^* \approx 2\sqrt{\alpha_a D_h} \tag{A.71}$$

where α_a is the arithmetic mean of intrinsic growth rates in the two kinds of patches, and D_h is the harmonic mean of the two diffusivities. Note how similar this formula is to the asymptotic rate of spread in the Fisher model (Equation A.63), which is the special case of Equation A.71 for homogeneous space. Interestingly, the relevant summary statistic for diffusion rate is a harmonic mean, which is always less than the arithmetic mean. This result suggests, therefore, that environmental variation in diffusivity will have a disproportionate effect on slowing down the spread of an invading species. The model of Shigesada et al. was formulated for a special kind of environmental variation. However, its general results may hold for a wider variety of spatial heterogeneity patterns, since an arbitrary function can be represented as an infinite sum of periodic functions (the Fourier series).

RATE OF SPREAD IN THE TELEGRAPH EQUATION   The telegraph equation is the partial differential equation model that arises as a continuum approximation of the correlated random walk process (see Section 4.3.1). The pattern of spread in the reaction-telegraph model (Equation 3.8) with logistic population growth, $f(u) = \alpha u(1 - u/K)$, was investigated by Holmes (1993). She found that traveling wave solutions exist, and that the critical velocity is given by

$$c^* = \begin{cases} \frac{2\gamma\sqrt{2\alpha\lambda}}{\alpha+2\lambda} & \text{for } 0 < \sqrt{\alpha/2\lambda} \leq 1 \\ \gamma & \text{for } 1 \leq \sqrt{\alpha/2\lambda} \end{cases} \qquad (A.72)$$

As expected, numerical solutions indicate that the critical velocity c^* is actually the velocity with which waves travel.

The case $1 \leq \sqrt{\alpha/2\lambda}$ is not biologically very interesting, because it basically says that the time to reverse direction is of the same order of magnitude as the time to produce a new individual. Generally speaking, behavioral events such as direction reversals occur on a much faster time scale than events affecting population change such as reproduction. Thus, we need to focus only on the more biologically-relevant first case ($0 < \sqrt{\alpha/2\lambda} \leq 1$).

Holmes (1993) investigated the numerical difference between the rate of spread c^* predicted by the telegraph equation versus that predicted by a diffusion approximation of the telegraph equation. She found that the ratio of these two rates of spread was

$$\frac{c^*_{\text{tele}}}{c^*_{\text{diff}}} = \frac{1}{1 + \alpha/2\lambda} \qquad (A.73)$$

That is, the more disparate are the time scales of reproduction versus behavior (as measured by the ratio $\alpha/2\lambda$), the closer are results of the telegraph model and its diffusion approximation. Applying the two models to a number of data sets on the spread of organisms ranging from the Black Death to gypsy moths, Holmes (1993: Table 1) found that the difference in predicted velocities were mostly around 1%, and always < 10%. Thus, both theoretical and empirical results agree that there is little need for refinements involving the telegraph equation when predicting the rate of spread of invading organisms.

A.4.3   Spatial contact processes

We have seen in the preceeding sections that the approach based on diffusion models has been very fruitful for a theoretical investigation of the spread of invasions. It has been particularly useful in generating analytical insights about the quantitative effects of nonlinear population growth and nontrivial dispersal on the rate of spread. The analytical power of the approach, however, has its costs. First, continuum reaction-diffusion models represent population density as a continuous variable and population spread as a completely deterministic process. Second, diffusion is, in a certain sense, a *local dispersal* model. We need to investigate the robustness of predictions made by the diffusion-based theory using models with different assumptions. Spatial contact models (Section 3.7.6) provide a framework for this kind of an investigation.

EFFECTS OF STOCHASTICITY   A stochastic model is essential when numbers are small (Mollison 1986). Stochastic effects are particularly important during the establishment of an invading population. Thus, deterministic and stochastic models of establishment give fundamentally different answers. Providing that the intrinsic rate of population growth is positive, a deterministic model would predict that only one outcome is possible—a steady increase of the invading population. A stochastic model, by contrast, will correctly predict that there is a certain chance of extinction, whose magnitude will increase as the initial number of invaders is decreased. A deterministic model, therefore, will be of little use in this kind of setting. Another situation where we expect stochastic factors to be significant is at the very edge of the spreading population, where population density is sparse. If the advance of the invasion front is "pulled" by population processes occurring at the edge (which is the case with, for example, the Fisher model), rather than "pushed" from behind by population pressure from well-settled regions (as is the case in the Allee populations), then stochastic effects may significantly affect the qualitative (mode of spread) and quantitative (rate of spread) aspects of the invasion (Mollison 1986).

Before comparing stochastic and deterministic models, however, we need to discuss what the rate of spread is in the stochastic context. There are several possible aspects of spread that we may want to focus on. One aspect of velocity is concerned with individuals; for example, tracking the distance to the farthest individual through time. Mollison (1977) refers to this quantity as the *front velocity*. The front velocity with its emphasis on individuals at the forefront of spread may be the appropriate variable to focus on in situations where just one individual getting to a certain locality may have a big impact, for example, the spread of a very virulent pathogen. Another quantity of potential interest is the spread of the expectation of the numbers of individuals at position x, measured by the *expectation velocity* (Mollison 1977). Since expectation of population numbers in a stochastic process is analogous to the population density of deterministic continuum models, the expectation velocity is most directly comparable to the deterministic rate of spread, c^*.

QUALITATIVE ASPECTS We have seen (sections A.4.1 and A.4.2) that a general qualitative prediction from the diffusion-based models is that as time goes on a definable front of population density is established, and this front advances with a velocity that approaches some constant asymptotic value, c^*. Stochastic contact processes such as the simple epidemic (Equation 3.12), on the other hand, can exhibit a greater variety of qualitatively different spread patterns. In particular, the qualitative pattern of spread depends in a critical way on the shape of the contact distribution $V(s)$. If $V(s)$ has *an exponentially bounded tail* [that is, $V(s)$ decreases faster than $\exp[-s]$ as $s \to \infty$], then the stochastic spread process will behave in a manner qualitatively similar to a diffusion spread process, such as the Fisher model; and there will be a front advancing with steady velocity (Mollison 1972; see results of simulations in his Figures 3, 6, and 9 illustrating the nature of stochastic spread).

An exponentially-bounded tail means that dispersal is, in a certain sense, a local process. Consider, for example the Gaussian contact distribution, which decreases to zero as $\exp[-x^2]$, and therefore has a "thinner" than exponential tail. Most of dispersing end points are contained within 2–3 standard deviations σ from the point of origin (to be precise, 95–99%). Beyond 3σ, the probability of finding an individual begins to decrease so rapidly with additional distance that we essentially do not need to worry about it. An even more extreme example of a local contact distribution is when movement is restricted to the nearest neighbors, so that the probability of moving beyond them is simply zero.

In contact distributions with exponentially-unbounded tails, by contrast, the probability of moving far decreases only gradually with distance. Such contact distributions may be appropriate in modeling the spread of organisms characterized by long-distance dispersal, such as windborne pathogen spores that may disperse through the atmosphere across a continent. Mathematically, we need to distinguish two cases: (1) tails of $V(s)$ are not exponentially bounded, but $V(s)$ has a finite variance; and (2) $V(s)$ has an infinite variance. In the more extreme second case, the rate of spread does not converge to any constant value, instead it increases without bound through time (Mollison 1972). Simulations of such a stochastic process show progress in a series of "great leaps forward" that get increasingly out of hand (see Mollison 1972: Figure 12). In the first case, when $V(s)$ has a finite variance, the pattern of spread is intermediate between the two extremes of local diffusion and $V(s)$ with an infinite variance. This case is characterized by episodic "great leaps forward," but between these leaps, the process settles down to a roughly constant velocity (see Mollison 1972: Figure 4). Thus, the rate of spread in this process does not increase to infinity.

In addition to the pattern of advance, another interesting qualitative aspect of spread is the shape of the area colonized (or infected) at any given time (Mollison 1977). In continuum models, diffusion tends to round any roughness or irregularity in the initial distribution of the founder population, so that the shape of the invasion area becomes increasingly more circular as time goes on (e.g., see Lewis and Kareiva 1993). In certain stochastic models, the invaded area asymptotically also becomes "circular" (Mollison 1977). However, intuitively we might suppose that in stochastic models the boundary of the invasion area may become very irregular. On the basis of their computer simulations of a birth-death contact process, Williams and Bjerknes (1972) suggested that this is indeed the case, since the simulated boundary had a fractal dimension slightly greater than 1. Whether this result has any practical significance for ecological applications remains an open question.

QUANTITATIVE ASPECTS   Mollison (1977) reviews the results on the rate of spread obtained from stochastic spatial contact models, and contrasts them with the results of deterministic models. We can summarize his results for linear models in continuous time, such as the contact birth process, as follows. If the contact distribution has an exponentially bounded tail, then the rate of spread is finite. Both the front velocity and expectation velocity converge to the same asymptotic value, c^*. Looking back to the diffusion approximation of the contact birth process (Equation 3.11), and identifying D with $\alpha\sigma^2/2$, we see that in the diffusion-approximation $c^*_{\text{diff}} = 2\sqrt{\alpha D} = \sqrt{2}\,\alpha\sigma$. For the contact process, c^*_{cont} is also proportional to $\alpha\sigma$, but the constant of proportionality varies depending on the shape of the contact distribution. Table 1 of Mollison (1977) lists proportionality constants for some common contact distributions. Thus, for nearest-neighbor $V(s)$, $c^* = 1.509\alpha\sigma$. For Gaussian $V(s)$, $c^* = 1.568\alpha\sigma$. For exponential distribution, $c^* = 1.851\alpha\sigma$. We notice that the diffusion approximation underestimates c^*, and that the fatter the tail of the contact distribution, the stronger is the bias. The borderline exponential distribution (borderline because distributions with fatter tails imply infinite spread velocity) exhibits an approximately 30% faster rate of spread, as compared to that predicted by the diffusion approximation.

In discrete time models, the shape of the contact distribution affects the relationship between c^* and α. For a nearest-neighbor $V(s)$, the expectation velocity does not depend on α at all. For a Gaussian $V(s)$, $c^* \sim \sqrt{\alpha}$, and for $V(s)$ with an exponential tail, $c^* \sim \alpha$. I will return to this contrast between continuous-time and discrete-time results in the context of the R&D kernel models.

Turning to nonlinear (density-dependent growth) models, we should expect that their rates of spread would be less than or equal to the velocities predicted by corresponding linear approximations. This should occur because the number of individuals in density-dependent models is limited. Thus, there are fewer offspring originating from behind the advancing front compared to linear models in which population numbers beyond the front grow without bounds. This point can be illustrated by considering an extreme case—a simple epidemic (Equation 3.12) in a discrete space with only one individual allowed at a spatial node, and the nearest-neighbor contact distribution (this stochastic model is equivalent to a percolation process, Mollison 1977; it is also similar to the interacting particles example in Section 3.7.5). In one-dimensional space, the rate of spread in this model is only one-third of that predicted by the diffusion approximation. The reason is that each organism has only two positions on which to deposit its offspring. Chances are that one or both of these positions will be occupied, leading to death of the offspring. Thus, the reproduction rate is effectively reduced, but the diffusion approximation misses this point, since it does not deal with discrete individuals. In two-dimensional space, the severity of this problem is reduced, since there are twice as many sites on which to deposit an offspring. In the two-dimensional case, thus, the diffusion approximation overestimates the rate of spread by a factor of less than two. If we allow more individuals at each site, the rate of spread will increase, and in the limit where $K = \infty$ the rate of spread becomes the same as in the contact birth process (these are simulation results, see Mollison 1977: Table 1).

A.4.4 The R&D kernel models

The reproduction-and-dispersal (R&D) kernel framework is an elegant and general mathematical approach for analyzing the spatial spread of populations, which was developed by Thieme (1977) and Diekmann (1978), and popularized and applied to data by van den Bosch et al. (1990a, 1992). The R&D kernel is a generalization of the contact distribution $V(s)$. Where $V(s)$ reflected the dispersal characteristics of the species under study, the R&D kernel models both its dispersal and its demographic characteristics. The R&D kernel model belongs to the general class of structured population models. Actually, we have been dealing with structured models all along in this book, since the primary dynamical variable of interest, population density $u(x,t)$ is spatially structured. In the R&D kernel model we go one step further, and allow population density to be structured both in space and in age. A systematic exposition of mathematical methods for formulating and studying structured population models can be found in Metz and Diekmann (1986).

The derivation of the R&D kernel model follows the logic of the derivation of the spatial contact process (see Section 3.7.6), but we keep track of not only where an organism came from, but also when it was born. The central idea is to relate the number of births at time t and position x, $b(x,t)$, to the number of births in the past at all possible positions (see van den Bosch et al. 1992). The equation for the birth rate is

$$b(x,t) = \int\limits_{\mathcal{R}^2}\int\limits_{0}^{\infty} b(t-a, x-s)L(a)m(a)V(a,|s|)\, da\, ds \qquad (A.74)$$

Because we are dealing with two-dimensional space, both x and s are vectors (s is a variable reflecting all possible displacements from the birth point to x). There are three key pieces in this equation. Age-specific survivorship $L(s)$ is the probability that an individual is still alive at age a. Age-specific fertility $m(a)$ is the rate of offspring production of an individual of age a. $V(a,|s|)$ is the conditional probability that an individual born at location $x - s$ is living at location x, given that it is still alive at age a. It is assumed that the environment is homogeneous and dispersal has no preferred direction; thus, $V(a,|s|)$ depends only on distance traveled ($|s| = \sqrt{s_1^2 + s_2^2}$). Integration is over all possible ages (a between 0 and ∞), and over the complete two-dimensional space denoted with $\mathcal{R}^2$ (that is, both s_1 and s_2 vary from $-\infty$ to ∞).

The equation for population density follows from Equation A.74 (van den Bosch et al. 1992)

$$u(x,t) = \int\limits_{\mathcal{R}^2}\int\limits_{0}^{\infty} b(t-a, x-s)L(a)V(a,|s|)\, da\, ds \qquad (A.75)$$

Some useful summary statistics are

$$R_0 = \int_0^\infty L(a)m(a)\,da$$

$$\tau = \frac{1}{R_0}\int_0^\infty aL(a)m(a)\,da$$

$$\sigma^2 = \int_0^\infty \int_{-\infty}^\infty \int_{-\infty}^\infty L(a)m(a)s_1^2 V(a,|s|)\,ds_2\,ds_1\,da$$

The net reproduction R_0 is the average number of female offspring produced by each mother (the R&D kernel model only keeps track of females, assuming that males are never in short supply). The mean age at child bearing τ can be interpreted, to a first approximation, as the generation time. The parameter σ^2 is the variance of the marginal dispersal density. It can be interpreted as the variance of each individual's displacement from birth to death, measured along one particular spatial axis (say, x_1; since dispersal is rotationally symmetric, σ^2 does not vary with the direction of the line along which it is measured). The parameters R_0, τ, and σ^2 have the following approximate relationships with the intrinsic rate of increase α and the diffusion rate D

$$R_0 = e^{\alpha\tau}$$
$$\sigma^2 = 2D\tau \tag{A.76}$$

The R&D kernel model is a density-independent model, and thus it cannot exhibit true traveling waves (see Section A.4.1). The essential features of its behavior are well captured by the Skellam model, although quantitatively the rate of population increase and spread will depend on the details of the reproduction and dispersal submodels. Thus, we are interested in whether the R&D kernel model, like the Skellam model, exhibits fronts advancing at an asymptotically constant velocity. As discussed by van den Bosch et al. (1992), it can be proved that this is indeed the case, and that there is an asymptotic velocity c^*, as long as the initial population distribution is confined within a finite area. This result appears to hold for non-rotationally symmetric dispersal, for example, the presence of drift and anisotropic dispersal, although it lacks a formal mathematical proof (van den Bosch et al. 1990a).

Furthermore, van den Bosch et al. (1990a) argue that the results of the linear R&D kernel model will hold for its density-dependent, nonlinear modifications, as long as (1) population growth is logistic-like (in particular, there are no Allee-like effects), and (2) the influence of an individual on the environment far from its present position is negligible. This is the so-called *linear conjecture* (Mollison 1991). We are familiar with the first condition in the context of diffusion models (Section A.4.1). The second condition is automatically satisfied by diffusion-based models because population density effects in them are completely local, since the birth/death term $f(u(x))$ depends only on conditions at x, and not at $x + \epsilon$, no matter how small ϵ is. In integro-differential models, one can make the growth term a function of density averaged within some finite unit of space. The second condition basically says that the nonlinear model behaves like the linear one at the front, where population numbers are small (Mollison 1991). Since it is the population dynamics at the front that determine propagation velocity in "pulled waves," the c^* of the linear model provides a good approximation for the c^* of the nonlinear one.

Returning to the linear R&D kernel models, we can now ask: under what conditions does the diffusion equation provide a good approximation of the propagation velocity c^* in the R&D kernel model? And what is c^* when the diffusion approximation fails? Van den Bosch et al. (1992) provide the following answers to these questions.

1. First, let us assume that organism movement can be described by a diffusion process (in particular, individuals do not tend to settle in a particular territory). The probability distribution of finding an individual at time a after birth (a is age) is Gaussian, with variance that increases linearly with age. The age-specific dispersal kernel is

$$V(a, |s|) = \frac{1}{2\sqrt{\pi D a}} \exp \frac{-|s|^2}{4 D a} \tag{A.77}$$

We are essentially assuming that population redistribution is simple diffusion, but unlike the Skellam model, we allow nontrivial age-dependent survival and fertility functions. The intrinsic rate of population increase is defined (implicitly) by the Euler equation (e.g., Roughgarden 1979)

$$1 = \int_0^\infty e^{-\alpha a} L(a) m(a) \, da \tag{A.78}$$

The asymptotic rate of population spread for this model is (van den Bosch et al. 1992)

$$c^* = 2\sqrt{\alpha D} \tag{A.79}$$

which is, of course, the same as c^* for the diffusion equation with exponential growth. Thus, the Fisher-Skellam rate of population spread is a robust result with respect to arbitrary $L(a)$ and $m(a)$ functions. In other words, adding age-structure to the diffusion model does not affect its prediction about the rate of spread (at least in linear, density-independent models, although the linear conjecture suggests that this result will also hold for various logistic-like population growth functions).

2. The above result was found for a special kind of the R&D kernel. Generalizing to an arbitrary R&D kernel, but assuming a small reproductive capacity, van den Bosch et al. showed that the asymptotic rate of spread is approximately

$$c^* \approx \frac{\sigma}{\tau} \sqrt{2 \ln R_0} \qquad (A.80)$$

If we identify $r = \ln R_0 / \tau$ and $D = \sigma^2 / 2\tau$ (see Equation A.76), then the velocity of population expansion given by Equation A.80 is identical to the Fisher-Skellam rate of spread. As van den Bosch et al. point out, however, there is a virtue in keeping the form of Equation A.80 (rather than the Fisher-Skellam form), since its parameters are more closely connected to the performance and behavior of individuals, than are r and D.

Van den Bosch et al. showed that Equation A.80 is accurate for $R_0 \leq$ 1.5. For greater reproductive capacity, the formula becomes increasingly less accurate.

3. For species with larger net reproduction and non-Gaussian R&D kernels, the diffusion approximation fails. The asymptotic velocity of spread can be calculated from implicit relationships (van den Bosch et al. 1990a: Equation 3.11) using numerical methods. An alternative tactic, followed by van den Bosch et al. (1990a), was to derive an approximation involving higher-order moments of the reproduction and dispersal probability distributions

$$c^* \approx \frac{\sigma}{\tau} \sqrt{2 \ln R_0} \left\{ 1 + \left[\left(\frac{\nu}{\tau} \right)^2 - \beta + \frac{\gamma}{12} \right] \ln R_0 \right\} \qquad (A.81)$$

where ν^2 is the variance in the age of reproduction, γ is the kurtosis of the marginal dispersal density, and β is a measure of the interaction between dispersal and reproduction (these quantities are defined in van den Bosch et al. 1992: formulas 3.9–3.11). This approximation is valid for a much greater range of R&D kernels than is Equation A.80. In particular, it gives accurate approximations for $R_0 \leq 7$ and $\nu/\tau \leq 0.06$. Equation A.81 gives more accurate predictions in practical applications than the Fisher-Skellam formula (see Section A.4.4).

A.4.5 Population spread and species interactions

We now progress from single-species models to models of population spread in the context of species interactions. Species-interactions models are too complex to study with analytical stochastic methods (apart from certain problems that can be reduced to a single-species equation, e.g., simple epidemics), and therefore all analytical results for spread in multispecies communities are based on diffusion models.

MODELING SPREAD OF A BUDWORM INFESTATION   A model of balsam fir–spruce budworm–generalist predator interaction (Ludwig et al. 1978, 1979) provides a good starting point for this section, because it can be reduced to a single-species equation and solved using essentially the same methods as in Section A.4.1. The aspatial version of the model was developed in Ludwig et al. (1978)

$$\frac{du}{dt} = f(u) = \alpha u \left(1 - \frac{u}{K}\right) - \frac{gu^2}{u^2 + h^2} \qquad (A.82)$$

Here u is the budworm density. The first term on the right-hand side is a logistic term, with carrying capacity K proportional to the surface area of balsam fir branches. We assume that K is approximately constant at the temporal scale of interest, since it takes several years for budworms to significantly reduce the amount of their resources, and our primary interest is in what happens during the initiation stage of a budworm outbreak. The second term on the right-hand side gives the rate of consumption of budworms by generalist predators, such as birds and mammals. At high levels of u this term saturates to the rate g because we assume that predators do not respond numerically to the elevated abundances of prey. Thus, g is the product of the predator density and the maximum consumption rate of an individual predator. At low budworm density the consumption rate drops sharply because the predators switch to alternate prey (Ludwig et al. 1979). In ecological literature, this kind of consumption rate is known as Type III functional response (Holling 1965).

A combination of logistic growth and Type III functional response terms may produce a complex, highly nonlinear shape of the birth/death function $f(u)$. Population dynamics in Equation A.82 are governed by the two attractors, u_1 and u_3, which are stable equilibrium points, and by the unstable equilibrium point u_2, which separates the domains of attraction associated with each of the two stable points. If the population density is initially $0 < u(0) < u_2$, then the solution will be attracted to the *endemic* stable equilibrium, u_1. If, on the other hand, $u_2 < u(0) < \infty$, then the solution will be attracted to the stable point u_3, which is the *epidemic* equilibrium.

To study spatio-temporal dynamics of budworm outbreaks, Ludwig et al. (1979) added a simple diffusion term to Equation A.82. Their analysis of the resulting reaction-diffusion model focused on whether there was a critical (minimal) size of a forest patch that could support a budworm outbreak. Since we are interested in the spatial spread of populations, we turn to the analysis by Murray (Section 11.5 in Murray 1993).

Murray (1993) considered the following scaled version of the Ludwig et al. (1979) model

$$\frac{\partial u}{\partial t} = \alpha u \left(1 - \frac{u}{K}\right) - \frac{u^2}{1 + u^2} + D\frac{\partial^2 u}{\partial x^2} \tag{A.83}$$

This model has two spatially uniform stable solutions, the endemic state $\tilde{u}(x) = u_1$, and the epidemic state $\tilde{u}(x) = u_3$. There also can be a variety of wave solutions, connecting any two of the four possible steady states $(0, u_1, u_2, u_3)$ in various combinations (Murray 1993). We are interested in whether a localized outbreak surrounded by an endemic budworm population will spread, or not. Thus, the appropriate wave to investigate is the one that connects u_3 to u_1. Murray (1993) showed that the direction of spread of such a wave (that is, whether the outbreak spreads or shrinks) depends on the sign of $\int_{u_1}^{u_3} f(u)\, du$.

The mechanism for the outbreak spread can be understood by considering the interface between the epidemic and endemic regions. Insects will diffuse from higher to lower population density, pushing density up on the endemic side of the front, while depressing it on the epidemic side. If the threshold point u_2 is closer to u_1 than to u_3, insects "spilling over" from the epidemic region will tip the endemic region over the threshold, and into the outbreak. The overall effect will be of the outbreak spreading. On the other hand, if the threshold point u_2 is closer to u_3, then diffusion will not be able to tip the endemic region into the outbreak. Moreover, density in the epidemic region will decrease below the threshold, and the net effect will be of the outbreak contracting.

POPULATION SPREAD AND INTERSPECIFIC COMPETITION So far we have assumed that an invading species moves into what is essentially a competition-free habitat. How is the rate of spread affected, if the invading exotic species has to displace an established native competitor (assuming that the invader is the superior competitor)? To answer this question, Okubo et al. (1989) considered a model of Lotka-Volterra competition with simple diffusion:

$$\frac{\partial u_1}{\partial t} = D_1 \frac{\partial^2 u_1}{\partial x^2} + \alpha_1 u_1 (1 - g_1 u_1 - a_1 u_2)$$
$$\frac{\partial u_2}{\partial t} = D_2 \frac{\partial^2 u_2}{\partial x^2} + \alpha_2 u_2 (1 - g_2 u_2 - a_2 u_1) \tag{A.84}$$

where u_i are the densities of the invading and the native species; D_i, α_i, and g_i are species-specific diffusivities, intrinsic rates of increase, and the coefficients of intraspecific competition (subscripts 1 and 2 refer to the invader and the resident, respectively); and a_i are the interspecific competition coefficients. Okubo et al. (1989) showed that the invading species will spread in a wavelike fashion, and the velocity of spread is given by

$$c^* = 2\sqrt{\alpha_1(1 - a_1/g_2)D_1} \qquad (A.85)$$

We see that interspecific competition does not qualitatively affect the spread dynamics (at least, in this simple competition model), since Equation A.85 differs from the Fisher-Skellam formula only in one particular: instead of α_1, it involves $\alpha_1' = \alpha_1 - a_1/g_2$. The quantity α_1' is the population growth rate of the invader when the invader's population density is near zero, and the resident's density is near the carrying capacity. Thus, a quantitative effect of competition is to slow down the rate of spread, since $\alpha_1' < \alpha_1$.

SPREADING WAVES IN PREDATOR-PREY SYSTEMS   Dunbar (1983, 1984; see also Murray 1993: section 12.2) studied the following general model of predator-prey interaction in space

$$\begin{aligned} \frac{\partial u}{\partial t} &= \alpha u \left(1 - \frac{u}{K}\right) - auv + D_1 \frac{\partial^2 u}{\partial x^2} \\ \frac{\partial v}{\partial t} &= \gamma auv - \delta v + D_2 \frac{\partial^2 v}{\partial x^2} \end{aligned} \qquad (A.86)$$

where $u(x,t)$ is the density of the prey, and $v(x,t)$ is the density of the predator. This model is based on the Lotka-Volterra predator-prey model, so that a is the rate of prey capture by predators (assuming a linear functional response), γ is the conversion rate of the captured prey biomass into the predator biomass, and δ is the death rate of the predators. There are two modifications of the Lotka-Volterra model in Equation A.86. First, the model assumes logistic growth of the prey population in the absence of prey with carrying capacity K. Secondly, the model adds simple-diffusion terms for the prey (with diffusion rate D_1) and the predators (with diffusion rate D_2).

The Lotka-Volterra predator-prey model has a pathological mathematical property of being neutrally stable (see, e.g., May 1981). Adding the self-limitation logistic term in the prey equation causes the model to stabilize. In fact, Equation A.86 without diffusion terms has globally stable point equilibrium that is approached in either an exponential or an oscillatory fashion depending on parameter values (Murray 1993).

Let us now ask the following question. Suppose that an exotic predator species invades an area where the prey are at the equilibrium K. What are the qualitative patterns of spatial predator-prey dynamics, in particular, patterns of spread? Analysis of the full model (Equation A.86) is difficult because it involves the study of a four-dimensional phase space. In many practical situations, however, prey dispersal occurs at a much reduced rate compared to the rate of predator dispersal. Thus, we can assume that D_1/D_2 is close to zero. A useful mathematical trick in such situations is to study the behavior of the simplified system in which the diffusion rate of the prey is set to zero. It can be shown that the dynamic behavior of such a system will be qualitatively similar to the behavior of the full system with non-zero, but small D_1 (Dunbar 1984).

We are interested in the spreading wave of the invading predator. Thus, far ahead of the wave front the prey density is at K and the predator density is 0. Behind the front, the prey and predator densities approach the stable steady state. Dunbar (1983) showed that such waves exist and will propagate with the critical velocity

$$c^* = 2\sqrt{(\gamma aK - \delta)D_2} \qquad (A.87)$$

Interestingly, a little algebra shows that this is the Fisher-Skellam velocity! Note that the second equation of Equation A.86 is of the form

$$\frac{\partial v}{\partial t} = g(u,v) + D_2\frac{\partial^2 v}{\partial x^2} \qquad (A.88)$$

Arguing by analogy with the spread in a one-species model, we might conjecture that the rate of predator spread will be determined by its growth and diffusion dynamics in front of the wave. If this is in fact true, then we can approximate Equation A.88 with a linear model of the Skellam form

$$\frac{\partial v}{\partial t} = g_v(K,0)v + D_2\frac{\partial^2 v}{\partial x^2} \qquad (A.89)$$

Here $g_v(K,0)$ is the partial derivative of $g(u,v)$ with respect to v evaluated at $u = K$ and $v = 0$—it is the "intrinsic rate" of predator population increase, which occurs ahead of the advancing front, where the predator density is close to zero and the prey density is at the prey carrying capacity. The spread velocity in Equation A.89 is $c^* = 2\sqrt{g_v(K,0)D_2}$, which turns out to be the same as Equation A.87, since $g_v(K,0) = \gamma aK - \delta$. Thus, the critical wave velocity in Dunbar's (1983) predator-prey model, $c^* = 2\sqrt{g_v(K,0)D_2}$, is equivalent to the Fisher-Skellam $c^* = 2\sqrt{f'(0)D}$.

However, there is one fundamentally new feature of spread that distinguishes predator-prey models from single-species equations. Single-species models (in continuous time) cannot exhibit limit cycles or stable oscillations. By contrast, predator-prey models have an inherent propensity to oscillate (May 1981). Thus, population spread in predator-prey models is not limited to a single wave front, but may involve a series of traveling waves following each other. Since the aspatial version of Equation A.86 is globally stable, its spatial version exhibits simple dynamics. More complex growth and interaction terms, that are capable of inducing limit cycles and chaos, generate much more intricate dynamical patterns in space and time.

Bibliography

Abramowitz M, Stegun I. 1964. Handbook of mathematical functions with formulas, graphs and mathematical tables. National Bureau of Standards, Washington (reprinted by Dover Publications, New York).

Akey DH. 1991. A review of marking technologies in arthropods and an introduction to elemental marking. Southwestern Entomologist Suppl No 14: 1-8.

Akey DH, Hayes JL, Fleisher SJ. 1991. Use of elemental markers in the sudy of arthropod movement and trophic interactions. Southwestern Entomologist Suppl No 14.

Alt W. 1980. Biased random walk models for chemotaxis and related diffusion approximations. J Math Biol 9: 147-177.

Alt W. 1985. Models for mutual attraction and aggregation of motile individuals. Lecture Notes Biomath 57: 33-38.

Alt W. 1990. Correlation analysis of two-dimensional moving paths. Pp 254-268 in Alt W, Hoffmann G (eds). Biological Motion: proceedings of a workshop. Springer Lecture Notes in Biomath, Springer Verlag, Berlin.

Aluja M, Prokopy RJ, Elkinton JS, Laurence F. 1989. Novel approach for tracking and quantifying the movement patterns of insects in three dimensions under seminatural conditions. Environ Entomol 18: 1-7.

Ammerman A, Cavalli-Sforza LL. 1973. A population model for the diffusion of early farming in Europe. Pp 343-357 in Renfrew C (ed). Institute of Archeology Research Seminar. Duckworth, London.

Andow DA, Kiritani K. 1984. Fine structure of trivial movement in the green rice leafhopper *Nephotettix cincticeps* (Uhler) (Homoptera: Cicadellidae). Appl Entomol Zool 19: 306-316.

Andow DA, Kareiva PM, Levin SA, Okubo A. 1990. Spread of invading organisms. Landscape Ecol 4: 177-188.

Andreassen HP, Halle S, Ims RA. 1996a. Optimal design of movement corridors in root voles – not too wide and not too narrow. J Appl Ecol 33: 63-70.

Andreassen HP, Ims RA, Steinset OK. 1996b. Discontinuous habitat corridors: effects of male root vole movements. J Appl Ecol 33: 555-560.

Andrewartha HG, Birch LC. 1954. The distribution and abundance of animals. Univ Chicago Press, Chicago.

Andryszak NA, Payne TL, Billings PM, Benenati JM. 1982. Effect of flight activity on laboratory response of the southern pine beetle to an attractant. J Georgia Entomol Soc 17: 456-460.

Antolin MF. Strong DR. 1987. Long-distance dispersal by a parasitoid (*Anagrus delicatus*, Mymaridae) and its host. Oecologia 73: 288-292.

Aris R. 1975. The mathematical theory of diffusion and reaction in permeable catalysts. Oxford Univ Press, Oxford.

Aronson DG. 1980. Density-dependent interaction-diffusion systems. In Stewart et al. (eds). Dynamics and modelling of reactive systems. Academic Press, New York.

Aronson DG. 1985. The role of diffusion in mathematical population biology: Skellam revisited. Lecture Notes Biomath 57:2-6.

Awerbuch TE, Samson R, Sinskey AJ. 1979. A quantitative model of diffusion bioassays. J Theor Biol 79: 333-340.

Baars MA. 1979. Patterns of movement of radioactive carabid beetles. Oecologia 44: 125-140.

Bach CE. 1980. Effects of plant density and diversity on the population dynamics of a specialist herbivore, the striped cucumber beetle *Accalymma vittata* (Fab.). Ecology 61: 1515-1530.

Baker MC, Mewaldt LR. 1978. Song dialects as barriers to dispersal in white-crowned sparrows *Zonotrichia leucophrys nuttali*. Evolution 32: 712-722.

Banks HT. 1981. Parameter identification techniques for physiological control systems. Pp 361-383 in Hoppensteadt F (ed). Lectures in Applied Mathematics (vol 19). Amer Math Soc, Providence.

Banks HT. 1985. On a variational approach to some parameter estimation problems. Pp 9-23 in Kappel F, Kunisch K, Schappacher W (eds). Distributed parameter systems. Lect Notes Control Info Sci (vol 75). Springer, Berlin.

Banks HT, Fitzpatrick BG. 1990. Statistical methods for model comparison in parameter estimation problems for distributed systems. J Math Biol 28: 501-527.

Banks HT, Kareiva P. 1983. Parameter estimation techniques for transport equations with application to population dispersal dispersal and tissue bulk flow models. J Math Bio 17: 253-273.

Banks HT, Kareiva PM, Lamm PK. 1985. Modeling insect dispersal and estimating parameters when mark-release techniques may cause initial disturbances. J Math Biol 22: 259-277.

Banks HT, Kareiva PM, Murphy KA. 1987. Parameter estimation techniques for interaction and redistribution models: a predator-prey example. Oecologia 74: 356-362.

Banks HT, Kareiva PM, Zia L. 1988. Analyzing field studies of insect dispersal using two-dimensional transport equations. Environ Entomol 17: 815-820.

Banks HT, Kunisch K. 1989. Estimation techniques for distributed parameter systems. Birkhauser, Boston.

Barkham JP, Hance CE. 1982. Population dynamics of wild daffodil (*Narcissus pseudonarcissus*) III. Implications of a computer model of 1000 years of population change. J Ecol 70: 323-344.

Bateman AJ. 1947a. Contamination of seed crops. I. Insect pollination. J Genetics 48: 257-275.

Bateman AJ. 1947b. Contamination of seed crops. II. Wind pollination. Heredity 1: 235-246.

Bateman AJ. 1947c. Contamination of seed crops. III. Relation with isolation distance. Heredity 1: 303-306.

Batschelet E. 1981. Circular statisitics in biology. Academic Press, London.

Beier P. 1993. Determining minimum habitat areas and habitat corridors for cougars. Conserv Biology 7: 94-108.

Beier P. 1995. Dispersal of juvenile cougars in fragmented habitat. J Wildl Manage 59: 228-237.

Bell WJ. 1991. Searching behaviour: the behavioural ecology of funding resources. Chapman and Hall, London.

Bell WJ, Tortorici C, Roggero RJ, and others. 1985. Sucrose-stimulated searching behaviour of *Drosophila melanogaster* in a uniform habitat: modulation by period of deprivation. Anim Behav 33: 436-448.

Belthoff JR, Ritchison G. 1989. Natal dispersal of Eastern Screech Owls. Condor 91: 254-265.

Bennet RB, Borden JH. 1971. Flight arrestment of tethered *Dendroctonus pseudotsugae* and *Trypodendron lineatum* (Coleoptera: Scolytidae) in response to olfactory stimuli. Ann Entomol Soc Amer 64: 1273-1287.

Bennett AF, Henein K, Merriam G. 1994. Corridor use and the elements of corridor quality – chipmunks and fencerows in a farmaland mosaic. Biol Conserv 68: 155-165.

Berg H. 1983. Random walks in biology. Princeton Univ Press, Princeton.

Berry JS, Holtzer TO. 1990. Ambulatory dispersal behavior of *Neoseiulus fallcis* (Acarina: Phytoseiidae) in relation to prey density and temperature. Exp Appl Acarol 8: 253-274.

Bibby CJ, Burgess ND, Hill DA. 1992. Bird census techniques. Academic Press, London.

Blanché S, Casas J, Bigler F, Janssen-van Bergeijk KE. 1996. An individual-based model of *Trichogramma* foraging behaviour: parameter estimation for single females. J Appl Ecol 33: 425-434.

Bond AB. 1980. Optimal foraging in a uniform habitat: the search mechanism of the green lacewing. Anim Behav 28: 10-19.

Boonstra R, Krebs CJ, Gaines MS, and others. 1987. Natal philopatry and breeding systems in voles (*Microtus* spp.). J Anim Ecol 56: 655-673.

Box GEP, Cox DR. 1964. An analysis of transformations. J Roy Statist Soc B26: 211-252.

Box GEP, Draper NR. 1987. Empirical model-building and response surfaces. Wiley & Sons, New York.

Box GEP, Jenkins GM. 1976. Time series analysis: Forecasting and control. Holden Day, Oakland, California.

Broadbent SR, Kendall DG. 1953. The random walk of *Trichostrongylus retortaeformis*. Biometrics 9: 460-466.

Brodie C, Houle G, Fortin MJ. 1995. Development of a *Populus balsamiferae* clone in subarctic Quebec reconstructed from spatial analyses. J Ecol 83: 309-320.

Brooks MI. Butlin RK. 1994. Estimates of male dispersal in *Yponomeuta padellus* (Lepidoptera: Yponomeutidae), the small ermine moth, by means of simulation. Heredity 73: 207-214.

Brown AC. 1961. Physiological-ecological studies on two sandy-beach gastropoda from South Africa: *Bullia digitalis* Meuschen and *Bullia laevissima* (Gmelin). Z Morph Okol Tiere 49: 629-657.

Brown KJ, Lacey AA (eds). 1990. Reaction-diffusion equations : the proceedings of a symposium year on reaction-diffusion equations. Clarendon Press, Oxford.

Brownlee J. 1911. The mathematical theory of random migration and epidemic distribution. Proc Roy Soc Edinburgh 31: 262-289.

Brussard PF. 1971. Field techniques for investigations of population structure in a "ubiquitous" butterfly. J Lepid Soc 25: 22-29.

Buechner M. 1987. A geometric model of vertebrate dispersal: tests and implications. Ecology 68: 310-318.

Bunnell FL, Harestad AS. 1983. Dispersal and dispersion of black-tailed deer: models and observations. J Mammal 64: 201-209.

Cain ML. 1989a. The analysis of angular data in ecological field studies. Ecology 70: 1540-1543.

Cain ML. 1989b. Pattern of Clonal Growth in *Medeola virginata* and *Solidago altissima*. Ph. D. Thesis, Cornell Univ, Ithaca, New York.

Cain ML. 1990. Models of clonal growth in *Solidago altissima*. J Ecol 78: 27-46.

Cain ML, Eccleston J, Kareiva P. 1985. The influence of food plant dispersion on caterpillar success. Ecol Entomol 10: 1-7.

Cain ML, Pacala SW, Silander JA, Fortin MJ. 1995. Neighborhood models of clonal growth in the white clover *Trifolium repens*. Amer Natur 145: 888-917.

Cappuccino N, Price PW (eds). Population dynamics: new approaches and synthesis. Academic Press, San Diego.

Cardé RT, Elkinton JS. 1984. Field trapping with attractants: Methods and interpretation. Pp 111-129 in Hummel HE, Miller TA (eds). Techniques in pheromone research. Springer-Verlag, New York.

Carslaw HS, Jaeger JC. 1959. Conduction of heat in solids (2nd ed). Clarendon Press, Oxford.

Casas J, Aluja M. 1997. The geometry of search movements of insects in plant canopies. Behav Ecol, 8: 37-45.

Caswell H, Etter RJ. 1993. Ecological interactions in patchy environments: from patch-occupancy models to cellular automata. Pp 93-109 in Steele J, Powell TM, Levin SA (eds). Patch Dynamics in Terrestrial, Marine, and Freshwater Ecosystems. Springer-Verlag, Berlin.

Chatfield C. 1989. The analysis of time series: an introduction. Chapman and Hall, London.

Clark JS. 1998. Why trees migrate so fast: confronting theory with dispersal biology and the paleorecord. Ecology, in review.

Clark JS, Fastie C, Hurtt G, and others. 1998a. Dispersal theory offers solutions to Reid's Paradox of rapid plant migration. BioScience, in press.

Clark JS, Macklin E, Wood L. 1998b. Stages and spatial scales of recruitment limitation in southern Appalachian forests. Ecology, in press.

Cochran WW, Warner DW, Tester JR, Kuechle VB. 1965. Automatic radio-tracking system for wild animals. J Wildl Management 27: 9-24.

Cohen DS, Murray JD. 1981. A generalized diffusion model for growth and dispersal in a population. J Math Biol 12: 237-249.

Cook SP, Hain FP. 1992. The influence of self-marking with fluorescent powders on adult bark beetles (Coleoptera: Scolytidae). J Entomol Sci 27: 269-279.

Crank J. 1975. The mathematics of diffusion (2nd ed). Oxford Univ Press, London.

Crawley MJ, May RM. 1987. Population dynamics and plant community structure: competition between annuals and perennials. J Theor Biol 125: 475-489.

Crist TO, Guertin DS, Wiens JA, Milne BT. 1992. Animal movement in heterogeneous landscapes: an experiment with *Elodes* beetles in shortgrass prairie. Functional Ecol 6: 536-544

Crist TO, MacMahon JA. 1991. Individual foraging components of harvester ants: movement patterns and seed patch fidelity. Insectes Sociaux 38: 379-396.

Cronin JT, Turchin P, Hayes J, Steiner CA. 1998. Intra- and inter-infestation dispersal by the southern pine beetle. Ecol Appl, in review.

Crumpacker DW. 1974. The use of micronized fluorescent dusts to mark adult *Drosophila pseudoobscura*. Amer Midl Natur 91: 118-129.

Curry GL, Feldman RM. 1987. Mathematical foundation of population dynamics. Texas A&M Univ Press, College Station, Texas.

Davey JT. 1956. A method for marking isolated adult locusts in large numbers as an aid to the study of their seasonal migration. Bull Entomol Res 46: 797-802.

Davis MB. 1976. Pleistocene biogeography of temperate deciduous forests. Geoscience Man 13: 13-26.

Dempster JP. 1957. The population dynamics of the Moroccan locust. Anti-Locust Bulletin 27.

Denn MM. 1975. Stability of reaction and transport processes. Prentice-Hall, Englewood Hills, New Jersey.

Dethier VG. 1989. Patterns of locomotion of polyphagous arctiid caterpillars in relation to foraging. Ecol Entomol 14: 375-386.

Diekmann O. 1978. Thresholds and traveling waves for the geographical spread of infection. J Math Biol 6: 109-130.

Dingle H. 1996. Migration: the biology of life on the move. Oxford Univ Press, New York.

Dmowski K, Kozakiewicz M. 1990. Influence of shrub corridor on movement of passerine birds to a lake littoral zone. Landscape Ecol 4: 99-108.

Doane CC, Cardé RT. 1973. Competition of gypsy moth males at a sex-pheromone source and a mechanism for the terminating searching behavior. Environ Entomol 2: 603-605.

Dobzhansky T, Wright S. 1943. Genetics of natural populations. X. Dispersion rates in *Drosophila pseudoobscura*. Genetics 28: 304-340.

Dobzhansky T, Wright S. 1947. Genetics of natural populations. XV. Rate of diffusion of a mutant gene through a population of *Drosophila pseudoobscura*. Genetics 32: 303-324.

Doucet PG, Wilschut AN. 1987. Theoretical studies on animal orientation. III. A model for kinesis. J Theor Biol 127: 111-125.

Dow H, Fredga S. 1983. Breeding and natal dispersal of the goldeneye, *Bucephala clangula*. J Anim Ecol 52: 681-695.

Drake VA. 1991. Methods for studying adult movements in *Heliothis*. Pp 109-121 in Zalucki MP (ed). *Heliothis*: Research methods and prospects. Springer-Verlag, New York.

Drake VA, Farrow RA. 1988. The influence of atmospheric structure and motions on insect migration. Ann Rev Entomol 33 183-210.

Drake VA, Gatehouse AG (eds). 1995. Insect Migration: tracking resources through space and time. Cambridge Univ Press, Cambridge.

Drilling NE, Thompson CF. 1988. Natal and breeding dispersal in House Wrens (*Trogodytes aedon*). Auk 105: 480-491.

Durrett R, Levin S. 1994a. Stochastic spatial models: a user's guide to ecological applications. Phil Trans Roy Soc London B 343: 329-350.

Durrett R, Levin S. 1994b. The importance of being discrete (and spatial). Theor Pop Biol 46: 363-394.

Dusenbery DB. 1989. Optimal search direction for an animal flying or swimming in a wind or current. J Chem Ecol 15: 2511-2519.

Dwyer G. 1992. On the spatial spread of insect pathogens: theory and experiment. Ecology 73: 479-494.

Dye C. 1983. Insect movement and fluctuations in insect population size. Antenna 7: 174-178.

Edelstein-Keshet L. 1988. Mathematical models in biology. Random House, New York.

Efron B, Tibshirani RJ. 1993. An introduction to the bootstrap. Chapman and Hall, New York.

Elkinton JS, Cardé RT. 1980. Distribution, dispersal, and apparent survival of male gypsy moths as determined by capture in pheromone-baited traps. Environ Entomol 9: 729-737.

Elkinton JS, Cardé RT, Mason CJ. 1984. Evaluation of time-average dispersion models for estimating pheromone concentration in a deciduous forest. J Chem Ecol 10: 1081-1108.

Elkinton JS, Cardé RT. 1988. Effects of intertrap distance and wind direction on the interaction of gypsy moth (Lepidoptera: Lymantriidae) pheromone-baited traps. Environ Entomol 17: 764-769.

Elkinton JS, Childs RD. 1983. Efficiency of two gypsy moth (Lepidoptera: Lymantriidae) pheromone-baited traps. Environ Entomol 12: 1519-1525.

Elton C. 1927. Animal Ecology. Sidgwick and Jackson, London.

Fagan WF. 1997. Introducing a "boundary-flux" approach to quantifying insect diffusion rates. Ecology 78:579-587.

Ferrer M. 1993. Ontogeny of dispersal distances in young Spanish imperial eagles. Behav Ecol Sociobiol 32: 259-263.

Fife PC, McLeod SB. 1975. The approach of solutions of nonlinear diffusion equations to travelling wave solutions. Arch Rat Mech Anal 65: 335-361.

Fisher NI. 1993. Statistical analysis of circular data. Cambridge Univ Press, Cambridge.

Fisher RA. 1937. The wave of advance of advantageous genes. Ann Eugen 7:355-369.

Fitt GP, Boyan GS. 1991. Methods for studying behavior. Pp 122-150 in Zalucki MP (ed). *Heliothis*: Research methods and prospects. Springer-Verlag, New York.

Fleischer SJ, Bridges JR, Ravlin FW, Thoeny WT. 1991. Elemental marking in deciduous and coniferous tree systems. Southwestern Entomologist Suppl No 14: 49-56.

Foppen R, Reijnen R. 1994. The effects of car traffic on breeding bird populations in woodland. II. Breeding dispersal of male willow warblers (*Phylloscopus trochilus*) in relation to the proximity of a highway. J Appl Ecol 31: 95-101.

Forsee E, Solbreck C. 1985. Migration in the bark beetle *Ips typographus* L.: duration, timing, and height of flight. Z Ang Entomol 100: 47-57.

Forsman ED. 1980. Habitat utilization by spotted owls in west-central Cascades of Oregon. Ph.D. thesis, Oreg State Univ, Corvallis, OR.

Fourcassie V, Coughlin D, Traniello JFA. 1992. Fractal analysis of search behavior in ants. Naturwissenschaften 79: 87-89.

Frampton VL, Linn MB, Hansing ED. 1942. The spread of virus diseases of the yellow type under field conditions. Phytopathology 32: 799-808.

Freeman GH. 1977. A model relating numbers of dispersing insects to distance and time. J Appl Ecol 14: 477-487.

Gadgil M. 1971. Dispersal: population consequences and evolution. Ecology 52: 253-261.

Gara RI, Coster JE. 1968. Studies on the attack behavior of the southern pine beetle. III Sequence of tree infestation within stands. Cont Boyce Thomp Inst 24: 77-85.

Gardner RH, O'Neill RV, Turner MG, Dale VH. 1989. Quantifying scale-dependent effects of animal movements with simple percolation models. Landscape Ecol 3: 217-227.

Gibson G. 1985. Swarming behaviour of the mosquito *Culex pipiens quinquefasciatus*: a quantitative analysis. Physiol Entomol 10: 283-296.

Glansdorff P, Prigogine I. 1971. Thermodynamic theory of structure, stability and flucutations. Wiley & Sons, New York.

Godt MJW, Hamrick JL. 1993. Genetic diversity and population structure in *Trnadescantia hirsuticalis* (Commelinaceae). Amer J Botany 80: 959-966.

Gottwald TR. 1995. Spatio-temporal analysis and isopath dynamics of citrus scab in nursery plots. Phytopathology 85: 1082-1092.

Goel N, Richter-Dyn N. 1974. Stochastic models in biology. Academic Press, New York.

Goldstein S. 1951. On diffusion by discontinuous monements, and on the telegraph equation. Quart J Mech and Appl Math 4: 129-155.

Goodenough JL, McKinion JM (eds). 1992. Basics of insect modeling. Amer Soc Agric Engineers, St Joseph, Michigan.

Goyer R, Hayes J. 1991. Understanding the southern pine beetle. Forests and People 1991 (4th quarter): 10.

Gregg WW, Walsh JJ. 1992. Simulation of the 1979 spring bloom in the Mid-Atlantic Bight: a coupled physical/biological/optical model. J Geophys Res 97C: 5723-5743.

Gregory PH, Read DR. 1949. The spatial distribution of insect-born plant-virus diseases. Ann Appl Biol 36: 475-482.

Green DG. 1989. Simulated effects of fire, dispersal and spatial pattern on competition within forest mosaics. Vegetatio 82: 139-153.

Greene DF, Johnson EA. 1989. A model of wind dispersal of winged or plumed seeds. Ecology 70: 339-347.

Greene DF, Johnson EA. 1992a. Fruit abscision in *Acer saccarinum* with reference to seed dispersal. Can J Bot 70:2277-2283.

Greene DF, Johnson EA. 1992b. Can the variation in samara mass and terminal velocity on an individual plant affect the distribution of dispersal distances? Amer Natur 139: 825-838.

Greene DF, Johnson EA. 1995. Long-distance wind dispersal of tree seeds. Can J Botany 73: 1036-1045.

Greenwood PJ, Harvey PH, Perrins CM. 1979. The role of dispersal in the great tit (*Parus major*): the causes, consequences and heritability of natal dispersal. J Anim Ecol 48: 123-142.

Griffin DR, Hock RJ. 1949. Airplane observations of homing birds. Ecology 30: 176-198.

Grindrod P. 1988. Models of individual aggregation in single and multispecies communities. J Math Biol 26: 651-660.

Grindrod P. 1991. Patterns and waves. The theory and applications of reaction-diffusion equations. Clarendon Press, Oxford.

Gross LJ, Rose KA, Rykiel EJ, van Winckle W, Werner EE. 1992. Individual-based modeling: summary of a workshop. Pp 511-522 in DeAngelis DL, Gross LJ (eds). Individual-based models and approaches in ecology: Populations, communities and Ecosystems. Chapman and Hall, New York.

Grünbaum D. 1994. Translating stochastic density-dependent individual behavior with sensory constraints to an Eulerian model of animal swarming. J Math Biol 33: 139-161.

Grünbaum D. 1998. Advection-diffusion equations for generalized tactic searching behaviors. J Math Biol, in press.

Guevara S, Laborde J. 1993. Monitoring seed dispersal at isolated standing trees in tropical pastures – consequences for local species availability. Vegetatio 108: 319-338.

Gurney WSC, Nisbet RM. 1975. The regulation of inhomogeneous populations. J Theor Biol 52: 441-457.

Gurtin ME, McCamy RC. 1977. On the diffusion of biological populations. Math Biosci 33: 35-49.

Gutiérrez RJ, Franklin AB, Lahaye W, Meretsky VJ, Ward JP. 1985. Juvenile spotted owl dispersal in neorthwestern California: preliminary results. Pp 60- 64 in Gutiérrez RJ, Carey AB (eds). Ecology and management of the spotted owl in the Pacific Northwest. Gen Tech Report PNW-185. USDA Forest Service, Pacific Northwest Forest and Range Station, Portland, Oregon.

Gutiérrez RJ, Harrison S. 1996. Applying metapopulation theory to spotted owl management: a history and critique. Pp 167-185 in McCullough DR (ed). Metapoplations and wildlife conservation. Island Press, Covelo, California.

Gutiérrez RJ, Ward JP, Franklin AB, Turchin P, Lahaye WS. 1998. Juvenile northern spotted owl dispersal: process and pattern. In review.

Haas CA. 1994. Dispersal and use of corridors by birds in wooded patches on an agricultural landscape. Conserv Biology 9: 845-854.

Hadeler KP, Rothe F. 1975. Traveling fronts in nonlinear diffusion equations. J Math Biol 2: 251-263.

Hagen BW, Atkins MD. 1975. Between generation variability in the fat content and behavior of *Ips paraconfusus* Lanier. Z ang Entomol 79: 169-172.

Hain FP, Anderson RF. 1976. Some response and attack behavior of *Ips grandicollis*. J Ga Entomol Soc 11: 153-157.

Halliday TR. 1996. Amphibians. Pp 205-217 in Sutherland WJ (ed). Ecological Census Techniques: a handbook. Cambridge Univ Press, Cambridge.

Hamilton WD, May RM. 1977. Dispersal in stable habitats. Nature 269: 578-581.

Hampton J. 1991. Estimation of southern bluefin tuna *Thunnus maccoyii* natural mortality and movement rates from tagging experiments. Fish Bull 89: 591-610.

Hanski I, Gilpin ME. 1991. Metapopulation Dynamics. Academic Press, San Diego.

Hare JA, Cowen RK. 1996. Transport mechanisms of larval and pelagic juvenile bluefish (*Pomatomus saltatrix*) from South Atlantic Bight spawning grounds to Middle Atlantic Bight nursery habitats. Limnol Oceanogr 41: 1264-1280.

Harrison S. 1989. Long-distance dispersal and colonization in the bay checkerspot butterfly, *Euphydryas editha bayensis*. Ecology 70: 1236-1243.

Harrison S, Taylor AD. 1997. Empirical evidence for metapopulation dynamics. Pp 27-42 in Hanski I, Gilpin ME (eds). Metapopulation biology. Academic Press, San Diego.

Hassell MP. 1978. The dynamics of arthropod predator-prey systems. Princeton Univ Press, Princeton.

Hassell MP, Comins HN, May RM. 1991. Spatial structure and chaos in insect population dynamics. Nature 353: 255-258.

Hawkes C. 1972. The estimation of the dispersal rate of the adult cabbage root fly (*Erioischia brassicae*) in relation to *Brassica* crop. J Appl Ecol 11: 83-93.

Hayes JL. 1991. Elemental marking of arthropod pests in agricultural systems: single and multigenerational marking. Southwestern Entomologist Suppl No 14: 37-47.

Hengeveld R. 1989. Dynamics of biological invasions. Chapman and Hall, London.

Heinrich B. 1979. Resource heterogeneity and patterns of movement in foraging bumblebees. Oecologia 140: 235-245.

Herben T, During HJ, Krahulec F. 1995. Spatio-temporaldynamics in mountain grasslands – species autocorrelations in space and time. Folia Geobotanica and Phytotaxonomica 30: 185-196.

Hestbeck JB, Nichols JD, Malecki RA, 1990. Estimates of movement and site fidelity using mark-resight data of wintering canada geese.

Hilborn R. 1990. Determination of fish movement patterns from tag recoveries using maximum likelihood estimators. Can J Fish Aquat Sci 47: 635-643.

Hilborn R, Mangel M. 1997. The ecological detective. Princeton Univ Press, Princeton.

Hilborn R, Walters CJ. 1991. Quantitative fisheries stock assessment. Chapman and Hall, London.

Hobbs R. 1992. The role of corridors in conservation: solution or bandwagon? TREE 7: 389-392.

Hodges JD, Elam WW, Watson WF, Nebecker NE. 1979. Oleoresin characteristics and susceptibility of four southern pines to southern pine beetle (Coleoptera: Scolytidae) attacks. Can Entomol 111: 889-896.

Holling CS. 1965. The functional response of predators to prey density and its role in mimicry and population regulation. Memoirs of the Entomol Soc of Canada 45: 5-60.

Holmes EE. 1993. Are diffusion models too simple? A comparison with telegraph models of invasion. Amer Natur 142: 779-795.

Horn H. 1978. Optimal tactics of reproduction and life-history. Pp 411-429 in Krebs JR, Davies NB (eds). Behavioral ecology: an evolutionary approach. Blackwell Scientific, Oxford.

Horvitz CC, Shemske DW. 1994. Effects of dispersers. gaps, and predators on dormancy and seedling emergence in a tropical herb. Ecology 75: 1949-1958.

Hoy JB, Globus PA, Norman KD. 1983. Electronic tracking and recording system for behavioral observations, with application to toxicology and pheromone assay. J Econ Entomol 76: 678-680.

Hoy MA. 1994. Insect molecular genetics: an introduction to principles and applications. Academic Press, San Diego.

Hughes RD. 1979. Movement in population dynamics. Pp 14-34 in Rabb RL, Kennedy GG (eds). Movement of highly mobile insects: concepts and methodology in research. North Carolina State Univ, Raleigh.

Hull DL. 1989. Science as a process. Univ of Chicago Press, Chicago.

Inghe O. 1989. Genet and ramet survivorship under different mortality regimes – a cellular automaton model. J Theor Biol 138: 257-270.

Ingliss G, Underwood AJ. 1992. Comments on some designs proposed for experiments on the biological importance of corridors. Conserv Biol 6: 581-586.

Inoue T. 1978. A new regression method for analyzing animal movement patterns. Res Popul Ecol 20: 141-163.

Ims RA. 1995. Movement patterns related to spatial structures. Pp 85-109 in Hansson L, Fahrig L, Merriam G (eds). Mosaic landscapes and ecological processes. Chapman and Hall, London.

Ims RA, Yoccoz NG. 1997. Studying transfer processes in metapopulations: emigration, migration and colnization. Pp 247-265 in Hanski I, Gilpin ME (eds). Metapopulation dynamics: ecology, genetics and evolution. Academic Press, San Diego.

Ishii T. 1979. Attempt to distinguish migration of fish propulation with survival parameters from tagging experiment data by the simulation method. Inv Pesq 43: 310-317.

Ito Y, Miyashita K. 1965. Studies on the dispersal of leaf and planthoppers. III. An examination of the distance – dispersal rate curves. Japan J Ecol 15: 85-89.

James IR. (1978). Estimation of the mixing proportion in a mixture of two normal distributions from simple, rapid measurements. Biometrics 34: 265-275.

Johnson AR, Milne BT, Wiens JA. 1992. Diffusion in fractal landscapes: simulations and experimental studies of tenebrionid beetle movements. Ecology 73: 1968-1983.

Johnson CG. 1969. Migration and dispersal of insects by flight. Methuen, London.

Jones RE. 1977. Movement patterns and egg distribution in cabbage butterflies. J Anim Ecol 45: 195-212.

Jones RE, Gilbert N, Guppy M, Nealis V. 1980. Long-distance movement of *Pieris rapae*. J Anim Ecol 49: 629-642.

Jones WT. 1987. Dispersal patterns in kangaroo rats (*Dipodomis spectabilis*). Pp 119-127 in Chepko-Sade BD, Halpin ZT (eds). Mammalian dispersal patterns: the effects of social structure on population genetics. Univ of Chicago Press, Chicago.

Jones WT. 1989. Dispersal distance and the range of nightly movements in Merriam's kangaroo rats. J Mammal 70: 27-34.

Kaiser H. 1976. Quantitative description and simulation of stochastic behavior in dragonflies (*Aeschna cyanea*, Odonata). Acta Biotheretica 25: 163-210.

Kareiva P. 1982. Experimental and mathematical analyses of herbivore movement: quantifying the influence of plant spacing and quality on foraging discrimination. Ecol Monogr 52: 261-282.

Kareiva P. 1983. Local movements in herbivorous insects: applying a passive diffusion model to mark-recapture field experiments. Oecologia 57: 322-327.

Kareiva P. 1985a. Finding and loosing host plants by flea beetles: patch size and surrounding habitat. Ecology 66: 1809-1816.

Kareiva P. 1985b. Patchiness, dispersal, and species interactions: consequences for communities of herbivorous insects. Pp 192-206 in Diamond J, Case T (eds). Community Ecology, Harper & Row, New York.

Kareiva P. 1990. Population dynamics in spatially complex environments: theory and data. Phil Trans Roy Soc London B 330: 175-190.

Kareiva P, Andersen M. 1988. Spatial aspects of species interactions: the wedding of models and experiments. Pp 35-50 in Hastings A (ed). Community Ecology. Springer-Verlag, New York.

Kareiva P, Odell GM. 1987. Swarms of predators exhibit "preytaxis" if individual predators use area restricted search. Amer Natur 130: 233-270.

Kareiva PM, Shigesada N. 1983. Analyzing insect movement as a correlated random walk. Oecologia 56: 234-238.

Karlin S, Taylor HM. 1975. A first course in stochastic processes (2nd ed). Academic Press, New York.

Kawasaki K. 1978. Diffusion and the formation of spatial distribution. Mathematical Science 183: 47-52 (in Japanese).

Kearns CA, Inouye DW. 1993. Techniques for pollination biologists. Univ Press of Colorado, Niwot, CO.

Keller AF, Segel LA. 1970. Initiation of slime mold aggregation viewed as an instability. J theor Biol 26: 399-415.

Keller EF, Segel LA. 1971. Model for chemotaxis. J Theor Biol 30: 225-234.

Kennedy JS, Way MJ. 1979. Summing up the conference. Pp 446-456 in Rabb RL, Kennedy GG (eds). Movement of highly mobile insects: concepts and methodology in research. North Carolina State Univ, Raleigh.

Kettle DS. 1951. Some factors affecting the population density and flight range of insects. Proc Roy Entomol Soc London A 26: 60-63.

Kierstead H, Slobodkin LB. 1953. The size of water masses containing plankton bloom. J Mar Res 12: 141-147.

Kindvall O. 1996. Dispersal in a metapopulation of the bush cricket, *Metripotera bicolor* Philippi (Orthoptera: Tettogoniidae).

Kindvall O, Ahlén I. 1992. Geometrical factors and metapopulation dynamics of the bush cricket, *Merioptera bicolor* Philippi (Orhtoptera: Tettigoniidae). Conserv Biol 6: 520-529.

Kinn DN, Parresol BR. 1998. Seasonal changes in southern pine beetle flight potential and energy reserves. Environ Entomol, in review.

Klassen W, Ridgway RL, Inscoe M. 1982. Chemical attractants in integrated pest management programs. Pp 13-130 in Kydonieus AF, Beroza M (eds). Insect suppression with controlled release pheromone systems (vol 1). CRC Press, Boca Raton, Florida.

Koehl MAR, Powell TM, Dairiki G. 1993. Measuring the fate of patches in the water: larval dispersal. Pp 50-60 in Steele J, Powell TM, Levin SA (eds). Patch Dynamics in Terrestrial, Marine, and Freshwater Ecosystems. Springer-Verlag, Berlin.

Koenig WD, van Vuren D, Hooge PN. 1996. Detectability, philopatry, and the distribution of dispersal distance in vertebrates. TREE 11: 514-517.

Kolmogoroff AN, Petrovsky IG, Piscounoff NS. 1937. Etude de l'equation de la diffusion avec croissance de la quantite de matiere et son application a un probleme biologique. Bull de l'Univ d'Etat a Moscou (ser intern) A, 1(6): 1-25.

Kornberg H, Williamson MH. 1986. Quantitative aspects of the ecology of biological invasions. Phil Trans of Roy Soc London B 314: 501-742.

Korpimäki E, Lagerström M. 1988. Survival and natal dispersal of fledglings of Tengmalm's owl in relation to fluctuating food conditions and hatching date. J Anim Ecol 57: 433-441.

Koshland D. 1980. Bacterial chemotaxis as a model behavior system. Raven Press, New York.

Kot M, Lewis MA, van den Driessche P. 1996. Dispersal data and the spread of invading organisms. Ecology 77: 2027-2042.

LaHaye W, Gutiérrez RJ, Akcakaya HR. 1994. Spotted owl metapopulation dynamics in Southern California. J Anim Ecol 63: 775-785

Lamberson RH, Noon BR, Voss C, Mckelvey KS. 1994. Reserve design for territorial species - the effects of patch size and spacing on the viability of the northern spotted owl. Conserv Biology 8:185-195.

Lapidus IR, Levandowsky M. 1981. Mathematical models of behavioral processes. Pp 235-260 in Levandowsky M, Hunter SH (eds). Biochemistry and Physiology of Protozoa (vol 4). Academic Press, New York.

La Polla VN, Barrett GW. 1993. Effects of corridor width and presence on the population dynamics of the meadow vole (*Microtus pennsylvanicus*). Landscape Ecol 8: 25-37.

Laymon SA. 1988. Ecology of the spotted owl in the central Sierra nevada, California. Ph.D. thesis. Univ of California, Berkeley.

Lee JE, White GC, Garrol RA, Batmann RM, Aldridge AW. 1985. Assessing accuracy of radiotelemetry systems for estimating animal locations. J Wildl Manage 49: 658-663.

Levandowsky M, Klaffer J, White BS. 1988. Feeding and swimming behavior in grazing microzooplankton. J of Protozoology 35: 243-246.

Levandowsky M, White BS. 1977. Randomness: time scales, and the evolution of biological communities. Pp 69-161 in Hecht MK, Steere WC, Wallace B (eds). Evolutionary Biology (vol 10). Plenum Press, New York.

Levin SA. 1974. Dispersion and population interactions. Amer Natur 108: 207-228.

Levin SA. 1980. Mathematics, ecology, and ornithology. Auk 97: 422-425.

Lewis M. 1994. Spatial coupling of plant and herbivore dynamics: the contribution of herbivore dispersal to transient and persistent "waves" of damage. Theor Pop Biol 45: 277-312.

Lewis MA, Kareiva P. 1993. Allee dynamics and the spread of invading organisms. Theor Pop Biol 43: 141-158.

Lidicker WZ. 1975. The role of dispersal in the demography of small mammals. Pp 103-128 in Golley FB, Petrusewicz K, Ryszkowski L (eds). Small mammals: their productivity and population dynamics. Cambridge Univ Press, Cambridge.

Lidicker WZ. 1995. The landscape concept: something old, something new. Pp 3-19 in Lidicker WZ (ed). Landcape approaches in mammalian ecology and conservation. Univ of Minnesota Press, Minneapolis.

Lima SL, Zollner PA. 1996. Towards a behavioral ecology of ecological landscapes. TREE 11: 131-135.

Lingren PD, Sparks AN, Raulston JR, Wolf WN. 1978. Applications for nocturnal studies of insects. Bull Entomol Soc Amer 24: 206-212.

Lotka AJ. 1925. Elements of physical biology. Williams and Wilkins, Baltimore.

Lubina J, Levin S. 1988. The spread of a reinvading organism: range expansion of the California sea otter. Amer Natur 131: 526-543.

Ludwig D, Aronson DG, Weinberger HF. 1979. Spatial patterning of the spruce budworm. J Math Biol 8: 217-258.

Ludwig D, Jones DD, Holling CS. 1978. Qualitative analysis of insect outbreak systems: The spruce budworm and forest. J Anim Ecol 47: 315-332.

MacArthur RH, Wilson EO. 1967. The Theory of Island Biogeography. Princeton Univ Press, Princeton.

Mack RN. 1981. Invasion of *Bromus tectorum* L. into western North America: an ecological chronicle. Agro-Ecosystems 7: 145-165.

Manasse RS. 1992. Ecological risks of transgenic plants: effects of spatial dispersion on gene flow. Ecol Appl 2: 431-438.

Mann CC, Plummer M. 1993. The high costs of biodiversity. Science 160: 1868-1871.

Marsh LM, Jones RE. 1988. The form and consequences of random walk movement models. J Theor Biol 133: 113-131.

Masaki T, Kominami Y, Nakashizuka T. 1994. Spatial and seasonal patterns of seed dissemination of *Cornus controversa* in a temperate forest. Ecology 75: 1903-1910.

Mascanzoni D, Wallin H. 1986. The harmonic radar: a new methodology for tracing insects in the field. Ecol Entomol 11: 387-390.

Mason RR. 1969. Behavior of *Ips* populations after summer thinning in a loblolly plantation. For Sci 15: 390-398.

May RM. 1981. Models for two interacting populations. Pp 78-104 in May RM (ed). Theoretical ecology: principles and applications (2nd ed). Sinauer Associates, Sunderland, Massachusetts.

McCulloch CE, Cain ML. 1989. Analyzing discrete movement data as a correlated random walk. Ecology 70: 383-388.

McMullen LH, Safranyik L, Linton DA, Betts R. 1988. Survival of self-marked mountain pine beetles emerged from logs dusted with fluorescent powder. J Entomol Soc Brit Columbia 85: 25-28.

Mech LD. 1983. Handbook of animal radio-tracking. Univ of Minnesota Press, Minneapolis.

Mech LD. 1987. Age, season, distance, direction, and social aspects of wolf dispersal from a Minnesota pack. Pp 55-73 in Chepko-Sade BD, Halpin ZT (eds). Mammalian dispersal patterns: the effects of social structure on population genetics. Univ of Chicago Press, Chicago.

Metz JAJ, Diekmann O (eds). 1986. The dynamics of physiologically structured populations. Lecture Notes Biomath 68. Springer-Verlag, Berlin.

Metz JAJ, van den Bosch F. 1995. Velocities of epidemic spread. Pp 150-186 in Mollison D (ed). Epidemic models: their structure and relation to data. Cambridge Univ Press, Cambridge.

Miller GL, Carroll BW. 1989. Modeling vertebrate dispersal distances: alternatives to the geometric distribution. Ecology 70: 977-986.

Miller GS. 1989. Dispersal of juvenile northern spotted owls in western Oregon. M.S. Thesis, Oregon State Univ, Corvallis.

Miller GS, Small RJ, Meslow EC. 1997. Habitat selection by spotted owls during natal dispersal in western Oregon. J Wildl Manage 61:140-150.

Milne B. 1991. Lessons from applying fractal models to landscape patterns. Pp 199-235 in Turner MG, Gardner RH (eds). Quantitative methods in landscape ecology. Springer-Verlag, New York.

Mollison D. 1972. The rate of spatial propagation of simple epidemics. Proc Sixth Berkeley Symp Math Statist Prob 3: 579-614.

Mollison D. 1977. Spatial contact models for ecological and epidemic spread. J Roy Statist Soc B39: 283-326.

Mollison D. 1986. Modelling biological invasions: chance, explanation, prediction. Phil Trans Roy Soc London 314: 675-693.

Mollison D. 1991. Dependence of epidemic and population velocities on basic parameters. Math Biosci 107: 255-287.

Molofsky J. 1994. Population dynamics and pattern formation in theoretical populations. Ecology 75: 30-39.

Morreale SJ, Standora EA, Spotila JR, Paladino FV. 1997. Migration corridor for sea turtles. Nature 384: 319-320.

Morris WF. 1993. Predicting the consequences of plant spacing and biased movement for pollen dispersal by honey bees. Ecology 74: 493-500.

Morris WF, Mangel M, Adler FR. 1995. Mechanisms of pollen deposition by insect pollinators. Evol Ecol 9: 304-317.

Murdoch WW. 1963. A method for marking Carabidae (Col.). Entomol Mon Mag 99: 22-24.

Murdoch WW. 1994. Population regulation in theory and practice. Ecology 75: 271-287.

Murlis J, Bettany BW, Kelley J, Martin L. 1982. The analysis of flight paths of male Egyptian cotton leafworm moths, *Spodoptera littoralis*, to a sex pheromone source in the field. Physiological Entomol 7: 435-441.

Murray BG. 1967. Dispersal in vertebrates. Ecology 48: 975-978.

Murray JD, Stanley EA, Brown DL. 1986. On the spatial spread of rabies among foxes. Proc Roy Soc London B 229: 111-150.

Murray JD. 1993. Mathematical Biology (2nd ed). Springer-Verlag, Berlin.

Naefdaenzer B. 1994. Radiotracking of greate and blue tits—new tools to assess territoriality. home-range use and resource distribution. Ardea 82: 335-347.

Neary J, Cash K, McCauley E. 1994. Behavioral aggrgation of *Daphnia pulex* in response to food gradients. Functional Ecol 8: 377-383.

Nelson SC. 1995. Spatiotemporal distance class analysis of plant disease epidemics. Phytopathology 85: 37-43.

Newton I, Marquiss M. 1983. Dispersal of sparrowhawks between birthplace and breeding place. J Anim Ecol 52: 463-477.

Nicholson AJ, Bailey VA. 1935. The balance of animal populations. Proc Zool Soc London 3: 551-598.

Norris KR. 1957. A method for marking Calliphoridae (Diptera) during emergence from the puparium. Nature 180: 1002.

Noss RF. 1987. Corridors in real landscapes: a reply to Simberloff and Cox. Conserv Biology 1: 159-164.

Nossal R, Weiss GH. 1974. A generalized Pearson random walk allowing for bias. J Stat phys 10:245-253

Odendaal FJ, Turchin P, Stermitz FE. 1988. An incidental-effect hypothesis explaining aggregation of males in a population of *Euphydryas anicia* Amer Natur 132: 735-749.

Odendaal FJ, Turchin P, Stermitz FR. 1989. Influence of host-plant density and male harrassment on the distribution of female *Euphydryas anicia* (Nymphalidae). Oecologia 78: 283-288.

Odiyo PO. 1979. Forecasting infestations of a migrant pest: the African armyworm *Spodoptera exempta*. Phil Trans Roy Soc London B 287: 403-413.

Okubo A, Chiang HC. 1974. An analysis of the kinematics of swarming of *Anarete pritchardi* Kim (Diptera: Cecidomyiidae). Res Popul Ecol 16: 1-42.

Okubo A. 1978. Horizontal dispersion and critical scales of phytoplankton patches. Pp 21-42 in Steele JH (ed). SPatial Pattern in Plankton Communities. Plenum, New York.

Okubo A. 1980. Diffusion and ecological problems: mathematical models. Springer-Verlag, Heidelberg-Berlin-New York.

Okubo A. 1984. Critical patch size for plankton and patchiness. Pp 456-477 in Levin SA, Hallam TG (ed). Mathematical Ecology. Lecture Notes Biomath 54.

Okubo A. 1986. Dynamical aspects of animal grouping: swarms, schools, flocks, and herds. Adv Biophys 22: 1-94.

Okubo A, Bray DJ, Chiang HC. 1981. Use of shadows for studying the three-dimensional structure of insect swarms. Ann Entom Soc Amer 74: 48-50.

Okubo A, Chiang HC, Ebbesmeyer CC. 1977. Acceleration field of individual midges, *Anarete pritchardi* (Diptera: Cecidomyiidae), within a swarm. Can Entom 109: 149-156.

Okubo A, Levin SA. 1989. A theoretical framework for data analysis of wind dispersal of seeds and pollen. Ecology 70: 329-338.

Okubo A, Maini PK, Williamson MH, Murray JD. 1989. On the spatial spread of the grey squirrel in Britain. Proc Roy Soc London Ser B 238: 113-125.

Othmer HG, Dunbar SR, Alt W. 1988. Models of dispersal in biological systems. J Math Biol 26: 263-298.

Pacala SW, Silander JA. 1985. Neighborhood models of plant population dynamics. I. Single-species models of annuals. Amer Natur 125: 385-411.

Paris OH. 1965. Vagility of P^{32}-labeled isopods in grassland. Ecology 46: 635-648.

Parrish JK, Turchin P. 1997. Individual decisions, traffic rules, and emergent pattern: a Lagrangian analysis. Pp 126-142 in Parrish JK, Hamner WM, Prewitt CT (eds). Animal Aggregations: Three-Dimensional Measurement and Modeling. Cambridge Univ Press, Cambridge.

Patlak CS. 1953a. Random walk with persistence and external bias. Bull Math Byophys 15: 311-338.

Patlak CS. 1953b. A mathematical contribution to the study of orientation of organisms. Bull Math Byophys 15: 431-476.

Payne TL. 1980. Life history and habits. *In:* Thatcher RC, Searcy JL, Coster JE, Hertel GD (eds). The Southern Pine beetle. USDA-Forest Service Tech Bull 1631.

Pearson K, Blakeman J. 1906. Mathematical contributions to the theory of evolution. XV. A mathematical theory of random migration. Drapers' Company Research Mem Biometric Series III, Dept Appl Math, Univ College, London.

Pech RP, McIlroy JC. 1990. A model of the velocity of advance of foot and mouth disease in feral pigs. J Appl Ecol 27: 635-650.

Pedgley DE (ed). 1981. Desert locust forecasting manual. Centre for Overseas Research, London.

Pedgley D. 1982. Windborne pests and diseases: Meteorology of airborne organisms. Ellis Horwood Publishers, Chichester.

Pedgley DE, Reynolds DR, Tatchell GM. 1995. Long-range insect migration in relation to climate and weather. Pp 3-29 in Drake VA, Gatehouse

AG (eds). Insect Migration: tracking resources through space and time. Cambridge Univ Press, Cambridge.

Phipps MJ. 1989. Dynamical behavior of cellular automata under the constraint of neighborhood coherence. Geographical Analysis 21: 197-215.

Pielou EC. 1977. Mathematical Ecology (2nd ed). Wiley & Sons, New York.

Platt T, Denman KL. 1975. A general equation for mesoscale distribution of phytoplankton in the sea. Mem Soc Roy des Sci Liege, 6th serie 7: 31-42.

Polymenopoulos AD, Long G. 1990. Estimation and evaluation methods for population growth models with spatial diffusion: dynamics of mountain pine beetle. Ecol Model 51: 97-121.

Porter JH, Dooley JL. 1993. Animal dispersal patterns: a reassessment of simple mathematical models. Ecology 74: 2436-2443.

Portnoy S, Willson MF. 1993. Seed dispersal curves: behavior of the tail of the distribution. Evol Ecol 7: 25-44.

Possingham HP, Roughgarden J. 1990. Spatial population dynamics of a marine organism with a complex life cycle. Ecology 71: 973-985.

Press WH, Teukolsky SA, Vetterling WT, Flannery BP.1992. Numerical recipes in FORTRAN. The art of scientific computing (2nd ed). Cambridge Univ Press, Cambridge.

Price MV, Kelly PA, Goldingay. 1994. Distances moved by Stephens' kangaroo rat (*Dipodomis stephensi* Merriam) and implications for conservation. J Mammal 75: 929-939.

Price PW. 1984. Insect Ecology (2nd ed). Wiley & Sons, New York.

Rabb RL. 1979. Regional research on insect movement: Initial consideration. Pp 2-12 in Rabb RL, Kennedy GG (eds). Movement of highly mobile insects: concepts and methodology in research. North Carolina State Univ, Raleigh.

Rainey RC. 1951. Weather and the movements of locust swarms: a new hypothesis. Nature 168: 1057-1060.

Rainey RC. 1979. Interactions between weather systems and populations of locusts and noctuids in Africa. Pp 109-119 in Rabb RL, Kennedy GG (eds). Movement of highly mobile insects: concepts and methodology in research. North Carolina State Univ, Raleigh.

Rausher M. 1979. Coevolution in a simple plant-herbivore system. Ph.D. Thesis, Cornell Univ, Ithaca, New York.

Reed DD, Liechty HO, Burton AJ. 1989. A simple procedure for mapping tree locations in forest stands. Forest Sci 35: 657-662.

Ribble DO. 1992. Dispersal in a monogamous rodent, *Peromiscus californicus*. Ecology 73: 859-866.

Ribbens E, Silander JA, Pacala SW. 1994. Seedling recruitment in forests: calibrating models to predict patterns of tree seedling dispersion. Ecology 75: 1794-1806.

Risch S. 1981. Insect herbivore abundance in tropical monocultures and polycultures: an experimental test of two hypothesis. Ecology 62: 1325-1340.

Rodgers AR, Klenner WE. 1990. Competition and geometric model of dispersal in vertebrates. Ecology 71: 818-822.

Roff DA. 1974a. Spatial heterogeneity and the persistence of populations. Oecologia 15: 245-258.

Roff DA. 1974b. The analysis of a population model demonstrating the importance of dispersal in a heterogeneous environment. Oecologia 15: 259-275.

Roland J, McKinnon G, Backhouse C, Taylor PD. 1996. Even smaller radar tags on insects. Nature 381: 120.

Root RB. 1973. Organization of a plant-arthropod association in simple and diverse habitats: the fauna of collards (*Brassica oleracea*). Ecol Monogr 43: 95-124.

Root RB, Kareiva PM. 1984. The search for resources by cabbage butterflies (*Pieris rapae*): ecological consequences and adaptive significance of markovian movements in a patchy environment. Ecology 65: 147-165.

Roughgarden J. 1979. Theory of population genetics and evolutionary ecology: an introduction. Macmillan, New York.

Rvachev LA, Longini IM. 1985. A mathematical model for the global spread of influenza. Mat Biosci 75: 3-22.

Saunders DA, Hobbs RJ. 1991. The role of corridors. Surrey Beatty, Chipping Norton, New South Wales, Australia.

Schaefer GW, Bent GA. 1984. An infra-red remote sensing system for the active detection and automatic determination of insect flight trajectories (IRADIT). Bull Entomol Res 74: 261-278.

Schlyter F. 1992. Sampling range, attraction range, and effective attraction radius: Estimates of trap efficiency and communication distance in coleopteran pheromone and host attractant systems. J Appl Entomol 114: 439-454.

Schneider JC. 1989. Role of movement in evaluation of area-wide insect pest management tactics. Environ Entomol 18: 868-874.

Schneider JC. 1998. A diffusion-based model for dispersal of a highly vagile insect in a heterogeneous environment. In review.

Schneider JC, Roush RT, Kitten WF, Laster ML. 1989. Movement of *Heliothis virescens* (Lepidoptera: Noctuidae) in Mississippi in the spring: Implications for area-wide management. Environ Entomol 18: 438-446.

Schultz ET, Cowen RK. 1994. Recruitment of coral-reef fishes to Bermuda: local retention or long-distance transport? Mar Ecol Prog Ser 109: 15-28.

Schwalbe CP. 1981. Disparlure-baited traps for survey and detection. Pp 542-548 in Doane CC, McManus ML (eds). The gypsy moth: research toward integrated pest management. USDA-Forest Service Tech Bull 1584. Wash, DC.

Segel LA. 1977. A theoretical study of receptor mechanisms in bacterial chemotaxis. SIAM J Appl Math 32: 653-665.

Segel LA. 1978. Mathematical models for cellular behavior. Pp 156-190 in Levin SA (ed). Studies in Mathematical Biology (vol 15). Mathematical Association of America.

Segel LA. 1984. Modeling dynamic phenomena in molecular and cellular biology. Cambridge Univ Press, Cambridge.

Shigesada N. 1980. Spatial distribution of dispersing animals. J Math Biology 9: 85-96.

Shigesada N, Kawasaki K, Takeda Y. 1995. Modeling stratified diffusion in biological invasions. Amer Natur 142: 229-251.

Shigesada N, Kawasaki K, Teramoto E. 1979. Spatial segregation of interacting species. J Theor Biol 79: 83-99.

Shigesada N, Kawasaki K, Teramoto E. 1986. Traveling periodic waves in heterogeneous environments. Theor Pop Biol 30: 143-160.

Sibert JR. 1984. A two-fishery tag attrition model for the analysis of mortality, recruitment, and fishery interaction. Tuna and Billfish Assessment Programme, South Pacific Commission, Noumea, New Caledonia. Tech Report No. 13. 27 p.

Simberloff D, Cox J. 1987. Consequences and costs of conservation corridors. Conserv Biology 1: 63-71.

Simberloff D, Farr JA, Cox J, Mehlman DW. 1992. Movement corridors: conservation bargains of poor investments? Conserv Biology 6: 493-504.

Siniff DB, Jessen CR. 1969. A simulation model of animal movement patterns. Adv Ecol Res 6: 185-217.

Skellam JG. 1951. Random dispersal in theoretical populations. Biometrika 38: 196-218.

Skellam JG. 1973. The formulation and interpretation of mathematical models of diffusionary processes in population biology. Pp 63-85 in Bartlett MS, Hiorns RW (eds). The mathematical theory of the dynamics of bilogical populations. Academic Press, London.

Smith JNM. 1974. The food searching behavior of two European thrushes. I. Description and analysis of search paths. Behaviour 58: 276-302.

Sokal RR, Rohlf FJ. 1981. Biometry. WH Freeman, New York.

Sorensen K, Bell WJ. 1986. Responses of isopods to temporal changes in relative humidity: simulation of a 'humid' patch in a dry habitat. J Insect Physiol 32: 51-57.

Sork V. 1984. Examination of seed dispersal and survival in read oak, *Quercus rubra* (Fagaceae), using metal-tagged acorns. Ecology 65: 1020-1022.

Soulé ME, Gilpin ME. 1991. The theory of wildlife corridor capability. Pp 3-8 in Saunders DA, Hobbs RJ (eds). Nature conservation. 2. The role of corridors. Surrey Beatty, Chipping Norton.

Southwood TRE. 1972. The role and measurement of migration in the population system of an insect pest. Trop Sci 13: 275-278.

Southwood TRE. 1978. Ecological Methods (2nd ed). Chapman and Hall, London.

Stanton ML. 1982a. Spatial patterns in the plant community and their effects upon insect search. In Ahmad S (ed). Herbivorous insects: host seeking behavior and mechanisms. Academic Press, New York.

Stanton ML. 1982b. Searching in a patchy invironment: foodplant selection by *Colias p. eriphyle* butterflies. Ecology 63: 839-853.

Stenseth NC, Lidicker WZ (eds). 1992. Animal dispersal: Small mammals as a model. Chapman and Hall.

Stimmann MW. 1991. A personal history of the development of the rubidium marking technique. Southwestern Entomologist Suppl No 14: 9-13.

Stone ND. 1990. Chaos in individual-level predator-prey models. Natur Res Modeling 4: 1-15.

Strong AM, Bancroft GT. 1994. Postfledging dispersal of white-crowned pigeons: implications for conservation of deciduous seasonal forests in the Florida Keys. Conserv Biology 8: 770-779.

Sutherland WJ (ed). 1996a. Ecological Census Techniques: a handbook. Cambridge Univ Press, Cambridge.

Sutherland WJ. 1996b. Mammals. Pp 260-280 in Sutherland WJ (ed). Ecological Census Techniques: a handbook. Cambridge Univ Press, Cambridge.

Swihart RK, Slade NA. 1985. Testing for independence of observations in animal movements. Ecology 66: 1176-1184.

Swingland IR, Greenwood PJ (eds). 1983. The ecology of animal movement. Oxford Univ Press, Oxford.

Taylor GI. 1921. Diffusion by continuous movements. Proc London Math Soc 20: 196-212.

Taylor LR, Taylor RAJ. 1977. Aggregation, migration and population mechanics. Nature 265: 415-421.

Tayor LR, Woiwood IP, Taylor RAJ. 1979. The migratory ambit of the hop aphid and its significance in aphid population dynamics. J Anim Ecol 48: 955-972.

Taylor RAJ. 1978. The relationship between density and distance of dispersing insects. Ecol Entomol 3: 63-70.

Taylor RAJ. 1980. A family of regression equations describing the density distribution of dispersing organisms. Nature 286: 53-55.

Taylor RAJ. 1981a. The behavioural basis of redistribution. I. The Δ-model concept. J Anim Ecol 50: 573-586.

Taylor RAJ. 1981b. The behavioural basis of redistribution. II. Simulation of the Δ-model. J Anim Ecol 50: 587-604.

Taylor RAJ, McManus ML, Pitts CW. 1991. The absolute efficiency of gypsy moth, *Lymantria dispar* (Lepidoptera: Lymantriidae), milk-carton pheromone traps. Bull Entomol Res 81: 111-118.

Thieme HR. 1977. A model for the spatial spread of an epidemic. J Math Biol 4: 337-351.

Thoeny WT, Tiarks AE, Hayes JL, Bridges JR. 1992. Marking the southern pine beetle (Coleoptera: Scolytidae) with rubidium within loblolly pine for dispersal studies. Environ Entomol 21: 1377-1385.

Thomas CFG, Hol EHA, Everts JW. 1990. Modelling the diffusion component of dispersal during recovery of a population of linyphiid spiders from exposure to an insecticide. Funct Ecol 4: 357-368.

Thorarinsson K. 1986. Population density and movement: a critique of Δ–models.Oikos 46: 70-81.

Timofeef-Ressovsky NW, Timofeef-Ressovsky EA. 1940. Populationsgenetische Versuche an *Drosophila*. I-III. Z i A V 79: 28-49.

Tourtellot MK, Collins RD, Bell WJ. 1991. The problem of movelength and turn definition in analysis of orientation data. J Theor Biol 150: 287-297.

Turchin P. 1986. Modelling the effect of host patch size on Mexican bean beetle emigration. Ecology 67: 124-132.

Turchin P. 1987. The role of aggregation in the response of Mexican bean beetles to host-plant density. Oecologia 71: 577-582.

Turchin P. 1988a. The effect of host-plant density on the numbers of Mexican bean beetles, *Epilachna varivestis*. Amer Midl Natur 119: 15-20.

Turchin P. 1988b. Models for aggregating populations. Pp 101-127 in Hallam TG, Gross LJ, Levin SA. Mathematical Ecology: Proceedings of the Autumn Course Research Seminars. World Scientific, Singapore.

Turchin P. 1989a. Population consequences of aggregative movement. J Anim Ecol 58: 75-100.

Turchin P. 1989b. Beyond simple diffusion: models of not-so-simple movement in animals and cells. Comments in Theor Biol 1:65-83.

Turchin P. 1990. Rarity of density dependence or population regulation with lags? Nature 344: 660-663.

Turchin P. 1991. Translating foraging movements in heterogeneous environments into the spatial distribution of foragers. Ecology 72: 1253-1266.

Turchin P. 1996. Fractal analyses of animal movement: a critique. Ecology 77: 2086-2090.

Turchin P, Kareiva P. 1989. Aggregation in *Aphis varians*: an effective strategy for reducing predation risk. Ecology 70: 1008-101.

Turchin P, Odendaal FJ, Rausher MD. 1991. Quantifying insect movement in the field. Environ Entomol 20: 955-963.

Turchin P, Odendaal FJ. 1996. Measuring the effective sampling area of a pheromone trap for monitoring population density of southern pine beetle (Coleoptera: Scolytidae). Environ Entomol 25: 582-588.

Turchin P, Reeve JD, Cronin JT, Wilkens RT. 1997. Spatial pattern formation in ecological systems: bridging theoretical and empirical approaches. Chapter 6 in Bascompte J, Solé R (eds). Modelling Spatiotemporal Dynamics in Ecology. RG Landes, Austin, Texas.

Turchin P, Simmons G. 1997. Movements of animals in congregations: an Eulerian analysis of bark beetle swarming. Pp 113-125 in Parrish JK, Hamner WM, Prewitt CT (eds). Animal Aggregations: Three-Dimensional Measurement and Modeling. Cambridge Univ Press, Cambridge.

Turchin P, Thoeny WT. 1993. Quantifying dispersal of southern pine beetles with mark-recapture experiments and a diffusion model. Ecol Appl 3: 187-198.

Turing AM. 1952. The chemical basis of morphogenesis. Phil Trans Roy Soc London B 237: 37-72.

Turner MG, Gardner RH. 1991. Quantitative methods in landscape ecology: an introduction. Pp 3-14 in Turner MG, Gardner RH (eds). Quantitative methods in landscape ecology. Springer-Verlag, New York.

Turner MG, Wu Y, Romme WH, Wallace L. 1993. A landscape simulation model of winter foraging by large ungulates. Ecol Modelling 69: 163-184.

Turner MG, Wu Y, Wallace L, Romme WH, Brenkert A. 1994. Simulatiung winter interactions among ungulates, vegetation, and fire in northern Yellowstone Park. Ecol Appl 4:472-496.

Unruh TR, Chauvin RL. 1993. Elytral punctures: a rapid, reliable method for marking colorado potato beetle. The Canadian Entomologist 125: 55-63.

Van den Bosch F, Zadoks JC, JAJ Metz. 1988a. Focus expansion in plant disease. I. The constant rate of focus expansion. Phytopathology 78: 54-58.

Van den Bosch F, Zadoks JC, JAJ Metz. 1988b. Focus expansion in plant disease. II. Realistic parameter-sparse models. Phytopathology 78: 59-64.

Van den Bosch F, Frinking HD, JAJ Metz, Zadoks JC. 1988c. Focus expansion in plant disease. III. Two experimental examples. Phytopathology 78: 919-925.

Van den Bosch F, JAJ Metz, Diekmann O. 1990a. The velocity of spatial population expansion. J Math Biol 28: 529-565.

Van den Bosch F, Verhaar MA, Buiel AAM, Hoogkamer W, Zadoks JC. 1990b. Focus expansion in plant disease. IV. Expansion rates in mixtures of resistant and susceptible hosts. Phytopathology 80: 598-602.

Van den Bosch F, Hengeveld R, JAJ Metz. 1992. Analyzing the velocity of animal range expansion. J Biogeogr 19: 135-150.

Volterra V. 1926. Fluctuations in the abundance of a species considered mathematically. Nature 118: 558-600.

Waddington KD, Heinrich B. 1981. Patterns of movement and floral choice by foraging bees. Pp 215-230 in Kamil AC, Sargent TD (eds). Foraging behavior: ecological, ethological, and psychological approaches. Garland STPM Press, New York.

Wadley FM. 1957. Some mathemtical aspects of insect dispersion. Ann Entomol Soc AM 50: 230-231.

Wallace B. 1966. On the dispersal of *Drosophila* Amer Natur 100: 551-563.

Wallin H, Ekbom BS. 1988. Movements of carabid beetles (Coleoptera: Carabidae) inhabiting cereal fields: a field tracing study. Oecologia 77: 39-43.

Walters CJ, Hall N, Brown R, Chubb C. 1993. Spatial model for the population dynamics and exploitation of the western Australian rock lobster, *Panulirius cygnus*. Can J Fish Aquat Sci 50: 1650-1662.

Waser PM. 1985. Does competition drive dispersal? Ecology 66: 1170-1175.

Waser PM. 1987. A model predicting dispersal distance distributions. Pp 251-256 in Chepko-Sade BD, Halpin ZT (eds). Mammalian dispersal patterns: the effects of social structure on population genetics. Univ of Chicago Press, Chicago.

Way NJ, Cammell MW, Taylor LR, Woiwod IP. 1981. The use of egg counts and suction trap examples to forecast the infestation of spring-sown field beans, *Vicia faba*, by the black bean aphid, *Aphis fabae*. Ann Appl Biol 98: 21-34.

Wegner JF, Merriam G. 1979. Movements by birds and small mammals between a wood and adjoining farmland habitats. J Appl Ecol 16: 349-357.

Weiss GH. 1983. Random walks and their applications. Amer Scientist 71: 65-71.

Welch D, Miller GR, Legg CJ. 1990. Pp 122-131 in Bunce RGH, Howard DC (eds). Species dispersal in agricultural habitats, Belhaven Press, London.

Wellington WG. 1945. Conditions governing the distribution of insects in the free atmosphere. Can Entomol 77: 7-74.

Wells KD, Wells RA. 1976. Patterns of movement in a population of the slimy salamander, *Plethodon glutinosus*, with observations on aggregations. Herpetologica 32: 156-162.

White GC, Garrott RA. 1990. Analysis of wildlife radio-tracking data. Academic Press, San Diego.

Wiens JA, Crist TO, Milne BT. 1993a. On quantifying insect movements. Environ Entomol 22: 709-715.

Wiens JA, Stenseth NC, Van Horne B, Ims RA. 1993b. Ecological mechanisms and landscape ecology. Oikos 66: 369-380.

Wiggett DR, Boag DA. 1989. Intercolony natal dispersal in the Columbian ground squirrel. Can J Zool 67: 42-50.

Williams EJ. 1961. The distribution of larvae of randomly moving insects. Aust J Biol Sci 12: 598-604.

Williams T, Bjerknes R. 1972. Stochastic model for abnormal clone spread through epithelial basal layer. Nature 236: 19-21.

Wilson EO. 1975. Sociobiology. Belknap Press, Cambridge, Massachusetts.

Wilson EO, Willis EO. 1975. Applied biogeography. Pp 523-534 in Cody ML, Diamond JM (eds). Ecology and evolution of communities. Harvard Univ Press, Cambridge, Massachusetts.

With KA. 1994. Using fractal analysis to assess how species perceive landscape structure. Landscape Ecol 9: 25-36.

Wolfenbarger DO. 1946. Dispersion of small organisms. Amer Midl Natur 35: 1-152.

Wolfenbarger DO. 1975. Factors affecting dispersal distance of small organisms. Exposition Press. Hicksville, New York.

Wolfram S. 1983. Statistical mechaniscs of cellular automata. Physica D 10: 1-35.

Wolfram S. 1988. Mathematica: a system for doing mathematics by computer. Addison-Wesley, Redwood City, California.

Woodbridge B, Finley KK, Bloom PH. 1995. Reproductive performance, age-structure, and natal dispersal of Swainson's hawks in the Butte Valley, California. J Raptor Res 29: 187-192.

Wright S. 1931. Evolution in Mendelian populations. Genetics 16: 97-159.

Wright S. 1969. Evolution and the genetics of populations (vol 2). The theory of gene frequencies. Univ of Chicago Press, Chicago.

Wroblewski JS, Richman JG, Mellot GL. 1989. Optimal wind conditions for the survival of larval northern anchovy, *Engraulis mordax*: a modeling investigation. Fishery Bulletin 87: 387-398.

Zalucki MP, Abel D, Pearson J. 1980. A novel device for tracking butterflies in the field. Ann Entomol Soc Amer 73: 262-265.

Zalucki MP, Kitching RL. 1982. The analysis and description of movement in adult *Danaus plexippus* L. (Lepidoptera: Danainae). Behaviour 80: 174-198.

Glossary

Absolute direction: direction measured with respect to North. (Also known as "compass direction.")

Advection: A mathematical representation of *drift* in a diffusion model.

Aggregation: population redistribution that leads to an uneven spatial distribution of organisms so that some spatial localities are characterized by elevated population densities (*aggregations*) and others by decreased density.

Bias: see *directional bias*.

Biased correlated random walk (BCRW): a random walk in which the direction of each move is influenced by both the direction of the previous move and the absolute direction (long-distance attraction). See also *correlated random walk*.

Congregation: aggregation as a result of behavioral responses of organisms to conspecifics. Thus, to *congregate* means to gather *together*, as opposed to *aggregate*, which is to gather *at* some locality. Congregating organisms may respond directly to neighbors using visual, acoustic, or chemical (pheromones) stimuli, or indirectly to population density cues, such as feeding damage on a host plant.

Coordinate fix: a complete specification of the spatio-temporal position of an organism. For example, when organisms move in two-dimensional space, a coordinate fix will consist of one temporal and two spatial coordinates.

Correlated random walk (CRW): a random walk in which the directions of subsequent moves are autocorrelated.

Diffusion: a kind of mathematical models used in representing population redistribution of organisms. Diffusion models are formulated as partial differential equations. They range from the simple diffusion model with one parameter (diffusion constant) to models of arbitrary complexity—*generalized* *diffusion models.*

Diffusivity or diffusion rate: the parameter in the Fickian diffusion equation that quantifies the rate of population spread. It is analogous to *motility* in the Fokker-Planck diffusion model. If diffusion rate is constant in space, it is refered to as the diffusion constant or coefficient. (Also known as Fickian diffusivity.)

Directional bias: tendency of individuals to move in a nonrandom direction. More precisely, when individual movement is affected by a directional bias the frequency distribution of absolute move directions is not uniform. (Also known as external bias, or long-distance attraction.)

Directional persistence: autocorrelation between directions of subsequent moves. Alternatively, a nonuniform frequency distribution of the turning angle.

Dispersal: population redistribution that leads to spatial spread of organisms. This definition differs from that used in the majority of ecological books, in which dispersal is equated to *population redistribution.*

Dispersal tail: abbreviation for the tail of the frequency distribution of dispersal distances.

Displacement: see *net displacement.*

Drift: the population-level manifestation of *directional bias* in individual movements of organisms. In diffusion models, drift is modeled with an *advection* term.

Fix: see *coordinate fix.*

Generalized diffusion models: a family of models, formulated as partial differential equations, that can be used to

Motility: the parameter in the Fokker-Planck diffusion equation that quantifies the rate of population spread. It is analogous to *diffusivity* in the Fickian diffusion model. (Also known as Fokker-Planck diffusivity.)

Move: in organisms that periodically interrupt their motion, a segment of the path between two consecutive stopping points. See Section 5.2.1 for how to define a move for paths traced by continuously moving organisms.

Movement: the process by which individual organisms are displaced in space over time. In this book, this term is used in its most general sense, including both dispersal and aggregation of organisms.

Net displacement: the straight-line distance from the beginning to the end point of a path.

Path: the complete spatio-temporal record of a followed organism, from the beginning to the end of observations. Each path is represented as a series of straight-line *moves*.

Population redistribution: the population-level consequence of movement by individual organisms.

Quasihomogeneity: the spatial scale of environmental heterogeneity is less than the scale of dispersal. In such a case, assuming spatial homogeneity may be a good approximation.

Random walk: a mathematical description of the probabilistic movement process underlying trajectories of individual organisms. It is assumed that movement is governed by a mixture of stochastic and deterministic influences. See also *correlated random walk* and *biased correlated random walk*.

Reaction-diffusion: models for spatial population dynamics that include movement (diffusion), birth, death, and population interaction terms.

Step: a displacement between two successive *coordinate fixes*.

Common Symbols

a	A constant or parameter
$A(t)$	Acceleration
ACF	Autocorrelation function
b	A constant or parameter
c^*	Asymptotic rate of population spread
C	Number of marked organisms that are recaptured
const.	Some undefined constant
D	Diffusion rate (diffusivity, coefficient of diffusion)
$E(\cdot)$	Expectation of the quantity in the parentheses
K	Carrying capacity
i	Index or counter variable
j	Index or counter variable
k	Index or counter variable
l_i	Length of move i
L	Probability of moving left
m_1	First moment of the move length distribution (mean)
m_2	Average squared move length
$M(\lambda, x, t)$	Frequency distribution of move length λ
n	Total number, or sample size
N	Probability of not moving
N_0	Initial number of individuals
$O(\cdot)$	Higher-order terms
$P[\cdot]$	Probability of some event
$p(x, t)$	Probability of finding an individual at x, t
r	Distance from the origin in the polar system of coordinates
R	Probability of moving right
R	Rate of direction reversal
$\bar{R}_n^2$	Mean net squared displacement

s	Distance moved (a dummy variable in the integral)
t	Temporal coordinate
t_i	Duration of move i
T	Characteristic time of directional autocorelation
$u(x,t)$	Spatio-temporal population density
$\tilde{u}(x)$	Equilibrium distribution in space (as $t \to \infty$)
v	Velocity
$V(s)$	Contact distribution (probability of moving distance s)
x	A spatial coordinate
$X(t)$	Vector of spatial coordinates as a function of time
y	A spatial coordinate
z	A spatial coordinate (height)
α	Intrinsic rate of population growth
α	Probability of giving birth
α	Effective sampling area or rate
α_i	Absolute direction of move i
β	Bias (or drift) coefficient
γ	Shape parameter of the move length distrubtion ($\gamma = m_2/m_1^2$)
Γ	Dynamical level
δ	Disappearance, death, or settlement rate
ϵ	Environmental potential
θ	Power exponent (transformation parameter)
θ_i	Turning angle of move i
λ	Step size or move length
μ	Motility
$\pi(x,t)$	Probability of moving in a unit of time
$\rho(x)$	Residence index
σ^2	Variance (standard deviation squared)
τ	Mean move duration
τ	Time interval
ϕ	Mean cosine of move direction
χ	Coefficient of chemotactic (preytactic) sensitivity
ψ	Mean cosine of the turning angle (directional persistence)

Index